God Knows, Everything is Broken:

The Great (Gnostic) Americana Songbook of Bob Dylan

Aubrey L. Glazer

© 2018-19 *Panui Publications*

Photograph: Chris Bradford

Cover Design: Aubrey L. Glazer & Elyssa N.
Wortzman

ISBN: 9781073495375

IN MEMORIAM:

Jane Ellen Kahn

בתיה יונה בת זאב ואסתא מלכה

צֶדֶק צֶדֶק תִּרְדֹּף...
"Justice, justice, you shall pursue ..."
(Deuteronomy 16:20)

November 23, 1954—December 26, 2018
י"ח טבת, תשע"ז
ת.נ.צ.ב.ה.

IN MEMORIAM:

Anne H. Meyer
חנה בת שמואל ופרומיט

אֵשֶׁת-חַיִל, וַתַּעַשׂ, בְּחֵפֶץ כַּפֶּיהָ, עֹז-וְהָדָר לְבוּשָׁהּ
פִּיהָ, פָּתְחָה בְחָכְמָה; וְתוֹרַת חֶסֶד, עַל-לְשׁוֹנָהּ
A valiant woman, adaptive and resilient, garbed in strength and dignity,
Speaking wisdom; and the teaching of kindness on her tongue.

י"ד באייר, תשע"ח
ת.נ.צ.ב.ה.

DEDICATED TO:
George & Colin
Take a deep breath, feel like you're chokin'…
God knows you can rise above the darkest hour…

CONTENTS

Acknowledgments

The through-lines of my thinking that have come to compose this analysis of the Dylan songbook have been singing themselves to me and through me for some time. Creativity is cataclysmic, and new beginnings are always challenging. I am grateful to the many midwives of my thinking this book reflects, as fragile and tentative as it still feels...

First and foremost, I am deeply grateful to Jeff Gabel for reconnecting me with Bob Dylan's lawyer, Jeff Rosen along with David Beal who responded with alacrity and devotion, ensuring that the legacy of Dylan's lyrical songbook will remain an inspiration and thus are herein analyzed and reprinted with generous permission. This act of deep generosity has allowed this project to see the light of day, and nothing could be more important than ensuring that yet another reading of Dylan's luminally dark songbook could continue to shimmer on through this ever-darkening world. Thanks to the visionary Brooklyn painter, Jac Abshalom Lahav for sharing his two Dylan Portraits (2006, 2007) which served as inspiration to my ultimate cover design. To that end, I am grateful to photographer Chris Bradford who was also so generous with his Dylan photo that served as the image for the final cover design. I am grateful to my love and life-partner, Elyssa Wortzman, for collaborating on the revised cover design before you.

Amidst my trials in serving as a pulpit rabbi in San Francisco, it was in jamming through an inspiring monthly set of Americana music that culminated in Dylan's "You Ain't Goin' Nowhere" accompanied by a few men of peace with "harmonious tongue[s]" and hands "full of grease" that allowed me to see the signs of the end of that road just as it was beginning to blossom. As I was trying to hold onto my practice as a scholar-rabbi amidst a ship of fools heading through a whirlpool to Tarshish, sage advice was shared with me by my teacher, colleague and dear friend, Elliot R. Wolfson, who understood the meaning of "the writing on the wall" in Daniel 5:25, and gently guided me through my numbered days in San Francisco with these words from Dylan: "Aubrey, strap yourself to a tree with roots!" While much of this constellation of thinking has already been alluded to in Wolfson's pioneering research on kabbalah, my intention here was to merely "show-and-tell" this open secret. I gratefully acknowledge the moment in our ongoing *sprachedenken* when Elliot guided my reading of these lyrics away from the original prophetic lens, re/turning towards more of a Gnostic lens. My deep gratitude for the infinite conversation within and beyond his afterword.

Shaul Magid has always been there, even as my ship's cargo was getting flung overboard. Only such a fiercely loyal friend and critic would continue encouraging me to ride off into new horizons with this book and I am grateful for that. This led me to rethink American Religion, which began together in New York, both in Harrison and Fire Island all the way to Jerusalem, as well as extending to a new conversation partner in San Francisco, the generous and affable Marc Dollinger. While in San Francisco, I benefited from wonderful conversations together with Marc on the larger historical context of American Judaism and his ability to continually "complicate the narrative" continues to inspire me. Along with the *bimah*-dialogue he so graciously engaged with Shaul, Marc was masterful in "complicating the narrative" of our *bimah*-dialogue dedicated to celebrating the jubilee anniversary of the *House of Love and Prayer* just down the way on 347 Arguello Street. In addition to Marc, I am grateful to Jay Michaelson for his thoughtful back cover blurb.

Along this journey of new horizons, I was blessed to reunite with fellow Gnostic traveler and scholar of mysticism, Jeff Kripal. There was a sensation of homecoming in reaching Jeff in the midnight hour of this project, when he generously showed me the way back to redeeming sparks of light I was quickly losing grip of in the process. His deep listening and empathy for my critical study of religion through the modality of music inspired me to continue through the stormy waters of uncertainty and doubt, so I am grateful for his ongoing excitement, inspiration. Just as I was about to abandon ship altogether, I continued onwards in my quest to unlock the Gnostic secret of the Dylan songbook.

My first encounter with Gnosticism came in my encounters with Harold Bloom. His generosity of spirit emerged when we were both published together in volume 11 of *Kabbalah Journal* from 2004 that paired his review of Gershom Scholem's newly discovered poetry along with my correlation of poetics in Haviva Pedaya's poetry with *Beit Lehem Yehudah*; from there Harold agreed to serve on my doctoral dissertation committee at University of Toronto. Those encounters solidified a strange loyalty, I daresay, a conspiracy of Jewish Gnostics. Decades later it even more clear to me how Harold's audacity truly inspired my first step, and I am grateful for his heartfelt missive about this project many years later. I lament Harold never lived to see this publication, but the sparks ascend in his memory for strong reading in the world of gnosis where he is now lecturing.

Somewhere along the road back from Tarshish, circling a whirlpool, I discovered the scholarship of Kathryn Lofton. She threw me a buoy, with her deeply insightful, and constructive critique that allowed me to revise my thinking on the historiography of American Religion as well as the category of Gnosticism. Katie was remarkably encouraging and I am grateful to her insight, acumen and generosity of scholarly spirit.

I am grateful once again to Dara Nachmanoff and Glenn Chertow, dear San Francisco *hevre*, for their ongoing support, always ensuring that I had a retreat space to continue writing this project to its near completion amidst the redwood forest in Guerneville. Michael Bien and Jane Kahn, *o.b.m.* were there through thick and thin, in friendship and counsel, as well as Howard Haberman and Marc Meyers, Garry Rayant and Kathy Fields. Their friendship knows no bounds. Some early readers of emerging chapters include Steven Goode and Mark Gunther and I remain grateful for their enthusiastic feedback. Jeremy Brown has been a fellow traveler from San Francisco (to Montreal) and remained encouraging and inspiring. Deep gratitude to my student and friend, Jeff Brandstetter, who has dedicated countless hours as counsel to ensure *Panui* is alive and doing its work from San Francisco to the world, including the publication of this inaugural volume! And I remain deeply grateful to Mark and Pat Gordon for their generosity in providing seed funds to begin this larger project of *Panui* while still in New York.

I am both hopeful and grateful to be so quickly embraced as a scholar-rabbi in my new community at *Congregation Shaare Zion* in Montréal. The dream of homecoming could not be more heartfelt, and I grateful to my lay leadership, including Suzanne Grant, Peter Yaffe, Gilla Geiger, Jimmy April, Ken Adessky, Neil Bernstein, Jason Tanny, David Budman, Arthur Sanft, Susan Abramowitz Rosenfeld, Geoffrey Ungar, Lon Dubinsky, and Gary Shapiro, as well as my clergy team Cantor Adam Stotland and Reverend Asher Tanenbaum. Especially exciting for me are the emerging inspiring collaborations to realize the musical journeys of the spirit with Cantor Adam Stotland (which hopefully will include some kind of musical celebration of this book too!)

I am grateful to fellow Bob-cats, Ryan Peck and Stephen Hazan Arnoff, who intermittently re-ignited my passion for Dylan through the years together whenever our paths would cross. I recall re-uniting with Ryan while living in Toronto, especially that road trip we took together to see Dylan in some strange casino in Verona, New York. Almost every visit to Jerusalem includes a Dylan "check-in" with Stephen to see how this shared passion for Bob can inspire community-building in unexpected ways. Their shared passion for Dylan and all things scriptural allowed me to realize the importance of deepening and problematizing the correlation at the core of this book as well as insuring there was a scriptural index to my analysis of Dylan's lyrics. Hopefully, Martin Cohen, my scholar-rabbi brother who "knows not Dylan" will be amused, and I'm grateful for his insights and ongoing support along the way!

I am grateful "more than blood" to my brother, Colin, who has been on this long journey through it all. His courage and coaching through all the drama, (both real and unintended) remains invaluable, as are our fly-fishing trips with our father, Bruce. So many wonderful "new mornings" on the stream to "catch rainbow trout". And especially to my father, Bruce, who knows his "Gunsmoke" and got me hooked on good vinyl from a young age.

In the end, the writing of this book has been on the wall since the day I left home in Toronto to live in New York—that's when treks to West Village became part of my weekly regimen. Sure enough, the Dylan songbook really came off the page for me during my seminary years in New York, over many coffees at

Café Reggio with Elliot Wolfson, and especially through my dear, friend, Cantor George Mordecai. Dylan's melodies were his mother's milk and his interpretations also nourished me in unique ways over our decades together in New York. It is with a torn heart that I dedicate this birdsong to you, on your return to your homeland of Australia, for you "[d]ried the tears up from my dreams and pulled me from the hole" like only a soul-mate could and I remain forever in song with you. Weathering all the deepening darkness of our serendipitous journeys back and forth to Tarshish remains interwoven within each line and beneath every word, as we continue to sing that song of our souls...

IN MEMORIAM:

Jack Haberman

יעקב בן משה הכהן

דער מענטש טראַכט און גאָט לאַכט.

Man plans and God laughs.

...הֱוֵי מְקַבֵּל אֶת כָּל הָאָדָם בְּסֵבֶר פָּנִים יָפוֹת

Always receiving every person with a
pleasant countenance.

(b. 1926- d. August 7, 2016)

תרפ"ו-כ"ח בַּאֲדָר ב' ,תשע"ו

ת. נ. צ. ב. ה.

*Howard's uncle Jack in his grandparent's family photo, which includes
(from left): his grandparents (the two adults in the center), and the rest,
are his uncles and aunts: Ann, Jack (on the stool), Rose, and Joe (who
was Howard's uncle who married his aunt Pauline, from Montréal).*

Dedicatory Preface

When I think of Jack, the first thing that comes to mind is something he often said about someone: "s/he makes me laugh!" I wasn't laughing much in those days, and I suspect he showed me, by example, that laughter can be OK, perhaps recalling that renowned Yiddish expression: "Man plans and God laughs". Jack could feel the laughter of others and in himself because he could also feel the divine laughter that fills so much of life.

Jack may be the only sibling with a college degree, as the family came of age during the depression. Jack studied chiropractic, and then some years later studied medicine in Milan, Italy. My father encouraged me to contact Jack after Jack came back to New Jersey after his medical training, and satisfied the New Jersey requirements for medical practice. Everybody loved him because he cared for everyone—Jack was always there. Late evenings with Jack, when I stayed with him, were frequently interrupted by calls of friends asking for medical conversation or advice. I remember going to Jack's wedding when I was quite young; the marriage was short-lived. When I connected with Jack, he was living in Union, New Jersey. I don't remember if this was before or after my move to San Francisco, but I remember staying with him when I was in NJ, and he became a combination of uncle, and older brother.

My father died in 2001, and I came back to New Jersey for a week or so, nearly every month for probably a dozen years, to facilitate management of my father's business. Jack moved to Spring Lake, a "cozy" Jersey Shore town, and I spent a lot of time with him in Spring Lake, on most of my New Jersey trips. Jack met Benchawan, probably when he lived in Union, as she was the niece of the owner of a Chinese restaurant Jack frequented. Benchawan was (and is) a gem!

And I, too, came to rely on him for advice, as well as friendship. Jack shared with me his interest in Jewish mysticism without saying it. To sum up, the Jack Haberman I came to know and love is encapsulated in his seeing the bright side of life, and being a valued friend to many. May his memory shine on, and may our laughter join his in the cosmic laughter that fills the universe; may it bring us smiles.

–Howard Haberman
(beloved nephew)

Preface:

Does it Really Even Matter?
Dylan's Haunting, and Haunted, Legacy

Dylan lyrics analyzed include: "Master of War," (*The Freewheelin' Bob Dylan,* 1966); "Tangled Up in Blue" (*Blood on the Tracks,* 1974); "Every Grain of Sand," (*Shot of Love,* 1981); "Visions of Johanna," (*Blonde on Blonde,* 1966); "Tombstone Blues," (*Highway 61 Revisited,* 1965); "One More Cup of Coffee (Valley Below)," (*Desire,* 1975); "A Hard Rain's A-Gonna Fall," (*Freewheelin' Bob Dylan,* 1963); "I'm not there," *The Bootleg Series, Vol. 11: The Basement Tapes Complete,* 2014); "Not Dark Yet," (*Time Out of Mind,* 1997).

Preface:

Does it Really Even Matter?
Dylan's Haunting, and Haunted, Legacy

Most great figures have humble beginnings. It seems providential, or an exercise in divine humor, that the "masses" are more apt to produce greatness than the aristocracy. As so it is with Robert Zimmerman, son of Abraham, a merchant from the hardscrabble Iron Range of postwar America, a land of hard-working immigrants, mostly from northern Europe and a smattering of Jews who took advantage of cheap land and a quiet life away from the bustling cities and the fear of anti-Semitism.

It seemed Robert had pretentions of grandeur early on, rock and roll his ticket out of Dodge. Listening to the great Hank Williams, The Carter sisters (Mabelle and Sarah), Ralph and Charlie Stanley, Big Bill Bronzy, Mississippi John Hurt, Muddy Waters and many others on scratchy AM radio shows like "The Health and Happiness Hour" out of Nashville, and a little later Jerry Lee Lewis, Buddy Holly, Roy Orbison, and Little Ricard, the young Zimmerman, like so many of his generation, envisioned himself a musician.

But those humble beginnings in Hibbing would not suffice; not in an era of Woody or Neal Cassidy, of Allen Ginsburg or Langston Hughes and so Zimmerman had to create mythic beginnings, he needed a story. And so, he became a runaway child, travelling with a circus through the west, the first mask of many. He hides his face before anyone is even looking at him. And so, the name-change to Dylan, also obscure, the high-minded Welch poet, Dylan Thomas or the American Marshal, Matt Dillon, in charge of Dodge City in "Gunsmoke", that 1950s TV Western. It depends who you ask, and when you ask. Dylan might respond, "Is there a difference?"

There was really only one place to go: Greenwich Village, that cluster of old New York houses where in the late 1950s and early 1960s you could create your own story. Many said the village was already passé by the 1930s when the Communists left and many of its black inhabitants had moved north to the Harlem Renaissance. But it left cheap housing for young vagabonds and poets like Dave Van Ronk, and entrepreneurs like Izzy Young of "The Folklore Center" and Moe Asch the music impresario (Moe was the son of the great Hebrew and Yiddish write Scholem Asch). Musicians such as Berl Ives, Pete Seeger and The Weavers, and younger kids like Phil Ochs and Neil Diamond were selling their wares in cheap coffee-house like Café Wha and Kettle of Fish for meager coins in a pass-around basket, like a secular church promoting a new liturgy. The Hootenanny was he great revival meeting and Washington Square Park the outer court of the Jerusalem Temple.

Young Bobbie shows up, early twenties but looking just north of his bar mitzvah, and joins the party, couch surfing long before the term existed, learning songs and the folk repertoire from Dave van Ronk the "Mayor of MacDougal Street."[1] But this one had a knack for lyrics and a voice channeling Woody who was by then paralyzed in a hospital in New Jersey, his room a pilgrimage for aspiring troubadours. With an Iron Range twang, a fertile imagination, and a drive for fame, something just sparkled there. Those days the folkies were divided into a few groups; there were the political activists like Seeger and Ochs, and then the folk aficionados like Van Ronk and Izzy Young, devoted to the folk tradition above all else. Dylan really didn't fit into any of those. The irony is that the author of "Master of War"[2] the great ant-war anthem, really didn't care that much about the war. And Dylan wanted to write his own songs and not be bound by the folk tradition (even as he became quite expert at it).

And so, when the folk scene whimpered, drowned out by Elvis, the screaming teenage Beatles' fans and the Rolling Stones, Dylan plugged in and left Van Ronk's couch behind. He had already elbowed his way past Ochs, who set off for more radical pastures in the revolutions in South America, or Gary Carawan, who went to the post-Jim Crown South to fight for civil rights. Dylan wanted to be a star and if that meant plugging in, so be it. The village was, in the end, a small "Kettle of Fish."

What I find so distinctive about Dylan is the way he could not quite abandon anything that touched him. But he also refused to own any of it. Teaming up with The Band, a group re-inventing American traditional music in a new register, Dylan never stopped hearing the songs of his youth. He wrote like a poet and often thought like a steel worker. Woody and Cisco Houston gave him fodder for an American myth that he never really lived, and European poets like Rimbaud, Dylan Thomas, or the anonymous "Italian Poet from the Fifteenth Century"[3] pushed his literary imagination. To my mind the only postwar American songwriters who could match Dylan were Leonard Cohen (who was Canadian), the urban Jewish bard who was so deeply Jewish he never had to deny it and also never had to embrace it, and Townes Van Zant, maybe the truest American of them all, the Whitmanean lyricist who could match Dylan's pain and darkness without the mask. But unfortunately never without the bottle. But as we moved into the late 1960s and 1970s it was clear that Dylan was the chosen one. Ochs suffered a tragic death, as did Van Zant later on; others faded into obscurity "some were mathematicians and some were carpenter's wives," [4] but Dylan played on because what Dylan cared about was Dylan. You can't blame him, who else should the "prophet of the generation" care about when the generation started reaching middle age and largely became what they protested against. Dylan followed suit, he bought a house in Malibu.

In an early sixties interview in San Francisco, Dylan, with a smirk, defined himself as a "song and dance man," and in the end that's what he became. The songs were brilliant, the timing and musical changes simple but also subtle, and the audience never tired of any of it, even when the music was stilted and the shows confusing. Some Jews found his Christian period annoying but one has to admit that "Every Grain of Sand"[5] is as good as "Visions of Johanna"[6] or "Tombstone Blues[7]," or "One More Cup of Coffee,"[8] or "A Hard Rain's A-Gonna Fall,"[9] maybe even better...

Some say longevity is a mixed blessing because you get to witness your own obsolescence. In Dylan's case, it is that you get to witness your own becoming an icon. And so, Dylan's youthful masks now came in handy. As the youth matured and received their graduate degrees and the drugs wore off, people began seeing Dylan as transgenerational; not of his generation but a representative who extended beyond it. From this was born Dylanology, a library of analysis, speculation, and vain attempts to unwrap what Churchill described Soviet foreign policy in 1940, "an enigma wrapped in a paradox." But Dylan was ready as ever, responding, "I'm not there."[10] Which, of course, he wasn't, and yet he was, presence in his absence, etc.

This may be one of the reasons he found the Lubavitcher Rebbe so appealing, and curious; also, a lonely transgenerational figure trapped in his own paradox. Yes messiah, no messiah— does messiah mean anything at all? But of course, the apparatchik nature of the Hasidim was too stultifying for Dylan, you can't have more than one paradox at a time ("one says to the other, no man sees my face and lives"). And so, he moved on.

As the books piled up, from the banal to the sublime, Dylan seemed to pay little attention. After his life-threatening heart ailment, he thought of quitting. Then Jerry Garcia said to him during the Dylan and Dead Tour, "go out and play the same thing every night, differently."[11] That was just too Dylanesque for Dylan to pass up (Garcia was close to Dylan's heart and could match Dylan's ironic wit without imitating him). So that's what he did, and The Unending Tour was born. In his spare time, mostly on his tour bus, Dylan hosted a radio show on the history of American music (quite beautiful at times, always well informed), took up metal sculpting, and then making whiskey. Dylan seemed to be trying to shut out the world – like Jesus chasing away his disciples - and with every attempt, more books were published.

Aubrey Glazer's *God Knows, Everything is Broken* is the latest iteration of the paradox. Or is it the enigma? Taken from the title of a song where, for a moment, Dylan seems to remove the mask, Glazer takes up Dylan's Songbook the way he did Leonard Cohen's in his previous book *Tangle of Matter & Ghost.*[12] Unlike the plethora of books about Dylan this does not try to explain him or disentangle his lyrical poetry. Rather, it puts him in conversation with a variety of enigmatic figures, mostly from the Jewish tradition. Dylan's "Jewishness" can be compared to the way the Musar teacher described his disciple's attempt to run away from the haughtiness attributed to "honor" (*kavod*). "Yes," says the master, "You keep trying to run away from it. But the problem is, you keep looking back to make sure it is following you?

Glazer wants to trace that chase, and chase that trace, not to say that Dylan's work is "Jewish" in any discernible way, but to say that Dylan touches on themes that can be pulled into the Jewish tradition both to illumine it, and to be illumined by it. There is no "Jewish" Dylan that is not also a "Christian" Dylan. Or a godless Dylan. The only Dylan is the one that lives "outside the law" and to do that, he says, "you must be honest."[13] But, as he says in Martin Scorsese's film *Rolling Thunder:* "only a person wearing a mask will tell you the truth."[14]

In the subtitle of this book before us, Glazer calls it *The Great (Gnostic) Americana Songbook of Bob Dylan*, an American wagon trail of dust and dusk, where "It's not dark yet…but it's getting there"[15] meets "these visions of Johanna are now all that remain."[16] But in spite of Dylan's mask, his masks upon masks, we continue to stare. Some with the hope of a glimpse of the real, or the truth. Some with the hope that they will be noticed. Some simply because it's there. But how many times does Dylan have to say it, "I'm not there."[17] Which is precisely why this story continues to haunt us; as it haunts him.

—Shaul Magid
(Dartmouth College, New Hampshire)

Author's Preface:
Dismissing My Delusions via Ophelia's Religion

Chapter at a glance: To imagine and then analyze American Religion is to dismiss delusions—this lies at the heart of this Great Americana Songbook of Bob Dylan. American Religion will never be the same since Bob Dylan crossed over all cultural boundaries in winning the Nobel Prize for Literature. The controversy over whether indeed Dylan's Songbook constitutes literature sets us off on an important cultural question, challenging not only that the false dichotomy between high and low culture or elite art and popular culture must be dismissed as an illusion, moreover, it provides a window into the current trajectory of American Religion in relation to the Great Americana Songbook. It demands that we return to the primary question of the role of criticism to begin with and how it carries forward Bloom's reading of Gnosticism in relation to American Religion as an exemplar of "Ophelia's religion" alluded to in Dylan's "Desolation Row" and woven throughout his entire songbook.

Dylan lyrics analyzed include: "What Can I Do For You," (*Saved*, 1980); "It's Alright Ma (I'm Only Bleeding)," (*Bringing It All Back Home*, 1965); "Need a Woman", (*Bootleg Series* Vol 1-3, 1982); "Nettie Moore" (*Modern Times*, 2006); "Last Thoughts on Woodie Guthrie, (*Bootleg Series* Vol 1-3, 1982); "Jolene," (*Together Through Life*, 2009); "Simple Twist of Fate," (*Blood on the Tracks*, 1974); "Only a Pawn In Their Game", (*The Times They Are a Changin'*, 1963); "Man in the Long Black Coat," (*O Mercy*, 1989); "Forgetful Heart," (*Together Through Life*, 2009); "Not Dark Yet," (*Time Out of Mind*, 1997); "When You Gonna Wake Up," (*Slow Train Coming*, 1979); "Jokerman," (*Infidels*, 1983); "Man of Peace," (*Infidels*, 1983); "Gates of Eden", (*Bringing it All Back Home*, 1965); "Every Grain Of Sand," (*Shot of Love*, 1981); "You Ain't Goin' Nowhere," (*Greatest Hits, Volume II*, 1967); "Ain't Talkin'" (*Modern Times*, 2006); "Neighborhood Bully" (*Infidels*, 1983); "Narrow Way," (*Tempest*, 2012); "Soon After Midnight," (*Tempest*, 2012).

Author's Preface:
Dismissing My Delusions via Ophelia's Religion

> "Her profession's her religion
> [Ophelia's] sin her lifelessness"[18]

> "Religious criticism can begin ...
> by disposing with any ambition to dismiss illusions or
> delusions."[19]

To be an effective critical thinker requires humility; but to dismiss delusions of grandeur requires clarity. Clarity suggests light and perspicacity—the search for which in a songbook marks the journey of this book. Before you is a book that challenges our assumptions about what it means to live and think in diverse, often contradictory reading communities we encounter called American Religion. My unorthodox turn here is to argue that this act of dismissing delusions lies at the heart of this great American songbook of Bob Dylan— a crooked path that cannot be easily straightened. This very Janus-faced American Religion,[20] however, will never be the same since Bob Dylan crossed over, winning the Nobel Prize for Literature—the ultimate acknowledgment of secular posterity woven within a larger unraveling fabric of the sacred.[21] As I examine this weaving throughout the argument of this book, I open respectfully with the sardonic response from Harold Bloom when I shared my excitement about this burgeoning project with him:

Dearest Aubrey,

... My problem is that I know nothing and care less about Bobbie Dylan. I don't like his voice and don't want to read his songs.

With warm regards,

Harold [22]

Such a courteous dismissal from one of the great (Gnostic) American literary critics of this century bespeaks the bigger picture controversy over whether indeed Dylan's songbook constitutes real literature worthy of critical analysis and gnostic critique beyond mere questions of category.[23] Listening deeply to Dylan's songbook demands iconoclastic critique, such that the false dichotomy between high and low culture or elite art and popular culture as well as between sacred and secular, must all dissolve as illusion if any analysis is possible of the current trajectory of American Religion and its relationship to the Great American songbook. The role of criticism in reading a living cultural moment of myth-making is astonishingly clear in the soliloquy of one of the great unsung feminist music critics, Ellen Willis, and what Dylan's record, *Love and Theft*[24] calls us to reconsider that: "[t]he American imagination will be taxed with demands for unquestioning unity and generic patriotism, will be burdened or inspired by our sense of loss and defiance, identification and separateness, new tensions between individual and collective. And irony (which in some quarters has been prematurely pronounced dead) will be very, very important...You can't get any more mythically American than that."[25] While Willis may have no direct interest in religious criticism, *per se,* even though she admits to Dylan's "flirtations with religion," [26] still her cultural critique of American myth-making through music remains remarkably visionary and succinct. She reminds us that part of Dylan's timeless appeal is his serving as our psycho-pomp who guides us and: "descends into the hell, or purgatory, or limbo, of America's mysterious rural past, which seems to be located mainly in the South."[27] This succinct insight of Willis opens the door for deeper reflection on the religiosity of the Dylan songbook by reminding us that: "From the earliest years of his career Bob Dylan has had a passionate impulse to obliterate his personal identity. ...much of his [Dylan's] work has been defined by an apparent desire to unload the baggage of his own experience and become a vessel, channeling American music."[28]

Listening deeply to this journey of Americana music, after all these years, Willis is showing us there is much more at play in the Dylan songbook than meets the eye and the ear. The paradoxes and tensions point to something more emerging in this Great Americana Songbook of Dylan, considering that: "Of course, the counter-impulses have also been strong: Dylan has an indelible signature, not to mention indelible ego. The essential tensions in his music have never been about electric versus acoustic but about personal and idiosyncratic versus collective and generic; topical and profane versus primordial and sacred; transcendence as excess versus transcendence as purgation; *Blonde on Blonde* versus *John Wesley Harding; Blood on the Tracks* versus *Time Out of Mind*."[29] Moreover, in proposing this creative tension within the songbook itself, this feminist rock-critic provides a remarkable roadmap for our entire journey of religious criticism. My ensuing analysis will build on these latter dialectics in the Dylan songbook of "topical and profane versus primordial and sacred; transcendence as excess versus transcendence as purgation" [30] through the lens of Gnosticism.[31]

So, before turning to the role of such religious criticism, we must first reflect on what we really mean by "religion" and "gnostic". Some philosophers of religion have argued that there is actually no such thing as religion per se, rather all that exists is "culture". If so, then what we read as religion is merely an arbitrary agglomeration of aspects of "culture" and labeled as "religion" but it is all a construct rather than a lived experience, as J. Z. Smith famously quipped that: "Religion is solely the creation of the scholar's study...created for the scholar's analytic purposes by his imaginative acts of comparison and generalization. Religion has no existence apart from the academy."[32]

In scouring the Dylan songbook and re-reading the lyrics as literature through a prism of strangeness and "defamiliarization" [33] through which to analyze aspects of the American spiritual journey, I continue to be subjectively engaged within this musical journey of the spirit along its Americana landscape that intertwines with my own experience. I am however returning to J.Z. Smith's clarion call to engage in crossing the boundaries that we too often place on the study of religion, especially American Religion *per se*, so that even the apocalyptic nightmare of Jonestown must be critically analyzed: "For if we do not persist in the quest for intelligibility, there can be no human sciences, let alone, any place for the study of religion within them."[34] This then is a quest for intelligibility in critically reflecting upon why there remains such a deep resonance of the Dylan songbook with so many spiritual seekers in post-secular America.[35] Moreover, as I share lyrics as allusions to cultural moments in the shifting landscape of American Religion with fellow seekers, I often wonder whether this returning to the wellspring of the Dylan songbook constitutes its own sort of religion?

How can Dylan's allusion to what he calls "Ophelia's religion"[36] provide an interpretive key to unlock the present gnostic interpretation of his Great Americana songbook? This surrealist stanza from "Desolation Row" dedicated to a twenty-two year old maiden-spinster, Ophelia will prove important within my reading of Dylan's songbook as we dawn and discard the masks of a cast of hybrid characters surrounding the watchtower, guarding the tower of song. Before attending to this question of Ophelia's "religion", I will offer a working definition of Gnosticism,[37] oscillating between its ancient and American context. Given that Gnosticism remains a perennial form of awakening that is alive and well in the habits at the heart of American Religion it serves as another interpretive key in reading the Dylan songbook. By Gnosticism I mean that sensibility that transcends any particular religion, characterized by dualism, alienation, esotericism, as well as the conviction that transcendent Creator *could* redeem the human creation from the very machinations of the evil forces engulfing them and managed by a demiurge, but the Creator chooses otherwise.[38] In searching for a countercultural paradigm of spirituality that best describes the soundtrack of Americana religion playing throughout the Dylan songbook, I will need to further unpack the meaning of Gnosticism, both academic and New Age.[39]

Firstly, using a Gnostic lens to interpret American Religion allows us to confront a false but recurring dichotomy between the categories of the secular and the sacred. This strange side of the phenomenon of American religion is that it remains avowedly secular in its approach to the sacred encounters of religion. Even in the midst of apparent secularism there remains a gossamer thread of metaphysics that is woven through this fabric of secularism in America.[40] In modern America religion transforms is: "all but equivalent to the aspirations of a progressive, enlightened nation-state." To be American means that even citizenship itself becomes "utterly consistent with particular versions of piety and moral transformation."[41] This suggests that secular modernity in America has been highly imprinted by Protestant practices and its particular metaphysical commitments in which "the truly religious and the truly secular were inscribed, seamlessly and simultaneously, with the mark of the real." [42] Such an experience of reality tightly intertwines the warp of the religious within the woof of the secular means essentially that as living in America one can be buoyed by a religious feeling all the while living in an avowedly secular age. Given that this kind of reality is neither "totalizing nor utterly determinative",[43] Dylan's songbook is adept at channeling this strange lightness of being, whereby "...people don't live or die, people just float."[44]

Secondly, using a Gnostic lens to interpret American Religion requires redressing assumptions about the very category of Gnosticism, for: "what often passes as the primary characteristics of Gnosticism—dualism, alienation, esotericism, and the like—do not appear nearly as central as the Gnostics' conviction that God had acted to save people from the machinations of the evil forces that surrounded them."[45] While this noble revaluation of Gnosticism attempts to reposition it from the margins to the center of our concerns, it may already be irrelevant to American religion, however, where such boundaries have long ago dissolved in the face of heterodox reality rather than orthodox living. The threat of ancient heresies to a "single, uniform religion"[46] called Christianity as argued in the polemical writings of Church father (like Iraenaeus) falls upon deaf ears in this post-secular age of American Religion. What the Gnostic myth once provided seekers of truth was a certain "story of return" to an "original state of fullness, harmony" while remaining aware of how "the entirety falls into lack, discord and ignorance, and yet the original state of perfection will be achieved once again, thanks to the world of immortal beings."[47] The Dylan songbook draws inspiration from this Gnostic myth reverberates in various keys, from life to death and rebirth as he sings, for: "Soon as a man is born, you know the sparks begin to fly/He gets wise in his own eyes and he's made to believe a lie".[48] Nothing is more Gnostic in its impulse than such a lucid awareness that these "sparks begin to fly" but which way do they fly? Do these sparks diminish the human stature of the soul into lack, discord and ignorance or do they fly back to a state of restoration? The genius of this lyric is its re-reading of an enigmatic verse in the book of Job: "But man is born unto trouble, as the sparks fly upward."[49] Whereas the Hebrew bible envisions these sparks in ascent that "fly upward" returning to their source, the Dylan songbook leaves open the question of the direction. It is possible these sparks either ascend or descend in their flight,[50] given that strange lightness of being, whereby "…people don't live or die, people just float."[51] This condition of spiritual floating in the lightness of being in Dylan's lyrics oscillates between this verse in Job and the Gnostic prayer, "Summer Harvest" by Valentinus (100-160 CE): "I see in spirit that all are hung/I know in spirit that all are borne/Flesh hanging from soul/Soul clinging to air".[52]

Just as originality demands iconoclasm with Gnostic theologians like Valentinus, who unabashedly bases his teachings upon his own unique mystical experience rather than shrouding it in the authoritative garb of past figures like Adam, Zoraster or John the Apostle, [53] so too, Dylan as singer-songwriter unabashedly bases his music on his own unique mystical experience rather than shrouding it in the authoritative garb of past folk music figures like Woodie Guthrie, Harry Belafonte, Peter, Paul & Mary or any contemporary "city-billies" playing at Gerde's

Folk City, [54] or Newport Folk Festival.[55] Dylan's mystique as a song-writer lies in his gift in conjuring an "aura of the uncanny" and the deep knowing that all great "folks songs grew of out of mysteries."[56] Just as Valentinus was perceived by the orthodoxies of his day to "speak like us, but think differently," [57] so too, was Dylan's music perceived as sounding like folk and rock, but engaged in an entirely different "musical thinking."[58] After Dylan switched out his acoustic guitar and went electric at Newport, he was henceforth censured by the folk orthodoxies of his day, never to be invited back to the canonical folk stage at Gerde's. It is this constant reinvention of self through unique lyrics that emerges from Dylan's songbook that I refer to throughout my analysis as Gnostic Americana. [59]

Yet even in light of such affinity and influence, still there is no escaping that unrelentingly negative vision of the material world as portrayed in the Dylan songbook which goes darker and disrupts deeper than even the most original, renegade and overly optimistic gnostic thinkers like Valentinus. While the gnostic impulse holds that the created material world may very well be "the result of some sort of mistake or error by a feminine figure", Valentinus sees this very personification of Error as "the feminine origin of materiality"[60] without displacing the ultimate unknowable, true reality as God. The strong sense of divine immanence as presented above in "Summer Harvest" by Valentinus also stands apart from standard gnostic thought, embracing more of a "Stoic pantheism"[61] that sees the term 'god' as being constituted by and of the cosmos as well as this global individual enacting its own periodic history-cycles, creating its own fate. And yet, such a closed system that feeds upon and loops back upon itself would likely rustle the feathers of that pioneering spirit that is supposed to undergird our perceptions of American Religion.

The contours of American metaphysical religion and its history are broad and ingrained within the terrain.62 Undoubtedly, questions will remain as to how contemporary religious criticism can even utilize terms like "Gnosticism".63 In light of the metaphysical texture of American secularism, Albanese's misgivings over the Gnostic lens hinges on sociological rather than theological grounds about the fluid profile of 'members' in a changing network of believers and practitioners whereby Gnosticism is the religion of Americans.64 While Albanese focuses on the "magic [that] still dwells"65 within the metaphysics of American religion, Bloom's analysis of American religion dispels any residual magic within the metaphysical imagination of mind. Gnosticism serves as a cleansing agent of deep cynicism, fearless in being enshrouded in the darkness of American religious existence where magic no longer to dwells, where "people just float."[66]

And yet, still no matter how "forgetful" that heart may ultimately be,[67] it remains open to the inspiration within the landscape of American religion. A different facet of this journey of the heart is recounted, again from the perspective of the sociology of religion, but in his renowned *Habits of the heart: individualism commitment in American life,* Robert N. Bella traces the contours of these habits of the heart that oscillate between individualism and communitarianism, between "biblical religion and civic republicanism, that have provided resources for countering extreme individualism by holding aspirations to solidarity."[68] This creative tension between challenging our aspirations for solidarity while rallying and revolting against republicanism is ever-present in the Dylan songbook. A disintegration of social capital is strongly felt when there is a decline in associational membership and erosion of public trust, which then tends to leave the individual their own devices. To contextualize the early chapters of the Dylan songbook, is to be left wondering just how those "city-billies" of which Dylan was part and parcel of in the Greenwich folk scene, managed to make it work. Was there really enough solidarity emerging from their shared revolt to create a communitarian ethos? Looking back at those "city-billies", as in the Cohen brothers' film *Inside Llewyn Davis* (2013), suggests a dystopian side of this associational membership.[69] As the trust between folk bards eroded, leaving each solitary singer searching for their singular break in the Greenwich Village folk scene, we witness the darkness of alienation from this ingathering of "city-billies" already in the early 1960s.

Is this sense of alienation just a function of the economy, stupid?[70] The rupture for Dylan runs much deeper, for this is a rupture that cannot be divorced from values which privilege worshipping the sovereign self. The deep divide tearing Americans apart, now as then, Bella points out "in terms of economic prosperity, Americans have imagined individualism is self-sufficient moral and political God. In times of social and birth of the present, you're tempted to say that is up to individual to look after their own interests."[71] So when Dylan's songbook redresses this growing alienation that emerges as a by-product of the American Dream with "The Times They Are A-Changin'", these lyrics must ultimately return to the biblical tradition, because it resonates with most Americans. Such a tip-of-the-hat to Scripture allows an affirmation of "the intrinsic value of individuals because of their relationship to the transcendent".[72] Such scriptural homage interwoven throughout the Dylan songbook reveals more preferred patterns of prophetic texts in the Hebrew Bible and New Testament,[73] rather the Hibbing bard is consistently misquoting so as to paint things darker, even if it is "Not Dark Yet".[74] Dylan's return to the biblical tradition is a pathway of eminent darkening within darkness where the transcendent is out of reach and withdrawn from walking any longer in the Garden of Eden. While Dylan, the music making machine may rally against republicanism and champion individual quest for meaning, notice how he also succumbs to precisely the neo-capitalism he appears to be critiquing[75] — from the lothario leering into a Victoria's Secret lingerie, to tasting Chobani yoghurt, to driving Chrysler automobiles and even using Apple computers, finally reaching an impasse with IBM's Watson. And just when you thought Dylan had "sold out" to every possible peddler, now there is even his own line of whiskey, called *Heaven's Door*.[76] While Dylan's scriptural predilections may not appear that dissimilar from the American gospel of self-enrichment,[77] it remains difficult to disentangle the original vagabond who is simultaneously "tangled up in blue" as he is "tangled up" in *green*. Is Dylan's "sell out" just another jab at the American dream, given that "from the neo capitalist point of view, privatization in the service of economic competitiveness is the solution to almost all difficulties"?[78]

And despite the American decline of social capital and the conviction that "all government social programs have been disastrous failures," [79] whereby Bella then asks: "can we pray that God is doing the same [as Ezekiel in "renewing a heart of flesh"] for us in America today?"[80] While the questions of sociologists of religion like Bella are already somewhat clichéd by1996, by contrast, the Dylan songbook has been asking this question from its inception. There is not necessarily a rigid chronology in the Dylan songbook, insofar as the challenge was posed early on: "It's easy to see without looking too far/That not much is really sacred".[81] As we shall discover, the challenge of prayer—of praying to pray— within the framework of Ophelia's religion hovers over the deeper mystery of divine absence in a world where "not much is really sacred". Singing in the shadow of Ezekiel's diasporic call for prophetic renewal is here transposed to the landscape of American Religion, a place of *non-place* that can imagine hosting an American Post-Judaism,[82] which once again, Dylan has already transcended and included from the outset.

The piece of this puzzle that continues to resurface is the time-honored question of every Gnostic: "How are we to live? How do we think about how to live? Who are we, as Americans? What is our character..."[83] The answer, my friend, that pervades the Dylan songbook points to the reality that the only constant is change, and that it is we as fellow travelers of the original vagabond who are ready to confront the reality that it is we who are nothing but a process of transformation exemplified by the myriad of masks Dylan dawns and discards.[84] This process of transformation of consciousness that is a process of reconstituting the social world, however, is not merely to "make America great again", but for America's greatness to be recovered, it must begin by involving individual action.[85] Dylan's songbook is warning about the need to awaken if one is really at all concerned about the transformation of collective American consciousness that requires individual accounting, where "even the president of the United States/Sometimes must have to stand naked"[86]—all the more so, each individual must be accountable. Dylan's lyrics are not a playbook in becoming accountable, but this music of protest against the status quo resonates for the constant need to wake up to a greater accountability, as he croons: "When you gonna wake up and strengthen the things that remain?"[87]

In searching for a countercultural paradigm of spirituality that best describes American religion, I necessarily return to Gnosticism— both academic and New Age— deeply interwoven in the habits at the heart of American Religion. While the case for a "Modern Psychedelic Gnosis" by Christopher Partridge astutely traces the "gnostic impulse" felt by Allen Ginsburg, in a long lineage including Aldous Huxley, Alan Watts, Gerald Heard, and Timothy Leary, it is unclear whether the Dylan songbook neatly fits into such a category. Surely such a "gnostic impulse" would not have been unfamiliar to the circle Dylan was rambling with, especially the powerful cleansing the doors of perception through entheogenic sacraments that was serving to liberate spiritual seekers from consumer culture of the 1960s.[88] Moreover, in moments of breakdown, as Deconnick has argued, where "romance with traditional politics and cultural structures disintegrate[s]" leaving a vacuum, whether under the brutal imperialism of first century Rome or during the 1960s in America, Gnosticism re-emerges *en toute force*.[89] The challenge before the religious critic is to clarify a clear Gnostic link across diverse times and spaces, showing how the themes of one age can reappear in another, despite their differences of cultural context and historical periodization.[90] Without flattening the complexities of each cultural moment, Deconick convincingly argues for a "shared metaphysical orientation common of past and present."[91]

American Religion is at home with a tempered Gnostic universe, replete with the best-case scenario of a God who unfolded himself into lower and lower forms of life. It is this tempered form of Gnosticism, not the forms that framed our world as a dark, demonic place, but became the undercurrent of Western spirituality. [92] The abiding loyalty of a fan-base of such diverse listeners to the Dylan songbook allows the religious critic to then appreciate just how far its theology is from such a "tempered form of Gnosticism" of the Hermetics, rather the hold this songbook has on its listeners comes in part, perhaps from its deep dive into singing through "our world as a dark, demonic place", all the more in line with the undercurrent of Western Spirituality. If indeed we are currently still experiencing a fourth gnostic awakening that began in the mid-twentieth century,[93] then this "unprecedented renaissance of Gnostic spirituality in America... has fueled skeptical, spiritual-but-not-religious sensibilities, which condemn conventional organized religious satisfaction and direct experiences of the holy."[94]

While the religious critic cannot avoid confronting the reality that there is indeed an "unprecedented renaissance of Gnostic spirituality in America",[95] it is important to distinguish America within its North American context. As this current "Gnostic awakening has fueled skeptical, spiritual-but-not-religious sensibilities" those are critical and curious forces that do not manifest in the same ways north of the border.[96] The revolutionary spirituality of Gnosticism that takes root in the American landscape of the soul or its "soulscape"[97] requires more than just that pioneering spirit[98] but an openness to provocation, risk, questioning, incitement and a willingness to be part of a process of ongoing change.[99] The American landscape is fertile ground for such religiosity and this is very much in line with the provocative nature of arousal at the core of the Dylan songbook. The gnostic impulse is unafraid to critique the stagnant forms of religion and to awaken the soul of every seeker that has fallen dormant, "waiting to be awakened, cultivated, and reunited with the divine source of all." [100]

The arc of the Dylan songbook is critical of most opiates, including religion, insofar as they enslave the authentic self from realizing its true freedom. And yet, once Dylan's music awakens us to our calling to be free, there appears to be little, if any, transcendence at the end of this road. The most transcendence Dylan is willing to let abide is a dialectical play between "transcendence as excess versus transcendence as purgation." [101] This process of identifying, opening, smashing and purging all the layers of excessive illusion enables the listener to realize how freedom must emerge from knowing the deeper truth, especially if it is hidden, dormant, unexpressed and forgotten. What remains for the Dylan songbook is a confrontation with very essence of nothingness as the source of all, rather than the seeking some ultimate reality which can also be imagined by some Gnostics as a "God of goodness and love (that) transcends all cards in all religions." [102]

The contours of the counter-cultural revolution that Gnosticism once sought, and continues to seek, lead to the inversion of ritual and liturgy. [103] It is therefore important to at least sketch out in broad terms exactly what theological worldview that Gnostics were overturning and then consider its ramifications on the Dylan songbook as an exemplar of American Religion. There were three main types of spirituality that dominated the religious scene before the emergence of the Gnostic counter-cultural revolution and Deconick categorizes those as one of the following: (1) servant spirituality; (2) covenant spirituality; and (3) ecstatic spirituality. [104]

In what follows I will rehearse Deconick's categories of precursor spirituality that pave the way for the counter-cultural revolution of Gnosticism:

(1) **Servant spirituality** represents "[t]his metaphysical orientation views the human being as a moral creature crafted by a more powerful being or god who is immortal. As the god's creature, the human being is the god's property to do with as the god wishes, even arbitrarily...The onerous job of maintaining cosmic stability and peace fell to humans under the direction of a leader or king who was believed to operate in the best interests of the gods, either as their representative or as their son."[105]

(2) **Covenant spirituality** is "The idea that a god would enter into a covenant agreement with his human servants... as an actual legal agreement between God and human [servants]". [106]

(3) **Ecstatic spirituality** "...encourages humans to seek knowledge of the gods through two avenues. The first avenue is human discernment, when we try to read the signs that the gods leave for us in the natural world...the second avenue is more traumatic because it involves trying to transmute the human being into a creature divine enough to enter the otherworld and communicate directly with the gods."[107]

What becomes readily apparent, and perhaps served as a key motivating factor for the spiritual revolution was the plain fact that: "[t]he religions that the ancient people constructed out of servant, covenant and ecstatic forms of spirituality are based entirely on metaphors of subservience, bondage, humiliation and fear." [108] So the more the Gnostics became aware of another reality altogether, then the over-arching religious criticism of Gnosticism becomes an interrogation of the status quo by inverting the stagnant forms that abide in past paradigms of religion. [109]

It is precisely in this inversion of the status quo that the Dylan songbook provides iconoclastic challenges along Gnostic lines of interrogation and critique. The Dylan songbook shares that uniquely Gnostic intention of creating a viable posture of worship that is turned upside down reflecting a world that is inside out. In seeing the chaotic ruptures in the spirit that have been ensuing since the 1960s to the present as continuous rather than discontinuous, I follow Deconick's insight here that views these as perennial expressions of "a rift that causes religious dissociation", even if we are now choosing to call it "secularism".[110] The move towards secularism, and especially now what is evinced by the acceleration of post-secularism, both suggest that such categories are insufficient to really appreciate the operative spirituality in the growing number of those seekers turning away and becoming "unchurched" who self-identify on surveys of today as S.B.N.R., and in the 1960s would have been more generally lumped into the Woodstock era.

The ebb and flow of Gnosticism, present throughout decades of the Dylan songbook is not susceptible to syncretism but it is a lyrical whole that can never be limited to the sum of its parts. It is akin to the Gnostic "religious buffer" which allows for a tagging, contesting, and blending of "a variety of religious revelations, spiritual sensibilities, religious experiences, and metaphysical speculations" that consolidates into "a new, viable way of being religious…" [111] So what emerges is something new altogether, while what is new sounds ancient, and the rhythm and cadence settles us into a place of solace and even comfort at the sounds, even while the words themselves may be jarring. The reason why these lyrics have such strong staying power is: "[b]ecause it is useful or meaningful in some novel way, the memory stabilizes as a new concept and the emergent spiritual orientation sticks." [112] And the reason why the listening community of the Dylan songbook continues expanding and growing is that its condition of the "religious buffer is available to all people in a given society, but the people who usually innovate religion from its assortment of religious sentiments are those on the margins of traditional religion." [113] As the dissatisfaction with status quo society and its given religious forms continues to rise, so too does the compelling pull of the Dylan songbook.

Dissatisfaction with the status quo can easily manifest through protest. Such a revolt against the status quo is a search for something more, and possibly the realization that this something more than the material and political world might point to a more sublime and concealed layer of life known as the spiritual. It is in this process of revolt and then awakening to another way of being in the world where we feel so strongly the pull of the Dylan songbook in its gnostic impulse. It is this impulse which has the power to arouse the otherwise dormant psyche within from its "state of isolation, latency, and stupor. It lies there pained, waiting to be awakened, cultivated, and reunited with its source, the supreme God." [114]

Liberation from the all-too human blanket of unexpressed, and forgotten emotions can be experienced through the Gnostic path of sound, chant, and song. [115] The power of song abides in the Dylan songbook, and the abiding question revolves around the vector of this return from awakening. Namely, does the Gnostic awakening affect the return as a reunion to "its source, the supreme God", the demonic demiurge, or into the oblivion of nothingness? Song has the power to heal the shared, human trauma of separateness, [116] which the Dylan songbook sings time and time again to its diverse communities of listeners.

The healing that may happen through sound does not necessarily catalyze a return to the supreme God, unless of course, that divinity is seen as the source of all sound leading to the creative process of making the music itself.

Person as path, soul as a process—this kind of openness to the endless journey where the only constant is change serves as a recurring motif in the Dylan songbook.[117] Rather than reaching a destination, the journey along Dylan's self-described "Desolation Row" is a process whereby each person becomes the path, every one of us is that original vagabond. What I am arguing is that the path of the original vagabond in the Americana songbook has strong parallels to the Gnostic path within American Religion, insofar as the Gnostics—both in antiquity and today— fancy themselves as guides initiating others upon a shamanic quest to: "invade the wholly other realm of the holy Other…to take their initiates on virtual cosmic journeys, beginning with a harrowing of hell." [118] The Dylan songbook initiates its listeners on a cosmic journey that ends where it begins— in the harrowing hell of "Desolation Row".

Are we then to believe that such a seemingly circular journey is some kind of trick? Who better to ask than the trickster! That is, Dylan's trickster who is "born with a snake in both your fists while a hurricane was blowing" known as "Jokerman".[119] Dylan refers to this elusive and duplicitous presence of "Jokerman" as the one who can be both a spiritual "man of the mountains" that can "walk on the clouds" while simultaneously down to earth "manipulator of crowds" and a "dream twister". Oscillating between the messianic and the demonic this figure who "Could be the Führer/Could be the local priest"[120] is the one who dupes seekers while calling out the duplicity of religion itself. Dylan's songbook is at home playing the role of

"Jokerman" to call out just how much "the traditional religious communities ha[ve] been duped by trickster gods who were really demons or fallen angels." [121]

Channeling this Gnostic impulse to its unique rhythm, the Dylan songbook calls out the duplicity of religion itself as capricious and malicious, without necessarily duping its listeners into some other transient protest movement as a substitute for religion. Any modicum of faith the original vagabond encountered within the folk scene as a protest movement, from the get go, was a fraud to Dylan. The faith each rebel claims to have lost is already an illusion for, as he already observed early on to wit: "You say you lost your faith/...You had no faith to lose". [122] To call out the fakes and the frauds requires a willingness to also undercut the faith that undergirds any such system of orthodoxy requiring the allegiance to some creed. And so, the lyrics of Dylan consistently revel in the art of such critique through inversion of convention, both of American religion and the American songbook. This double-edged critique early on made his incessant reinvention of form and sound a near enemy to the orthodoxies and creedal faiths of the folkies and others along the way. To harness the power of music resonating from the depth of one's soul is to see oneself as an extension of these sacred sounds that cannot be contained, categorized and compartmentalized, to "no longer trick us into believing otherwise"—that "we are children of the wholly Other." [123]

In confronting the darker reality of life as being nasty, brutish, short, dark and deeply depraved requires a certain resoluteness. To have clear "visions of sin" is one of the Hibbing bard's great gifts, as Ricks duly notes, but the abiding question remains whether the Dylan songbook points the way to redemption from such darkness. If so, and many listeners might agree, there needs to be an acknowledgment of the ways in which Dylan's lyrics allow us to gain a sense of control over otherwise chaotic lives, and to then focus on the "task of overthrowing the cosmic powers" of oppression. This songbook has a certain power to alleviate "the anxieties and fears that plague all of us [as they] live deep within our unconscious, where the deep self, the spirit, is buried." [124] So too, the same generative process of creation that "inevitably embeds the one into the many" and is imagined often in Gnostic mythology as a cataclysm, serves as a clarion call to the power of sounds of music to restore this separateness from one's root, and to recover deeper connection to transform one's "delusions, emotions, and damaging appetites." [125]

Differences still abide between Gnosticisms of antiquity and modern America. What was once seen as "the deviant and the cursed" in Gnosticism of antiquity is somewhat "inverted and breached" so that the "Gnostic message of the God within is no longer a terrifying and distant one of defiance against the gods." Modern Gnostic reformulations of religion offer a less threatening "quest for spiritual wholeness" which is welcomed insofar as it "has supplanted religion's older parameters of forced servitude to powerful gods."[126]

The arc of heresy present in American Gnosticism is tempered, if not somewhat tamed, by the encroachment of a deeply secularist mentality that suffuses and appears to be mitigating the influence of religion within so much of contemporary culture. And yet, the spiritual impulse still abides strongly within the American landscape. What does this reality really look like? Consider that nine-in-ten Americans believe in a higher power, but only a slim majority believe in God as described in the Bible. [127] These trends point to rising numbers of Americans who on the one hand, may reject a traditional, and cliched image of a bearded man on a throne in the sky while embracing other spiritual forces, or images of a supreme being elsewhere in the bible and beyond. In this sense, America is not necessarily witnessing a decline in belief in God, for even as doubts and uncertainties abound, it is more that "I don't believe in that God as bearded man on a throne in the sky!" If indeed "nearly three-quarters of religious "nones" (72%) believe in a higher power of some kind, even if not in God as described in the Bible" [128] then the Dylan songbook is opening a journey through the Americana soul-scape that is searching for a higher power. That higher power that influences the course of their life's journey is no longer "omnipotent, omniscient, benevolent and active in human affairs." [129] And yet, there is an abiding sense of the influence of that power throughout the highs and lows of life. The American seeker tends to be more open to a higher power that is protective and rewarding rather than judgmental and punitive. [130] So just what kind of seeker is the Dylan songbook speaking to really?

At first blush, it may feel that the major arc of the Dylan songbook is most concerned with the darkening corners of life, where any such higher power is more judgmental and punitive and less protective and rewarding. More as riffs than as verbatim references does one encounter the patterns of how the Dylan songbook references scripture, always searching for the places that are not dark yet, but getting darker. This Gnostic impulse for transforming scripture by "transgressing the very foundation of covenant spirituality and scriptural interpretation" is a recurring theme in the Dylan songbook, one that is also "obsessed with explaining a crack that they perceived in the biblical narrative…"[131]

For example, that hairline crack uncovered in scriptural verses exists classically in the creation narrative recounted in Genesis 1:26: "And God said: 'Let us make a human [*adam*] in our image, by our likeness..." What is most strange about this verse is not that *adam* points to the origin of humankind and is a generic term for human beings without automatically suggesting *de facto* maleness,[132] rather stranger still is that this higher power speaks in the plural and announce: "Let us" – which acknowledges a possible plurality of divine powers that creates the first human in the divine imprint. This allusion to a plurality of divine powers is but one of many examples that allows the Gnostics to build the case that something is awry in the Garden of Eden and that while humanity traverses this same landscape of existence and suffers, it is the Gnostic view that YHVH is responsible for this corruptible creation that suffers, and that surely there must be somewhere out there, beyond the realm of suffering, a more supreme and transcendent God. This is a dark view of the cosmos that needs rupture as part of the plan of creation to work. And this darkness works well for the Dylan songbook.

Perhaps the recurring motif of darkness as a motivating influence for creativity in the Dylan songbook is what inclines its arc towards descent, rather than ascent is that for some Gnostics "[a]scent is presented as a withdrawal to the self, a self-imposed silence that results in coming to know the divinity, praising and blessing him." [133] What these lyrics seek by contrast is to dawn and unveil many masks in the process of descent through the harrowing hell of self, so that one emerges with a realization of greater fragmentation of who "I" am in relationship to the ways one walks through the circus of life. To leap beyond the boundaries of self and the folk song, Dylan intentionally follow the path of *"dérèglement de tous les sens"*[134] as espoused by French symbolist poet, Arthur Rimbaud, the Dylan songbook seeks out the fragments where "I is *other*". [135] By challenging these forms of selfhood and folk music and simultaneously through a process of complete renewal, Dylan announces a formal novelty of unknown and new forms in his music. Just as Rimbaud was critiquing his precursor Baudelaire for not having gone far enough in his complete renewal with a poetics that remained too <<*mesquine*>>, Dylan is critiquing his fellow "citi-billies" and folk music aficionados for not having gone far enough. By daring to explore the "inventions of the unknown in new forms" [*les inventions d'inconnu réclament des formes nouvelles*], both Rimbaud and Dylan are introducing formal novelty as anarchic poetics, whereby the newness of the form exposes rather than suppresses "the life of the body as instantiated (not represented) in rhythmic sound, in a way that defeats the *regulation* of the body made possible, precisely, by images and figures. As *enfants terribles,* both Rimbaud and Dylan yearn to renew their language through the infantile sound-play of every vowel and consonant, that becomes "an overture to a more liberatory [*sic*] sexual politics in which the conventional images (and they are always images) of sexual relations and sex-roles are inadequate to the ecstasies of the rhythmic body." [136] Both Rimbaud and Dylan dare to imagine and sing that rhythmic body, as unsocialized and asocial, not repressed but on the contrary instantiated by meter. [137]

While there is often a yearning in the Dylan songbook has the power to "awaken, purge, mature, and integrate the damaged self into a stable state of primal and permanent wholeness", [138] notwithstanding the great assortment of musical masks it dawns and discards, there is not necessarily a final realization of this yearned for integration. I would argue that the purpose of the Dylan songbook is to point us to those darkened places of rupture within the soul that need healing before they can be re-integrated back into a possible sense of wholeness.

While Joan Baez and Joni Mitchell had real reasons for doubting the direction of the "two-timing" original vagabond,[139] early on the Dylan songbook was already betraying more ancient resonances than just the Americana landscape. The new-ancient pathway of betrayal has deep resonances with a group of the oldest Gnostics known as the Peratics, who were known simply as their namesake suggests, as Travelers. Rather than fitting into the box of Gnostics seen as elitist, to be a Peratic is to dare venturing upon the "route through the underworld and cosmic realms, ... to traverse mortality."[140] What we sometimes forget is that Dylan's original vagabond is a traveler, akin to a Peratic, who also has a "seed of divine potential" [to] be roused from its dormancy and [to be] grown into its full divine form so that it can journey back to its transcendent home."[141] And yet, the exact location of this "transcendent home" of the original vagabond's quest remains unnamed, in the offing, down the endless road.

This overall sense of rupture begs the question of dislocation, exile and separation— but from what exactly? Gnostic mythology suggests creation as an act of original rupture from the great chain of being. The divine family of the Father and the Mother are ruptured, when the Father unfolds into a great chain of being, necessitating a divorce from his partner, Sophia. This rupture is necessary for the unfolding of the infinite into the finite so that human beings might exist, and yet the process of the spirit descending into matter is traumatic. What this Gnostic mythological structure provides the Dylan songbook is a vision of the human being as the nexus between cosmic, material and celestial realms. The Dylan songbook traces this intertwining journey, tangled up in all colors of the spectrum, creating a weave of earthly spirit, psychic matter and the human as the cross-roads of this journey itself. [142] Those who listen carefully to the stations of the Dylan songbook realize this is not the liturgy of any sort of spiritual gnostic church, per se, but there are at times strange resonances. The more surreal the contrast, the better, especially while "the groom is still waiting at the altar", [143] as with Gnostic ritual wedding envisioned by Marcus, where the rotating leader of the day pours their blood red wine into the chalice and prays:

> "Prepare yourself as a bride awaiting her bridegroom, so that you be what I am and I may be what you are. Consecrate the seed of light in your bridal chamber. From me, receive (your) bridegroom. Hold him and be held by him. Behold grace has descended upon you. Open your mouth and prophesy." [144]

The ritual theatre of Gnosticism would seem to resonate with moments in the Dylan songbook, especially in his inter-song sermons from 1979-1981, in channeling the spirit of becoming such a "community's prophet of the day". While it's unclear what, if any, substance Dylan was imbibing, upon drinking the overflowing, bubbling chalice, Marcus' Gnostic community prophet of the day embodied through this process of imbibing the sounds of these prayers in uniting with her divine avatar. Recall that the Vineyard Fellowship steered clear of Gnosticism, and as such, one remains hard pressed to find such ritual displays of redemptive reunion taking place almost anywhere in the Dylan songbook. This sense of straddling, of living approximately, between and betwixt Eden and exile, is so apparent in the Dylan songbook, insofar as while "there are no sins inside the Gates of Eden" still "there are no truths outside the Gates of Eden".[145]

In grappling with this state of being betwixt and between, not only Eden but also Adam remains in question. Exactly what was the creation of this primordial Adam really all about? Never mind the conflicting stories in Genesis, there is something at play about the consciousness of primordial Adam and its soul that continues to concern us as seekers. For example, in Mandaeaen Gnosticism, it is the soul that contains and refracts fragments of the soul of Adam as evinced in this prayer:

> "O soul, arise, go forth,
> Enter the body and be chained in the palace.
> The rebellious lion will be changed by you, the rebellious, unruly lion.
> The dragon will be changed by you,
> the evil one will be slain where it is.
> But you, O soul, the king of darkness will be bound, against whose might no one can prevail."[146]

In this world of oppositional forces that proliferates Gnosticism, light competes for primacy with the overwhelming hold of darkness. The question that emerges in the Gnosticism of Mandaean theology is whether or not darkness will prevail or whether the weight of the soul is able to overcome the prevailing darkness. Just as this uncertainty hangs in the balance within this branch of Gnostic theology, I would argue this same question hangs in the balance in the Dylan songbook, which more often than not, seems to find itself at the crossroads where light and darkness meet. The Dylan songbook is in a perpetual search for light amidst the darkness, and leaving open the question as to whether there is any real chance that the light of the soul will break through the deepening darkness, as sung in the aptly titled song, "Not Dark Yet": "I was born here and I'll die here against my will/...Don't even hear a murmur of a prayer". [147]

While the hunger of American Religion and its perennial seekers is not easily quenched, yet another way Gnostic spirituality rubs moderns the wrong way—the frequent misconception about Gnosticism being highly irrational. A more nuanced appreciation of Gnostic spirituality suggests its appeal lies in "spontaneous religious experience." Whereas Gnostics are searching for a transcendent state called, "God Beyond All Gods", the Dylan songbook struggles to routinize rapture, instead struggling with ecstasy and an inability to transcend the quagmire of self. [148] Granted that the creative process the drives the inspiration behind so much of the Dylan songbook emerges from this need to be spontaneous. Throughout countless reflections both biographical and analytical, one thing remains consistent with Dylan as a singer-songwriter—the "first-take" of a song usually says it all and playing live is where it all happens. Whether Dylan would describe the magic that happens in the first-take is a form of "spontaneous religious experience". For Dylan, it's all about the music as gnostic process itself.

Another compelling quality of the Gnostic impulse within American Religion is its enabling a critical view of religions as human constructions, known as a transtheistic perspective, distinguished from the view that all religions are expressions of the same God, known as a perennialist perspective. [149] What separates the perennialist view from "the transtheistic Gnostic experience"—the endless, anarchic search for truth as a process—is precisely what demarcates the Dylan songbook. These lyrics are

Gnostic insofar as they artfully try to capture what cannot be captured and reveal the fragility of that elusive process that is always: "...hanging in the balance of the reality of man/Like every sparrow falling, like every grain of sand".[150] The deeper we delve into the decades of prolific lyrical inspiration within the Dylan songbook, we realize these lyrics channel a gnostic impulse upon a long and winding road where the process supersedes the destination.

So, where does Dylan really stand along this journey to redemption? Is redemption every realizable? Rallying against every institutional expression of religion within the metaphysics of secularism that typifies this original vagabond, Dylan's songbook strikes us a solitary soundtrack—yet "lonely missives to God [are] constituting a mediasphere."[151] When spirituality becomes a "mode of haunting and a means of disenchantment"[152] there is a deeper inspiration that fuels the imagination at work here. The current mediasphere that emerges along this lonely landscape is one full of wayfarers and god-fearers as I learned upon publishing a short essay on Dylan, entitled, "Bob Dylan, the messiah and personal redemption."[153] I had no idea how deep the rabbi's hole of the mediasphere went, until almost instantaneously there emerged a community of "wayfarers" and "god-fearers".[154] While my reflections seemed uncontroversial in challenging the messianic elements within Dylan's songbook as well as his journey as a singer-songwriter, immediately I was confronted with two divergent reading communities and their reactive discourse. On the one hand, representing the wayfarers of Dylan's Jewish scriptures was pioneering Dylanologist, Stephen Pickering, who in the comments section of the essay came to the defense of my position on Dylan's messianism with prolific polemic in word and photos, even reproducing the photo of Dylan in a hoody at a "devotional gathering" called a *fabrengen* with the Lubavitcher rebbe at 770 Eastern Parkway, in Crown Heights, New York. This photo was proof that Dylan had frequented not just Chabad rabbis, but the Lubavitcher rebbe himself, who by some in the Chabad world is revered as a messianic figure himself.

On the other hand, representing the god-fearers was Scott Marshall, who contacted me through this mediasphere of a global Dylan discussion group called *Expecting Rain*.[155] Marshall appears to hover somewhere in a space that values the approbations of the American evangelical camp, including Pat Boone, Jimmy Carter and Robert Hudson amongst others that figure prominently in lauding his publication on Dylan's spiritual odyssey.[156] While I politely declined his request for me to write an approbation, I realized quickly that this Dylan mediasphere was not so lonely after all, rather it was a lively and regular communal gathering space for "lonely missives to God" that are shared all over the globalized virtual world. The spiritual quest that the Dylan songbook engenders is itself an ingenious "mode of haunting and a means of disenchantment"[157] for those with an "appetite for something like religion."[158] While Leonard Cohen would call this riff on religion "something like" it but not quite, Dylan names it as Ophelia's religion which distinguishes the anchor of the present analysis.

"Desolation Row" displays elements of Dylan's self-reflection over time spent in the Greenwich Village folk scene, the time and place where Beatniks like Jack Kerouac and sidekick, Neil Cassady found refuge—but as always, these lyrics may have emerged from and been inspired by such a context yet continue pointing to something more. "Desolation Row" is indeed a place of refuge for every listener seeking the truth and the song becomes shelter from the storm of untruth. But if it is that place described by T. S. Elliot and Allen Ginsberg, then it is a place of deepening darkness—the former imagining America as "The Wasteland", and latter imagining America through a singular "Howl" over the death of its own dream. In the end, "Desolation Row" suggests that no matter how much one seeks after truth, no one ultimately cares enough to make real, radical change within the infrastructure of American culture. After all, who would want to be in living in a time and place where the youthful, beauty of every Cinderella is that of an old maid? Where Ophelia wears an iron vest. *Let's rewind that last image...*

However far the expanse of "Desolation Row" reaches, surely it extends beyond this-worldly, first hand memories of the Greenwich Village folk scene. I am arguing that what I will refer to as Dylan's gnostic view sees the entire created world, in all its desolation and deprecation as worthless and thus unworthy of redemption. If one chooses to live "open-eyed" to the corrosion of truth that is the reality of this-world, then life has an overwhelming feeling of desolate cruelty to it that is inescapable—this is Ophelia's religion. And it is here that the Dylan Songbook serves as the score to a vanishing American Religion. The ideal setting for "Desolation Row" is when "the moon is almost hidden/the stars are beginning to hide." [159] This time of the occluding moon—a kabbalistic symbol of the feminine divine and her capacity to redeem this world—is recast here in a pessimistic light. The world is damned to darkness that no light can infiltrate to ever redeem.

And what of Ophelia? While Shakespeare in general wrote female roles with the men in mind who would be playing them on stage, in particular, Ophelia the noblewoman stands as a profoundly tragic symbol of the feminine as a bit character in *Hamlet*. Ophelia's unrequited love for Hamlet appears to remain unconsummated which may have led to her to take her own life, while such a religion would then be a tragic ascetic piety. When such a beloved yearns for her beloved, where is God in the process of reuniting with the missing piece of one's soul? In Ophelia's religion, is the world devoid of the divine? Or is there merely an eclipse of the divine in moments like these? Dylan's songbook hovers between such a vacuum and an eclipse of the divine in this world, and thus early on Ophelia's religion stands as a scathing critique of organized religion as lifeless. Once the experience which resists definition is institutionalized through religion, the life of the experience itself is dead.[160] And so Ophelia falls into the pit of pessimism and ultimately drowns as she wades in the waters of her unrequited love. Death in Ophelia's religion is stronger than love, inverting the encouragement of the Song of Songs, wherein: "Love overpowers death's sting."[161]

Ophelia's religion is Dylan's Gnosticism—namely that process of wading in the waters of unrequited love that drowns the seeker in a world of deepening darkness beyond anything imaginable. Dylan's songbook follows Ophelia's religion in allowing this pessimism to kill the spirit. This pathway is unlike Camus in the face of the absurdity of life, because at least the philosopher dedicates to living life fully to redeem what remains. These remnants on display in "Desolation Row", align with darker sentiments later: "Well, my sense of humanity has gone down the drain/Behind every beautiful thing there's been some kind of pain" [162] much like the Psalmist, who sings that: "all of humanity is deplorable"[163] while praising all sentient beings of creation. Once one has seen through the looking glass darkly, it becomes all the more challenging to muster the courage and clarity to see through the speculum that shines. Tragedy knows no boundaries, so that the

East Coast Greenwich Village, New York landscape of "Desolation Row" complements the West Coast landscapes of flophouses, honky-tonks, scattered lots and sardine canneries of Monterey Bay in John Steinbeck's *Cannery Row*,[164] as well as Jack Duluoz's journeying from the Cascade Mountains to San Francisco, Mexico City, New York, and Tangier in Jack Kerouac's *Desolation Angels*,[165] inspiring Dylan's pathway is ultimately a site of deeper tragedy as he sings: "Behind every beautiful thing there's been some kind of pain."[166]

Ophelia's religion occupies a tension between her symbolizing the eternal virgin, that untouchable vessel of morality who is also cast by Shakespeare as both loyal wife and nourishing mother. Of course, this archetype of the Great Mother has many layers, and Ophelia stands in as but one of many such masks she wears throughout the ages.[167] While Ophelia is accused by Hamlet of being a prostitute, she symbolizes a deeper tension within the soul oftentimes referred to as the anima, the symbol of the maiden or feminine aspect of the masculine soul.[168] She symbolizes a condition of the soul "that is drowsily nymphic, neither asleep nor awake, neither self-sustainingly virginal nor faithfully conjoined, lost and empty, a tabula rasa". This state of the soul serves as a muse for the Dylan songbook, oftentimes "only an object created by projection, an Eve reborn of Adam's sleep, without independent soul, fate and individuality."[169] While Ophelia as maiden and mother is ultimately lost and empty, still to the prince of Denmark and darkness—she remains a sexual object, epitomizing the corrupt and deceitful lover! Recall Ophelia confesses to her father, Polonius that her forlorn lover, Hamlet has indeed told her that he loves her and that she actually believes him. This is why Polonius calls her a "green girl"—which is nothing short of an accusation of her naiveté in judging Hamlet's sincerity. Just around this time, Ophelia escapes her unrequited love by climbing into a will tree by the brook, hanging on a branch that breaks, catapulting here to drown in the water below—why?[170] Queen Gertrude claims this noblewoman's death-drive overtakes her will-to-live because Ophelia appears incapable of overcoming her own distress at being betrayed by her lover, Hamlet. What ultimately drives Ophelia to drown—by accident or intention—remains an unresolved, but dangling on the branch of the Tree of Life seems a dangerous proposition. No wonder Dylan's lyrical warning resounds so strongly here—if only Ophelia had listened: "Strap yourself/To the tree with roots."[171]

Hopelessness sets in as a cornerstone of Ophelia's religion as a function of sexless, manless, fatherless status, ultimately drowning herself in the waters of unrequited love. Ophelia's "iron vest" is either a chastity belt or her knight's armor—but neither protect her from the fate of unrequited love. The religion of Ophelia, akin to Dylan's gnostic songbook, is a pathway to the lost and empty soul awaiting creative vision to carry on. But with such a dark world view—why bother caring enough to carry on? Despite this deepening darkness, the Dylan songbook invites us to strip ourselves of any sense of self-deception and pride. The sovereign self can be asphyxiating, but if the right covenant woman can unconditionally redeem every soul singer, then the song of every soul can sing on.

Even if God is not fully eclipsed and religion exists, those truths are so distance from "Desolation Row" that the world of here and now feels like chaos and void. It is this aspect of gnostic theology I am arguing to consider as a lens in reading the Dylan songbook. For if indeed "there are no truths outside the

Garden of Eden"[172] then the quest for truth's luminosity known as *gnosis* in the Dylan songbook remains singularly quixotic, if not alien to the world of here and now. If there is ultimately no light and no love to redeem the seeker from this deepening darkness, then the gnostic myth itself is fragmentary and incomplete. The most I could argue for then in reading Dylan's songbook as gnostic is that it emerges from and remains tied to the World of Chaos.

The more limited gnostic lens I seek to see through resonates in what kabbalah calls the world of *Tohu*—the initial, primordial form of the world of consciousness known as *Atzilut*. While some strains of kabbalah see *Tohu* emerging in two stages: firstly, from a more "stable form" (*Akudim*) while remaining in tension with and followed by a more "unstable form" (*Nekudim*). While most gnostic theologies depict this primordial scene of creation as deeply darkening, even in the world of *Tohu* there are "great lights". The problematic moment of this myth that deeply imprints upon religious and literary criticism is when these "great lights" enter premature "vessels which then results in the "breaking of the vessels" (*shevirat hakelim*).[173] While *Tikkun* is the spiritual process of retrieving the fragments of light trapped within the material realm, this process of restoring the world to its initially intended state of perfection is never contemplated in the Dylan songbook.[174]

Now let us return to the grounding question: why engage in criticism of religion? How does religious criticism allow us to grow as human beings amidst our search for meaning? Religious criticism, after Bloom, aims "to build bridges across gaps, to explain in particular the very curious relations that generally prevail between theology and actual religious experience, in whatever faith…"[175] As a scholar-rabbi, I incline more to "bridge building" than to utter deconstruction. The critical aspect of "bridge building" allows for the reality that "[t]heologies will fall away, and the varieties of religious experience will begin to suggest subtler demarcations, keener sounds than earlier could have been apprehended."[176] Theology as a reflection on the personal quest to connect with the creative spirit evolves most meaningfully when it engages critical thinking. Such a correlation of thinking and theology is possible precisely in opening the ears of the heart to these "suggest subtler demarcations, keener sounds" that "uncovers the winding paths that link together [antithetical] faiths" which paradoxically enables the "culmination of the growing inner self."[177] Religion, when read in this way, serves as the poetry of the masses. Criticism—whether it be of belief or poetry, [178] must necessarily share in the experiential nature of what is being studied. While both religious and literary criticism are modes of interpretation, unlike the critic of imaginative literature, the critic of religion is not primarily an interpreter of texts. What the religious critic is tasked with is to compare perceptions represented by imaginative literature or by religion, and specifically how they emerge as the product of poetry or belief.

The book before you is a work of a religious criticism, a call to take more seriously Dylan's Great American songbook as an evolving soundtrack to the evolution of American Religion. It is important to realize the centrality of the Great American songbook in Dylan's imagination. While it refers to a period of profound creativity, between the 1920s and 1950s when songs were being written and performed to great acclaim,[179] for Dylan it means more than canonization—it is part of his mythology. Dylan consider his songs to be extensions of the melodies of these earlier classic songs that become standards in the

Great American songbook were written by the likes of: Irving Berlin; George Gershwin; Jerome Kern; Richard Rogers; Cole Porter; Duke Ellington; Arthur Schwartz; Harry Warren; Hoagy Carmichael; Richard Whiting; Vincent Youmans; Walter Donaldson; Jimmy McHugh.[180] This burst of creativity in songwriting emerged in "Tin Pan Alley" spanning one city block of New York City, between Broadway and Sixth Avenue on West 28th street.[181] Fittingly, Dylan's latest series of cover song recordings,[182] are more than merely a "tip of the hat" to the Great American Songbook, including his own covers of standards by Frank Sinatra, Dean Martin and Big Joe Turner to the Stanley Brothers and country duo Johnnie & Jack. Dylan's genius is at work here in repurposing motifs and inspiration from the Great American songbook of standards, as he writes his own classics all figuring as part of an evolving soundtrack of American Religion. Just as literary criticism must take the work of literature as text in context and beyond to appreciate precursors and strong readings that carry the vision forward, so too religious criticism must take religious experiences in their context and beyond to appreciate precursors and strong readings that carry their luminous sounds forward.

This calling in religious criticism came into clearer relief for me after completing my recent book on post-secular mysticism in Leonard Cohen's songbook.[183] I realized at numerous musical book-talks I was giving in collaboration with local musicians, especially in Israel, just how much Cohen's songbook was satiating those who have "an appetite for something like religion." That is part of the grace and splendor of Cohen's lyricism, which is really what aligns him with the great liturgical poets of bygone eras in arousing the soul from its slumber and showing us the way home. If Cohen's lyricism could be seen as a true American *payytan* or liturgical poet, Dylan's songbook wanders outside synagogue walls. As the Original Vagabond, Dylan wanders the pathless paths of mystical precursors—whether the Beat poets of the 1960s or the *Hevraya* of the Zohar in the fourteenth century— each of whom set out on the road to find that creative spirit of inspiration.

From inception to execution, distilling the insights gleaned from personal pilgrimages can come quickly but take a lifetime to render in an accessible and comprehensible to others. When renowned beat, Jack Kerouac, set out to write up his experience on the road as a novel, *On the Road,*[184] legend has it that he typed it almost nonstop for three weeks on a 120-foot roll of paper.[185] While no Kerouac, I do realize my style may strike many readers as meandering, and it reflects my own search through Dylan's songbook that for so many of us has accompanied a personal pilgrimage. "For Guthrie, the road was habitat; for Dylan, metaphor." [186] As a result, there will be many comments and analyses of these rich metaphors you will find intriguing, surprising, interesting, even at times arresting. I do not however want you to feel that there is a prerequisite fund of knowledge without which you cannot read this book. I will challenge you, but I invite you to stay on for the ride. On the one hand, I will hope that you are in some way intrigued by Bob Dylan, given that many of you will be hard-core Dylan fans who actually do know all the details in depth like scripture, while other readers will need many more of those details to be filled in. That is not the primary purpose of this book, but a great beginning is the canonical work of Clinton Heylin, *Behind the Shades*, which provides an exhaustive and integrated intellectual biography of Bob Dylan.

When writing a book, it is important at the outset to acknowledge one's perspective. This *circonfession* leads me to admit myself as a scholar-rabbi, who is very invested in the larger religiosity versus spirituality question—namely, what's at stake in the question of the "born-again Dylan" versus the "Jewish Bobby Zimmerman" (aka *Shabbetai Zisl ben Avraham*) versus the "Original Vagabond- spiritual-but-not-linked-to-any-specific-religious-tradition" Dylan. This is the undercurrent of this entire book, but may not always appear as explicitly as in other studies. For the sake of context, I will briefly outline some moments along that journey that can be known with any sense of certainty, given the notorious obfuscation that Dylan continues to play with. And in doing so, I acknowledge my debt to the remarkable biographical research of Heylin,[187] and more recently, Margotin and Guesdon.[188] Regardless of their prowess as biographers with encyclopaedical knowledge of nearly every living aspect of Dylan's life as well as descriptive details about the production of almost track, still they both fall prey to what new criticism calls "biographical fallacy" in interpreting the Dylan songbook. I will unpack what biographical fallacy means critically in a moment, but it boils down to realizing that even if you can prove that Albert Grossman may have inspired the "thief" in "All Along the Watchtower"[189] and Suze Rotolo may have inspired heartbreak laments like "Cry a While" and "It Ain't Me Babe"[190] it leads to a reductive interpretation that limits these lyrics in the Dylan songbook as the grand works of art.

The issue of interpretation is a great challenge, especially as in any work of religious criticism. How objective can the scholar be towards texts that by their nature describe and invite subjective experience? My approach is hybrid, insofar as I am a scholar-rabbi, which means I have been trained both in the rigors of objective critical scholarship, both literary and theological, while also having been trained to be a communal leader subjectively invested in the text and its implications. A turning point in my journey from pure academe to my "calling" happened while studying the literary criticism of French thinker, Roland Barthes. In his prolific analysis of French literature and American culture, when Barthes spoke about the mystery of interpretation in the face of the "Death of the Author", I was awestruck.[191] To read, and in this case listen, to the text as "a tissue of citations, resulting from the thousand sources of culture"[192] opened up a whole new way of analyzing cultural artifacts. If every work of art by extension is "the text" which itself "is a tissue of citations", then the ongoing issue that often plagues Dylan's creative repurposing of a myriad of texts is artistry not theft. But at the heart of the matter lies the enigma of the author, made even more complicated for the present venture in religious criticism, given that Bob Dylan is not yet dead. The "Death of the Author" happens, however, symbolically, from the critic's perspective as soon as the creative work is completed. For once the text is completed, for all intents and purposes it no longer belongs to the artists and as such is dead: "Once the Author is gone, the claim to "decipher" a text becomes quite useless..."[193] In this sense, the present analysis is not an exercise in deciphering, rather it remains a bold act of interpretation.

From his earliest press conferences to this day, Dylan remains highly suspect of any message of "AuthorGod" in deciphering his songbook. For now, suffice it to say that beyond dodging any interviewers questioning the meaning behind any of his lyrics, Dylan's "I'm Not There" really lays bare a crucial key to interpreting this songbook. "The Author is gone" even if he is still alive; the creative act of song-writing as an art form means that the song stands on its own, separate from its creator. The critic is toiling in vain to recover and decipher the intent of the author to then solve the questions of interpretation by closing the text, even though "...the space of the writing is to be traversed, not penetrated: writing ceaselessly posits meaning but always in order to evaporate it: it proceeds to a systematic exemption of meaning" [194] That closure Barthes is alluding to in weak interpretation is the tendency to fall prey to reading any work of art, especially text, as a reflection of the events in the life context of its author. This interpretive closure is so dangerous not only because it reduces the work to a single essential way of reading but it also shuts down the journey of the imagination. Even and perhaps especially for religious criticism, there is need to remain open to the cues of the imagination, for without such openness the sacred itself remains inaccessible. [195]

On the side of Jewish religious criticism, I have been greatly inspired by writers like Seth Rogovoy whose prolific criticism is primarily interested in Dylan as a Jewish singer-songwriter. [196] On this line of criticism, Rogovoy has more than ample evidence to argue his case. Recall Robert Zimmerman grew up near the Canadian border in the iron-mining town of Hibbing, Minnesota. Most of the nuclear and extended Zimmerman family lived in Hibbing or the nearby port city of Duluth. Dylan went through the rite de passage of bar mitzvah in 1954, and also guided his sons through this *rite de passage* for Jakob at the Kotel in Jerusalem. My divergence with Rogovoy is the moment he places the mantle of "Jewish prophet" upon Dylan. [197] In the course of my reflections that unfold throughout this book, I will respond critically to these kinds of claims that attempt to pigeon-hole the Original Vagabond whose journey cannot be contained by such concepts or labels. Put simply, just because an artist re-reads and extrapolates poetic inspiration from prophetic literature does not make the artist a prophet.[198] By suggesting that Dylan has "in large part adopted the modes of Jewish prophetic discourse as one of his primary means of communication, determining the content of his songs, the style of delivery, and his relationship to his audience",[199] is an essentializing move by Rogovoy that I will critique. While I appreciate the investment intrinsic to a loyalist critique when he earnestly asks: "Was Dylan at his best as a Christian"[200] and then goes on to review the recently released bootlegs of Dylan's "born-again" period 1979-1981, I remain in doubt. Rogovoy shares "shivers of fear" mixed with love, as he boycotted Dylan from that moment in 1979 at Jewish summer camp onwards.[201]

The last taboo for a self-professed member of the Jewish tribe as loyal as Rogovoy, is the blurring of the borderline between Judaism and Christianity. The 1970s were ripe with opportunities for spiritual seekers, especially American Jews, to search for spiritual practice absent in mainstream synagogues, through Americanized import of Eastern spirituality, from the Rajneesh and Transcendental Meditation of Maharishi Mahesh, to the repackaging of Western religions from Sun Myung Moon's *Unification Church* (aka Moonies) to Jim Jones' Peoples Temple to Moishe Rosen's messianic *Jews for Jesus*. As the counter-cultural yearning for compelling spiritual practice spread like wild-fire, American Judaism was struggling to respond in a meaningful way to this need and Dylan's search needs to be contextualized within this greater arc. But the question remains: "Can a minority religion flourish if it presents itself as a pale imitation of the dominant civic culture, rather than as a counter-cultural movement?"[202] Moreover, what happens when the original vagabond from Hibbing transforms the counter-cultural movement into its own

American songbook?

Most curious, however, is that Dylan's search never took him through any of the anarchist doorways of the *havurah* movement. Jewish textual literacy in Hebrew and Aramaic which was so lacking in most mainstream synagogues became the counter-intuitive counter-cultural twist to the way that a searching segment of American Judaism responded whether through the *Ba'al Teshvuah* movement or the *havurah* movement. The latter path was more radical in its anti-institutional, D.I.Y. ethos by spreading far and wide with the publication of *The First Jewish Catalogue: A Do-It-Yourself Kit.*[203] Moreover, as the recent collection of its oral history suggests.[204] Clearly something was afoot during this period of Dylan's exploration of American Religion that offered an intrinsically Jewish folk practice—for whatever reason, then and now, Dylan did not see Judaism as a religion to avail himself of as a D.I.Y. *practice.* Rather Dylan's subversive commitment always remains to the singular song of his soul. To be clear, I am not arguing that Dylan is merely "remixing Judaism" by subversive tinkering,[205] rather Dylan's subversion is wholesale and much more radical, insofar as it unapologetically returns to the biblical sources that birthed Judaism and Christianity as religions.

By now, it should be evident that my analysis is unconcerned with proving that Dylan *is* Jewish, for that is already a fact of the lineage that constitutes the reality of the "Jewish Bobby Zimmerman" (aka *Shabbetai Zisl ben Avraham*). To realize his *rite de passage* of bar-mitzvah, Dylan was trained by an itinerant rabbi who would appear and disappear in Hibbing, perhaps alluded to in his song "Man in the Long Black Coat."[206] Whether the man portrayed in this song was his bar mitzvah tutor, Rabbi Reuben Maeier, or it is the resurrected Lubavitcher rebbe,

Rabbi Menachem Mendel Schneerson, or it is the wandering incarnation of death itself—there remains something elusive in Dylan's lyrics. While laudable as a project of synthetic interpretation, the analysis of Philippe Margotin and Jean-Michel Guesdon in *Bob Dylan: All the Songs: The Story Behind Every Track,* it does give the religious critic pause before interpreting the song as scripture, limited to a singular meaning. If the Dylan songbook at its core is iconoclastic, then how can one book with endless one-page analyses that promulgate "one story" behind each song possibly do justice to the depth and breadth of the imagination operating in each lyric?

How then should an analysis of the Dylan songbook proceed? Critics like Rogovoy[207] and Pickering[208] have made compelling arguments about the need to analyze Dylan's work through their unique Jewish lenses to fully appreciate "the way in which it engages Jewish themes and thought in a process akin to *midrash,* the elaboration upon Jewish scripture as a form of commentary."[209] Rogovoy goes further in suggesting that Dylan's "complete *oeuvre* can also be read in large part as:

1) A reckoning with various loves and losses, most notably his relationship with his wife, Sara, before, during and after their marriage,

2) A commentary on topical concerns of American society and politics…and/or

3) A meditation on identity, with various characters and narrators that come to the forefront and disappear, and an obsession with the theme of the mask…[210]

As a popular critic who knows his Dylan songbook inside/out, Rogovoy draws a series of plausible maps of interpretation, but ultimately his wish comes through to downplay how "Dylan's work suggests a struggle or identification with a personal relationship with Jesus (as I hope to show, one that is at least subsumed by and doesn't discount his primary relationship with his Jewishness)."[211] This kind of hopeful apologetics betrays the very game of dawning and discarding masks that Dylan is engaged with.

Others remain concerned as to how Dylan's Judaism is expressed and to what degree he still self-identifies as a Jew? I want to interrogate these concerns by problematizing their underlying assumptions. Why would Dylan have visited the late, great Lubavitcher rebbe between 1979-1981? And why did an entourage of three of four rabbis, including the Lubavitcher rebbe come to study Torah with Dylan on his turf?[212] Why did the Lubavitcher rebbe refuse to acknowledge his presence in the Crown Heights headquarters at a celebratory *fabrengen* until Dylan immersed in a *mikveh* to re-enter the Jewish fold while in the midst of his Gospel years? Was Dylan's connection to Chabad as passionate and frenetic as his connection to the Vineyard Fellowship? Why then was Dylan pursuing scriptural studies with both groups simultaneously? Why did Dylan's son Samuel become bar mitzvah in 1982 at the Wailing Wall in Jerusalem? [213] Or why was the Orthodox Jewish outreach movement known as Chabad his "favorite organization"? Or was Dylan returning to ultra-orthodox Judaism in spending time with Chabad rabbis like Kasriel Kastel and Manis Friedman? And during that time did Dylan record an album of hasidic songs now lost? [214] Or does it matter that his daughter Maria married orthodox singer-songwriter, Peter Himmelman?[215] Or in recent years while on tour, Dylan has been seen attending Yom Kippur services? [216] The risks of authorial intention and biographical fallacy are already a minefield literary critics readily avoid, but when it comes to religious critics, sometimes the degree to which someone is drawn to religious experiences may predetermine their interpretation. This remains an occupational hazard of religious criticism.

On the other hand, Dylan can also be read through a Christian mask, either as embodied in his riffs on Western Literature or in an evangelical Christian key,[217] which will be redressed below. It should come as little surprise that Dylan was drawn into the Vineyard Fellowship in late 1978, given his inspiring coterie of female Gospel singers, including Helena Springs, Carolyn Dennis, and Mary Alice Artes.[218] That 1980 description of his "Precious Angel" who "mentioned a couple of things to me and one of them was Jesus" turns out to have been Artes. When Dylan returned to rethink their life together, Artes had already "changed her way of thinking" and committed to relocate to an immersive course of study at the Vineyard Fellowship in Reseda, California.[219] When Dylan was ready to join Artes at the Vineyard Fellowship's immersive School of Discipleship, they strategically dispatched a fellow musician, Larry Myers as his personal liaison.[220] It was more than a natural fit, given that Dylan's bandmates, David Mansfield, T-Bone Burnett, and Stephen soles had all fallen prey to the same charms.[221]

Whenever Dylan dawns a new mask he goes deep, as he remarks: "When I get involved in something, I get totally involved. I don't just play around on the fringes." [222] This artistic commitment to total immersion was also present in those painting classes with Norman Raeben from 1974-75 when Dylan makes the following self-discovery:

> "[My time with Raeben] locked me into the present time more than anything else I ever did... I was constantly being intermingled

with myself, and all the different selves that were in there, until this one left, then that one left, and I finally got down to the one that I was familiar with."[223]

Amidst this process of immersion that leads Dylan to self-discovery, requires a discarding of mask after mask, which will be addressed in terms of its mystical import later on. For now, it is important to simply appreciate the parallels here between the commitment to the artistry of painting as to religion. So here too, when Dylan drops deep into the Vineyard Fellowship's immersive School of Discipleship, he is already coming with many questions already formulated given his own vast exposure to scripture throughout his life's journey. One of his Discipleship teachers, Terry Botwick, recalls that Dylan as a student:

"...was a sincere and honest seeker, trying to understand and learn. What struck me about him was how deeply interested he was. My only frustration was keeping up with his questions. I'd go over five to six subjects each week, an Old Testament book like Isaiah 28, and he would've read ahead to chapter 43."[224]

Undoubtedly, there was a Pauline priority to the Vineyard Fellowship's immersive School of Discipleship focus on Isaiah 28. To understand Paul's proselytizing mission of the gospel to the gentile world in 1 Corinthians, one must know Isaiah 28 inside and out. The spiritual exhaustion and longing of the Jewish people Isaiah describes after the destruction of the Jerusalem temple in 70CE takes on an eschatological meaning, whereby Paul understands God as fulfilling Isaiah 28 in speaking to Israel through not only the invasive actions of the Assyrian armies but also through the gift of the Holy Spirit. Messianic Jews, in Paul's reading of Isaiah 28 through I Corinthians, then leaves little room for doubt that play a pivotal role in the salvation of the Jewish people.[225] While Dylan never intervened when *Jews for Jesus* decided to billet at some of his shows, [226] this does not appear to have been his primary interest and also explains why Dylan's thirst was not quite quenched with merely reading Isaiah 28 without seeing its correlation to Isaiah 43's renewal, redemption and ingathering of Jacob/Israel from the whole world. While Dylan's exegetically associative mind was too vast and expansive for his Vineyard Fellowship's immersive School of Discipleship teachers and their methods, there remains a certain sense of purpose with which Dylan continually immerses himself in scripture to inspire the messianic impulse undergirding his music, as he remarked in 1979:

> "All that exists is spirit, before, now and forever more. The messianic thing has to do with this world, the flesh world, and you got to pass through this to get to that. The messianic thing has to do with mankind, like it is…"[227]

This brand of messianism is a fusion of the Vineyard Fellowship's dualism between "the flesh world" and the end game of the world of the spirit coupled with a Chabad post-messianic messianism[228] of dealing "with mankind, like it is" in order to make a space for the divine to manifest where it already dwells.

Despite the cultic exterior of the Vineyard Fellowship's immersive School of Discipleship, Dylan was also at home in this learning environment because, as David Mansfield claims: "It was as intense as what was going on in fundamentalist circles, but it was culturally from an entirely opposite place." [229] To read scripture as a guide for self-help necessarily means that it is already being read as metaphor and poetry. This link to the bible as transformative literature had strong appeal for Dylan, especially in how often he would riff on and misquote scripture as it would morph in and out of his songbook. [230]

Reading Christianity and its scriptural beliefs as inspiration for strong literature, a compelling argument has been made by Christopher Ricks by taking seriously the theology of sin, insofar as: "Dylan's is an art in which sins are laid bare (and resisted), virtues are valued (and manifested), and the graces brought home".[231] While it appears to be sound criticism to analyze Dylan's songbook through the motif of sin that may haunt much of the songbook, yet as a critic, Ricks remains too sophisticated to fall into the essentialist trap of reading the entire Dylan's songbook through the lens of the seven deadly sins. As a literary critic, Ricks knows he must be more cautious and humbler in confessing: "The claim in this book isn't that most of Dylan's songs, or even most of the best ones, are bent on sin. Simply that (for the present venture in criticism) handling sin may be the right way to hold the bundle together."[232] If the Dylan songbook takes pride in making a mockery of songs *about ideas*, then the experiences it evokes must be *the thing itself.*[233] Effective criticism is sometimes a question of how well one navigates the road, steering clear of that myopic manhole of interpretation that would horrify the religious critic and scholar but please the believer. Many nuances hidden within this Christian mask are analyzed but still remain tone deaf to the Gnostic resonances hidden in plain sight.

As a religious critic, I dawn the Gnostic mask to read the Dylan songbook as an act of both cultural critique and disavowal. Reading these lyrics needs to evolve beyond interpreting the Dylan songbook as categorically Jewish, Christian, or Zionist. Once again, Heylin is helpful here in his recent reappraisal of the so-called "born-again" period of 1979-1981 by reframing it as *Dylan's Gospel Years* so as to recover *What Really Happened.*[234] Dylan is clear-headed and unapologetic in his disavowal of such pigeon-holing, claiming that "religious labels are irrelevant."[235] Every mask Dylan has dawned and discarded has only been for the sake of the music: "I find the religiosity and philosophy in the music...I don't adhere to rabbis, preachers, evangelists...I've learned more from the songs than I've learned from any of this kind of entity."[236]

While many readers will scratch their heads at the mention of Gnosticism in general, and Manichaeism in particular, most readers will know of its diluted resonances that grace bestsellers like *The Da Vinci Code.*[237] Surely the world is full of university-educated Americans who haven't ever heard of Manichaeism even while they enjoy being titillated by Tom Hanks redeeming the world in *The Da Vinci Code*! But Gnosticism remain unknown to most. While Gnosticism is the perennial quest for illumination, it is considered historically to be that heretical movement of the second century that the Christian Church could not ultimately contain or fully censor. Gnosticism derives from the desire for gnosis or knowledge as illumination. This search for a deeper truth comes by challenging the status quo, especially inspired by a need to overcome the perception that institutionalized religion is full of contradictions and hypocrisy.[238]

Gnosticism operates within a complex and dark mythology then sees the world as created and ruled by a lesser divinity, known as a *demiurgos* or demiurge. It is precisely this esoteric knowledge, known as *gnosis,* that enables the redemption of the human spirit. Although the myth of a creative god in tension with the demiurge and the theme of reawakened awareness of divine origins have parallels elsewhere in philosophy, oftentimes, the gnostic myths portray a sharper dualism. This sharpness also involves more darkness, more negativity toward the inferior creator god, the material cosmos, and the human body.[239] It is this dark, negative soundtrack in search of redemption that runs throughout Dylan's songbook. This demiurge comes alive for Dylan through the "prince of the power of air" which he encounters in the gospel of Hal Lindsey through the Vineyard Fellowship.[240] This reformulation of the earthly demiurge posits the "prince of the air" as "Satan [who] rules over the thoughts of the world system." [241]

This creative tension is present in all aspects of thinking for an artist wired to see the world through this dialectical lens of "topical and profane versus primordial and sacred; transcendence as excess versus transcendence as purgation." [242] Dylan sees himself completely engaged in this primordial battle as an artist, insofar as there:

> "...there are two kinds of thoughts in your mind...good thoughts and evil thoughts...Some people are more loaded down with one than the other. Nevertheless, they come through. And you have to be able to sort them out, if you want to be a songwriter."[243]

This supports my interpretive claim that Dylan sees himself as a songwriter engaged in this struggle between good and evil that produces a creative tension to then inspire his Great Gnostic American songbook.[244]

Gnosticism, however, is crucial to understanding the history of American religion in general, and American Judaism in particular. Gnosticism became less of a mystery lost to history with the discovery of the Nag Hammadi Library along with helpful guides, like critics of religion, Harold Bloom and Elaine Pagels.[245] The discovery by an Egyptian peasant in 1945 buried in a jar near the village of Nag Hammadi was a game changer because it means reuniting with fifty-two hidden scrolls including Gnostic Gospels. These gospels are variations on the more commonly read Synoptic Gospels of Matthew, Mark, and Luke. Recall that the Synoptic Gospels are so called because of their inclusion of similar stories, sequences and wording. But what Elaine Pagels cogently deciphered in the texts of the Gnostic Gospels had implications for hungry American seekers. Her award-winning book, *The Gnostic Gospels,*[246] puts Pagels in a unique position—on the hand, she is a renowned biblical scholar whose work has changed our understanding of the origins of Christianity and its heresies. On the other hand, these very heresies (or other choices) were what led her as a biblical scholar to return the origins of her own abandoned religion with new eyes.[247] So Dylan is not far off when he listlessly sings: "I practice a faith that's been long abandoned/Ain't no altars on this long and lonesome road".[248] Like Pagels, Dylan's songbook confesses that it takes time and distance to return to origins on one's own terms. Part of what amazes us reading these Gnostic Gospels today is how open its writers were to multiple perspectives of truth relating to the redeemer and redemption. Everything changes with what eventually becomes the new religion of Christianity. Some say that the pivotal moment that birthed Judaism in contradistinction from Christianity was the year 180 CE, when Bishop Irenaeus of Lyons denounced all gospels but Matthew, Mark, Luke and John as heretical— "an abyss of madness and of blasphemy."[249] We still live in the shadow of this canonical moment that sought to censor and forget that "abyss" and replace it with a newly unified religion and credo.

It is thus not hard to see why religion is so complicated. Moreover, when the quest for truth is obfuscated, lost or censored, we need maps to get there. Matters are made even more complicated by the reality that the inherited maps we currently have of religions are not territory. So, it is not surprising then that in the study of religion in America, the landmark inaugural lecture, called, "Map Is Not Territory" delivered by Jonathan Z. Smith's in 1974 changed the playing field. The danger in the study of religion is precisely the way we analyze religion and its texts through our own maps, whether locative or utopian, we can oftentimes fall prey to projecting our own "particular way of thinking about the world—of making sense of it and, thereby, of obtaining some sort of leverage over it." [250] So when I come as a religious critic to analyze a religious experience through a given text, there needs to be a self-awareness both by myself as well as the reader that the analysis at hand reflects a "particular way of thinking about the world"—that this is *my map*, even if only for this leg of the journey, and it is liable to evolve. Why does this matter when reading a book such as the one before you? Because "what is at stake is the infinite potential for new epiphanies to occur as the religious imagination continues to expand among the citizens of a world republic of letters"[251] and given the state of affairs at this hour, nothing feels more critical.

In my present analysis of the Dylan songbook, a motivating factor for returning to these forgotten Gnostic Gospels is to seek out a lens with a more multi-perspectival view of the truth. Dylan's songbook has embedded within it "the infinite potential for new epiphanies" and so my task as religious critic is to decipher this expansive religious imagination in the context of American Religion and it is Gnosticism that enables a fuller view of this perennial search. And yet in using the gnostic lens, I am not necessarily arguing for something like a "Jewish Gnosticism" as did scholar of Jewish mysticism, Gershom Scholem. His project was more of a reaction to the questionable proposition that "Christianity was rooted in Gnosticism and thus needn't be dependent on any Jewish sources" and as a result this was considered to be quite "damaging the very idea of a German Jewish culture".[252] And so, exiled from German having emigrated to Mandate Palestine, Scholem argued that there was a "Jewish Gnosticism" that eventually morphed into the religion known as Christianity. The borderlines of identity are much more fluid within the landscape of American Religion.

As we roll back the tape even earlier, the resonant complexities of identity sound clearer— especially in considering how the Dylan songbook dawns and discards the masks of Judaism and Christianity. The act of choosing one mask over another is considered to be heresy. Here it is most helpful to return to reflections on the birth of heresy by Boyarin. He points to "the very discursive effect of the mutual efforts to distinguish Judaism from Christianity that provided the major impetus for the development of heresiology in its different forms among the second-century church writers and the rabbis." [253] In this process of creating discursive distinctions between these burgeoning religions, Boyarin argues that the second-century church writers and the rabbis did not really suspect "that in struggling so hard to define who was in and who was out, who was Jewish and who was Christian, what was Christianity and what was Judaism, it was they themselves who were smuggling… the very discourses of heresiology and of religion as identity." [254] The question that dominates the iterations of Judaism(s) in American Religion today is less "Who is a Jew?" in terms of legal status and more "How is a Jew?" as a performative question. Given the fluid, hybrid nature of identity, what are the acts that constitute the dance of these different masks worn at once?

On the question of Dylan's religious identity as portrayed through his songbook, one could argue that: "[t]here is now virtually no way that a Jew can stop being a Jew, since the very notion of heresy was finally rejected and Judaism…refused to be, in the end, a religion." [255] The implications of rejecting the rigid boundaries of religion to determine identity have implications to this day for in: "[r]effusing to be different in quite the same ways, not a religion, not quite, Judaism…remained something else, neither quite here nor quite there. Among the various emblems of this different difference remains the fact that there are Christians who are Jews, or perhaps better put, Jews who are Christians, even up to this very day." [256] And so, when Dylan sings: "I practice a faith that's been long abandoned",[257] he is again acknowledging that this path is not one of religion *per se,* rather this is the songbook of a wandering identity, between faithfulness and faithlessness.[258]

Then there is the most intriguing (an ironically today the most heretical) Zionist mask, which like Gnosticism, serves as a bridge between Dylan's Jewish and Christian masks. Part of the draw for Dylan to the Vineyard Fellowship was its early adoption of millennial eschatology. The gospel of Hal Lindsey, another in a long line of misguided autodidacts, claimed in his best-selling, *The Late Great Planet Earth*, that the key to unlock St. John the Divine gnostic flights was through his interpretation of State of Israel's restoration in 1948.[259] *The Late Great Planet Earth* was already mainstream by the time Dylan encountered it, but its resonance with such a lapsed and wandering American Jew was all the more powerful, especially in light of Dylan's lineage as the son and grandson of Jewish emigres from Easter European pogroms at the turn of the century. The gospel of Hal Lindsey hit home with Dylan given that he presented a Jesus that spoke for Jews and Christians alike.[260] Notwithstanding the impact of the gospel of Hal Lindsey, it should be recalled that already in 1971 at thirty years old, during his second honeymoon with then wife, Sara in Israel, Dylan was photographed at the Wailing Wall in Jerusalem, coupled with his vigilant "desire to escape self-imposed identity reached such a height on this trip that he even considered entering a kibbutz with his family" so that by June "Dylan and Sara approached the *Kibbutz Givat Haim*, with a view of joining up for a year."[261] Although his band tours in Tel Aviv and Jerusalem challenged and confused audiences, Dylan continued pressing on with this relentless process of dawning and discarding his masks.[262] The Zionist mask is much more concerned with the religious facets of Zion than necessarily with its political facets, except as will be analyzed later on in "Neighborhood Bully."[263]

Just as Dylan learned while immersed in the Vineyard Fellowship's *School of Discipleship* that scripture could be read as great literature, so too, upon receiving the Nobel Prize, Dylan is now reading himself as a poet. While Dylan begins his 2016 Nobel Prize for Literature acceptance address in denial, claiming: "Not once have I ever had the time to ask myself, 'Are my songs literature?' [264] eventually he accedes that his lyrics are indeed "Homeric".[265] Like the great bards of antiquity, it is the lyricism of his songs that resonates with that shared lyre of the ancient bard, whereby songs are meant to be sung and not necessarily read. Somehow, the impact of Dylan's songbook as a kind seeker's scripture that transcends and includes American religion, reaching the world over, can thus indeed be read as great literature.

The lyricism of Dylan's songbook abides in the daily discovery that when words bridge heaven and earth— truth is spoken; and when words fall short— lies abound. As the late, great American poet, Walt Whitman responds to Dylan's uncertainty about his lyrics as literature: "Discovering to-day there is no lie, or form of lie, and can be none, but grows as/inevitably/upon/itself as the truth does upon itself."[266] What I am arguing here is how Dylan's songbook continually seeks after this truth to sing it through song. Yet, as complex as some of these lyrics may come across throughout my analysis, I am not suggesting that Dylan himself was necessarily familiar with the exegetical and mystical sources I cite (although he is riffing scripture incessantly like a mystic), nor the nuances of Gnosticism as being on his radar. Rather, I am arguing that on my own pilgrimage through the Dylan songbook I have discovered a compelling meaning behind his work—the song within the songs— by following an avenue of interpretation that goes back to the origin of each song in its composer's heart and mind. In other words, I am offering yet another way of reading Dylan's songbook that, like all great works of art, remains timeless.

From the timeless to this very moment in time of reading this book, hearing the echo of Dylan's snarl: "You got too many lovers waiting at the wall/If I had a thousand tongues I couldn't count them all."[267] Amidst the culture industry of Dylanology, some might see yet another book as one "too many lovers waiting at the wall". Since being awarded the Nobel Prize, the yearning to see the light behind the mask of darkness in Dylan's songbook resonates even deeper. Despite the shelves of Dylanology in my library, I still feel justified in my love for humbly offering my own analysis of an understudied aspect of Dylan's expansive songbook. As "I'm searching for phrases to sing your praises/I need to tell someone"[268] may these words make a bit more space for "the infinite potential for new epiphanies to occur as the religious imagination continues to expand."[269] My offering here is made not just as a scholar-rabbi, but also as a Levite dedicated to serving in the Jerusalem Temple. By enabling this offering through my Hebrew namesake, Aaron, I feel the reverberations of Aaron's perfect death as he transfers the priesthood over to his son, Eleazar as his soul passes from his body. The final note in this song of this soul's return is a kiss from the *Shekhinah,* who has been suffering with all of us through every moment of exile. Indeed, *God Knows, Everything is Broken*, but the *Shekhinah* and her suffering alongside each creative cataclysm makes healing possible, no matter how far in the offing. As a lost Levite searching for a vanishing broken-down palace in Jerusalem, what the Dylan songbook enables me to see with greater clarity is just how "soon after midnight" that the "day" of American Religion (that still bleeds across the border into the once immune northern hinterland) "has just begun"[270] may its song continue to be sung…

Rosh Hodesh Menachem Av, 5779
(yahrzeit of Aaron, the high priest)
Panui (Baka, Jerusalem)
Shaare Zion (Montréal, Québec)

Introduction:
God Knows, Everything is Broken

Chapter at a glance: *If God Knows, Everything is Broken, then how can life still have any meaning? Any attempt at analyzing the songbook of Bob Dylan requires a confrontation with paradox. To confront what God knows can be challenging if we never really think of God all that much. This introduction stakes out the claim that the Dylan songbook is Gnostic in its inclination to read the world as ever darkening without any hope of real redemption through light. If God Knows Everything is Broken, then this chapter argues that Dylan's songbook is a manual in negative direction that absorbs the disruption between and total reality is at the bottom of nihilism. The genius of Dylan's songbook is its uncanny ability to stare at the isolated selfhood, to which it condemns every human, along with the rupture, would abolish also the idea of human qua human, and still somehow the seeker carries on the search for meaning, for light. In embracing that paradoxical state of emergence from a luminous source while the sparks begin to fly, Dylan's songbook is willing to accept "That not much is really sacred" all the while searching to hover on a "third road", beyond self-estrangement, erasing humanity and the reality of a broken world that each song must perennially cry out in the darkness.*

Dylan lyrics analyzed include: "God Knows," (*Under the Red Sky*, 1991); "Everything is Broken," (*O Mercy,* 1989); "The Times They Are A-Changin'" (*The Times They Are A-Changin'*, 1965); "Things Have Changed" (*The Essential Bob Dylan*, 1999); "Wedding Song" (*Planet Waves*, 1973); "Full Moon and Empty Arms" (*Shadows in the Night*, 2015); , "Long Time Coming" (*Bootleg Series Volume 9: Witmark Demos 1962-64*, 2010); "Absolutely Sweet Marie," (*Blonde on Blonde*, 1966); "Huck's Tune," (*Tall Tell Signs: Bootleg Series 1989-2006*, 2007); "Ballad of a Thin Man," (*Highway 61 Revisited*, 1965); "It's Alright Ma (I'm Only Bleeding)," (*Bringing It All Back Home*, 1965).

Introduction:
God Knows, Everything is Broken

If *God Knows, Everything is Broken,*[271] then how can life still have any coherent meaning? Any attempt at analyzing the songbook of Bob Dylan requires a confrontation with such glaring paradox. To confront what God *knows* can be challenging if we never really *think* of God all that much.[272] What comes to mind with first part of this clause, *God Knows* resonates with American Jewish novelist, Joseph Heller's *God Knows*[273] where there is an urgency to meditate upon one's mortality through the deathbed memoirs of old man David—purportedly the memoirs of King David himself! The absurdity of life to be meditated upon, by Heller in his novel, is in no ways linear but often hilariously fractured. It is precisely in the rupture where God knows that humor can emerge. Despite his deep admiration for that "secret cord that pleased the lord,"[274] Dylan is no David! As legend has it, in conversation with the truly modern Davidic singer-songwriter Dylan discovers that the writing "Hallelujah" had taken Leonard Cohen over five years, with dozens of verses drafted and discarded, so Cohen told Dylan:

> "I really like 'I and I,'" [a song that appeared on Dylan's album *Infidels*].
> "How long did it take you to write that?"
> "About fifteen minutes," Dylan said.[275]

Sometimes songs come like prayers, other times they appear like jokers—it all depends on the hand you are dealt, as one bard admits to another. And yet, Dylan's songbook has us turn and turn again to this cliché in his lyric "God knows" as a highly paradoxical expression because it captures so much of the Dylan songbook—at once emphasizing that one does not know something, while, on the other hand, it is used to emphasize the truth of a statement. *How can something be at once true and unknowable?*

It is from within this paradox of truth and its unknowability, the secret and its necessary disclosure[276] through a song that Dylan continues to be prolific in his exploration of timeless themes within the long and winding road of the American Dream and its unfolding songbook. But it is an America that is a "post-September 11 America, [where] the inescapably topical is also enveloped in history and myth."[277] From where does the wisdom come, that spans "the American Revolution, and beyond, back before the New World, the New Eden was envisioned"[278] that still inspires this American bard, Bob Dylan, to continue creating and covering this unfolding songbook? There is *something more* than meets the eye and it requires a step back into the thicket of American Religion before proceeding into Dylan's songbook. That *something more*, perhaps what God knows, is what drives this American bard to explore "the gap where the towers used to be [where there] rise many ghosts".[279] An abiding aspect to the genius of Dylan's songbook aligns strongly with the poetic ambivalence at the heart of the *American Sublime* as Bloom calls it to be addressed further on.[280] Right from the moment Dylan's lyrics encapsulated the ethos of the folk scene with "The Times They Are A-Changin'" while he had already moved on: "The chance won't come again/And don't speak too soon"[281] for the open secret can easily be misconstrued. This shift inevitably happens once the singer realizes he has already moved on from the euphoric moments of utopia, because in his own subjective experience: "I'm locked in tight, I'm out of range /I used to care, but things have changed".[282]

If one is mindful of the arc of Dylan's musical wanderings as the "Original Vagabond",[283] it comes as little surprise that he is perceived as a betrayer. Female companions, like Joan Baez and Sara Noznisky live to see that betrayal already by 1975 when "we talked for hours about those days when the Original Vagabond was two-timing us."[284] Off stage and on stage, the betrayal was felt deeply, especially by Joan as lover and collaborator. [285] But the betrayal ran deeper, eliciting that infamous caterwaul by Keith Butler tarring Dylan as "Judas" during those early years of going electric at the Albert Hall concert in 1966. [286] For in the eyes of those who wanted to hold onto Dylan's prophetic impulse that elevated the social justice aspect of the folk scene, especially its hard core adherents, like Phil Ochs and Dave Von Rank, the Original Vagabond betrayed the folk scene from which he emerged in Greenwich Village. But truth be told, this pattern continued with every genre the Original Vagabond has passed through, completely absorbing its ethos and shedding it in search of only one thing— his singular voice within the Great American songbook. In close hindsight, Dylan's songbook reflects upon this perception so common to his early folk audience, that this singer-songwriter was doing anything more than passing through the scene: "It's never been my duty to remake the world at large/Nor is it my intention to sound a battle charge".[287]

Even before Bloom could call it the *American Sublime*, Joan Baez, who knew Dylan too well, put her finger on that poetic ambivalence at the heart of his songbook in an ingenious moment of flashback to their time together: "And at keeping things vague/'Cause I need some of that vagueness now".[288] It is this gift for ambivalence or what Baez sings to her forlorn lover as "vagueness" that demarcates Dylan genius. This also set Dylan's lyrics apart from the folk scene that he was already taking leave of while he still hovering within it. His uncanny ability to absorb an entire genre or persona, beginning with the likes of Woody Guthrie, and then recreating his singing and songwriting arc that transcends and includes everything he touches right up to Frank Sinatra's "Full Moon and Empty Arms"[289] as part of his wandering through the American songbook writ large, most recently, with *Triplicate.* [290]

As the ashes of the folk scene gave way to the Summer of Love, there were multiple streams seeking liberation and power. As Black Power was emerging with its own gravitas, there was an equally powerful emergence of Jewish Power that spread in numerous directions.[291] There were other Jew on the margins of the folk scene who attempted to translate the Summer of Love into the core message of the emerging future of American Judaism. The broken mirrors of Reb Shlomo Carlebach with the House of Love and Prayer as well as Reb Zalman Schacter-Shalomi with the Aquarian Minyan, each attempted translating the power of the music during the times that are a changin' into a renewed chapter of American Religion.[292] It is no coincidence that both of these rabbis were sent as emissaries to draw back the wandering Jews of the 1960s to return to the American Religion of Judaism as envisioned by the Lubavitcher rebbe. [293] While Chabad-Lubavitch hasidism was never foreign to Dylan, he translated American Religion in a different key. One can see a stronger, albeit much less artful parallel, with the strident translation of social justice as a cornerstone of American Judaism in the liturgizing of Rabbi Arthur Waskow. In watershed moments like his American freedom *seder* prophetic moment. While Waskow takes up the prophetic mantle transforming American Judaism on the margins, Dylan is in the spotlight and remains more interested in transforming an intertextual Americana songbook in his own image, [294] rather than any practice *per se.*

At this point, having been tarred as a heretical "Judas" to so many orthodoxies, many feel that Dylan is the false prophet *par excellence.*[295] If so, perhaps it is worthwhile for the moment, to subject him to the test of false prophecy. Undoubtedly, at its core, the Judaism from which Dylan was birthed requires a fealty to the prophets. While the prophets always sang their songs an octave just above what those listening in their generation could really absorb, still the prophet establishes his/her credibility by either performing a wonder or by consistently predicting future events. If and when the prophet establishes him/herself, then that generation of listeners are required to obey the instructions. And yet as Jewish history shows time and time again, the authority of the prophet is not absolute nor may s/he really revise the commandments of the Torah. Notwithstanding such fences around the law, still it does not preclude a temporary suspension of a specific law.

Recall Dylan and his search for prophetic roots:

"Check on Elijah the prophet. He makes rain.
Isaiah the prophet, even Jeremiah, see if their
brethren didn't want to bust their brains for
telling it right like it is, yeah—these are my
roots, I supposed. Am I looking for them? ...
I ain't looking for them in synagogues, with
six-pointed Egyptian stars shining down from
every window, I can tell you that much." [296]

Just how might one "check on Elijah" I wondered. As listeners to the Dylan songbook we are now being beckoned to hear the echoes of the challenge by the Hebrew prophet to the priests of the Ba'al. Such a curious moment of sacred theatre passed over in hastily reading scripture. Think about what's at stake in this moment: if Elijah challenges these neighbourhood priests to prepare a sacrifice that will rival his own, he must know something they do not know! As the scene unfolds, we see how this showdown between priests and prophet culminates in offering fiery prayers to their respective deities in hope that something catches fire. The priests of Ba'al take up the challenge and call upon their god to alight their offering, and after their mortifying failure, Elijah takes the stage with his offering. Doused with water, raising the stakes, the prophet then sings the song of his soul and makes his offering. At that moment, a flame descends from heaven and the offering is enshrouded in flames. The prophetic song of Elijah, akin to Dylan going electric in the face of the folk scene, emphatically proves the authenticity of the song of his soul against the naysayers.[297]

Folk purists would all agree that Dylan violated the folk ethos, in the same way the Sages suggest that Elijah violated the Torah in his challenge to the priest of Ba'al. For Elijah ends up defeating the priests of the Ba'al by offering a sacrifice outside of the Jerusalem Temple. If there is only one place and one way of making the offering of song, whether those offerings are to be made upon the altar of the Temple or through the conventions of the folk scene—Dylan and Elijah are iconoclasts. However, what the Sages note in the case of Elijah is that a prophet can still temporarily suspend a command in order to preserve the overall integrity of Torah. In Elijah's case there is a suspension of the prohibition of offering sacrifices outside of Jerusalem Temple so as to discredit the worship of the Ba'al and to return the Israelites to the core of Torah.[298] Yet the suspension of the prohibition against idolatry in order to preserve the Torah is an oxymoron.[299] If Dylan does not fall squarely into the category of false prophet, perhaps the Original Vagabond still succumbs to a certain kind of idolatry in the process of singing his own *Great, Gnostic Americana Songbook*?

Is it possible that such a false prophet could be deemed worthy of a Nobel Prize in Literature? More than merely a question of bad faith, Dylan swerves in and out of the persona of the false prophet in establishing his credibility as a folk prophet as he has been performing wondrous music and through this music predicting future events, proven time and time again by the ubiquity and flexibility of his songbook to respond to current events. But with the whole controversy surrounding his acceptance and appearance to receive the Nobel Prize, has Dylan the prophet not exposed himself as a charlatan?[300] While the prophetic impulse within Dylan's songbook has not necessarily directed the people to adopt idolatrous practices, from each musical period of discovery and re-invention, many feel betrayed by a fraud.

If *God Only Knows*, then how can such a fraudulent provocateur be granted the freedom to perform wondrous musical sets or even predict the future of Americana music? In other words, if *God Only Knows*, why not protect the true listeners and believers from such confusing musical tests? Perhaps, allowing this fraudulent provocateur to achieve recognition and even acclaim as a prophet, even winning the Nobel Prize, is all part of a plan to test whether we can be fooled by this impostor. False musical prophets, like Dylan are necessary in every generation insofar as s/he presents such a catalyst-challenge. This false musical prophet, by virtue of his/her stature within the culture becomes regarded as that sacred figure, especially needed within the secular cultural context of American Religion. Dylan sheds the prophetic mantle early on by declaring his intention: "But I know I ain't no prophet/An' I ain't no prophet's son".[301] And so, Dylan's immense courage, and enduring confidence in his convictions make his songbook nearly impossible to resist and oppose. The recurring resistance and denouncing this established American bard as a charlatan may only be possible through the very process of soul-searching that his music catalyzes for us.

Clearly, if one dares to dip into the sea of the burgeoning cottage industry known quaintly as Dylanology, there is an abiding frustration as to how to best pigeon-hole Dylan—born again Christian? *Ba'al teshuva* Jew? Zen master? Joker? Infidel? — and it stems from a larger issue of American Religion hidden in plain sight. The proclivity of American Religion, as suggested by literary critic Harold Bloom, to constantly focuses upon Gnosis, that two-millennia-old belief system that emphasizes knowledge of "the God within" bespeaks a certain messianic preoccupation.[302] Not unlike Dylan, but less artfully, Bloom oscillates between the brilliant and the half-baked in his insistence that that many Americans are "Gnostics without knowing it" and that the country's "rampantly flourishing industries" of astrology, dream divination and angel worship are "the mass versions of an adulterated or travestied Gnosticism."[303] If Bloom's critique of American Religion is correct, then we need to further understand what his idiosyncratic definition of Gnosticism looks like.

This task is made more accessible thanks to an American classic from 1939 called, *As A Driven Leaf*—a pioneering work of historical fiction but none other than an rabbi and author named Milton Steinberg.[304] The Americanization of Gnosticism that emerges in this novel stems from Steinberg's painstaking translation of its presence hovering throughout rabbinic Judaism as well as the abiding influence of his teacher, Mordechai Kaplan who was deemed a heretic by his orthodox brethren. It is no coincidence that Milton Steinberg and his teacher Mordechai Kaplan each in their day, as well as David Wolpe who writes the updated forward, are all Conservative rabbis. (That irony is not lost upon the author of this study who is also caught in the thicket of this Americanization of Gnosticism!)

Not unfamiliar to the rabbis of the Talmud often referred to as the Pharisees, who are credited with creating post-Second Temple Judaism, this esoteric doctrine of Gnosticism became influential around the second century CE. For Steinberg, the heretic par excellence in *As A Driven Leaf,* is Elisha ben Abuya aka *Aher*, not because he is a gnostic but given his passion for Greek philosophy. The real gnostic in Steinberg's rendering is Elisha's colleague, Ben Azzai. But in Biale's reading of Steinberg, there is a larger project at work here, namely that:

> "Steinberg clearly wants to construct a Judaism that will allow liberty of the mind to coexist with revealed religion. Rather than a heretic intent on destroying Judaism, Steinberg's *Aher* seeks what in Steinberg's view will only become possible two millennia."

What emerges in Biale's analysis of Steinberg is the insight that "[i]n constructing modern identities, whether Jewish or not, the hold of tradition, with its now-complicated categories of orthodoxy and heresy, remains a subterranean reality."y contrast, for Bloom American Gnosticism is much more deep seated impulse. Whereas Steinberg was struggling with assimilation through the model of Elisha's Hellenization, Bloom's American Gnosticism is already predicated upon a darker view of our fallen world of "death camps and schizophrenia" that was not created by the real, hidden God, but by a rebellious *Demiurge,* what Bloom refers to sardonically as a "bungler" who is responsible for our fall from Eden. If humankind predates the Fall, then a divine spark of the real God exists in everyone's deepest self, which leads to a deeper focus on "the God within. Bloom traces the traditional American emphasis on individuality with the Emersonian belief that whatever "gives me to myself" is best. Still, as Bloom points out, self-reliance has a way of devolving into mere selfishness or self-absorption, as he pontificates:

> "Our contemporary debasement of Gnosticism goes under the name of the New Age, a panoply wide enough to embrace Shirley MacLaine and Arianna Huffington, in which Ms. MacLaine worships Ms. MacLaine (with some justification) and Huffington reveres Huffington (with perhaps less)."[309]

While Dylan has not yet written any lyric about MacLaine or Huffington (although an ode to R & B diva, Alicia Keys has been made),[310] his songbook remains deeply immersed in travelling down Highway 61. Rather than mimicking legendary Blues guitarist Robert Johnson and his meeting the devil at the crossroads that sealed his soul and promised genius,[311] after Bloom and Steinberg, I will argue American Gnosticism is not entirely debased, rather it remains the appropriate *vade mecum* in approaching Bob Dylan's songbook.

As a thoroughly American bard, Dylan's acceptance speech for the Nobel Prize in literature reminds us why his songbook continues to captivate us—the inimitable process of making what is familiar

"Dylanified" and thus strange.[312] Dylan absorbs the mythic stories of modernity by making them sing the song of his soul. Of the three pivotal novels that influenced his song writing most, it is Melleville's *Moby Dick* that aligns him most with the American Sublime. In his analysis of the American Sublime, Bloom points to its main ingredient—ambivalence. Dylan's songbook could seamlessly fit into such a description of ambivalence caught in the thicket of time: "A selfhood endlessly aspiring to freedom from the past [that] is bound to resist actual over-determination that binds us all in time."[313] Dylan's songbook is marked, time and time again, by its uncanny yet ambivalent ability to add strangeness to beauty. And yet it is an abiding strangeness of meaning that continues to haunt us in "America, the Evening Land" that favors such "drastic sublimities".[314]

Even as an exemplar of the American Sublime, still there remains an enigmatic quality to the joker-genius of Dylan's songbook. On the one hand, the elusive quality of his genius speaks to his songbook's universal appeal of all seekers; while on the other hand, there is his songbook's refusal to be pigeon-holed in the tribal tradition of Judaism that has formed much of his worldview. Dylan's songbook fits well into the category of negative theology to which we will return throughout this analysis, insofar as it can only really be defined by what it is not— *not* folk protest music; *not* affirming love songs; *not* universal songs of peace; *not* tribal Jewish music; *not* born-again Christian evangelism, etc. So, what then exactly is Dylan's songbook, if it continues to refuse categorization while captivating listeners?

Many valiant attempts at analysis of Dylan's songbook have already been made, whether as scholarly literature,[315] as scriptural theology,[316] as mystical prophesy,[317] as the musings of a Zen master,[318] or as wanderings through a "self-directed study of Jewish scripture." [319] Yet part of the tension remains whether to analyze the Dylan songbook as high or low art, namely, to suggest that the literary analysis is somehow caught in the "thicket of academic obfuscation" is to completely miss the point of such an in-depth literary analysis.[320] Clearly the Dylan songbook deserves this kind of in-depth intertextual analysis worthy of other greats in the canon of English literature and it is by no means hyperbole to see his work as "rock's equivalent of James Joyce."[321] On the side of Jewish critique, the Dylan songbook has evolved into a kind of "contemporary sacred text". [322] And yet Dylan's songbook remains intentionally elusive, insofar as "Jewishness might be *one of many prisms* that Dylan uses for reflecting the world and himself back to his audience, but it is a stretch to claim that he is primarily Jewishly motivated as an artist". [323] The only critical voice willing to admit the shortcomings in the myopic Jewish analysis of the Dylan songbook to date is Arnof, who indeed calls out the sore "apologetic for a single Jewish critical narrative to explain Dylan".[324] It is this critique which points to the reality that any future analysis of the Dylan songbook needs to be "engaged with a range of generative disciplines, not only produce sophisticated interpretations of the many layers of their source material, but also encourage rapt audiences to hear voices echoing beyond the original intent of the texts they love."[325]The Dylan songbook necessarily negates by transcends and includes its intrinsically Jewish origins. One must pause here and reflect on the afterlife of the Dylan songbook upon its community of listeners insofar as one is attuned to hearing "voices echoing beyond the original"[326]— this is the sign of the highest and most transcendental art.

I aim to be more generative here in exploring

the depth and breadth of Dylan's songbook in still other registers, building on the insightful critique of Arnof. At first blush, these registers sound digressive, if not heretical. And yet, it will become self-evident within the course of this investigation that brokenness is what God knows and thus sheds light on the alienation of the seeker in the Dylan songbook. What are the implications of Dylan's self-reflection that: "...as the eighties progressed his faith seemed to only reinforce him in his view of a world gone mad, or just plain wrong"?[327] The present swerve to the mystical theology of Gnosticism is an attempt to understand precisely what it means to live in a darkening world gone made in search of the light of meaning.[328]

I argue that "God knows" is less a cliché than it is a mystical truth in a gnostic key. This is an umbrella term derived from *gnosis*, the Greek word for "knowledge". Such knowledge is understood in terms of the radiance of luminosity. The thrust of the present analysis of the Dylan songbook through the mystical theological lens of Gnosticism suggests that God *knows* the world is broken, and then attempts to provide theological mechanisms for navigating the darkness towards the light of meaning as Dylan's lyric convey a deeper knowledge of how: "God knows you can rise above the darkest hour/Of any circumstance."[329]

The one who is able "to rise above the darkest hour" with great luminosity is the Gnostic, "the Knowing one", that is, the one who shares this knowledge of brokenness amidst the human experience of alienation from God and the world.[330] The challenge before "the Knowing one" is to discern how and with whom to share this intimate knowledge of luminosity. I suggest that it is the artist who can be best understood as "the Knowing one" who is able to make manifest the experience of luminosity through all their forms and symbols. It is precisely this radiant light in the Dylan songbook that draws us in. This way of seeing each song reflects a larger world view in which:

> "The universe is radiant light energy. As experiencers, we are already luminous beings living in the immediacy of these universal energies. We live in the world and live within this luminous sensuous nature as place and space. The immediacy of sheer experience is found nowhere else but within our daily experience, and within the ever present translucent symbolic reality of all that is."[331]

What this symbolic view of reality as radiant light energy made manifest suggests is that "these archetypal actualities are present within us" [332]—how and why else would we find ourselves pulled so strongly to its magnetism?

Another aspect of this sense of alienation emerges from a radically existentialist theology. Of course, the French existentialists and symbolists would have cringed at their implication in constructing any sort of theology whatsoever. And yet Dylan's abiding influences are felt in the thinking of Albert Camus and Arthur Rimbaud within his anarchic songbook. The former allows for a "God who cheats the entire world along with him, and myself too" [*Dieu triche, tout le monde avec lui, et moi-meme*].[333] What this God is cheating the world of is one thing— justice. And so, the bard's clarion call is clear on this front— "But to live outside the law, you must be honest".[334]

The latter allows for a view from the self towards the unknown as <<*Je est un autre*>>. This renowned poetic manifesto of Arthur Rimbaud explains the human conundrum of living with such radical knowledge influences not a few songwriters, including Dylan.[335] But Dylan's turn to Rimbaud is more than merely a bohemian rock star in need of "expressing individual visions"[336] rather this is a gnostic turn, insofar as the gnostic path is aligned with the poetic throughout his songbook. To be a poet, according to Rimbaud, requires that one become "a seer" or "a visionary" [*un voyant*]. To appreciate what Dylan's songbook is after, it is worth reflecting further upon Rimbaud's letter from May 15, 1871 addressed to Paul Demeney that describes the calling of the poet as visionary:

> "A Poet makes himself a visionary through a long, boundless, and systematized derangement of all the senses [*dérèglement de tous les senses*]. He searches himself for all forms of love, suffering, madness, exhausting within all poisons, and preserving their quintessences. Ineffable torment, where he will need the greatest conviction, a superhuman strength, where he transforms into all types of being– the great beggar, criminal, accursed–and even the Supreme Savant [*le suprême Savant*]! For he attains the unknown! Because he has cultivated his soul, already rich, more than anyone else! He attains the unknown [*à l'inconnu*], and if, mad [*affolé*], he finally loses any understanding of his visions, at least he will have seen them! So, what if he is destroyed in his ecstatic flight through the unheard of and the ineffable [*les choses inouïes et innombrables*]: other horrible workers will come; they will begin at the horizons where the first one has fallen! ... So the poet, therefore, is truly a thief of fire."[337]

To decry "I am other" in relation to the divine housed within me is to acknowledge that I am *other* to myself. This constant shape-shifting persona was brilliantly captured in the strange bio-pic on Dylan, aptly titled, *I'm Not There* (2007). What screenwriters, Todd Haynes and Oren Moverman capture in this surrealist experiment is a six-fold cinematic lens into the various incarnations of Bob Dylan as: (1) actor; (2) folk singer; (3) troubadour playing electric; (5) French symbolist poet, Arthur Rimbaud; (5) the outlaw, Billy the Kid; and (6) folk legend, Woody Guthrie. The artist is a shape shifter, continuously morphing from one mask to another—I is other— whether as the son of Ramblin' Jack Elliott finding his Jesus; or handsome Robbie falling in love and then abandoning Claire; or as Woody escaping from foster care and singing his way through America; or as Billy awakening in a six-lane highway valley; or as Rimbaud rambling on; or as Jude being booed at Newport betraying his folk roots to turn to the electric guitar. What *I'm Not There* captures cinematically is what has eluded critiques— the dynamic nature of the singer-song writer known as Bob Dylan and the ensuing songbook. Every persona that this *I* takes on is but another layer of the *other* within that *I* have yet to uncover. The more I other myself, the more I know this deconstructive Creator— the God who subverts, cheats and destroys. Any sense of stability of persona is destroyed in a process of never-ending recreation of self.

I am less concerned with the historical questions around the origins of Gnosticism, yet it is worth noting that "modern scholars have advanced in turn Hellenic, Babylonian, Egyptian and Iranian origins and every possible combination of these with one another and with Jewish and Christian elements." [338] While a highly syncretic system, Gnosticism remains more than a "mere mosaic of these elements" so as to "miss its autonomous edge." [339] Returning to the opening paradox contained in the expression "God knows", that simultaneously acknowledges the truth of unknowing, here in Gnosticism, the object of knowledge itself refers to "the knowledge of God" as "the knowledge of something naturally unknowable and there itself is not a natural condition."[340]

One should also take note of "the violently anti-Jewish of the more prominent gnostic systems is by itself not incompatible with Jewish heretical origin at some distance."[341] To remain generative in our approach, the key to the gnostic lens for our present analysis is to appreciate the degree to which "the movement of [*Gnosticism*] itself transcended ethnic and denominational boundaries, and its spiritual principle was new." [342] So many of the lyrics in Dylan's songbook hover in the place of paradox, by transcending and including the ethnic and denominational boundaries he writes from to a place of non-place that is always new because it is ancient.

If there are any laws, by necessity these are "broken laws"[343] in light of all the corruption and suffering. And so, the law, called a *nomos*, is shattered. The integrity of such shattering can only be understood in the midst confronting the myth of Gnosticism. But what is Gnosticism and how on earth does it relate to the Dylan songbook—God knows!?! "Subversion of the idea of the law, of nomos, leads to ethical consequences in which the nihilistic implication of the gnostic acosmicism, and at the same time the analogy to certain modern reasonings, become even more obvious than in the cosmological aspect."[344] The Gnostic path posits that: "[p]sychical man can do no better than abide by a code of law and strive to be just, that is properly 'adjusted' to the established order, and thus play his allotted part in the cosmic scheme. But the *pnematicos*, 'spiritual' man, who does not belong to any objective scheme, is above the law, beyond good and evil, and a law unto himself in the power of his 'knowledge'." [345] And so Dylan's songbook early on acknowledges this subversive pathway for 'spiritual' seeker is through the law, insofar as: "to live outside the law, you must be honest."[346]

The mood of "homelessness, forlornness and dread" [347] that recurs throughout the Dylan songbook represents a coherent gnostic mystic theology of the alienated soul estranged from the world, seeking to return home. The challenge before this analysis of *God Knows Everything is Broken* is to cogently argue that the Dylan songbook sets into relief this "estrangement between man and the world" [348] as a perennial battle of darkness against light as a gnostic quest. To appreciate how this perennial struggle manifest in the Dylan songbook, we will turn to the insight of one of Heidegger's children, Hans Jonas, and the epilogue to his thinking through Gnosticism.[349] In confronting the darkening eclipse after modernity, it is in this pioneering reconsideration of Gnosticism in light of modern existentialism in relation to ancient nihilism that allows Jonas to suggest that ancient nihilism sets into relief modern nihilism.[350] If nihilism symbolizes the death of god, the metaphysical basis of gnostic nihilism suggests that " 'the God of the cosmos is dead'—is dead, that is, as a god, has ceased to be divine for us and therefore to afford the lodestar for our lives."[351]

To search for that star to guide the course the ship of our thinking is no small task amidst the deeply darkening heavens. And yet, in the ashes of the *Shoah*, it is at this nexus in reading Hans Jonas' critique of his teacher, Martin Heidegger, that I must return to the thinking of my teacher and colleague, with Elliot Wolfson, to listen more deeply to his critique of "a god, has ceased to be divine for us". My argument is that listening more deeply to what is so great in the American Gnostic songbook of Dylan is that lyrical gift which can encapsulate a philosophical translation of the gnostic myth, [whereby] the human being is that alienation within the great fortuitiveness of being.[352]

Despite the deep alienation expressed in this modern Gnosticism, amidst this simplicity and aloneness of being, there remains a paradoxical possibility of unison. Language is an intimate house of being as "the haven of solitude and the womb of relationality"[353] because it can make space for that dance between alienation and unison that hovers throughout Dylan's songbook.[354] This very creative tension recurs throughout the Dylan songbook, coming across most forcefully in the masterful ways in which Dylan's lyrics encapsulate this Gnostic dilemma: "In this version of death called life/... Behind every tree, there's something to see".[355] It is this deepening darkness, beyond the Tree of Knowledge, more evil than good, which permeates the lyrical palette. Ultimately, contrary to Song of Songs, such lyrics privilege the power of darkness — namely, death is stronger than love and life itself. The Gnostic seeks to recover and ready the light amidst this overwhelming darkness, given the knowledge: "...that the ladder of law has no top and no bottom."[356] If the law— which in Judaism is the Torah— is also a symbol and source of light accessible to human beings, why is that light not available to shine through the Dylan songbook? After all, as Rogovoy's writing suggests, Dylan's journey is suffused with and marked by his Jewish identity. This light of the terrestrial Torah is not accessible in this darkened world then all that remains is the knowledge of a pristine light hidden away from the darkness of this world in what Jewish mystics call "Primordial Torah" (*Torah Kedumah*).[357] It is this

Primordial Torah that "has no top and no bottom" insofar as it has no beginning and no end, unlike the exoteric scroll of the Torah that is commonly known and read in Jewish communities across the globe. When we correlate these two lyrical visions from the Dylan songbook together, it strongly aligns with the gnostic myth. But Dylan's songbook is less concerned with the law as spiritual practice and more with navigating broken world through an illumined pathway—akin to Nietzsche's madman but much, much darker:

> "Have you not heard of that madman who lit a lantern in the bright morning hours, ran to the market place, and cried incessantly: "I seek God! I seek God!" — As many of those who did not believe in God were standing around just then, he provoked much laughter. Has he got lost? asked one. Did he lose his way like a child? asked another. Or is he hiding? Is he afraid of us? Has he gone on a voyage? emigrated? — Thus, they yelled and laughed."[358]

Perhaps the voyage of *Original Vagabond* in Dylan's songbook is a search for a hidden god in world of deepening darkness. Yet time and time again, the divine is absent in retreat or present in all its brokenness.[359] Rather than stand denuded before the abyss emptied of all absence, it is merely in confronting the gap that in any meaningful, coherent correlation between the human being, the world and God emerges at the heart of gnostic mystical theology.[360] If the divine force that created the world is but a *deus absconditus,* a power and will that is concealed from the world, [361] then in this concealment, the divine remains Unknown. This in turn creates "the feeling of an absolute rift between man and that in which he finds himself lodged—the world." [362] This rift has implications both for the cosmos and humankind, as Jonas notes: "[c]orrespondingly, in its cosmological aspects it states that the world is not the creation of God but of some inferior principle whose law it executes; and, in its anthropological aspect, that man's inner self, the *pneuma* ('spirit' in contrast to 'soul' = *psyche*) is not part of the world, of nature's creation and domain, but is, within that world, as totally transcendent and as unknown by all worldly categories as is its transmundane counterpart, the unknown God without." [363] The demiurge responsible for creating the world out of ignorance and passion is seen as an inevitable perversion of the Divine. What matters then is that the world itself is seen as "the product, and even the embodiment, of the negative of knowledge." [364] It is this sense of the vulnerability of creation hovering on the precipice of its momentary destruction is that: "God knows it could snap apart right now/Just like putting scissors to a string". [365]

At this juncture, I return to the pioneering analysis of the Dylan songbook as a series of Zen musings. [366] While Heine's deep analysis of the apophasis at play in the Dylan songbook is an important contribution to a fuller understanding of this *oeuvre*, it needs further layering. That deepening is found in what Bauer sees as the symbolic view of reality as radiant light energy made manifest so that "these archetypal actualities are present within us." [367] Further embedded within this gnostic lens is a realization that the absorption of time from Zen into the thinking through a philosophical temporality[368] that opens up new doorways of perception of this luminosity. [369]

It is this seeming paradox that "in time we will find ourselves having facility with being in timeless awareness and in time simultaneously" which Dylan's songbook so subtly captures, mesmerizing generations of listeners. This wobbling pivot in time allows us to then better understand why there is such a mood of "homelessness, forlornness and dread" [370] that recurs throughout the Dylan songbook. This sense of being homeless at home or on a trackless path[371] tends to emerge from "the mindlessness of this will is the spirit of the world, which bears no relation to understanding and love." [372] The only way forward for the one seeking meaning is by way of holding onto a "knowing in the midst of unknowing, of light in the midst of darkness, and this relation is at the bottom of his being alien, without companionship in the dark vastness of the universe." [373] Dylan's songbook seeks to recover this loss of understanding and love in a darkening universe, and pointing to such darkness, the bard continues singing "[u]nder this pitiless sky, which no longer inspires worshipful confidence" precisely because of his being "conscious of his utter forlornness." [374] The genius of Dylan's songbook is its capacity to transform the dread the soul's self-estrangement in the world into a song of awakening from this inner self slumber in the world. Dylan has the self-awareness that the process of awakening from such slumber can be dangerous, as he quipped in 1997 that: "For some reason, I am attracted to self-destruction. I know that personal sacrifice has a great deal to do with how we live or don't live our lives."[375] The need to live an authentic life in search of the light of meaning is aspirational, even amidst the slumber to which the seeker succumbs. Whereas the gnostic approach to redemption is to overcome the degraded world through power, for Dylan's songbook the dread is overcome through songs of yearning. Rather than the countering the degraded power of the world with more authentic power, it is the song which points to the possibility of redemption through its continually being written and sung.

The path to redemption from the midst of the brokenness of the world requires a knowledge of the unknowable that points to freedom through such knowing. What this means in gnostic terms is that "the authentic freedom of the self, it is to be noted that this freedom is a matter not of the 'soul' (*psyche*), which is as adequately determined by the moral law as the body is by the physical law, but wholly a matter of the 'spirit' (*pneuma*), the indefinable spiritual core of existence, the foreign spark."[376] It is from this collection and dispersal of these of sparks within one's inner spirit that defines human existence in the Dylan songbook, as the bard sings about this spark and its loss: "Soon as a man is born, you know the sparks begin to fly/He gets wise in his own eyes and he's made to believe a lie".[377] Although the sparks of the seeker disperse throughout the course of existence, it is that potential for greater illumination that alludes to an origin in luminosity, so that "in the gnostic formula it is understood that, though thrown into temporality, we had an origin in eternity, and so also have an aim in eternity." [378] It is here that the Dylan songbook resonates more strongly with being placed in the "inner-cosmic nihilism of the Gnosis against a metaphysical background which is entirely absent from its modern counterpart." [379] This means that despite the darkening sense of self-estrangement in the Dylan songbook, the loss of sparks still paradoxically points to an origin and aim to return to a lost source in eternity which sets his lyrics in sharp contrast to modern nihilism. Dylan's songbook sings around the contours of "the absolute vacuum, the really bottomless pit" without succumbing completely to its nihilism. Rather his lyrics give directionless direction, despite it all, a kind of "negative direction, to be sure, but one that has behind it the sanction of negative transcendence to which the positivity of the world is the qualitative counterpart." [380] Negative direction embraces the given paradox while pointing beyond it. Dylan echoes this subtle journey in reflecting on the writing of this song itself: "It's like a ghost writing a song like that. It gives you the song and it goes away, it goes away."[381] The singer himself is negated in the journey of songwriting itself as another Jewish mystic quipped: "the song sings itself."[382] This negative transcendence is captured through all its poetics counterparts throughout the bard's journey of life within and beyond the 1960s: "With no direction home/Like a complete unknown."[383] In negating the very knowledge of knowing even what the creator creates in his own songbook— "Because something is happening here/But you don't know what it is"[384]— there is a directionless direction home to the place of no-place.

If *God Knows Everything is Broken*, then I can only continue to argue is that Dylan's songbook is a manual in negative direction that absorbs "[t]he disruption between and total reality is at the bottom of nihilism."[385] The genius of Dylan's songbook is its uncanny ability to "stare at the isolated selfhood, to which it condemns man…along with the rupture, would abolish also the idea of man as man,"[386] and still somehow the seeker carries on the search for meaning, for light. In embracing that paradoxical state of emergence from a luminous source while the sparks begin to fly, Dylan's songbook is willing to accept the challenge that: "It's easy to see without looking too far/That not much is really sacred"[387] all the while searching on a "third road", beyond self-estrangement, erasing humanity and the reality of a broken world. Each song illumines "a million miles" of the trackless road ahead "by candlelight" even "if there's a heaven" and "it's out of sight"— "God knows".[388]

(1) *I & I* as *Eheyeh*: Knowing Thyself Through Shades of I & Masks of Other

Chapter at a glance: *When am I who I really am meant to be, and when do I feel other than my true self? What is the constitution of identity—human and divine—as one comes to be caught in this dialectical dance? This chapter explores the theological and philosophy resonances in Bob Dylan's "I and I" through the lenses of Rastafarian theology and selected exemplars in Jewish mysticism to realize that god is a process of becoming called Eheyeh. It is this mysterious name revealed in the book of Exodus— Eheyeh Asher Eheyeh— that both Moses and Dylan encounter in their lyrical seeking. This creative tension within the song as a whole moves beyond Rastafarian theology, returning to its biblical source in this mysterious name of Eheyeh Asher Eheyeh— "I will be that which I am becoming". What Dylan's lyric ingeniously extrapolates from Jewish process theology is not only that God is a verb rather than a noun, but what God is much less important than what God does in our lives. If my life is constantly in flux and the divine is constantly emerging from moment to moment as an abiding presence with me, then the divine is necessarily in flux—God is godding. This chapter suggests that through the oscillation in Dylan's I & I, the initial dialectic between the I who is other reveals itself as a godding process of "I will be that which I am becoming". Ultimately, in the journey from I to I, from all concepts of the ego to the realm beyond conception, what remains in returning home is the realization there is no longer any other but I in the fullness of its very emptiness.*

Dylan lyrics analyzed include: "I and I" (*Infidels*, 1983).

(1) *I&I* as *Eheyeh*: Knowing Thyself Through Shades of I & Masks of Other

How do I understand myself in relationship to everything that is not my *self* that is beyond, yet seemingly so much within reach? Philosophers through the ages have sought to define the nature of identity through the lens of "self-knowledge". The way to "Know thyself" is through knowledge of my own sensations, thoughts, beliefs, and other mental states. But the role of the oracle was not limited to politics and reached all aspects of life, public and private.[389] Before us stands a singer-songwriter, Bob Dylan, one seeks this truth in song through the messiness of life, precisely in that blurry boundary between philosophy and religion.[390]

And yet, most philosophers have suggested that my knowledge of my own consciousness is a different kind of knowing than my knowledge of the external world. From here I come to realize a distinction between my own consciousness of self and everything that is not my *self* that is beyond yet seemingly so much within reach, this becomes known as *other*. The nature of the relation between *self* and *other* in Dylan's songbook is a perennial concern. No song captures this mystical transformation of multiple masks and many identities as "I and I".[391] Far from being a "confessional" what is important here is to see anew the mystical experience of the name of *Eheyeh Asher Eheyeh* which the biblical prophet Moses encounters in the Exodus 3:14 theophany in order to appreciate the ingenuity of its lyrical subversion in the gnostic songbook of Dylan.

Is Dylan pointing to the practice of lived philosophy that emerges from a theology the Hebrew bible alludes to but never completes? Can the *self* fuse with the *other* to the point where there is no longer a distinction between "you and I", rather everything becomes absorbed into the greater "I" in surrender to complete oneness? Dylan's adaptation of the traditional "I and I" subverts our expectations as readers of the biblical text which is highly monist, which then allows the lyrics to open a tension of dual identity that remains irreconcilable as in the refrain of the song itself:

> "I and I
> In creation where one's nature neither
> honors nor forgives
> I and I
> One says to the other, no man sees my face
> and lives"[392]

What is this lyric attempting to accomplish by challenging this classical Rastafarian theology which is highly monist, that is, singular in its view of all of being as a unified and intertwined whole? The lyric is ingenious in allowing this dialectic of identity to stand as part of a larger ethos in the Dylan songbook that returns to Rimbaud's 1871 radical statement <<*Je est un autre*>> dissolves the philosopher's attempt at constructing boundaries of "self-knowledge" in relation to all else that is external to self, by decrying that "I is other".

In the second section of the refrain in the aforementioned lyric: "In creation where one's nature neither honors nor forgives" there is a rapid shift into negative theology of creation. Whereas philosophers and theologians have spilt much ink in grappling with what it means for God as Creator to create the world and make space for humanity to exist within it, this lyric negates the yearning of the individual for honor or forgiveness. The sense of radical alienation of the human being from a God that can bring one honor or forgiveness is striking. But such alienation as negation cannot be fully appreciated without the given context of negative theology. I argue that Dylan's lyric here is a form of *via negativa*, that is, of a human life in negation rather than the divine life in negation.

To gain a better appreciation of what is at stake, let us turn briefly to one of the most renowned attempts at wrestling meaning from human language that cannot approximate the infinitude of the divine. It is found in the medieval Jewish philosophy that dares to claim that statements like "God lives" or "God is powerful" are simply nonsense. If so, then how does a human being express prayerful yearnings, either in poetry, liturgy, or even in lyrics? These statements can only function as disguised negations, so that "God is powerful" really means "God is not lacking in power." This tendency towards negation through language, or what is referred to in theological language as apophasis is often misunderstood.[393] Is this merely a language game, whereby a double negative indicates a positive? What remains elusive with this kind of negative theology is how deep is the proposed form of negation. Returning to the previous statement that "God is powerful" then comes to mean that "God does not lack power" or that "God does not possess power in a comparable way". The depth of negation here is meant to recognize that the power to create the whole universe is truly incomparable and so far beyond human comprehension and experience that any comparison is only misleading. This ultimately leaves those in search of truth through negative theology in a deeper quandary, as a modern philosopher once quipped: "What we cannot speak about we must pass over in silence."[394] Negating the modern philosopher's acquiescence into silence, Dylan instead fully embraces the paradox through song.

Also, notice in the second section of the refrain in the aforementioned lyric: "One says to the other, no man sees my face and lives" there is an evocation of both the biblical archetypes of David and Moses, as exemplars of the dialectical nature of the soul itself. Moreover, as these archetypes of David and Moses evolve in Jewish mystical literature, each of them displays a deeper affinity to the hovering feminine of the "I" within the "I" of self, what Jung would call the "anima",[395] or mystics call *Shekhinah*, namely that feminine counterpart of the masculine soul which is hovering amidst its exile. This tincture of the feminine within the alienated masculine soul is heard from the outset in this lyric: "In another lifetime she must have owned the world, or been faithfully wed/To some righteous king who wrote psalms beside moonlit streams".[396] The gnostic dualism recurs here, insofar as love is lost and the singing voice is alienated from his feminine counterpart. The Dylan lyric imagines the masculine and feminine to be forever hovering in a dialectical tension. While it seems like there is temporal distance because it has: "Been so long since a strange woman has slept in my bed" the lyric is concerned with the presence of the feminine in this moment and invites the listener to "Look how sweet she sleeps, how free must be her dreams". By entering into this acoustic invitation to gaze, there is a peeling back the layers of mundane time into primordial time where: "how free must be her dreams". It is that freedom of the feminine that David seeks with Bathsheba,[397] that Moses seeks with Zipporah,[398] while ultimately that seeking "I" remains alienated in this very quest for unified consciousness.

Before the cataclysm of creation[399] "in another lifetime she must have owned the world or been faithfully wed" cracks open to the state where "everything is broken" and this feminine facet (*Sophia* or *Shekhinah*) is torn from her masculine counterpart, remaining in exile. There is further self-reflection as the "I" yearns to return to its origins, not merely limited to cosmic self before the cataclysm of creation, but also to a moment of prior to rebirthing. The singer recounts the journey along "an untrodden path once, where the swift don't win the race" rather he comes to see that truth takes time to unfold. Along this journey to truth, the seeker also learns how to "divide the word of truth" through the process of deep reading and self-reflection. Through that process of learning from a stranger, likely Dylan's teachers at the Vineyard Fellowship and Chabad respectively, the seeker develops the capacity "to look into justice's beautiful face" to see the secret hidden in plain sight. It is the secret of the self in relation to other from the place where there is more than one "I".

The "untrodden path" points to a search for truth which may very well have taken one of Dylan's prior "I"s through a conversionary moment, but has already disappeared and died, this moment of being reborn now looking for a new birthing. The present "I" looks back at its exoskeleton only to realize that the path to truth does not come to those demanding immediate gratification and transformation, rather truth comes to those "who can divide the word of truth". This process of division cuts counter to the unity at the core of monotheism. So here lies a crucial key to Dylan's songbook whereby the gnostic credo of "I is *other*" resists the unified "I and *I*". It is this searching "I" that sings to that space "In creation where one's nature neither honors nor forgives". To come to the ultimate realization that deeper within the self there is a residue of the divine imprint that is beyond status and reconciliation indicates a transcendence of human relations. If that sense of deeper self exists within the first layer of immanent "I", then it opens to the search for the transcendent "I", which turns back to the immanent "I" to reveal that in the transcendent sphere: "no man sees my face and lives". The chorus of "I and I" juxtaposes reconciliation and revelation without needing to synthesize either. Again, it is the embrace of the dialectic within each verse and then in relation to the other verse that abides so strongly here. In an attempt to achieve reconciliation, the present "I" looks back at its exoskeleton only to realize that the path to truth does not come to those demanding immediate gratification and transformation, rather truth comes to those who wait.

Yearning for revelation is a desire to see that divine countenance face-to-face through a process of dissolving the self. As the ego is shed, "I" can then dissolve into the Limitless "I".[400] It takes us as listeners all the way back to the first inkling of cosmic creation itself that can dust up again in any encounter, whether on the endless road or the trackless "train platform". Waiting for the train that never comes in spring, the singer witnesses two figures while "there's nobody in sight". To see the residue of self in the nothingness before him, the singer must search far and wide, and not give up hope amidst the endless waiting. This searching to transcend the "I" of immanent self encounters the other transcendent "I" on the tracks. The dark night of the soul is approaching as "The world could come to an end tonight" but the singing "I" is unflinching. For nestled deep within the singer there abides a trust that "She should still be there sleepin' when I get back—" that even amidst exile into this dark night that the soul will recover its dialectical tension of "I and I". Even and especially amidst the darkness, one must push on down the road, through "the darkest part/Into the narrow lanes." In this process of pressing on down the endless road in search of true self, the singer is restless, forever wandering because "someone else is speakin' with" his own mouth, while the singer is "listening only to" his heart. This tension of being there and not being there emerges in the very words being spoken from the other within the self, all the while the deeper self transcends these words, guided by the heart. The same tension is felt between the immanent "I" who "made shoes for everyone" while remaining "barefoot" in the realm of the transcendent "I". This push along the road, albeit narrowing, shows the "I" yearning to sing that the voice emerging is not his own, but true to the dialectic whereby the very feminine facet of the divine called *Shekhinah* talks by way of his throat. When Moses speaks, Dylan's lyric captures that feeling as if "Someone else is speakin' with my mouth" which the exegetes agree is the *Shekhinah* talking through him. In the presence of the divine mystery of the "bush all aflame yet not consumed",[401] Moses must go "barefoot" by removing his sandals.[402] It is this mysterious name of *Eheyeh Asher Eheyeh*[403] that both Moses and Dylan encounter in their lyrical seeking.

Is there a way of reconciling this dialectic between the *I* who is *other*? This creative tension within the song as a whole returns to Dylan's source of abiding truth of the bible of this mysterious name of *Eheyeh Asher Eheyeh*. Rather than translating this mysterious name as "I am that I am" as would Popeye the Sailorman, I suggest more of translating more of this dialectic between the *I* who is *other* — "I will be that which I am becoming". What Dylan's lyric ingeniously extrapolates from Jewish process theology[404] is not only that God is a *verb* rather than a *noun*,[405] but *what God is* much less important than *what God does* in our lives. If my life is constantly in flux and the divine is constantly emerging from moment to moment as an abiding presence with me, then the divine is necessarily in flux—God is *godding*. What I suggest is that through the oscillation in Dylan's I & I, the initial dialectic between the *I* who is *other* reveals itself as a godding process of "I will be that which I am becoming". Ultimately, in the journey from I to I, from all concepts of the ego to the realm beyond conception, what remains in returning home is the realization there is no longer any other but I in the fullness of its very emptiness.

.

(2) *Nothing is Better Than I'm Not There*:
Dylan's I Minus I as '*Ayin*

Chapter at a glance: *How can you claim being present
enough to any song if indeed you are not really there? Is
the whole project of singing the songbook of the soul all in
vain and nothing but an empty proposition? This chapter
explores the Dylan songbook as an Americanized
expression of the apophatic negation common to the Zen
Buddhist tradition, specifically in one of its pre-eminent
Soto Zen philosopher, Dogen (1200-1253). The Dylan
songbook is engaged in a perennial quest for truth through
the wisdom of negation, known as apophasis that remains
embedded in the Western rather than Eastern tradition.
This matters because even with the paradoxical, koan-like
quality of the Dylan songbook, contextualizing these lyrics
solely in the Eastern tradition risks ignoring a major
thread in the Western tradition—namely, 'God'. And if
indeed as I argue throughout, then it is precisely the No-
thingness of God that Dylan's songbook cannot escape.
This chapter briefly sketches out the mystical tradition of
being in a state of not being there, annihilation of the "I"
known as apophasis, and its specific rendering in Jewish
mysticism known as 'Ayin. This chapter then presents
three distinct layers of no-thingness in: (1) general
precursor mystics; (2) kabbalistic mystical texts; (3)
hasidic mystical texts. This chapter shows how the bard
can be present to sing "I'm Not There" while not being
there as a doorway into the underlying role of no-
thingness that holds this seeming paradox together.*

Dylan lyrics analyzed include: "I'm Not There," (*The Bootleg
Series, Vol. 11: The Basement Tapes Complete*, 2014); "Like a
Rolling Stone" (*Highway 61 Revisited*, 1965); "Not Dark Yet",
(*Time Out of Mind*, 1997); "It's All Over Now, Baby Blue"
(*Bringin' it all back home*, 1965); "You're Making a Liar Out of
Me", (*Trouble in Mind: Bootlegs* 1979-1981); "Nothing Was
Delivered", (1968).

(2) *Nothing is Better Than I'm Not There*: Dylan's I Minus I as *'Ayin*

How can Bob Dylan be present enough to sing a lyric like "I'm Not There"[406] if indeed he is "hardly there at all"? [407] This is curious, playful and deeply paradoxical—not only does such a lyric disrupt the dialogue between lover and beloved but the listener must rightfully ask: who then is singing if not that bard with "his I-am-America self-importance"? [408] Moreover, if "I'm Not There", why bother? Is the whole project of singing the songbook of the soul all in vain and nothing but an empty proposition? While most of the critical literature known as Dylanology has not really engaged this apophatic tendency in the Dylan songbook, there is one notable exception. The reading of the Dylan songbook as an Americanized expression of the apophatic negation common to the Zen Buddhist tradition, specifically in one of its pre-eminent Soto Zen philosopher, Dogen (1200-1253), is worthy of further consideration.[409] Still I will argue that the Dylan songbook is engaged in a perennial quest for truth through the wisdom of negation, known as apophasis that remains embedded in the Western tradition. This matters because even with the paradoxical, *koan*-like quality of the Dylan songbook, contextualizing these lyrics solely in the Eastern tradition risks ignoring a major thread in the Western tradition—namely, God. And if indeed as I argue throughout if *God Knows Everything Is Broken*, then it is precisely the No-thingness of God that Dylan's songbook cannot escape.

In what follows, I will briefly sketch out the mystical tradition of being in a state of *not being there*, annihilation of the "I" known as apophasis, and its specific rendering in Jewish mysticism known as *'Ayin*. To appreciate the nuances of nothing into which the Dylan songbook invites the listener, I will present three distinct layers of no-thingness in: (1) general precursor mystics; (2) kabbalistic mystical texts; (3) hasidic mystical texts. In so doing I endeavor to show how the bard can be present to sing "I'm Not There"[410] while not being there as a doorway into the underlying role of no-thingness that holds this seeming paradox together.

Already as early as the third century, this quest for no-thingness begins in a longing to seek something higher and beyond the nature of existence oftentimes referred to as being. It is at this moment of vertical seeking that we encounter a need to point towards something that is higher than being and thus begins to intimate beyond those ultimate heights a no-thingness in the neo-Platonic philosopher, Plotinus, who claims: "We say what [the One] is not, but not what it is.... [It is] higher than what we call 'being.'"[411] fifth-century, Christian mystic, Pseudo-Dionysius is searching for something beyond being by positing that God is "the cause of being for all, but is itself nonbeing, for it is beyond all being."[413] No-thingness as nonbeing is now perceived not only to be higher, but beyond all being, which effectively ensconces its primordial quality beyond even the ancient layering of any heavenly Father. Further along this path seeking no-thingness, it is fascinating to see how by the ninth-century, a Christian mystic like John Scotus Erigena then takes this notion a step further, in claiming that because of "the ineffable, incomprehensible and inaccessible brilliance of the divine goodness.... it is not improperly called 'nothing.'"[414]

With these apophatic precedents in mind, it is unsurprising that a twelfth-century Jewish philosopher can make the audacious claim that God "exists but not through existence."[415] He then champions this negation of apophasis as: "[t]he description of God ... by means of negations is the correct description.... You come nearer to the apprehension of God with every increase in the negations regarding God."[416] Is this theological claim of negation all that radical? Given the brief sketch of the precursor zeitgeist, it does not necessarily seem so. And this then brings us to reconsider what the Talmudic mind has Rabbi Yochanan teach: "Words of Torah endure only in a person who makes himself like one who is as nothing, as is said: (*Ve-ha-hokhmah me-ayin timmatse*), *Wisdom, where is it found? Wisdom comes into being from 'Ayin, nothing* (Job 28:12)."[417]

The remarkable influence of this negative theological thinking within the philosophical mysticism of Maimonides then sets the stage for a counterpoint within the mysticism of kabbalah.[418] It is in the later layers of kabbalistic mystical texts where we witness a remarkable moment of creative flourish in the process of creating and projecting a cosmological vision. This externalized mapping of the infinite becomes manifest through a series of ten spheres known as *sefirot*, but one cannot help but notice the paucity of attention paid to the transition between the infinite and no-thingness, relative to the robust renaissance of imagery relating to the other nine lower spheres, especially the *Shekhinah*, who presence is felt on almost every page of the mystical medieval classic like the Zohar. And yet the insight of the Talmudic mind that internalizes no-thingness as an expression of the human cultivation of humility is redirected externally to the source of humility in the divine essence.[419] That repositioning from the soul to the cosmos is evident insofar as "The inner power is called *Ayin* because thought does not grasp it, nor reflection," according to Asher ben David, a thirteenth-century Kabbalist. "Concerning this, Job said: *Wisdom, where [me-ayin] is it found? Wisdom comes into being from Ayin* (Job 28:12)."[420] This awareness of the primordial state of nothingness as a source of true knowing is important but not so simple to see. "*Ayin* (Nothingness) is more existent than all the being of the world," according to David ben Avraham ha-Lavan fourteenth-century Kabbalist. "But since it is simple, and every simple thing is complex compared with its simplicity, it is called *Ayin*."[421] The directness here of David ben Avraham ha-Lavan's realization is remarkable insofar as the awareness of the simplex helps to form a way of seeing no-thingness in all its fullness.

The challenge these mystics then face is how to convey the experience of nothingness through language. If language is limited by its given alphabet and syntax, how can it serve as a container for reflecting that which abides beyond limits? "The depth of primordial being ... is called Boundless...[b]ecause of its concealment from all creatures above and below, it is also called *Ayin* (Nothingness).... If one asks, 'What is it?' the answer is, '*Ayin* (Nothing),' meaning: 'No one can understand anything about it.' It is negated of every conception. No one can know anything about it—except the belief that it exists. Its existence cannot be grasped by anyone other than it. Therefore, its name is (*Ehyeh*), *I am* (Exodus 3:14)."[422] The entirely simple constitution of identity as "I am" normally the definition par excellence of what it means to be human is here suddenly expanded into a more simplex portrayal of this divine-human awareness residing within nothingness. But to reach that awareness, as thirteenth-century Kabbalist, Moses de León, comments, is a question of waiting in the divine: "That which abides in thought yet cannot be grasped is called (*Hokhmah*), Wisdom. What is the meaning of (*Hokhmah*)? (*Hakkeh mah*), 'Wait for what.' Since you can never grasp it, (*hakkeh*), 'wait,' for (*mah*), 'what,' will come and what will be. This is the sublime, primordial wisdom emerging from *Ayin*."[423]

Glancing at the struggle of medieval Jewish mystics, one encounters a challenge: is it really possible to access this experience of no-thingness through the very language that transcends it? That is, upon reaching this apophatic state and returning to normative consciousness, these mystics are deeply concerned with how one then translates this experience of nothingness into some form of accessible practice. This remarkable challenge is actually addressed by interrogating the paradoxical fullness of emptiness further, he realizes that: "[A true prayer is one in which] we have directed the words to the nothingness of the word."[424] Language itself looks different to the mystic upon returning from the realization of nothingness to then convey it through the apparent fullness of the alphabet. As energetic containers of meaning, the letters themselves can dissolve into nothingness. This is a prayerful posture that invites deeper contemplation of silence.

How can one be "a lone hearted mystic", as Dylan sings, and still "carry on"? [425] While the medieval Jewish mystics display a remarkable sensitivity for contemplating the truth of nothingness from a more externalized, cosmological perspective, that earlier strain of yearning to internalize this awareness we encountered in the Talmudic mind returns centuries after the kabbalah with the advent of Hasidism. It is precisely in these later layers of Hasidic mystical texts where we witness a process of internalizing the previous externalized cosmological projections of the kabbalistic mystical texts as a call to: "transform (*aniy*) "I" into (*ayin*), "Nothing."[426] What is different about this later transformation? To appreciate the nuance, we turn to a later mystical master who teaches: "When one sows a single seed it cannot sprout and produce many seeds until its existence is nullified. Then it is raised to its root and can receive more than a single dimension of its existence. There in its root the seed itself becomes the source of many seeds."[427] Nothingness then abides at the root of all existence but must remain simplex. And yet even while simplex at its core, awareness of this nothingness is what allows one to transform by letting go of layers of obfuscation: "Think of yourself as *Ayin* and forget yourself totally."[428]

Forgetting the *self,* you spend our life trying to construct is no small feat. But the realization that there is really no "independent self" and that "Everything was part of divinity"[429] is a key pivot in hasidic hermeneutics. This journey to awareness of the fullness of nothingness by letting go of egocentric holds on the heart-mind is crucial to appreciating the nuances at play in the Dylan songbook, to which now we will turn attention. One of Dylan's most sustained reflections on this paradoxical awareness of the fullness of nothingness by letting go of egocentric that holds on the heart-mind can be found in songs like, "I'm Not There" to which we shall turn momentarily as part of the *Basement Tapes*. To get there, let us consider a few shorter lyrical *koans* that move the listener in that paradoxical direction peppered throughout his songbook. Reflecting on the course of his life as a vagabond singer-songwriter, Dylan is known to return to his hometown of Hibbing and even as he would "spend time in the bedroom of his old house, presumably making contact with memories"[430] contemplating what it means to have "no direction home" while sitting right in it, when he sings: "When you got nothing, you got nothing to lose/You're invisible now, you've got no secrets to conceal".[431]

Directionless, the vagabond pivots homeward in his endless wanderings in search of the dying light amidst the deepening darkness: "I was born here and I'll die here against my will/...Don't even hear a murmur of a prayer"[432] Returning home is an impossible task, as is evading the inevitable darkness of death's shady abode, that very darkness that comes with the approach of one's autumn years.[433] And it is precisely in this awareness of the night setting in that the imagination paradoxically grows into its luminal darkness at this hour that has always been favored as a propitious time for creativity by mystics through the ages. [434] These attempted moments of returning to the place of being born and ultimately dying—that perennial search for who you were with your original face as one Zen *koan* puts it— suggest a limbo in search of meaning. Prayer is not possible in such limbo, but something more is needed to push through this appetite for self-transformation: "The vagabond who's rapping at your door/Is standing in the clothes that you once wore".[435] Along this search for the original "I" that transcends the everyday "I" can be as disarming as seeing your true self in the shadow of the an *other*.

With the more recent release of the bootlegs from 1979-1981, especially in the song "You're Making a Liar Out of Me", for example, in the rehearsal take, Dylan starts off singing: "I tell people, you just going through changes/And that you're acquainted both with night and day"[436] which opens up the possibility of self-transformation through "changes" in self. That very transformation begins in acknowledging how at key moments, one's life can feel utterly inauthentic: "And that you really do have all the best intentions/But you're making a liar out of me."[437] This inauthenticity is a plaguing darkness of living in a world of lies that pushes the authentic self into deeper conflict with the inauthentic veneer that passes as the quotidian self that must perform these lies to the world. Being "acquainted both with night and day"[438] suggests that such a knowing of the apparent difference between darkness and light no longer abides as the authentic self emerges into more fullness from this very emptiness. Then the lyric that captures that moment of self-transformation resonates even stronger: "Now that you're gone/I gotta wonder if you were ever here at all."[439] The singer as love appears to be addressing the sense of feeling abandoned by the beloved into a deeper dark night of the soul. By singing through that very darkness one becomes more "acquainted both with night and day"[440] so that as that dichotomy dissolves into oneness, so too does the dichotomy between lover and beloved, to then "wonder if you were ever here at all."[441]

A handful of neglected apophatic masterpieces[442] that maps out this journey of self-transformation through negation of the "I" were recorded in the spring of 1967 in the basement of Big Pink in Woodstock. Legend has it that Dylan ritualized a routine of coming by the house at one o'clock each day.[443] "As [Garth] Hudson cued up the tape to record, Dylan would begin to play, and the others—multi-instrumentalists, all of them—would join in, occasionally lending harmony vocals or trading phrases, as well as interjecting laughter or nonsensical lyrics."[444] I agree with both the characterizations of and that there was a process unfolding that produced paradoxical *koan*-like lyrics like: "Nothing is better, nothing is best/Take heed of this and get plenty rest".[445]

Rather than "nonsensical" which sounds irrational and silly enough to be dismissed, I argue there is process of paradoxical unfolding that is akin to the process of the *koan* in Zen Buddhism. To see with deeper clarity these Americana *koans* do is open "to the one who has an eye on the forehead to see it", which suggests that such a seeker must "abandon his usual relative point of view so that he can reach the absolute ground of all things."[446] The technique of clearing through the weeds of self by deep focus on the *koan* (combined with the sitting practice of *zazen*) is considered the domain and trusted technique in Zen.[447] What the *koan* practice, here akin to the lyrical paradoxes, invites is a state where "all the outer details are to be so controlled as to bring the mind into the most favorable condition in which it will gradually rise above the turbulence of passions and sensualities."[448] While the Zen practitioner needs to control the internal conditions of consciousness like posture and the breath, external conditions also need to be controlled, so that "naturally such places as the market, the factory or the business office may be better avoided."[449] While the setting of the basement of Big Pink sounds wholly unconventional for enabling such practice, Dylan's description is more in line with this contemplative space for songwriting he was seeking there in Woodstock, as the bard remarks on that period: "You know, that's really the way to do a recording—in a peaceful, relaxed setting, in somebody's basement, with the windows open and a dog lying on the floor." [450] If there could be something akin to a kind of "Woodstock Zen," if you will, the ritualized environment of the *Basement Tapes* must have been closest to that communal vision. I am suggesting that the heart of the *koan* practice, returning to its original meaning of "a public document" was being played with in the basement of Big Pink, offering a shedding of self, eating the document and in the process rediscovering the root of his calling as a gnostic bard: "It was almost as if Dylan were attempting to tap into some common constituency in American popular music in order to remind himself not only of his roots, but of his audience." [451] But very quickly through this process of unfolding, if "I'm Not There" then the distinction between roots of self and audience are already standing as an illusion.

This process of unfolding of the self could be seen as most remarkably culminating in songs like "I'm Not There" (1956) so that Rogovoy can claim that "the musicians respectfully accompany Dylan's mystical investigation of identity"[452] while Heylin suggests that Dylan was "[s]pontaneously experimenting with country and blues forms, he was mouthing line upon line of oblique images from the id…[as] a vision begins to fragment." [453] Despite their important comments here, Heylin and Rogovoy seem to only be willing to point to the door of the self that needs to still be opened through apophatic transformation. The basis for the present extended analysis of apophasis in the Dylan songbook relies on connecting the dots of these characterizations alluded to here as a process that had yet to flower and unfold. These ritualized sessions enabled a kind of automatic singing that relied heavily on musical "telepathy", [454] where, as Garth Hudson describes it: "Bob would make up [lyrics] as he went along…We'd play the melody, he'd sing a few words he'd written, and then make up some more, or else just mouth sounds or even syllables as he went along." [455] Amidst the domestic circus of these ritualized recordings in the basement of Big Pink, Dylan finds exactly the contemplative context for removing the mask of his joker by scraping down language and self-identity to its bare bones. This is the precisely the journey Dylan finds himself engaged in during these Woodstock retreat years, that give him the space and time to eradicate the ego entailed in "I'm Not There".

This same sense of the singer's "I" being present to the vagaries of darkness and light emerges again in "I'm Not There" that opens with this rendering: "In my neighborhood she cries both day and night/I know it because I was there."[456] Here again we encounter a forlorn lover lamenting his beloved, who herself is wailing both day and night. The lover experiences the suffering of his beloved, witnessing her sink deeper into her own dark night of the soul. As the lover continues in this process of witnessing, he has already extricated his sense of self from first to third person. He then sees the beloved in her suffering and wonders whether this suffering through her dark night of the soul might somehow be mitigated. The need to belong creates a sense of longing, if only she would be willing to care: "I believe where she'd stop him if she wants time to care/…But I don't belong there". [457]

It is at this juncture of witnessing the dissolution of his relatedness in love to her, where he then is ready to "go by the Lord". This pivot suggests a willingness to seek another layer of relatedness in this stance of deeper letting go to take hold of a new reality. Heylin suggests from a typescript of "I'm Not

There" that Dylan published much earlier circa 1956 in the *Telegraph* that the "our heroine is 'a drag queen…a drag-a-muffin…a drag' [that] is replaced by an exquisite remorse for the singer's inability to save her from herself." [458] By contemplating this face of the other, there is an "exquisite remorse for the singer's inability to save her from herself" that provides an opening for the divine in this journey from darkness to light. This then leads to a slight inversion of expectation of the beloved, whereby: "I wish I was beside her but I'm not there, I'm gone/Well, it's too hard to stay here and I don't want to leave". [459] The beloved is transformed into a "Christ forsaken angel", becoming fallen as she is separated from her lover. That exquisite remorse embedded in the lover's inability to save the beloved from herself is made even more complex when the earlier version of the beloved envisioned as a drag-queen is overlaid.

Already gone, the bard is always in a state of "I'm not there". As I have argued that what emerges through this process of unfolding is that the self dissolves into a deeper clarity of the absolute ground of nothingness. The Zen *koan* technique as well as the kabbalistic and hasidic techniques of contemplating *'Ayin* each serve as a helpful analogies to better appreciate what is at stake in a handful of lyrics from Dylan's *Basement Tapes*. Whereas the Jewish mystical masters contemplating *'Ayin* understood their experiences of no-thingness as reconnecting the seeker to the primordial divine sphere, the Zen master operates in an entirely other realm that excludes any hint of theism. Rather the danger of the *koan* of course is well known to the master, namely: "that the device of a *koan* was an artificiality and a superfluity; for unless Zen grew out of a man's own inner activity it could not be truly genuine and full of creative vitality as it ought to be. But even a semblance would be a blessing when the genuine thing is so difficult and rare to have; and, moreover, it was likely, if it is left to itself, to disappear altogether out of the lore of human experience."[460] It is this disappearing altogether that embodies the fullness possible when "I'm Not There"…

(3) *In the Garden, Outside Eden:* Singing From Snake Eyes

Chapter at a glance: What is the symbol of the snake doing slithering through the Dylan songbook? Lest the snake disappear from our imagination, the Dylan songbook is reminding us that both the bard and his song are always both creative and destructive, poisonous and healing, spiritual and material—utterly irreconcilable opposites. By reconsidering the fairy tale as a journey of the soul in Jungian archetypal psychology that enables the emergence of the soul within the collective unconscious. This process is a return from lost wholeness in second generation Jungian interpretations of the spirit's journey through the fairy tale. As one of the greatest American Gnostic artists of our time creating on a deeply intuitive level, Dylan's calling is to continue to animate the image of the snake through the sounds of his songs. Lest the soul remain even more unanimated after listening to the song than it was before, Dylan's songbook shows us how the search the meaning of life hinges upon our ability to stick with the animal image, rather than let it slither away. The greatest temptation from that moment in the Garden until the ink dries at the end of this book is that we are all just a bit too eager for conceptual meanings. In that all too human eagerness, we ignore the actual beast. We are no longer astounded by its facts, or wonder over its presence. The remarkable cry from the Garden of Eden that continues to concatenate to this day comes from this astounding and wonderful Americana Gnostic songbook.

Dylan lyrics analyzed include: "Man Gave Names to the All the Animals," (*Slow Train Coming,* 1979), "Wiggle, Wiggle," (*Under a Red Sky,* 1990), "Froggie went a Courtin'," (*Good as I been to You,* 1992), "Please Mrs. Henry," (*Basement Tapes,* 1967), "Angelina," (*Bootleg vol's 1-3,* 1961-1991, 1981).

(3) *In the Garden, Outside Eden:* Singing From Snake Eyes

"Slithering his way through the grass
Saw him disappear by a tree near a lake . . ."[461]

What begins here as a list of the animal kingdom in Dylan's seeming rock n' roll nursery rhyme appears to end with the ineffable. Dylan's lyric begins with the perspective of Adam in the garden who gives names to all the animals, by the final verse of the song, the most important animal in the garden—the snake— remains unnamed—*why?* To appreciate the depth of such a rock n' roll nursery rhyme, a fuller archetypal analysis would be in order. While a full-fledged discussion of archetypal psychology is beyond the scope of the present analysis, some summation is in order. I would argue that such an archeology of self as an exercise in excavating and interpreting these signposts of the soul's journey in such a rock n' roll nursery rhyme is invited by this songbook.[462] How does the Dylan songbook allow the emergence of the soul within the collective unconscious to return to its lost wholeness?

Truth be told, singing the snake into the song is a slippery feat. More than merely avoiding nightmares for the child to whom this rock n' roll nursery rhyme might be directed, even as adults, we remain terrified of the snake as "a symbol for the unconscious-psyche—particularly the introverting libido, the inward-turning energy that goes back and down and in." [463] There is something so seductive and repulsive about the snake that "draws us into darkness and deeps." [464] And what remains fascinating and so alluring about this primordial creature is that "[i]t is always a "both": creative-destructive, male-female, poisonous-healing, dry-moist, spiritual-material, and many other irreconcilable opposites."[465] Avoiding the snake and its symbolism is something we have mastered as moderns at our peril, but the Dylan songbook is snake-*ish* in this regard, always reveling in those "irreconcilable opposites". There is always the danger of over-interpretation, to the point where the image within the given lyric no longer resonates as art but fallows in the interpretive dust.[466]

This disappearance of the snake from the living movement of our imaginations is tragic and always nearly complete. Listening to the Dylan songbook on snakes is really an attempt at "keeping the snake around" and "imagined as a felt presence" whereby it is honored by our attentions. We can bring the snake closer by visualizing it, sensing its skin, its strength" and in so doing "[n]ow the imagination replaces meaning, and the human mind gives itself over to the animal presence." [467] I would argue that in listening deeply to Dylan's songbook, we are invited to "animate the sound" from over-interpretation. The genius of Dylan's songbook is how it straddles animating the sound as image in quite a revelatory fashion. Listen anew to these lyrics scattered throughout the Dylan songbook as it slithers through the image and sound of the snake into song:

> "Wiggle, wiggle, wiggle, rattle and shake
> Wiggle like a big fat snake."[468]

"Next to come in was a big black snake, Uh-huh.
Ate up all of the wedding cake,
Uh-huh."[469]

> "I can crawl like a snake."[470]

> "His eyes were two slits that would make a
> snake proud." [471]

Lest we forget the snake entirely, recall it has long served as the symbol of gnostic wisdom *par excellence*. And so what emerges in this song is that of all the animals that Adam knew in the Garden of Eden, it is the snake that remains most slippery, in terms of what it can see, given its perspective that must be confronted in this process of retelling the story of the Garden of Eden.[472] Try as it might, Dylan's songbook cannot seem to swerve the snake, especially in unsaying the snake in "God gave names to all the animals". Notwithstanding the slippery skin of the snake, we cannot escape its symbolic grasp, which eludes both Judaism and Christianity.[473] The book before you is also elusive, the by-product of a (post)modern gnostic intellectual reading the songbook of Bob Dylan—a (post)modern gnostic songwriter. One of the perennial plagues afflicting the most obsessive of Dylan scholarship (aka *Dylanology*) is the obsession as to whether *Shabetai Zisel ben Avraham*, born a Jew, remained a loyal Jew during his so-called "born again" period.

Dylan problematizes this reductionism already within his songbook for those who pay close attention. The already noted oscillation from the three "born again" recordings to its iconoclastic follow-up of *Infidels* (1982) critiques the entire project of ideology from the outset as inauthentic and a case of "bad faith". With his more recent swerve in accepting the *Nobel Prize*, Dylan makes as explicit as possible that his conviction is neither Jew nor Greek nor Christian nor shall he ever, after all these years, succumb to "bad faith". Dylan is not original in this sense of refuting public acclamation or recognition of his value, after all, it was Sartre, who already refused the *Nobel Prize* in 1968 as a case in point of "bad faith" to the point where both the writer and the singer must each refuse the temptation of accolades and awards that might transform their freedom into the shackles of an institution, even if this occurs under the most honorable circumstances.[474] Whether one is a singer-songwriter, or a waiter in a café, the main task for any existentialist is not fall into prey to the tempting state of inauthenticity.[475] Sartre has been observing the waiter while sitting in a café, insofar as all his behavior appears to be nothing more than a game. So, Sartre goes on to claim this person is trying to fit into that "waiter"-role which reeks of inauthenticity and "bad faith" [*mauvaise foi*]—why? After all, as a matter of "facticity" the man remains a waiter but is that all this person really is, a waiter and nothing else?!? This societal role cannot remain the be all and end all of his existence, for even as a waiter, this human being remains free because he can choose at any time to cease and desist acting in his role as a waiter. That is to say that his job as a waiter does not define or limit his human freedom. Whether waiter, or singer-songwriter, one must still make ultimate decisions about what to do with one's life. The irony here is not lost on the Dylan songbook that claims no matter how free you seem to be you still "gotta serve somebody".

Dylan's lyrics point to a desire to go beyond and even transcend his role as bard and singer, just as for Sartre, the one functioning as waiter can go beyond his role as a waiter. Whether waiter or bard, both are seen in terms of their facticity and their transcendence. What captures listeners in the Dylan songbook is this "double-bind" of being human—at once, an intricate and unique fusion of our facticity and our transcendence. If being a waiter or a bard means that such a person must deny this freedom, or play down one's transcendence and play up one's facticity, then there is no choice but to revolt. For turning oneself into a being-in-itself obviates the human experience of remaining awake and conscious — after all, there are tangible benefits and security of remaining a waiter and even a Nobel singer. Here is the rub— one yearns to be both a being-in-itself and a being-for-itself. To be in such a state, at once, being-in-itself and being-for-itself is to be simply put — God. Whether one is attempting to become a *Waiter God* or a *Singer God,* it is a reach for that security of being-in-itself, albeit impossible. Dylan here would agree with Sartre's conclusion that the more one attempts to emphasize one's facticity at the expense of one's transcendence or freedom, the more one remains chained in the condition of futility. I would argue that the genius of Dylan's songbook aims to disrupt the ruse that we know is otherwise than reality, in fooling ourselves about this desired double-bind of our facticity and our freedom.

This means that no one can circumscribe or even affirm my authenticity or value except myself. Dylan then chooses in his freedom to "up the ante" from the founding father of existentialism, because true to form: "Instead of declining the prize, he has simply declined to acknowledge its existence." [476] Recognizing this radical pathway of existentialism should already have disabused all Dylanologist from having to wade through any waters of doubt. In denying the existence of the prize, the genius songwriter here, Bob Dylan is also denying his own existence— simply, "I'm not there".[477] At the outset, we need to expand our horizons as to why it has never been a question of Dylan resisting categories of being "Jewish" or "Christian" or anything else for that matter. The whole enterprise is highly irrelevant given how porous the nature of identity really was during the formation of Judaism as a distinct way of being with the emergence of Christianity. So a border line term "Gnosticism" is necessary but not always sufficient.[478] I would argue that this is where the songbook of Dylan is at once refreshing and challenging. Here we have a modernist bard who eschews either category of "Judaism" and "Christianity" by exploring their porous natures as a gnostic. Dylan sheds all preconceptions and presumptions by embracing the slippery concealment of seeing the Garden from the eyes of the snake.[479]

How intriguing to discover that the rabbinic mind already envisioned that all the curses we encounter in life really "begin with the snake as the first animal to be cursed."[480] Here the serpent, long known to appear in Gnostic literature as the principle of divine wisdom, convinces Adam and Eve to partake of knowledge while the Lord threatens them with death, trying jealously to prevent them from attaining knowledge, and expelling them from Paradise when they achieve it. The Gnostic perspective retains ongoing relevance, especially in the study of religion.[481] There are three ways of knowing—faith, reason, or gnosis. Now consider that the distinguishing nature of gnosis as: "a form of intuitive, visionary, or mystical knowledge that privileges the primacy of personal experience and the depths of the self over the claims of both faith and reason traditionally in order to acquire some form of liberation or salvation from a world seen as a corrupt or fallen."[482] Dylan's songbook sheds any preconceptions of faith or reason in favor of embracing "of intuitive, visionary, or mystical knowledge" at all costs. This is in part what has confused adherents to any coherent religious system attempting to claim Dylan as their troubadour or redeemer. More than an adherent to any religion or denomination, Dylan's songbook is a case study in religious anarchism and the aesthetics is one open to channeling the radical amazement that so emerges in such a chaotic state.

So now when one encounters the lyrics about snakes in the Dylan songbook, ears must be attuned anew to its esoteric implications and anarchic challenges to the unveiling of truth: "You were born with a snake in both of your fists while a hurricane was blowing/Freedom just around the corner for you".[483] Whereas "[f]alse-hearted judge dying in the webs that they spin"[484] unable to arrive at and dispense the truth, this is a quest in discerning false prophets who transmit and channel a vision of the truth, but distorted.[485] But it is the true prophet who is already bitten by the viper and "born with a snake in both fists", more David than Daniel.[486] While there are floating associations in "Jokerman" to a series of symbolic registers from messiah as redeemer to god as redeemer, Dylan is not necessarily "...drawing himself closer to the faith of his ancestors separating himself from his dalliance with Christianity."[487] The tendency amongst critics is to oscillate on the religion pendulum, that is, reading Dylan and his lyrics as either having fully returned to Jewish roots or being fully reborn as a Christian.[488] Such allegiance is but another role for the bard, as clearly this would already run a fowl with the aforementioned "bad faith". The lyrics are painted from a theological palette, but colors which are not carried exclusively on the orthodox shelves of Jewish or Christian theologies. This is why I am arguing for this way of reading Dylan's lyrics as a "shifting theology"[489] in a Gnostic key.

If redemption is the final act already inscribed in the beginning of time, then it is not surprising to encounter the "howling wolf" in the deepest darkness of the end while the "king snake" returns us to the Garden of Eden: "Well, the howling wolf will howl tonight, the king snake will crawl/Trees that've stood for a thousand years suddenly will fall".[490] Amidst the deep dualism of Christian theology which envisions God being opposed by Satan as its own negative power, is origin in the Hebrew bible posits much less separate. The most salient trace of dual divine powers is glimpsed in the Book of Job, but even the case of or "Satan" posits that this prosecuting angel if fallen from its source to which it must—the ultimate God. By getting back home to the divine source has not merely one pathway for it may even involve dissolving into nothingness for: "She's a lone hearted mystic and she can't carry on/When I'm there she's alright but then she's not when I'm gone".[491] It is only possible for the singer seeking separation to set out alone, even in the midst of love, and to remain radically alone. So, the lover has already fallen away from the beloved, given that "She's my Christ forsaken angel" who no longer hears the cry of her lover. The sense of forsakenness stressed in Psalm 22 and then later in the gospel's depiction of the moment before crucifixion.

The lyrics of "Jokerman" point to a shadow side of the divine, as Dylan remarks in writing it that: "It's very mystical. The shapes there, and shadows, seem to be so ancient."[492] This is by no means a naive affirmation of the theological symbol of Satan serving as the anti-Christ, rather here the Dylan lyric complicates matters by blurring lines. We are left wondering: where does Satan end and God really begin?[493] The messianic allusions in the "post-conversion" both appearing on *Infidels* (1982) is no coincidence, insofar as these lyrics intentionally conjure a figure being "born with a snake in both of your fists" and that "the king snake will crawl". Snake as messiah emerges through Jewish mystical hermeneutics of numerology,[494] but it does not take such sophistication. This evocation of the snake as a messianic symbol could not be any clearer amidst its concealed disclosure. While appearing in all its regalia in the Garden of Eden, the snake then becomes more deeply concealed throughout the duration of the Hebrew bible in an attempt to demythologize its polytheistic, mythic origins.[495]

So, what remains of the snake after all these interpretive exoskeletons have been shed? Lest the snake disappear from our imagination, the Dylan songbook is reminding us that both the bard and his song are always both creative and destructive, poisonous and healing, spiritual and material—utterly irreconcilable opposites.[496] On a deeply intuitive level as one of the greatest American Gnostic artists of our time, Dylan knows his task remains to continue "animating the image" of the snake through the sounds of his songs. Lest he leave the soul even more unanimated after listening to his song than it was before, Dylan's songbook reminds us that "the search for meaning, and the meaning of life" hinges upon our ability to "stick with the animal image." [497] The greatest temptation from that moment in the Garden until the ink dries at the end of this book is that we are all just a bit too eager for conceptual meanings. In that all too human eagerness, we "ignore the actual beast. We are no longer astounded by its facts, or wonder over its presence..."[498] The remarkable cry from the Garden of Eden that continues to concatenate to this day comes from this astounding and wonderful Americana Gnostic songbook.

(4) Lovesick/Sick of Love: Love Lost & Found

Chapter at a glance: *Nowhere is the depth of mystical cynicism in Dylan's songbook more apparent than when his unique brand of Gnostic theology than when it comes to the dark side of love in his lyrical imagination. Love is tainted, sick, forgotten and almost irretrievable, from the very cataclysm which creates the world. Knowing how everything is broken means that there is a divine self-awareness within the Creator that the bliss of ultimately being alone enwrapped within oneself is eventually ruptured. This rupture emerges once the Creator begins creating a universe and creation that is separate from what was until that moment nothing but godliness everywhere. This persecuted heart withdrawing deeper into the stark, shadowy mindscape. The only resolution offered for the conflict between the mind and heart is that the door to the heart must be closed as nothing but an illusion all along. Whether the knowing mind will prevail over the forgetful heart remains a question but what continues to echo through this sparse Americana musical landscape is a unique lyrical solitude of darkening emptiness at the heart of it all.*

Dylan lyrics analyzed include: "Covenant Woman" (*Saved*, 1980); "The Groom's Still Waiting at the Altar" (*Shot of Love*, 1981); "Ain't Talkin'," (*Modern Times,* 2006); "Love Sick," (*Time Out of Mind*, 1997); "Gonna Change My Way of Thinking" (*Slow Train Coming*, 1979); "Spirit on the Water" (*Modern Times*, 2006); "I Believe in You," (*Slow Train Coming*, 1979); "Up To Me" (*Biograph,* 1974), "When the Deal Goes Down" (*Modern Times*, 2006); "Cry a While" (*Love and Theft*, 2001); "Down the Highway" (*The Freewheelin' Bob Dylan*, 1963); "It Ain't Me Babe" (*Another Side of Bob Dylan*, 1964); "Forever Young", (*Planet Waves*, 1974); "Rollin' and Tumblin'", (*Modern Times*, 2006); "Beyond the Horizon", (*Modern Times*, 2006); "Forgetful Heart", (*Together Through Time*, 2009).

(4) Lovesick/Sick of Love: Love Lost & Found

Nowhere is the depth and breadth of mystical cynicism in Dylan's songbook more apparent in his unique brand of Gnostic theology than when it comes to love. Love is tainted, sick, forgotten and ultimately lost, almost irretrievable. Such an overwhelming loss of love is encapsulated precisely in the very cataclysm which creates the world and thus allows for the *gnosis* of such to be that *God Knows Everything is Broken.* Knowing how everything is broken means that there is a divine self-awareness within the Creator that the bliss of ultimately being alone enwrapped within oneself is eventually ruptured. This rupture emerges once the Creator begins creating a universe and creation that is separate from what was until that moment nothing but godliness everywhere. Where O where then is the place for love? Attempting to counter the gnostic myth, the Hebrew bible goes on to proclaim that the Creator creates worlds from such a very source, as the Psalmist sings: "the world is built from love."[499] But the gnostic take on creation remains more skeptical about this possibility of love being the creative force for anything that could last forever— especially love.

Undoubtedly, Dylan's songbook presents a series of encounters with a formidable feminine force. Upon examination of Dylan's prolific songbook that now hovers in covers of classic homages to love as manifest in the American songbook, one should never imagine that the Hibbing bard is content with love. Love is always a battle. Throughout these lyric encounters, especially in "Covenant Woman"[500] and "The Groom's Still Waiting at the Altar",[501] one experiences an embrace and betrayal of love like no other. Just when you think that Dylan's lyrics can soften into romantic fantasy as evinced throughout the clichéd country homage in *Nashville Skyline*,[502] and even in apparently calmer moments of love domesticated through marriage throughout *Planet*

Waves, reaching its climax with the likes of "Wedding Song",[503] pay attention to how conflicted it feels, how: "Your love cuts like a knife" and the lover can confess: "I love you more than blood".[504] The lyrical contours of this love song are filled with surrealist imagery that is bound to disrupt and disturb: "[n]ot exactly your conventional images of marital bliss," as feminist critic, Ellen Willis has already pointed out. It is precisely the "remixing" of apparent clichés that camouflage Dylan's innovate lyricism.[505] While even a critic as sharp as Willis falls for the trap that this is a personal love saga and homage of Dylan to Sara, this gamble the critic loses emerges from distrusting her initial critique that was spot on—namely, "Dylan's mask has simply become subtler."[506] This subtlety becomes even more refined, beyond Sara, her alter-ego, Joan Baez or even every beloved in the audience as it reaches its apex with "Dirge" that confesses its lament for love lost: "I hate myself for lovin' you and the weakness that it showed/You were just a painted face on a trip down Suicide Road".[507] That such deep love can provoke such equally toxic hate is part of the gamble that is posed by falling in love. While the symbolism of "a painted face on a trip down Suicide Road" might seem embarrassing at first blush, such an intimate lament is intended to push deeper into the pathos of the pained heart. This poignant pain pushes beyond the clichéd dialectic that classifies women "as goddesses to be idolized or bitches to be mercilessly trashed".[508] Indeed Dylan's lyrical dirge transcends the stereotype to dwell deeper in the archetype of the mystic with the already explored in the recurring visions of sin throughout the Dylan songbook.[509] Love is "that foolish game" that exposes its players— both lover and beloved— to "[t]hat hollow place where martyrs weep and angels play with sin".[510]

That mercy emerges as a higher expression of love is little surprise to mystics, given that the "lower love" [*ahavah*] is a lower manifestation of the "higher love" of ever-flowing compassion [*hesed*]. To be touched by such mercy from another catches the lover by surprise, which then opens the channels of love deeper within only to be betrayed in that "lower" place of the human heart. The human heart becomes hollowed out for both martyrs and angels in the process of holding on too strongly to human love, when it is the "higher" love to which they both yearn to ascend. Amidst such dialectical tension within love, it is worthwhile to juxtapose this lyrical challenge with another text in the gnostic gospel library, as it sheds further light on the nature of the battle between masculine and feminine powers. In a gnostic gospel, entitled, *The Thunder, Perfect Mind,* there is a poetic depiction, spoken in the voice of a feminine divine power:

> "For I am the first and the last. I am the
> honored one and the scorned one.
> I am the whore and the holy one.
> I am the wife and the virgin....
> I am the barren one, and many are her
>   sons....
> I am the silence that is incomprehensible....
> I am the utterance of my name." [511]

This dialectic of the feminine, portrayed as "the whore and the holy one" as well as "the wife and the virgin" encapsulates precisely the struggle present in Dylan's songbook. As we have already seen, lyrics about love and the heart are at once pristine and abandoned, pure and watered down. This is a function of their deep gnostic symbolism, which embraces the paradox. There are number of ways, however, from the gnostic perspective, to see love's workings in the world. Witnessing and partaking of this love allows for light to emerge from an otherwise overwhelming darkness. In one of the Gnostic Gospels, for example, redemptive love is experienced as fraternal, integral, radically alone and what ultimately emerges from concealment through the disclosure of its secretly afflicted love. So we learn in the Gnostic Gospels that fraternal love comes when you: "Love your brother like your soul./Protect that person like the pupil of your eye."[512] From the intimacy of love shared in fellowship there is the love of gnosis and its divine source: "From what I tell you, you do not know/who I am,/but you have become like the Jews./They love the tree but hate its fruit/or love the fruit but hate the tree."[513] And love is radically alone insofar as: "Those who do not hate their father and mother as I do/cannot be my students,/and those who do not love their father and mother as I do/cannot be my students./For my mother gave me falsehood,/but my true mother gave me life."[514] And finally there is lost love found again as it is revealed from its concealment as the parable explains: "The kingdom is like a shepherd who had/a hundred sheep./One of them, the largest, went astray./He left the ninety-nine and looked for the one until he found it./After so much trouble he said to the sheep,/"I love you more than the ninety-nine."[515]In all these cases of preparing to receive gnosis, love transcends boundaries, barriers and hierarchies, for both the divine and human yearn for it and pursue it.

But the lost love being sought is already afflicted and sick in Dylan's songbook, akin to the malaise of a recurring French symbolist poet, Charles Baudelaire, whose influence can be felt throughout the songbook.[516] Love begins hopelessly in sight of death, given that it is already ruled by the force of evil called "the impious one" and it is amidst this very impiety that humanity cannot escape "the shameless laugh". The shame is at once succumbing to the power of love that weakens its swooning lovers, but moreover it is the shame of being in the sight of death amidst the throes of love. As the Song of Song contends, there is something at the root of love that is stronger than death, but here Baudelaire envisions an inversion whereby death overpowers love and thus rules over it. So "the impious one" can remain "shameless" in its quest to continually conquer and subdue lovers. While love nobly attempts to ascend to lofty heights "[a]t the ether's end", ascending this peak already catalyzes its descent like a dream: "The sphere, fragile and luminous,/Takes flight rapidly,/Bursts and spits out its flimsy soul/Like a golden dream." It is precisely this "sphere" of love that remains "fragile and luminous" and thus susceptible to corruption. Such corruption is a simple fact of existence—once the human created in the world, there is nothing but corruption of the pristine divine imprint. The decomposition of love is a sign of its loss already in the very moment of the first embrace. This simultaneity of love and its concomitant death fascinates the poet to contemplate the end inscribed in the beginning of each love:

"I hear the skull groan and entreat
At every bubble:
'When is this fierce, ludicrous game
To come to an end?
Because what your pitiless mouth
Scatters in the air,
Monstrous murderer — is my brain,
My flesh and my blood!"[517]

The poet hears the "fierce, ludicrous game" being played out already in the beginning of a lover's call for the beloved which marks its very own demise in death. Love is a "Monstrous murderer" that cannot be contained or avoided but must be confronted as a function of being human. What love murders is the very will to think freely and truly feel after being betrayed by the very loss of love.

So, with this sinfully sweet layering in mind, it now becomes that much more apparent how Dylan's lyrics, for example, in "Ain't Talkin'," evoke the site of those evil flowers plucked from the garden of lost love in all its affliction. In the guise of First Adam, the original vagabond has returned to the Garden of Eden and feels: "The wounded flowers were dangling from the vines" while "passing by yon cool and crystal fountain" he is hit from behind.[518] Who strikes Adam in the Garden? Is Adam love struck from behind, or is love struck from the human being altogether as a capacity it can really hold onto? Such a stroll through the melancholic spleen of life lived through loves lost opens a further pathway in his ode to Song of Songs, called, "Love Sick": "I'm walking through streets that are dead/Walking, walking with you in my head".[519]

It becomes quickly apparent that the state of being "Love Sick" for Dylan is a return to its ancient resonance, meaning that when the lover falls into the throes of love it appears as if such swooning is akin to a sickness. Just as one feels out of control and unable to think straight when in the frenzy of a fever, so too does the lover feel out of control and unable to think straight while in the frenzy of love for the beloved. By playing with this layer of meaning in this expression, Dylan recovers the deepening darkness at the core of what it means to be lovesick. This recurrent portrayal is remarkable insofar as the love sickness of radical amazement in the Song of Songs immediately sours so that the Hibbing bard that can also wander in search of love, but it quickly turns from "wounded flowers" to a psychic landscape where the "streets that are dead".

The pathetic fallacy evoked here in "Love Sick" has the both the landscape of "mystic garden" and the natural order as "the clouds are weeping" to reflect the inner turmoil and darkness of the poet who is "tired" and "wired" only to be "hit from behind" with a flash of insight amidst his solitude. There is that same sense of wanderlust recurs in the Song of Songs, as the lover searches for his beloved:

> "Tell me, my only love, where do you pasture
> your sheep,
> where will you let them rest/in the heat of
> noon?
> Why should I lose my way among the flocks
> of your companions?"[520]

The question of the beloved appears at first blush in the Song of Songs that she simply wants to know the whereabouts of her lover at noontime, a period is associated with rest and relaxation. Rather than see lyrics like "Love Sick" as expressing a search for a fleeting love, the lyric takes us into a state of mind, emptied of that possibility. Namely, that whatever fleetingness once was has already fled forever and the singer is emptied and left abandoned, which is radically different than the erotic interplay of hide and seek between lover and beloved throughout the Song of Songs, culminating in the lover once again fleeing in the final chapter with the beloved chasing after him. Her rendezvous flutters to and fro between fantasy and reality in the midday heat. And yet her language suggests "a certain air of threat and tease".[521] The volatility of this "threat and tease" foreshadows trouble down the road that shifts to the underside of the love song as a lament.

The language of lament is canonized in the Hebrew Bible too near the love song to be a coincidence. The scroll of Lamentations is a language of exasperated interrogation so difficult to translate. Yet this exasperation approximates the questioning of both "where" as well as "how". And so, the love song of Song of Songs can only be understood in its fullness when read as a prelude to love and its loss through the ashes. Only when the lost lover begins to ask the question: how is it possible to have been led down this road to loss that the nuances of *eros* and *thanatos,* love and death can be fully appreciated. This simultaneity is a creative tension felt by strong poets, beginning

124

with the Song of Songs: "Let me lie among vine blossoms,/in a bed of apricots! I am in the fever of love."[522]

And so, it is by merely alluding to this selfsame verse from the Song of Songs that one of the most nuanced and complex erotic homages to love and its loss is found in the Hebrew poem of Yehudah Amichai known as "Love Gifts": "As it is written in the Song:/persecute me in a bed of apricots/so we might lie among vine blossoms." [523] It is this willingness to tear into the difference that seemingly separates love from its death that allows Amichai's poem to so slyly evoke this biblical verse in an homage to gifts given in love that end in its death. And so here the turn to love's demise in Dylan's lyric is much more acute, without bothering to linger in the gifting quality of love, rather his lyric leaps directly to the spleen and skull of love subdued by death as ruled by the impious one: "I'm sick of love but I'm in the thick of it".[524] Just as throughout Baudelaire's *Flowers of Evil* portrays the paradoxical deep pull of love through the spreading of his spleen, here there is no escaping love amidst its paradoxical decomposition through death, as the bard is "in the thick of it" wish they had never met, just trying to forget it all despite being so enmeshed.

Rather than recall loves lost with a sense of longing leading to homage, Dylan's lyric is a cry out from the broken-hearted self that yearns to be emptied and freed of such longings that chain lovers to the eternal Song of Songs. In yearning to be freed from these feeling constantly calling out from that love song, the lover who has lost cries out to forget and erase the very star-crossed encounter that brought this lover and beloved together in love to begin with. The texture of this lyrical spleen is only deepened in "Love Sick" with that swampy Americana soundscape that producer Daniel Lanois has brilliantly framed this for the entire album, *Time Out of Mind*, which evokes a hopeless search for love lost and never found. The overwhelming sense of betrayal the lover feels in being separated from the beloved resonates in the "thunder" of the heavens and on the lonely "road" of the earth. By contrast, the beloved still hopes to catch a glimmer of the fleeting lover:

> "Before day breathes
> before the shadows of night are gone,
> run away, my love!
> Be like a gazelle, a wild stag on the
> jagged mountains."[525]

But just what do they portend for the bard? He can catch a similar glimmer of the "lovers in the meadow" or catch a glance of "silhouettes in the window" but they quickly dissolve, leaving the bard "hanging on to a shadow".[526] From this place of darkness, yearning for love along the gnostic path is what allow for disclosure of the concealed, insofar the heart serves as the vehicle for that very disclosure: "I shall give you what no eye has seen, what no ear has heard, what no hand has touched, what has not arisen in the human heart."[527] But the inability to receive Gnosis is directly related to lack of love: "...because they are blind in their hearts/and do not see." [528] This visionary quality of the mystic and poet, recalls Rimbaud's call to the *voyant*, as the seer who can indeed see through an open heart.

Sometimes, however, what the seer can see is paradoxically: "From the abundance of the heart/such a person brings forth evil."[529] Moreover, if the materiality of one's manifest reality seems like it is indeed enough of a vehicle to enable this deeper seeing whereby one lacks nothing, this ultimately is deluded thinking: "This is what he was thinking in his heart,/but that very night he died." [530] The mystical poet as bard then is the one who is tasked with bringing solace to the broken-hearted, and: "Blessings on you who have been persecuted in your hearts."[531]

Songs of the persecuted heart will often point towards its redemption, as seen in a number of songs from the so-called "born again" period. Redeeming the persecuted heart requires a reorientation,[532] identifying the "way into my heart", [533] daring then unlock it, [534] and then offering a renewed focus on its rebirthing and surrender to a new love so the bard can then sing: "I owe my heart to you".[535] Realize that Dylan's songbook tends to focus less on heart break[536] and more on the heart of darkness. The light of hope for the heart is rare, but glimmers through the darkness from time to time, especially when addressing the other as child who should remain "Young at heart"[537] rather than succumbing the foreboding quality of darkness the singer occupies in aging. Despite the darkness that sets in with love's betrayal over time, sparks of light abide in the fall and winter years of the forlorn lover, where there is a: "Heart burnin', still yearnin'/No one on earth would ever know".[538] Who knows this truth hidden within the depths of the heart but the Gnostic?

So, this tendency within his songbook to move in a gnostic key manifests this sense of the heart that is persecuted, "wretched"[539] and "sufferin'."[540] Dylan articulates one of his darkest gnostic reflections on the persecuted heart, questioning if there was ever any love for the open heart, in his collaboration with Robert Hunter. In "Forgetful Heart" [541] the source of love itself is interrogated for losing its power to recall any amorous feelings of: "The times we knew/Who would remember better then you". [542] The song opens in a dialogue between the self and the heart that is unable to remember loves past. In this chiding dialogue, a glimmer of hope remains if the heart is seen as merely being forgetful, rather than utterly forgetting or forgotten. And yet there is a cynicism that abounds as the self is pleading with the heart to fulfill its assigned role. The heart is the source that provides vitality throughout the circulatory system and thus best positioned to feel love. But the mind is meant to remember and recall past emotional experience. Without that integration of feelings in the heart imbedded as memories in the mind, the lover becomes withdrawn, and feels betrayed. When the lover recalls the deep love experienced in union with the beloved, then that experience of union itself serves as the answer to an otherwise lost prayer. The self that desires a prayerful life chastises the forgetful heart for its inability to make time count as "now you're content to let the days go by". Making time count from loves and other worthy experiences is what weaves a veritable "garment of days" which the soul is said to dawn in the time that is coming.[543] In this reckoning, not only are loves lost but so is the chance to make that time have counted for something more than withdrawal, exile, and solitude. Prayer is thus broken here insofar as the doorway to it has been obstructed. Once the heart is forgetful, it no longer fulfills its role as the human-divine organ that can be "the answer to my prayer...with all the love that life can give." The lament for love lost deepens into a dirge-like quality, as the self yearns for what once was and wonders why it can no longer be. In confronting the loss of the remembering heart and all its fecundity, the searching self wallows deeper into darkness. This wandering movement bespeaks more than merely a diminishing of virility but a loss of vitality and will to live, thus veering away from life onto the precipice of death.

The closing verse of this lyric, like the closing of the door forevermore, "If indeed there ever was a door",[544] sounds the final cynical Kafkaesque laughter that is devoid of consolation, with grave implications for any possibility of a loving heart.[545] An earlier lyrical reflection on love would playfully confess to be locked out of the sealed heart: "Yes, I can take him to your house but I can't unlock it/You see, you forgot to leave me with the key."[546] However, in this later lyric, there is the level of paradox, namely, how can a door be "closed forevermore" if its very existence is in question. "If indeed there ever was a door" present a kind of musical Zen *koan* that is a challenge to the entire proposition of the song that there is a doorway to and from the heart that can be opened and closed.[547] At the same time, this final verse of "Forgotten Heart" alludes to the messianic vision of the prophet, Isaiah, who sees the messiah as the one who: "shall open, and none shall shut; and he shall shut, and none shall open."[548] This enigmatic prophesy erases, for all intents and purposes, the very purpose of a door to begin with. For in the end, which is inscribed in the beginning, there never was, is, nor shall there be any door. And so, we see here how one verse in the course of the entire composition can swerve its apparent direction, swerving ingeniously between the paradox of a *koan* and the power of a prophecy.

What I have argued for here in the Dylan songbook is a gnostic vision of the pain of the persecuted heart that is withdrawing deeper into the shadowy mindscape which could not be starker. The conflict between the mind and heart is recalled here, and the only resolution offered here is that the door to the heart must be closed because it was nothing but an illusion to begin with. While it remains unresolved whether the knowing mind will ultimately prevail over the forgetful heart, what continues to echo through this sparse Americana musical landscape that aptly complements the lyrical solitude is a deepening darkening emptiness at the heart of it all.

(5) *Forever Young*:
Heartfelt Hymn Resting Upon Fatherly Trust

Chapter at a glance: *"Forever Young" remains a most
powerful prayerful poem that seemed to flow from Dylan
in an instant. From the place of unknowing, Dylan's
intuitive decision to finally allow this internalized
inspiration to be externally recorded as a slow acoustic
waltz is perhaps what allowed for the song's heartfelt,
hymnal quality to emerge. Dylan's muse here is his focus
on fatherhood. "Forever Young" poises the singer looking
at his son while blessing him, all the while addressing that
divine trace emerges through every encounter with the
face of the other. There are many layers to "Forever
Young" so to truly appreciate the depth of its exegetical
artistry, this chapter begins by first outlining the
contextual meaning of the Priestly Blessing from the book
of Numbers in light of recent archaeological discoveries
and then reflecting exegetically upon Dylan's "Forever
Young" as an extended translation of this ancient prayer.
"Forever Young" manifests a hope for an awareness of
nearby luminosity, rather than emanating from those
distant stars. Surrounding lights of family and loved ones,
once identified and blessed, then can be carried forward
upon your journey. This hopeful moment in Dylan's
songbook is highly unusual and lasts but a moment.
"Forever Young" is a remarkable moment that sets into
relief the proclivity for the preponderance of Dylan's
songbook to return deeper into the darkening misery,
loneliness and exile of existence. Darkness is momentarily
punctured by the bard's hopelessly hopeful moment of
blessing, however, fleeting, for the sake of his children,
and the world family.*

Dylan lyrics analyzed include: "Forever Young," (*Planet
Waves*, 1974).

(5) *Forever Young*:
Heartfelt Hymn Resting Upon Fatherly Trust

> "Forever Young" I wrote in Tucson. I wrote it thinking of my boys, not wanting to be too sentimental. The lines came to me, they were done in a minute. I don't know.[549]

Everyone in the studio was mesmerized by the riveting immediacy of this song captured in one take at the time during the recording of the slow version of "Forever Young",[550] especially engineer, Rob Fraboni. Why was this song so powerful? Dylan told Fraboni: "I been carrying this song around in my head for five years and I never wrote it down and now I come to record it I just can't decide how to do it." [551] From the place of unknowing, Dylan's intuitive decision to finally allow this internalized inspiration to be externally recorded as a slow acoustic waltz is perhaps what allowed for the song's heartfelt, hymnal quality to emerge. Dylan's muse here is his focus on fatherhood and his relationship to his sons (Jakob Luke, Jesse Byron, Samuel Isaac Abraham), if not all his children (Desiree Gabrielle and Anna). "Forever Young" poises the singer looking at his son while blessing him, all the while addressing that divine trace emerges through every encounter with the face of the other. There are many layers to Dylan's song, "Forever Young" but to truly appreciate the depth of its exegetical artistry, it is worthwhile to first outline the contextual meaning (*p'shat*) through translation of the "Priestly Blessing" itself, as follows:

> "May the Lord bless you and protect you!
> May the Lord deal kindly and graciously with
>   you!
> May the Lord bestow favor upon you and
>   grant you peace!

Thus, they shall link My name with the people of Israel, and I will bless them."[552]

Notice how Dylan's songwriting cuts to the chase by invoking "May You" from the third person "May the Lord" formulaic Priestly Blessing, much like Psalm 23:4 in its shift from third person to second person. The riveting immediacy of this ancient blessing comes into clearer relief when these words are seen in their historical context, as uncovered in recent archaeological discoveries at *Ketef Hinnom*—the very hill overlooking the Hinnom Valley to the southwest of the Old City of Jerusalem, the very site Dylan visited for the *bar mitzvah* celebration of his son, Samuel.[553] These ancient paleo-Hebrew benedictions were written on silver plaques found in these rock-hewn burial caves, dating from the end of the First Temple period (seventh century B.C.E.). Framing the Priestly Blessing is its concluding verse: "And they (the priests) shall place My Name on" (Numbers 6:27) demonstrates that the "Jerusalem the Priestly Benediction was worn on the body in the form of amulets… [so] that the Priestly Benediction delivered by the priests in the sanctuary was also to be placed on the Israelites as prophylactics." [554] This blessing is a placing of the divine Name by the priests upon the Israelites through song. These kinds of amulets do more simply protect the one wearing them: they bring the Divine Presence into one's life.

So, what is the song— as parents, as mentors, as co-workers— we hope to convey to our children, apprentices and the next generation? What is the song we hope they will continue to sing long after we are gone? The prophet Malachi warns that any blessing that emerges from hypocrisy, especially from the priests, is bound to die young:

"…will [God] lift your countenance (*ha-yissa panekha*)…that He may be gracious to us (*viḥanneinu*)…will He lift His countenance (*ha-yissa panim*)? Would that you not light (*ta·iru*). My altar in vain (*ḥinnam*)!"[555]

As the Children of Israel betray their priests who serve God, their Father in Heaven, so too, do we as children often betray our parents. The hope in Dylan's song is not only that this child's wishes may come true, but that a parent's wishes for their child also be fulfilled. To read this song as wishful blessing resting upon a further act of trust: that your wishes are and shall always be wise ones.[556] This is carried further in the verse: "May you build a ladder to the stars/And climb on every rung" [557] alluding to the cumulative effect of this hopeful blessing of a god-wrestler like Jacob (after all, the namesake of one of Dylan's sons is Jakob), rather than an esoteric kabbalistic ascension into celestial spheres.[558] The song is more concerned with trusting your own authenticity, as the parental blessing suggests: "May you be like Ephraim and Menashe" here reframed as "May you be *you*." The most disappointing and terrifying moment of life happens when you look yourself in the mirror and wonder why you have not been your authentic self.

So, be careful what you wish for, lest your wish be granted. But as to your prayers, may they all come true in your lifetime, and the lifetime of your children, and your children's children—*how?* By the way you live, moment to moment. This takes a certain wisdom of experience that only emerges with the patience of living in time and learning to wait patiently within it. May you be granted the gift of giving before getting. Then your getting is all the richer! What stops this? Mistaken pride and the illusion of happiness. Mistaken pride is what puts yourself before others, while Dylan reiterates time and again: "happiness is not on my list of priorities"[559]— namely, that the search for happiness is illusory. If this song is a way to bless your child, notice that "Forever Young" does not share the wish: "May you be happy!" The direct pursuit of happiness always leads you astray. The values this father sings to his son at this moment are values more lasting and less illusory than happiness.

This prayer resonates with such immediacy because it is authentic in its request and thus can be answered—all in a matter of time! That is the hope. "Forever Young" is dedicated to hope. In the ashes of 9/11 terror attack of 2001, Dylan remarked: "my mind would go to young people at a time like this..."[560] In the face of such terror, one can only continue to be hopelessly hopeful. "May you always know the truth"— here the call is to discover the truth, not necessarily your truth, but a higher truth. Truth is a lifelong quest, so father reminds his son to stay humble and within time, perhaps you will see the truth that unites us rather than dividing us. From this clarified point of view, then "see the lights surrounding you" in that more than one light shining manifests an overflow of generosity. May such lights always abide. The hope is for an awareness of these lights surrounding nearby, rather than emanating from those distant stars! These surrounding lights can be carried forward with you upon your journey. To see the lights surrounding you, especially when you know the truth, is to thus never lose sight of hope! This hopeful moment in Dylan's songbook is highly unusual and lasts but a moment. And yet, even in this evanescent moment, Dylan felt inspired enough to share it as an impromptu musical gift as blessing under the wedding canopy of his cousin, Linda Goldfine at the Temple Israel Camp in Minneapolis.[561] "Forever Young" then sets into relief the proclivity for Dylan's songbook to return deeper into the darkening misery, loneliness and exile of existence. Darkness is momentarily punctured by the bard's hopelessly hopeful moment of blessing, however, fleeting, for the sake of his children, and the world family.

(6) *Desolation Row*:
Mommy, Mommy, Wall, Wall…Consolation From Where?

Chapter at a glance: In the possibility of mourning the emptiness, just what kind of future remains? Could this very mourning of this emptiness set into relief the growing rupture between Diaspora and Israeli Jewry? In daring theological imagery drawn from mystical exegesis in Zohar Hadash on Lamentations, the Hibbing Bard is sending us another missive about the impossible possibility of consoling such mourning that began already in 1965 with "Desolation Row". This chapter attempts to join the orphans of Jerusalem as diaspora jackals and desert ostriches. The daring theological imagery of this medieval commentary has never rang truer, the more deeply devoid we feel of any possible consolation in the current ruins of a Jerusalem that is tearing the Jewish people apart— just makes you wanna cry! Precisely—that's the point of a real dirge! This chapter invites readers to listen more deeply to the caterwauling concatenation of the inconsolable child. Let us never forget that as a community of orphans we continue mourning the emptiness of our collective authenticity which is manifesting as a deep rupture between Diaspora and Israeli Jewry. This wandering and weeping within us all, wailing these words, "Mommy, mommy, wall, wall!" as a naive child would, he presses on, searching for his divine mother, long gone from the wall, so all that remains is this inconsolable wailing. Alas, the prophet Isaiah comes carrying "postcards of the hanging" and a torn heart to console each of us as orphaned children.

Dylan lyrics analyzed include: "Desolation Row," (Highway 61 Revisited, 1965).

(6) *Desolation Row*:
Mommy, Mommy, Wall, Wall...Consolation From Where?

"I lift my eyes yonder to the mountains, from where will my consolation come?" Unlike another brilliant "broken mirror" singer-songwriter,[562] Bod Dylan never set Psalm 121 to music, nor did he compose anything for *Shabbat Nachamu*, yet I've been rethinking his recent allegedly plagiarized Nobel Prize address as his own Americana *Nachamu*. To be clear, to me as a scholar-rabbi, nothing is more depraved than plagiarism, and yet I wonder, whether for an artist as adept as Dylan whether in this limited case, his plagiarizing is itself an exercise in exile – namely, I steal from others because I am and remain a truly Americana Jew bereft of ideas. Do we copy others as an act of mourning the emptiness of our own besieged self? The great tragedy is when we no longer remember we are thieves and act as if stolen property is our own. We make the obligation of returning lost objects impossible. I argue that Dylan proffers a spark of redemption in his thievery, as when they asked him about stealing lyrics from a Civil War song some years ago, he responded, "I never said I wasn't a thief." In that possibility of mourning the emptiness, just what kind of future remains? Could this very mourning of this emptiness set into relief the growing rupture between Diaspora and Israeli Jewry? I cannot escape the sense that the Hibbing Bard is sending us another missive about the impossible possibility of consoling such mourning that began already with "Desolation Row" in 1965: "Yes, I received your letter yesterday/(About the time the doorknob broke)/When you asked how I was doing/Was that some kind of joke?"[563]

Dylan's current missive recounts how he learned the way of the wanderer from Odysseus; *All quiet on the western front* showed him there is no consolation to the horrors humans continue to inflict upon one another; and *Moby Dick* showed him the American dream is about hunting down the dream and incubating it in the belly of the whale. It seems then that Dylan's songbook resides in such deeply darkening places. Akin to the child hobo in Overman's brilliant Dylan bio-pic, *I'm not there*, much of this darkening darkness where consolation feels out of reach, reminds me of another inconsolable child in an astonishing text I've recently discovered while teaching in Jerusalem. *Lamentations*, the core biblical text recited on the floor during the 9th of Av, is a phantasmagoric recounting the Jerusalem temples' destructions and thus our need for consolation this Shabbat so named. As a dirge, Lamentations focuses on the divine need for consolation. The God of the biblical Lamentations is either the wailing Daughter of Zion or the fallen God of War. But in the late medieval Spanish commentary, called *Zohar Hadash*, it is the inconsolable child who is wailing. Wandering through the ruins of Jerusalem, we run into these orphaned children sifting through the ashes of Jerusalem and crying out:

> "Every day we approach Mother's bed, but we do not find Her there. We ask after Her— no one heeds us. We ask after Her bed— overturned. We ask after Her throne— collapsed. We ask Her palaces—they swear they know nothing of Her whereabouts. We ask the dust—not footprints there." [564]

I hear the wailing of the real Children of Israel in *Zohar Hadash* who are crying: "We are the orphans, without Father or Mother! We cast our eyes upon the walls of our Mother's house, but it is destroyed, and we can't find Her..." No longer servants or children, we are now all orphans. After the destruction of the Jerusalem temples, we orphans bang our heads against a wall that is also wailing. We are like children crying out: "Mommy, Mommy, wall, wall!" I write these words that echo *Zohar Hadash*'s imagined barbed missives being sent back and forth by Babylonian Jewry to Israeli Jewry challenging each other's authenticity and calling out each other's "bad faith"! In choosing not to leave the diaspora of Babylon, you should weep for yourselves not the Temple you never frequented, quip the Israeli community. You chose your fate, you live in a place of darkness because your self-concern still over-rides your concern for the Jerusalem Temple, the Holy Land, so weep for your own sorry fate.[565] The response of Babylonian Jewry from the depths of diaspora comes later on, when they finally have enough courage to respond to their Israeli brethren:

> "It is fitting that you cry, and it befits you to eulogize and mourn when you see Mother's sanctuaries destroyed, the place of Her bed upended in mourning. She is absent, having flown away from you, leaving you unaware of Her whereabouts. You might say the She is with us in exile, dwelling among us. If so, we should rejoice, for indeed the prophet Ezekiel saw Her here with all Her legions. But actually, for this we must weep and eulogize, like jackals and desert ostriches. She has been banished from Her chambers and we are in exile. She comes to us in bitterness and sees us daily in all our afflictions, with all the statues and decrees they impose upon us constantly. But She cannot remove these scourges from us, nor all the ordeals that we suffer."[566]

So, we join the orphans of Jerusalem as diaspora jackals and desert ostriches. The daring theological imagery of this medieval commentary has never rang truer, the more deeply devoid we feel of any possible consolation in the current ruins of a Jerusalem that is tearing the Jewish people apart— just makes you wanna cry! Precisely—that's the point of a real dirge! So, as we enter this Sabbath of consolation, nicknamed *Nachamu,* let's all listen more deeply to the caterwauling concatenation of the inconsolable child. Let us never forget that as a community of orphans we continue mourning the emptiness of our collective authenticity which is manifesting as a deep rupture between Diaspora and Israeli Jewry. This wandering and weeping within us all, wailing these words, "Mommy, mommy, wall, wall!" as a naive child would, he presses on, searching for his divine mother, long gone from the wall, so all that remains is this inconsolable wailing. Alas, the prophet Isaiah comes carrying "postcards of the hanging" and a torn heart to console each of us child with these words: "*Nachamu, Nachamu*"—There, there, be consoled! Yonder is your consolation coming, O orphaned ones...

(7) *Long Time Gone*:
Time as Redemption & Loss

Chapter at a glance: So little time, yet so much love to know... yet time is a mystery that touches us all. What we remember, what we forget and what we forget to remember and remember to forget—it is all a matter of time. And the textures of time are so supple. I think about all the times I have considered emigrating over the past two decades to this Holy Land while remaining a rambler in my Diaspora—all those times away from this place, despite seemingly forever returning in a backwards inflected futurity, as "Ring Them Bells" encapsulates that: "time is running backwards and so is the bride." To frame our exploration of time in the Dylan songbook, it is important to appreciate the nuances and textures of time that permeate his songbook, including: The lonesome time of exile is what drives the "true man" to continue on the road in search of love lost. This perennial search below for love lost is echoed above, as the masculine divine presence searches from the exiled feminine presence in the ruins of the Jerusalem Temple. Jewish Gnosticism stresses the extended pain of this yearning most strongly in examining the traces of "divine coupling" of the masculine with the feminine. Amidst all the wandering of this rambling vagabond, always yearning to return home, there is eventually a realization that he can never truly return home. That realization allows for a certain beauty to emerge, even if it is already a long time gone.

Dylan lyrics analyzed include: "Ring Them Bells" (*O Mercy*, 1985); "Long Time Gone" (*Witmark Demos*, 1963); "Slow Train," (*Slow Train Coming*, 1979); "What Can I Do For You," (*Saved*, 1979); "Tomorrow Is A Long Time" (*Witmark Demos*, 1962-64, 1963).

141

(7) *Long Time Gone*:
Time as Redemption & Loss

So little time, so much love to discover... yet time is a mystery that touches us all. What we remember, what we forget and what we forget to remember and remember to forget—it is all a matter of time. All these textures of time are so supple. As I write these words of analysis on one Nobel laureate from 2017, Bob Dylan, so I encounter another Nobel laureate from 1966 here in Jerusalem café at 5 Salomon Yo'El Moshe Street, whose renowned 1945 novel, called *'Tmol Shilshom* — is the very namesake of this place. In writing, I am touched by all the times I have sat in this Jerusalem café space to read, write, and reflect upon living, loving and losing. Wandering later that same day through Valley of Ghosts known as *Emek Refaim,* I traverse the once abandoned train tracks, renewed as the First Station with the words originally used by novelist, S. Y. Agnon, aka Shmuel Yosef Halevi Czaczkes (1888-1970) from his novel, *'Tmol Shilshom,* about Jews emigrating from to Palestine, translated as *Only Yesterday* or even beyond that as *The Day before Yesterday* (1945). Agnon's words are now punched into re-purposed, corroding steel from the tracks unearthed, now serving as the pathway markers where the tracks once stood. I think about all the times I have considered emigrating over the past two decades to this Holy Land while remaining a rambler in my Diaspora—all those times away from this place, despite seemingly forever returning in a backwards inflected futurity, as Dylan's lyric encapsulates that: "time is running backwards and so is the bride."[567]

To frame our exploration of time in the Dylan songbook, it is important to appreciate the nuances and textures of time that permeate his oeuvre: (1) the time of the present momentum, (2) there is the time of the past, and (3) there is the time of the future. It is in turning to the fourth time, the time of timeless awareness that then brings forth this dimension into time for ourselves and others. Somehow human beings have developed the necessary facility with simultaneously being in timeless awareness while in time.[568] While the Dylan songbook may struggle with love in the present while toggling between its past losses and future hopes, there is clearly some other order of time altogether that emerges in this process— namely, the time of timeless awareness. I would argue that within the Dylan songbook in particular, and in music, generally, that the time of timeless awareness is what abides.[569] It is from this subtle awareness of the layers of time that we return to our analysis in a gnostic key.

Time portends its very own redemption while demarcating its loss. Loss is not always noticed in the darkness. So, the extent of this loss can be seen as a return of light lost from creation in the face of the overwhelming darkness of primordial chaos. As lost light now dissolves in the face of Redemption forever in the offing as described in the Gnostic Gospels.[570] Yet this loss can be seen, more damningly, with the emergence of *time itself.* Time emerges as a concept of human experience once Creation begins, for the beginning of temporality, torn apart from eternity, is what causes this loss of eternality. Time, in the Dylan songbook, emerges from within negativity— from death to life, from darkness to light. It is from such space of "loneliness, tenderness" time emerges as a dialectic of emotional tapestry. The liminal space that hovers between "loneliness, tenderness" can only be captured in dream-time— "when we were made of dreams". This texture in time is liminal, between pockets of conscious and subconscious time, precisely where dreams emerge. To appreciate the deeper depths of time's passage in the Dylan songbook, we will examine the way in which time emerges between redemption and loss.

Dawning the mythic mask of the rambler, Dylan's bard proclaims that: "I'm a long time a-comin'/I'll be a long time gone".[571] Time is measured in the distance between ingression and regression, between coming and going. It is necessary for this middle class Hibbing bard to claim his own myth of origins by reformulating them in claiming that: "When I was all so young/And I left my home the first time". [572] Despite the seeming monotonous repetition of being a rambler wandering through life on "carnival trains", here the singer admits seeing the pristine quality of the beginning of time before progressing onwards, namely: "I remember children's faces best/I remember travelin' on".[573] The innocence of childhood and its face it what is lost in wandering down the road, until one can surrender to the dialectic of being "…a long time a-comin'/…a long time gone".[574] What ruptures time from its source in eternity but love, as the bard confesses having "once loved a fair young maid" who broke his heart "ten or twelve" times.[575] This throw-away confession is important insofar as it foreshadows the never-ending experience of heart break that begins all the way back at the time of first love. Once the first love is lost, the time of the first heart break, then the rambler will forever encounter brokenness. Every time of future brokenness appears to already be implanted in that first experience of the heart breaking.

In the face of this interminable brokenness, it serves as the inspiration precipitating a journey towards the light within this darkness, the healing within this rupture. The journey takes multiple routes, with recurring motifs of the railroad that have been duly explore,[576] as well as the highway, the latter which I will now explore. Setting out on the road to meaning and redemption, hitchhiking is meandering pathway that demands the hitcher to remain utterly present. For the Beatniks like Jack Kerouac and Allen Ginsberg, the guide upon this pathway was strongly inflected with the Dharma of Buddhism.[577] By contrast, the Dylan songbook draws upon Americana music as its primary guide,[578] deriving its inspiration from Black Spirituals and Gospel that undergird this tradition. Both pathways— whether Buddhist, and to a lesser extent, Gospel— focus on presence within the moment, deferring meaning to the redemption that is coming, so that it is not about the destination but the journey itself. Redemption on the road is indeed a "slow train coming", so beware of anyone who might give you the definitive answer along this wandering space. Any answer, even from the artist, cannot be trusted, even if coded in numerical form![579] Deception about the current state of existence abounds as the unseen realm of light is obscured by the darkening darkness of the world. There is an element of deep displeasure with the current status of self within the world as it is that propels one to wander in exile, alone: "Sometimes I feel so low-down and disgusted/Can't help but wonder what's happenin' to my companions/Are they lost or are they found".[580] Wandering on the road—a metaphor for the search of an authentic life— is precisely the open space that allows the bard reflects how: "Many times by the highwayside/I tried to flag a ride/With bloodshot eyes and gritting teeth/I'd watch the cars roll by/The empty air hung in my head". [581] This "empty air" is only experienced wandering on the road—why? In line with the deferral of redemption, it is only the residue of "empty air" —what Jewish Gnostics refer to as the "empty void"[582]— that can point to what still remains from the cataclysm of creation.[583]

Redemption of the world created in time suffers from constantly distracted. The disgust that emerges is from the insight of the exiled "the true man", who knows intimately that as: "Soon as a man is born, you know the sparks begin to fly."[584] What the wanderer in the Dylan songbook, like the exiled Primordial Adam, is searching for that lost time that is no longer mired in the darkness of distraction, but is bathed in the light of eternity. Embedded within every human is the capacity for this yearning, and so, embedded within each moment is redemptive time in the offing. The ingenuity of this symbolism is woven into the Dylan songbook early on: "If today was not an endless highway/If tonight was not a crooked trail/If tomorrow wasn't such a long time/Then lonesome would mean nothing to you at all".[585]

Wandering again on the "endless highway" reveals what it truly means for the "true man" to be caught up in a "lonesome" state. And yet this loneliness of exile exists only as a function of time embedded in the moment called "today". The moment of redemption that is always in the offing as "tomorrow" could cure the wanderer's "lonesome" state if only "If tomorrow wasn't such a long time". But the darkness of exile that is "today" occludes the light of redemption of "tomorrow". The loss of "today" could be repositioned into moments of redemption through love: "Yes, and only if my own true love was waitin'/Yes, and if I could hear her heart a-softly poundin'/Only if she was lyin' by me/Then I'd lie in my bed once again".[586]

The lonesome nature of exile is what drives the "true man" to continue on the road in search of love lost. This perennial search below for love lost is echoed above, as the masculine divine presence searches from the exiled feminine presence in the ruins of the Jerusalem Temple. Jewish Gnosticism stresses the extended pain of this yearning most strongly in examining the traces of *hieros gamos* or "divine coupling" of the masculine with the feminine. Those traces are alive and well in the memories buried in the dust and the abandoned bed as described in the Zohar:

"At the hour of midnight, She enters Point of Zion, site of the holy of holies, and sees how it has been razed and defiled—the place of Her habitation and Her bed. Her wailing and sobbing rises from below on high, and from on high down below. She looks upon the domain of the cherubim, shrieking grievously. Raising Her voice, She cries, 'My bed, My bed, of My dwelling. Of this place is written: '[*On*] *my bed at night*' (Song of Songs 3:1). My bed—bed of *Matronita*. Wailing through Her weeping, She says, 'My bed, site of Temple, place of precious jewels...the world was sustained on your account, I was Master of the Universe."[587]

The bard casts himself as that solitary child, the "only son" cast adrift in the universe. Amidst all the wandering of this rambling vagabond, always yearning to return home, there is eventually a realization that he can never truly return home. That realization allows for a certain beauty to emerge, "skin deep" that will already "rot before your eyes" given it is "a long time gone."[588]

(8) *All Along the Watchtower*:
Where are the Watchers of Zion?!?

Chapter at a glance: *One may search, seemingly in vain, for the presence of Zion and the Land of Israel in the Gnostic theology of Dylan's songbook. And yet, it is precisely this sublimated motif that propels so much of the bard's wandering along Highway 61 is not merely a journey through the signposts of the American Dream, where a redeemed Zion remains in the offing even if Her exiles may be returning. This chapter analyzes Dylan's masterful lyrical re-reading of the archetype of the thief who reveals and the jokers who conceals the portrayal of Zion through the prophesy of Isaiah 62 in "All Along the Watchtower" and how it stands in conversation with the more explicit parable of modern Israel within the Middle Eastern in "Neighborhood Bully". Along the journey of performing his songbook, Dylan exposes his Tel Aviv and Jerusalem audiences to his several Christian songs appears strange at best, and an offensive anomaly at worst. What was Dylan after in the Holy Land? In the space of tripartite narratives competing for ascendency, yearning for singular power and unquestionable authenticity to invalidate the other, Dylan choses to blur the lines. Such borderlines were already conceived of in the face of blurring boundaries, lest one forget how the story really began this songbook comes to remind us again.*

Dylan lyrics analyzed include: "Ring Them Bells," (*O Mercy,* 1989); Bob Dylan, "Long Time Gone," (*Witmark Demos,* 1963); "Slow Train," (*Slow Train Coming,* 1979); "What Can I Do For You," (*Saved,* 1979); "Tomorrow Is A Long Time," (*Witmark Demos,* 1962-64, 1963); "Neighborhood Bully" (*Infidels,* 1983); "All Along the Watchtower" (*John Wesley Harding,* 1974).

(8) *All Along the Watchtower*:
Where are the Watchers of Zion?!?

One may search, seemingly in vain, for the presence of Zion and the Land of Israel in the gnostic theology of Dylan's songbook. And yet, it is precisely this sublimated motif that propels so much of the bard's wandering along Highway 61 is not merely a journey through the signposts of the American Dream, where a redeemed Zion remains in the offing even if Her exiles may be returning. In this chapter, I focus on Dylan's masterful re-reading of the archetype of the thief who reveals and the jokers who conceals the portrayal of Zion from Highway 61 breaking through to the prophesy of Isaiah 62 in "All Along the Watchtower"[589] and how it stands in conversation with the more explicit parable of modern Israel within the Middle Eastern in "Neighborhood Bully".[590] To appreciate Dylan's exegetical prowess operating in "All Along the Watchtower", it is necessary to understand the contextual meaning of the imagery in Isaiah. To begin, the song's title, "All Along the Watchtower" refers to First Isaiah's vision of Babylon's fall and the need for a "watchman" [*ha'metzapeh*] guarding the watchtower in Isaiah 21: 6-9—

> "For thus has the Lord said to me: Go, set a watchman [*ha'metzapeh*]; let him declare what he sees! And when he sees a troop, horsemen by pairs, a troop of asses, a troop of camels, he shall hearken diligently with much heed. And he cried as a lion: 'All along the watchtower [*'al ha'metzapeh*] Lord, I stand continually in the daytime, and I am set in my ward all the nights,' And, behold, there came a troop of men, horsemen by pairs. And he spoke and said: 'Fallen, fallen is Babylon;

and all the graven images of her gods are broken unto the ground.'"

This vision of "All along the watch-tower [*'al ha'metzapeh*]" can only be seen by the "watchman" [*ha'metzapeh*] and yet in Dylan's rendition this prophetic position of the watcher comes from those least trusted as outlaws—the joker and the thief, to whom we shall return later. Isaiah's vision likens the prophet to this sentry positioned with an overarching vision from the watchtower so as to foresee invasion before anyone else. For now, notice the apocalyptic sense of devastation coming with the approach of horsemen (21:9) is felt throughout the song. Moreover, the efficacy of setting watchmen along the watchtower which is meant to foresee what is coming remains deeply in question by the time this imagery recurs in Third Isaiah (62: 1-6):

"For the sake of Zion I will not remain silent,
For Jerusalem's sake I will not be still,
Till her victory emerge resplendent
And her triumph like a flaming torch.
Nations will see your victory,
And every king your majesty;
And you shall be called by a new name,
Which YHVH shall mark out.
You shall be a glorious crown of beauty
In the hand of YHVH,
And a royal diadem
In the palm of your God.
Nevermore shall you be called 'Forsaken'
Nor shall your land be called 'Desolate';
But you shall be called, 'I delight in her,
And your land, 'Espoused.
For YHVH delights in you,
And your land shall be espoused.
As a youth espouses a maiden,

Your sons shall be espoused.
And as a bridegroom rejoices over the bride,
So shall your God rejoice over you.

Upon your walls, O Jerusalem,
I have set watchmen,
Who shall be silent
By day or by night.
O you, YHVH's remembrancers,
Take no rest

And give no rest to Him,
Until He establish Jerusalem
And make her renowned song on earth."

The prophet can foresee Jerusalem and the
reversal of Her plight, from exile to redemption. But
there is an irony here, insofar as the postexilic context
of this prophetic vision can merely predict the
redemption of Zion that has not yet been realized, even
if some exiles have indeed returned. It is this irony that
is felt immediately in these opening verses, a limbo
between refusing to remain silent about Zion and
falling into inaction.[591] Zion is the center of Jerusalem
that will be renamed as she is reborn in her splendorous
and elevated state. Renaming a city like Jerusalem
happens to commemorate a noteworthy occasion of
divine revelation at its site, or due to its being rebuilt
or its conquest.[592] As Jerusalem is elevated in her new
royal status, she dawns the golden diadem and is
betrothed to God. The shift here taking place is from
Jerusalem's condition of being called "Forsaken" and
"Desolate indicating the divine abandonment of the
city,[593] to rise again to be called 'I Delight in Her'.
What emerges is the vision of salvation as a joyful
wedding ceremony, wherein espousal is inhabiting the
land.[594] In the act of enabling this redemptive vision,
God sets watchmen to along the perimeter walls of

Jerusalem to safeguard her from the raid of enemies. The wedding vow is a promise of ensuring that never again shall foreigners be allowed to penetrate the walls, looting the land and stealing the nation's harvest.[595] It is through the appointment of these watchmen all along the watchtower which is meant to ensure that these walls are not breached again, leading to the weeping walls of yesteryear.[596] These "watchmen" are sentinels posted atop the city walls that shall remain there standing vigil. These watchmen are never meant to rest but to remain vigilant like the divine who neither slumbers nor sleeps in the role of divine Guardian.[597] Much like the Levites whose task was to sound the trumpets to prod the Lord into constant action through song,[598] Dylan's lyric suggests that here too the watchmen and those who frequent the watchtower, like the joker and thief are the "true remembrancers". It is the duty of those who remember the music to sing the Lord into action through her "renowned song". Both outcasts stand to announce the proclamation through their song that the Deliverer is coming. [599] The roadway to redemption, a royal highway[600] must be carved out for the benefit of the returnees to Jerusalem along with the bestowal of new names on Jerusalem and the nation. [601] This is the dual task before the joker and the thief, at once to escape as well as to return with others in exile and reclaim a new name and destiny within this redeemed city.

This image of Zion is hidden in plain sight, especially in the passion at play in "All Along the Watchtower":

" 'There must be some way out of here,'
    said the joker to the thief
'There's too much confusion, I can't get no
    relief
Businessmen, they drink my wine, plowmen
    dig my earth

None of them along the line know what any
of it is worth.'
'No reason to get excited,' the thief, he
　　　kindly spoke
'There are many here among us who feel
　　　that life is but a joke
But you and I, we've been through that, and
　　　this is not our fate
So let us not talk falsely now, the hour is
　　　getting late' "[602]

The musical conversation between the joker and the thief stands as one of key structures to "All Along the Watchtower". While Dylan's songbook has a recurring interesting in the outlaw, here the joker and the thief are common allusions to the crucifixion in New Testament literature.[603] The question is how Dylan's lyric is re-reading these very exegeses on the original Isaiah prophesy. But I want to suggest another way of reading the thief. Imagine when the joker turns to the thief, and realizes the thief is actually a yeshiva student!?! And along the watchtower, this thief is most ingenious, with an innovative method of obtaining horses. For whenever this thief witnesses horses in the possession of people that do not look like their original owners, he yells out, "Hey! That's my horse!" More often than not, the accused horse-rider takes off and leaves the horse behind. The law states clearly regarding thieves and thievery that: "A thief is invalidated as a witness – even if the thief returned the item until he does some introspection."[604] But what of the thief who steals from a thief? The Sages suggest that paying an extra fine equal to the value of the stolen item only applies in the case where the item was taken from the owner itself and not from another thief.[605] The question remains – is one who steals from a thief is not considered a thief?

While it is true that the thief must return the item to the owner – it could be that he is not considered a thief and would be eligible to be a witness. Some suggest that one who partakes of something that was stolen from a thief is not rendered ineligible to testify.[606] The debate runs deeper. Another view suggests that one who steals from a thief is actually not considered a thief at all, but rather one who damages another.[607] In this light, the horse thief may still be a witness at his friend's wedding, but most certainly has the obligation to return the horse to the original owner, but only because he is a damager. A dissenting view suggests that there is a second theft here and that, especially in the case when the item is consumed – the second theft brought the item further still from the original owner.[608] Finally, there is the possibility that this is only exempting the second thief from the obligation of the imposed fine, but in regard to the principal of the item that was stolen – certainly he remains a thief![609]

How then might the second thief make amends? If the thief knows the real owner of the horse, then of course he should give it back. Otherwise, he should return it to the police and tell them that the item was in all probability stolen. But more than that, the thief comes to the realization that deeper introspection is needed known as *teshuva*. The more this song replays, the more possible it is to hear the thief turning back not only to the joker, but also in this turning to a place deeper inside to make space for regret, confession. In this process of *teshuva* as replaying, even the thief has the capacity to ensure that he does not go down this road of thievery again when standing at the crossroads. The thief can change through this process, and so could once again be eligible to be a witness at a wedding.[610] It is precisely through this transformation of the thief that Jerusalem can be elevated in her new royal status, dawning her golden diadem and is betrothed to God. The thief intimately knows what it means to exist in this condition of being called 'Forsaken' [*Ne'ezvah*] and 'Desolate' [*Shomemah*], to rise again in this vision of salvation as a joyful wedding ceremony, wherein espousal is a way of inhabiting the land.[611]

From this salvific vision of the land being wed to the divine, we turn to the ritual of wedding as a union of opposites. Whether wedding the land or another person it is a window into the very nature of relationship. There is clearly a concern elsewhere in the Dylan songbook, especially in the lyrics of "Wedding Song" and "The Groom's Still Waiting at the Altar" for this sacred encounter. In the former lyric, the wedding is a moment of that the lover can declare: "I love you more than ever, more than time and more than love".[612] But it is by entering into the wedding party where "the courtyard of the jesters, which is hidden from the sun" that the concealed space of luminosity emerges.

There is always a melody at the wedding that captures the "moment that the tune that is yours and mine will to play on this earth will play whatever it is worth…" So, the jesters are joined with the *klezmorim* known as the musicians whose melodies facilitate light emerging from darkness. Heylin analyzes "Wedding Song" to be a most personal account of the hard espousing his true love amongst all other overs to his beloved Sara, the moment before he returns back on the never-ending road tour. While highly possible as an interpretation, this reduces the majesty of Dylan's lyric only to the personal. But the prophetic and tradition from which Dylan draws always sees the personal as messianic and thus expanding to the national layer of Jerusalem as well as its cosmic implications. This is the power of every wedding and its ensuing song of love!

The texture of this love runs deep, so that the bard sings: "I love you more than ever, more than time and more than love"[613] I suggest this is evoking the very texture of the "equiprimordiality of time" [*Gleichursprunglichkeit*][614] that intertwines times past, present, and future all future emerging in the love being consecrated in this liminal moment of the wedding. The cosmic dimensions of wedding heaven and earth abide in this lyric "with a love that doesn't bend/and if there is eternity, I'd love you there again." [615] But the layers of time quickly begin to dissolve away in this rendition when the lover sing that: "I love you more than ever now that the past is gone" [616] suggesting that this love transforms temporality altogether, especially what has come before which shall be no more, dissolving even its traces as a memory.

And so, as this cosmic wedding takes place, we wonder all along the watchtower how do the joker and the thief contend with an even greater outlaw —the neighborhood bully? How far off is their road to redemption if life is but a joke? In this parable, Dylan's masterful lyric is in part a loyal exegesis of the prophecy imbedded in Third Isaiah (62:1-6), it could be the joker, the thief or the bully who asks the question with no answer.[617] The elixir to the stupefaction we all experience when what is sacred is inverted and turned against us as a weapon could be simply an abrasive finger, as is the habit of *Radiohead*'s lead singer Thom Yorke, who in the face of BDS protestors at their recent decision to play in Tel Aviv, "flipped the bird". Yorke goes on to describe the concert protest as "offensive" and "an extraordinary waste of energy," saying: "I don't agree with the cultural ban at all, along with J.K. Rowling, Noam Chomsky and a long list of others..."[618] Between Yorke's abrasive counterpunch and the Hillel rabbi's naïve hospitality, I kept wondering: *if Dylan we there, what song would he have sung to respond to Spencer's retort?* After all, Dylan is renowned for his spontaneous repartee with hecklers at his shows, especially the razor wit of his response to the Judas accusation of betraying his folk roots by going electric at the Albert's Hall performance in 1966. But here in the Hillel debate, *alt right fascist*, Richard Spencer is arguing that Jewish continuity is predicated on resistance to assimilation which he was seeking for the establishment of a White Zionist state within the U.S. On the other side of the fence, one encounters the awakening of the sleeping giant of Christian Evangelical Zionists, which did not quite coincide with Dylan's time with the *Vineyard Fellowship*.[619]

At first blush, there appears to be a lacuna in Dylan's gnostic mysticism in relation to a redemptive site like Zion and the Land of Israel, however, there are allusions worthy of reflection. Recall that C. Peter Wagner viewed three waves of the Holy Spirit's activity within the last century: (1) first wave of the Holy Spirit as the Azusa Street revival in Los Angeles which took place in 1906; (2) second of these waves was the Charismatic movement of the 1960's; (3) third wave as the rise of signs and wonders in the 1980's within the *Vineyard Fellowship* movement. Curiously it is this "third wave" that attracted Dylan. Coinciding with this period of constant touring:

"In [September 1982], [Dylan] returned to Jerusalem, in the company of his ex-wife, and again found himself back in the news, when he was photographed at the *bar mitzvah* of his son Samuel wearing a *yarmulke*. It was interpreted as considerably more than a sign of respect, and Dylan's next album would be recorded again a backdrop of religious crossfire from both sides of the messianic divide."[620]

If the mainstreaming of Christian Zionists had been happening in the 1980s, with the like of pastors like John Hagee, of Cornerstone Church, in San Antonio, Texas, who has become a fixture at AIPAC conferences, one could speculate that Dylan would likely have gravitated towards that conflation, but instead, Dylan wandered home through the Vineyard Fellowship.[621] In terms of Dylan's own journey, his highly misunderstood and purported "born again" period was short-lived, insofar as by March, he was already returning "to the religion of his forefathers"[622] and by early 1983 he was spending time with an ultra-orthodox hasidic sect known as Chabad, and even allegedly recorded an album of Hasidic songs, so now it appeared as though "Abraham's sons was about to bring it all back home."[623] There is a palpable tension here, in terms of how radically Dylan's pendulum swings—not merely from one orthodoxy to another. Rather from Christian Evangelism with some possible Zionist predilections, to the anti-Zionist, ultra-religious Chabad hasidism. Dylan's Chabad contact at the time, Rabbi Kasriel Kastel claimed: "He's been going in and out of a lot of things, trying to find himself. And we've just been making ourselves available. As far as we're concerned, he was a confused Jew. We feel he's coming back." [624] Of course it is fitting for a seeking Jew, who dabbled in messianic Christianity of the *Vineyard Fellowship* to find his way to return to through the backdoor of Chabad hasidism that is so deeply charged in terms of its messianic impulse. On *Infidels*, "Jokerman" continues Dylan's fascination with the *Book of Revelation* and specifically the need to separate false-messiahs from the "one true Messiah".[625] For Dylan, the return to his Jewish roots was just that—radical. Not in the sense of being a zealot, which Infidels clearly rejects, rather this was a return to the radical nature of the Jewish roots, devoid of orthodox ideology, [626] as he himself makes clear:

> "Roots man—we're talking about Jewish
> roots, you want to know more? Check on
> Elijah the prophet. He makes rain. Isaiah the
> prophet, even Jeremiah, see if their brethren
> didn't want to bust their brains for telling it
> right like it is, yeah—these are my roots, I
> supposed. Am I looking for them? ... I ain't
> looking for them in synagogues, with six-
> pointed Egyptian stars shining down from
> every window, I can tell you that much." [627]

This searching for roots, as a return to self, for many
was misunderstood as "a Dylan returned to secular
values, or even the faith of his father" which somehow
then:

> "...provided reassurance to the majority of
> (ex-) fans who preferred a world operation as
> a series of accidents, without purpose or
> reason, to 'a perfect, finished plan.' Perhaps
> their singing spokesman again accepted
> chaos. Even the more questioning of his
> constituency preferred a confused Judaic
> humanist to an unequivocal evangelist." [628]

From such comments, clearly most of his (ex-
)fans and critics simply misunderstood his search and
found the need to pigeon hole Dylan in the process.
Succumbing the inevitable preference of labeling
Dylan in an either/or dichotomy, that is, either as "a
confused Judaic humanist" or "an unequivocal
evangelist" serves to simplify and reduce his journey.
Heylin does pick up and then abandon the insight
before the labeling, namely, in his suggestion that
Dylan merely returns to being the perennial "singing
spokesman" of chaos. [629] The refocus on creation as the

blueprint for the messy and accidental meaning(lessness) of existence—the classic gnostic mysticism we discussed earlier on.

It is even more curious when we look for clues to Dylan's relation to Zion as the site of redemption, that Heylin chalks up the singular "Neighborhood Bully" as one of two "all-but-meritless-rants" [630] on *Infidels.* The artistic struggles around promoting Infidels seem to have centered precisely around this song, "[n]ot that the man behind Renaldo and Clara and Eat the Document was uninterested in the possibilities of the medium, it was just that a Zionist, 'David and Goliath' parable about the Battle of Armageddon might be fine hidden away on side two of the latest long-player, but not pumped into pubescents via cathodes and cables." [631] What happens when Dylan attempts to envision the site of redemption as Zion? Can this utopia be visualized or does it fall prey to the prohibition of what German-Jewish philosopher and music critic, Theodor Adorno called the *Bilderverbot?*[632]

"…We wanted to do 'Neighborhood Bully,' but [it's difficult] tryin' to explain to somebody what you see and drawin' up storyboards; I haven't really found anybody that really thinks a certain way that needs to be [done], like the German filmmakers, the English filmmakers. In the States there aren't people like that. They just don't exist… I visualized 'Neighborhood Bully'… there were certain segments which I just wrote down one night which I just wrote down one night which I thought would look great on film, and it would be like a Fassbinder film."[633]

To envision "Neighborhood Bully" as a Fassbinder film sounds more like a darkening dystopia rather than one of a number of conventional "all-but-meritless-rants" [634] on Zion. It is truly curious insofar as how one is meant to square this comment with Fassbinder's actual creations around Zion, especially plays like "Garbage, the City and Death" that emerged from street protests.[635] The disturbing element, typical of Fassbinder, is the casting of a character to play the old Nazi called, the Rich Jew, who describes himself in this way:

> "I buy old houses in this city, tear them down, build new ones and they move well. The city protects me, they have to. Besides, I'm a Jew. The police chief is my friend, in the broad sense of friend; the mayor invites me over. I can count on the city council."

As a provocateur, Fassbinder found himself assiduously defending his play as well as his films "in defense of minorities like homosexuals and Turkish workers in Germany - strenuously denied that 'Garbage' was anti-Semitic." Fassbinder was profoundly prescient of the alt right reality of America today when he asserted that "the 'taboo-izing'" of Jewish themes could spread anti-Semitism among young Germans" as the filmmaker remarked already in 1976: "The Jew in this play is the only person who is capable of loving. He is absolutely a figure with positive particulars." [636] It is worthwhile to reflect on Fassbinder's aesthetic briefly, especially in relation to Zion. As a provocateur in Germany, it is highly ironic that he chooses to reference to the sentimental, idyllic postwar genre of the *Heimat-film. The re-appropriation of the* homeland film by Rainer Werner Fassbinder aligns with his comment that he was trying to construct a house with his films, which is hard, enervating, and even dangerous work.[637]

     I would argue that Dylan is creatively constructing his own unique house with his songs, a kind of *Heimat-song.* That is most apparent in his ongoing love for Americana as inspiration and more recently in cover song projects.[638] The abiding question is why Dylan did not buy that homestead in Jerusalem and has remained on the never-ending tour, which is a dystopian road-trip that never really ends. That is, can there really be a homestead to which Dylan returns in homecoming. Is there a Zion to return to? Or is Zion a signpost, like in "Blind Willie McTell":

> "Seen the arrow on the doorpost
> Saying, "This land is condemned
> All the way from New Orleans
> To Jerusalem"
> I traveled through East Texas
> Where many martyrs fell
> And I know no one can sing the blues
> Like Blind Willie McTell"[639]

Or do the signposts reach beyond Highway 61 and the Americana journey, all the way to the liberation of Latin America, as in "Angelina"?

> "There's a black Mercedes rollin' through
>   the combat zone
> Your servants are half dead, you're down to
>   the bone
> Tell me, tall men, where would you like to
>   be overthrown
> Maybe down in Jerusalem or Argentina?
>
> She was stolen from her mother when she
>   was three days old
> Now her vengeance has been satisfied and
>   her possessions have been sold

He's surrounded by God's angels and she's
wearin' a blindfold"[640]

Whereas Dylan's vision of Jerusalem in "Blind Willie McTell" in *Infidels* (1982) is clearly transposed into an Americana landscape, something is already adrift in *Saved* (1980). A standard interpretation of "Solid Rock" is to read this song as yet another typological prefiguration for the return of Christ. But as usual, it is more complicated for Dylan insofar as the lyrics allude to the archetype of the solid rock "Made before the foundation of the world" and the need to not let go. To be "hangin' on to a solid rock" that predates creation, or is the archetypal plan from which the world was created, here Dylan inclines more towards Jerusalem as the navel of the universe, rather than towards Jesus. And as soon as one reads this as uniquely referring to Jerusalem, there is the shift again towards the Redeemer: "For me He was chastised, for me He was hated/For me He was rejected by a world that He created" [641] and what concerns Dylan here is the need to engage and ultimately transcend the either/or dichotomy. Then he returns to the need for discerning the True Messiah from the false messiahs: "Nations are angry, cursed are some/People are expecting a false peace to come."[642] The "New Jew" who fights to rebuild and defend the State of Israel is no messianic Zionist, but in Dylan's lyrical rendition transformed into a "Neighborhood Bully". This transformation of the "wandering Jew" motif returns here along with themes of exile and return to the Land of Israel as the natural effect of the cause of anti-Semitism.

"The neighborhood bully been driven out of every land
He's wandered the earth an exiled man
Seen his family scattered, his people

163

> hounded and torn
> He's always on trial for just being born
> He's the neighborhood bully" [643]

The imagery the marks the majority of the song alludes to the *Yom Kippur War* and the preceding wars in which the State of Israel is accused of using disproportionate force to fend off invading forces. This marks a moment whereby the war against enemies shifts soon thereafter into a war against terrorism. And yet even with this early criticism, the focus is upon how Israel targets sources of enemy attacks, including bombing a bomb factor that would have resulted in numerous casualties. The consequence of being singled by tendencies towards moral equivalency from the critics of Zionism who would not have seen themselves as anti-Semitic, is that any argument of proportional self-defense is insufficient. This pariah state of the Jews is forever being held to a double standard that no nation-state could ever live up to, and so Dylan's response drips with irony, being "surrounded by pacifists who all want peace/They pray for it nightly that the bloodshed must cease."[644] Lest one think this lyric is a shallow metaphor for the contemporary existential issues of the political State of Israel, Dylan complicates matters further, by blurring the boundary between the renaissance of the nation-state within a more ancient eschatological resonance inscribed by the biblical archetypes of Egypt, Rome and Babylon. Again, the shift to post-1948 reality of the State of Israel that was built upon the draining the swamps re-emerges here:

> "Now his holiest books have been trampled
>   upon
> No contract he signed was worth what it was
>   written on
> He took the crumbs of the world and he

turned it into wealth
Took sickness and disease and he turned it
into health
He's the neighborhood bully."[645]

After that moment at the Western Wall for his son's *bar mitzvah* ceremony, where was Dylan's search leading? Some of these circuitous path marks re-emerge during Dylan's tour to Tel Aviv and Jerusalem:

"In 1989, I watched in delight as he ended a New York City concert by jumping from the stage into the audience and dodging out by a side staircase. Before that, at his two debut performances in Israel in 1987, years after he had retreated from born-again evangelizing on his albums, he chose to give both his Tel Aviv and Jerusalem audiences several Christian songs, though his repertoire was wholly different the one night from the other. Who else could, or would, do that?"[646]

To expose his Tel Aviv and Jerusalem audiences to his several Christian songs appears strange at best, and an offensive anomaly at worst. What was Dylan really after in the Holy Land? In the space of tripartite narratives competing for ascendency, yearning for singular power and unquestionable authenticity to invalidate the other, Dylan choses to blur the lines, as such borderlines were already conceived of in the face of blurring boundaries,[647] lest one forget how the story really began.

This boundary-crossing comes to mind as I conclude writing this chapter in clear view of the *Ratisbonne Monastery* in the *Rehavia* neighborhood of Jerusalem. I wonder— is there a lesson embedded here in blurring of boundaries in the story of Marie-

Alphonse Ratisbonne? As a French convert from Judaism, this story began in 1874 on a barren hill, now in the center of West Jerusalem, together with his older brother Marie-Theodore, himself also a convert to Catholicism. I often wonder about whether Ratisbonne's noble intention indeed went awry, after all there seems to have been a genuine yearning to bring about a better understanding between Jews and Christians, and yet the urge to proselytize and convert the Jews and Muslims in Palestine already from 1855 onwards proved irresistible. Fast forward to May 1948, and *Ratisbonne Monastery* agrees to open wide its gates to women and children evacuated from *Gush Etzion* before they were moved to *Kibbutz Ma'ale HaHamisha.*[648] Ironically, day to day life was organized along the lines of a *kibbutz*: girls worked in the kitchen and laundry, and in child care, while a corner of the yard was fenced in for cows. Could this co-operative model of coexistence at a *monastery-kibbutz* have continued beyond wartime? It is a question that echoes through the boundary-crossing American Gnostic songbook of this bard all along the watchtower.

(9) *So Pray From the Mother*:
Choosing Life Withdrawn From the Garden

Chapter at a glance: *As human beings, every one of us is radically alone in the face of the one thing that marks existence in its singularity—death. One thing we certainly all share is the knowledge that each of us must die. This raises the deep existential question—what then does it mean to live and to choose life? In discerning the layers of the Great Mother and Mother Earth in Daryl Arnofsky's film, "Mother!" as correlated to Dylan's "Ain't Talkin' " as a compass to the journey back through the decomposing garden of Eden and is then correlated to the Tiberean hasidic commentary of Peri haAretz. As a relentless martyr, visionary, performer, pariah, and fool, Dylan's songbook remains enraptured by the elusive Lower Mother from whom it draws the inspiration to plead to pray. Dylan's lyrical return to the garden as a spleen-filled womb that oscillates between ecstasy and anguish, finds its fleeting fulfillment through erotic cycles of intoxication to conflict and revulsion to remembered tranquility nesting in the womb of the Great Mother and transmuted suffering within the Lower Mother's violated garden into great art, witnessed from a distance.*

Dylan lyrics analyzed include: "Ain't Talkin'," (*Modern Times*, 2006); "What Can I Do For You?" (*Saved*, 1980); "Born in Time," (*Under the Red Sky*, 1990).

167

(9) *So Pray From the Mother*:
Choosing Life Withdrawn From the Garden

As human beings, every one of us is radically alone in the face of the one thing that marks existence in its singularity—death. One thing we certainly all share is the knowledge that each of us must die. This raises the deep existential question—what then does it mean to live and to choose life? Yet there is *more than* the radical aloneness that comes with the singular experience of being a lone human, even as the singular artist. That *more than* is found in community. Philosophers realized early on that community is the counterbalance to the individual, analogous to the way that life is the counterbalance to death. Indeed, while Solomon sings that "stronger than death is love", it is collective life in community which transcends the delimitations of singular death. The experience of being together, more than just a couple, but as part of a collective is a kind of immanent transcendence that can never be exhausted, whereas the individual quest eventually ends and is thus exhausted on a certain level.[649]

One expression of the collective search for redemption is found through religion. It is the communal envelope of religion that often seeks to provide a framework for that collective kind of immanent transcendence that can never be exhausted, and yet too often it may feel exhausted. However, within the margins of many religious streams, there have been Gnostics who remain committed to finding light in these darkened forms of calcifying religion. Gnostics are those who seek gnosis or illumination, and so their quest, through the Abrahamic religions and beyond, remains a perennial search for luminosity amidst the darkness of existence. While some see Gnosticism returning in the modern period that embrace a version of existentialism featuring a deeper kind of nihilism than any earlier one,[650] others see the blind embrace of scientific materialism as the key to liberation of the mind as succumbing to the limited ideology that traps even Gnosticism.[651]

Modernity presents every seeker and every system with unending challenges in recovering the sacred and salvaging the light—even Gnosticism! And yet, in a landscape devoid of holy names that marks that deep absence of the presence of the divine, community too feels abandoned. [652] Consciousness can bring light but it can also dwell deep in luminal darkness. If consciousness is "not only a progressive and affirmative development toward light but also seen as an expulsion from the nocturnal bliss of sleep in the unconscious and—as, for example, in all world views of gnostic coloration—as loss of the original home",[653] then there is much to be ascertained from singer-songwriter Bob Dylan and his post-exilic wanderings to and from the Garden of Eden. An exhaustive study of this motif of wandering as a vagabond on a train as a metaphor for perpetual homelessness has been duly noted,[654] yet what I hope to further analyze are the implications of choosing life withdrawn from the Garden. Amidst this exile, there is a hope for the continued possibility of praying to pray from the deeper awareness of the Mother nesting in the womb of community.

To delve deeper into this aforementioned notion that there is both a Lower Mother Earth and a Higher Mother that nests in the womb of eternal time, that both a Higher and Lower Mother necessarily integrate the immanent and the transcendent, the natural and the supernatural will be attempted through some contemporary examples in Bob Dylan's songbook. Strolling through the mystic garden is a place to search for the Mother. Entry into this garden is both an ascent and a descent from this Paradise or

Pardes as described with dark and daring detail in Dylan's song "Ain't Talkin'".[655] The stanza sets up a visionary ascent, thus accidentally picking up on a theme known to scholars of ancient Jewish mysticism from the obscure work *Heikhalot Zutarti* ("The Lesser Palaces), [656] wherein the bard sings: "I was passing *yon* cool and crystal fountain/Someone hit me from behind." [657] It was here in the very mystic garden of *Pardes* that visions of ascent led to descent into heresy for mystical rabbis like Elisha ben Abuya who saw the "splendor of the marble plates" in the crystal fountain and, mistaking them for cascading water, called out: "Water! Water!"[658] and thus ruined his mystic experience by mistaking outer reality for inner essence. The danger in entering Paradise is to misperceive aspects of the garden as somehow unique and disjointed elements, leading to the heretical vision that there is more than one power competing within the other contained within separate forces of the godhead. Elisha is said to be "cutting at the roots" of the godhead by separating the force of God the Creator of the pristine garden and the force of the Demiurge that rules over the forlorn garden. So within the same stanza of Dylan's lyrical portrayal of the mystic garden, it also appears to be a return of descent to the post-exilic Garden of Eden: "As I walked out tonight in the mystic garden/The wounded flowers were dangling from the vines." [659] How precisely this descent occurs is not entirely clear, but there is some indication that life as lived outside the garden cannot fully support the quest for mystical ascent: "They will tear your mind away from contemplation/They will jump on your misfortune when you're down." [660] Yet he continues wandering on, living and choosing life amidst this darkening, forlorn garden of life.

Amidst the unsettling surroundings of "wounded flowers…dangling from the vines" there is a deep darkness that pervades this lone seeker who is not seeking "Father of Night".[661] The song opens with a surprise encounter of being struck "from behind" and closes in addressing the mysterious other by explaining to her that "There's no one here, the gardener is gone." [662] The identity of this female interlocutor is further explicated as the song progresses, identifying the source of prayer that has the power to help from the Mother. Praying from the Mother is meant to assuage and channel the evil spirit dwelling in the human heart. Despite best efforts to pray from the mother, the exasperation resounds: "But oh, mother, things ain't going well." [663] Here there is a clear shift from the "Father of Night" to the Mother of the Garden. I argue that it is this shift from the symbol of the Father to the Mother, namely the Great Mother in the Garden of Eden that allows the seeker to choose life. This symbol of the Great Mother presumes a nourishing and nurturing association with the maternal that wants to care for the child despite the opposite appearing to be lived experience. Dylan further raises the question as to what the difference is to "pray *from* the Mother" and not the expected "pray *to* the Mother". To appreciate this difference implied in praying *from* different from praying *to* requires a further understanding of the Great Mother.

This symbol of the Great Mother is often associated in many streams of Jewish mysticism with the *Shekhinah*. What She brings to the one wandering to return to the post-exilic Garden is the intimacy of prayer that partakes in Her suffering. Dylan as the perennial seeker is singing at this late stage in his songbook, with many loves lost: "Ain't talkin', just walkin'/Through this weary world of woe/Heart burnin', still yearnin'/No one on earth would ever know" [664]—what then remains?

When Dylan sings that as: "Soon as a man is born, you know the sparks begin to fly,"[665] he means that from the moment of being born, there is then a shift from containment in the womb to the expulsion of birthing which comes with beginning to live an independent life. As the seeker leaves that "old shell of existence" in the womb, exile from the garden must necessarily begin.[666] Being thrown into existence as described in Genesis 3:23 produces with it a deeper sense of "rejection by the mother".[667] Dylan envisions this process of birthing as being akin to the deprivation of love that comes as an individual is born and withdraws from the mother. It is through this withdrawal as individuation—mirroring cosmogenesis—that "the sparks begin to fly". The sparks that fly are simultaneously both giving and shedding the light that is life. Moreover, being "born in time"[668] is a process of inevitable corruption, in growing more and more distant from the source of that illuminating fire. By coming into existence, the fire of one's pneumatic soul diminishes until one is able to return to that mystic garden where the *Shekhinah* cries out, hovering alone in exile. The garden is here imagined through a looking glass darkly, where Adam and Eve have already been banished—so who and what then truly remain there east of Eden?

The entrance to the garden east of Eden is no longer guarded by the cherubim with the "ever-turning fiery sword to guard the path to the Tree of Life."[669] In Dylan's rendering then, it is upon returning to this post-exilic garden, at once emptied and forlorn "dangling with wounded flowers" where the question is inverted: "Where are you?"[670] It is not God asking the whereabouts of Adam hiding in the garden, but now it is exilic Adam returning to the garden in search of the divine. This is a return to the garden as a spleen-filled womb where only *fleurs du mal* will dangle in their decomposition.

The concluding poem, "Le Voyage," in *Les Fleurs du mal* (1861) best exemplifies what Baudelaire's spleen symbolizes as an elusive journey to true self that Dylan's songbook continually mirrors. In *"Spleen et idéal"* Baudelaire's poetic pontifications on the quest for art and beauty seduce the artist, are precisely what lead him to portray the artist alternately as "martyr, visionary, performer, pariah, and fool." [671] What is key to appreciating Dylan's lyrical return to the garden as a spleen-filled womb is this Baudelairean dialectic of sexual and romantic love that oscillates between ecstasy (*idéal*) and anguish (*spleen*). This oscillation of the Baudelairean dialectic finds its fleeting fulfillment through erotic cycles leading from intoxication to conflict and revulsion to an eventual ambivalent tranquility born of memory and the transmutation of suffering into art. [672] The attempt of the artist to be fulfilled through the fullness of love ends in utter emptiness, and so Baudelaire's *"Spleen et idéal"* culminates with an anguished poetic vision of the soul imprisoned within itself, a veritable gnostic theme. The only certainty here before the artist is a vision of suffering radically alone in the throes of death's erotic embrace. [673]

To continue crying out after all these years with this feeling of "heart burnin', still yearnin'" is precisely the desire for the Great Mother, but in Her stead is a plane of existence marked by withdrawal. This is a withdrawal of the Great Mother from the garden, as well as a withdrawal of Her love from the individual. Not only is She in exile, but so is Her love, which then "leads to pronounced feelings of loneliness, misery, and exile. Birth is experienced not only as a release into life but also a rejection of the uterine paradise." [674] Dylan's songbook grows and expands only to realize this tragic truth that the sparks of life and love are already flying away.

Return to the garden is a witnessing of the rejection by the Great Mother, a distancing of fire by fire, for She is the source of illumination. So that even if "the fire's gone" there is still the realization "but the light is never dying." While the immanent passion of the *Shekhinah*'s fire may have diminished from the very birthing of the seeker's soul, the Limitless Light continues to shine on. How then does the seeker walk through life knowing and living, even when confronting the fear of death intertwined within that its very source of life. For the mystic, this dialectic of life and death, fear and love are intrinsically imbedded within the symbol of the Mother, drawing from the Great Mother on the side of Judgment while manifest through the Lower Mother. What then does the seeker encounter by returning to this "mystic garden"? Which Mother is that "someone who hit me from behind"? That mysterious opening encounter feels like it is a collision with the Upper Mother, which then recurs at the conclusion of the song "Ain't Talkin'" as a reunion with the Lower Mother in this: "Excuse me Ma'am, I beg your pardon/There's no one else here, the gardener is gone." [675] Rather than merely pointing to the cherubim standing guard at the gate of the garden, the gardener is nowhere to be found—for all intents and purposes, the garden has been abandoned.

This gardener who tends the garden and its precious flowers in Jewish mystical literature symbolizes the masculine righteous one, called the *tzaddik* who serves as a shepherd dedicated to tending to the souls.[676] Whereas the Great Mother is the *Shekhinah*, also symbolized as the field of holy apples, who must be tended by her gardener, the masculine *tzaddik*. Whereas flowers can be seen as composed of precious petals like letters of words for prayer, in Dylan's dystopian gnosis flowers are wilted and evil. Whereas these flowers are gathered into bouquets that create the possibility of prayer for the *tzaddik* tending to these souls, for Dylan these flowers bring another kind of prayer—nothing but lament to the Great Mother. Whereas each generation births a *tzaddik* tending to the souls as a gardener tends to the garden

174

and can redeem all the flowers of language, Dylan find himself "in the last outback, in the world's end." [677]

Coming full circle from this brief wandering to and from the abandoned Garden of Eden where the Lower Mother abided, I wonder: *Is this gnostic quest a Jewish one?* As Scholem sought to redress the *gnostic quest* for the abandoned Garden of Eden in astonishment: "It is one of the marvels confronting the explorer in the field [of Jewish mysticism] that scholars who have been looking far and wide to establish the source from which [Gnosticism] has come have been remarkably reluctant, or rather, unwilling to allow the theory that Gnostics tendencies may have developed in the very midst of Judaism itself, whether in its classical forms or on its heterodox and sectarian fringes."[678] Scholem is courageous in seeking to prove that the quest for illumination or the *gnosis* known as Gnosticism emerged as an intrinsic part of Jewish mysticism rather than as being something derived from or influenced by a later religions known as Christianity. As far as Dylan's quest is concerned, this further complicates the claim he was ever "born again"—a mistaken claim negated by both himself and the larger arc of heretics who remained Jewish despite their attempts at self-exile from Judaism. The garden was long ago abandoned by the Lower Mother, so this relentless martyr, visionary, performer, pariah, and fool, who sings throughout Dylan's songbook. This voice remains enraptured by the elusive Lower Mother from whom it draws the inspiration to plead to pray. Dylan's lyrical return to the garden as a spleen-filled womb that oscillates between ecstasy and anguish, finds its fleeting fulfillment through erotic cycles of intoxication to conflict and revulsion to remembered tranquility nesting in the womb of the Great Mother and transmuted suffering within the Lower Mother's violated garden into great art. The attempt of the artist to be fulfilled through the fullness of love ends in utter emptiness, but Dylan's songbook never fully relinquishes the artist's as soul imprisoned within itself, rather the seeker can return to witness this state and sing about it from a distance. This thoroughly modernist vision of the suffering artist radically alone in the throes of death's erotic embrace is precisely the inspiration of the very beloved servant that Dylan encounters in that fateful night walking in the mystic garden long abandoned where she remains forever young.[679]

(10) *Father of Night*:
Nothing But Darkness to Love

Chapter at a glance: *The preponderance of darkness in the American Gnostic Songbook of Bob Dylan is manifest, especially during his so-called Rundown era of songwriting ranging from 1977's Street Legal through to 1982's Infidels. The nuances of this luminal darkness could not be contained to this 4 ½ years as evinced by his continually evolving oeuvre that remains focused on the textures of this very darkness. Only this darkness— "not perfect, not blessed, not divine"— remains for this bard to love. Reflecting here upon the Americana Gnostic songbook of Dylan brings us full circle, challenging whether the Gnostic "self-within-the self" is a knowledge that leads to freedom. Dylan's songbook is in perpetual search for this "uncreated self" as the light of the divine seed, the pearl. This spark of knowing being sung by the singer is the self-same substance of the divine. Perception of this spark is a sign of freedom, so that original sin falls to the wayside. This Americana Gnostic bard no longer measures his falling as a contingency or even flawed word made flesh, rather his songbook is a hearth of sparks amidst the lies. This chapter argues that within this Americana Gnostic songbook is a contradictory truth-seeking, but the genius of its paradox lies in its ability to sing of this seeming duality in experiencing the singer's self-within-a-self. The sublime lyrical genius of this Americana daemon is in unmasking and dawning anew the mask of the inexpressible one.*

Dylan lyrics analyzed include: "Father of Night," (*New Morning*, 1970), "Shot of Love," (*Shot of Love*, 1981), "Precious Angel," (*Slow Train Coming*, 1979); "If Not for You," (*New Morning*, 1970); "What Can I Do For You?" (*Saved*, 1980).

(10) *Father of Night*:
Nothing But Darkness to Love

"I don't have anything but darkness to love.
I'm way beyond that."[680]

The primacy of darkness in the American Gnostic songbook of Bob Dylan —even in his so-called Rundown era of songwriting ranging from *Street Legal* (1977) through to *Infidels* (1982)[681]— cannot be swerved. The nuances of this luminal darkness could not be contained to these four and a half years as evinced but his continually evolving oeuvre that remains focused on the textures of this very darkness. This America Gnostic cannot avoid the delving into the deepest darkness if there is any light to be redeemed. Only this darkness— "not perfect, not blessed, not divine"[682]—is all that remains for this bard to love.

This creative tension between darkness and light was not unfamiliar to the early rabbinic mind. Already in the Talmud —so imbued with Gnostic tendencies despite its better judgment[683]— there is a pride of place reserved for the ways in which "in the beginning there was darkness, and from this darkness light emerged!" What is fascinating to witness how through the ages Jewish mysticism attempts to dance between two strains of intensity of darkness within kabbalah. The parallel imaginal paths posit that darkness/evil is either an intrinsic part of the godhead or it is imagined as merely a byproduct of creation.[684] Either way Jewish mysticism cannot quite seem to shake the anxiety of Gnostic influence of a darkened world controlled by lower level god known as the *demiurgos* or demiurge.[685] God the Father remains above and beyond this corrupted world, for example:

"The One rule all. Nothing has authority over it.
It is the God.
It is Father of everything…
Nothing is above it.
Nothing rules it.
Since everything exists within it
It does not exist within anything."[686]

This image of God the Father as removed from the corruption of the human world is redolent in the Gnostic Gospels. Specifically, in this aforementioned we can appreciate that quality of monism whereby all of reality flows from and the only reality therein. While later in this gnostic myth with the fall, the world does become dualistic, but its origin is monistic in the beginning.[687] To be in this state beyond description beyond words as a pure point without dimension is possible but nothing yet has come into being. Yet all potential to be resides within this "Father of everything." [688] To know this quality of the ultimate oneness of reality that is within divine is to truly know joy for:

"The gospel of truth is joy for those who have received from the father of truth the grace of knowing him by the power of the word, who has come from the fullness and who is in the thought and the mind of the father….You see, all was inside of him, that illimitable, inconceivable one, who is better than every thought."[689]

There is a however real sense of distance between this ultimate reality and the nature of existence human beings live and experience. To lack the power of knowing this primordial power of the Father stems from ignorance and brings one to err along the path to truth:

179

"This ignorance of the father brought about terror and fear.... The forgetfulness of error was not revealed. It did not become light beside the father. Forgetfulness did not exist with the father, although it existed because of him. ...Since forgetfulness existed because the father was not known, if the father comes to be known, from that moment on forgetfulness will cease to exist."[690]

Knowing the Father and singing of this ultimate reality for the bard is the key to illuminating the darkness of existence. Being called to sing this song comes to the one who has been called and responds by turning towards this ultimate reality.[691] This deeper knowing of the ultimate reality as the Father is what allows the singer to restore his own identity within the world of darkness by no longer being blinded by that very tenebrous ignorance. [692] And yet if *God Knows Everything Is Broken*, then there is a space that remains open to suffering in this world, despite knowledge of that ultimate, blissful reality.

The song that the bard must sing amidst his own deep darkness is the song whose pathways lead to the hidden light. How long will this dark night of the fallen soul remain before the light of dawn springs forth? *New Morning* can be seen as that awakening for the bard, here reacting to the lingering questions of the night, where knowledge of the father becomes the dawn.[693] What we see from glancing at the Gnostic Gospels is a certain prominence of the spiritual archetype of the Father as a channel of light from deep darkness that encompasses everything within it as the ultimate reality. The quandary lying at the heart of monotheism is present in its gnostic prevarications.[694] And it is precisely in this resignation to the predominance of darkness that we encounter Dylan's "Father of Night":

"Father of night, Father of day
Father, who taketh the darkness away
Father, who teacheth the bird to fly
Builder of rainbows up in the sky
Father of loneliness and pain
Father of love and Father of rain

Father of day, Father of night
Father of black, Father of white
Father, who build the mountain so high
Who shapeth the cloud up in the sky
Father of time, Father of dreams
Father, who turneth the rivers and
streams"[695]

The call to the Father, rather than to the Mother (as we have seen earlier on in the previous chapter nine) suggests an openness to finding that paternal figure in a devotional mode. The Father as ultimate reality being sought throughout this song is the Inexpressible One, we have encountered earlier in the Gnostic Gospels rather than the biblical psalms.[696] Part of the mythos of the American vagabond in Dylan's lyrics is meant to suggest a violent rupture from the home, being thrown into an abusive reality of living in a world without a father, for example: "You've only murdered my father, raped his wife/Tattooed my babies with a poison pen/Mocked my God, humiliated my friends".[697] To see through the darkness of death and apparent emptiness of a universe devoid of any father figure, Dylan must beckon the angelic presences swirling around this tenebrous maelstrom: "Shine your light, shine your light on me/Ya know I just couldn't make it by myself/I'm a little too blind to see".[698]

In confronting his own blindness, the singer realizes the importance of seeing the role that love plays in releasing his alienated self from falling into a deeper darkness. In seeing through the heart, it is then possible to see that "pure light no eye can bear to look within".[699] But the contours of this luminous love are different than anything we have yet encountered in this songbook as Father of Night is now seen as Father of Day:

"If not for you
Babe, I'd lay awake all night
Wait for the mornin' light
To shine in through
But it would not be new
If not for you

If not for you
My sky would fall
Rain would gather too
Without your love I'd be nowhere at all
I'd be lost if not for you
And you know it's true"[700]

By relating his "I" to a second person "you", the singer is able to make it through the dark night of the soul, where he would "lay awake all night/Wait for the mornin' light". Waiting through the long stretch of darkness does not necessarily lead to light, even if the natural world refracts the sun's light, for this lover is laying in "Wait for the mornin' light/To shine in through". Dylan's gnostic songbook here displays a remarkable willingness to persevere within the darkness. Living life in a state of such long suffering bespeaks a commitment to transforming this darkness into something more than falling into a blacker abyss.

This brief reflection on the Gnostic songbook of Dylan brings us full circle, swerving back to the challenge posed by Harold Bloom in his *The American Religion*, where he sees another salient aspect of Gnosticism that: "is a knowing, by and of an uncreated self, or self-within-the self, and [this] knowledge leads to freedom...."[701] The revelation being sought through this American Gnostic songbook is the awakening that emerges in knowing that something within the bard remains uncreated. Dylan's songbook is in perpetual search for this "uncreated self" as the light of the divine seed, the pearl. This spark of knowing being sung by the singer is the self-same substance of the divine. Once the bard comes to truly perceive the gnosis of this spark, then he realizes despite it all that he remains truly free. Here is where original sin falls to the wayside insofar as this American Gnostic bard no longer measures his falling as a contingency or even flawed word made flesh, rather his songbook is a hearth even though "Soon as a man is born, you know the sparks begin to fly/He gets wise in his own eyes and he's made to believe a lie."[702] I have been arguing that this American Gnostic songbook is truth seeking while holding within it endless contradictions, but the genius of its paradox lies in its ability to sing of this seeming duality in experiencing the singer's self-within-a-self. What marks the sublime genius of Dylan's American *daemon*[703] is precisely this ability to continually unmask and dawn anew the mask of the inexpressible one.

(11) Candle's Flame Lit into the Sun: Inflaming the Imagination of Love, *Approximately*

Chapter at a glance: In exploring the arc of the dreaming being points towards a futurity of the human being—is the future being dreamt of in the Dylan songbook one of darkness or light? The futurity of the flame and its source in creative fire was channeled by a forgotten precursor French Dadaist, Tristan Tzara, who envisioned fire as generative as it is consuming, to the point of demolishing all the values of modern civilization. This chapter considers how these Dadaist concerns with embodied awareness of illumined consciousness in his epic poem, Approximate Man, correlated with lyrics in Dylan's songbook as well as his lesser known novel, Tarantula. By considering how Tzara's approximate man sees "eyes, ambassadors of fire", it becomes evident that in Dylan's lyrics one can feel the "heat and flame" while confessing: "all I see are dark eyes". The search for "love that's pure" which burns as "an eternal flame" is always illuminating the darkened paths of lovers on the search for light. Even though the flames of reverence, catharsis and humility flicker frequently, there remains precious little protection along the darkening path of life.

Dylan lyrics analyzed include: "Watered-down love," (*Shot of Love*, 1981); "Love Minus Zero/No Limit," (*Bringing it all Back Home*, 1965); "Ballad of Thin Man," (*Highway 61 Revisited*, 1965); "Queen Jane Approximately", (*Highway 61 Revisited*, 1965); "Every Grain of Sand," (*Shot of Love*, 1981); "Pay In Blood," (*The Tempest*, 2012); "It's alright ma, I'm only bleeding," (*Bringing it all back home*, 1965); "Let me die in my footsteps," (*Bootleg Series Volume 1: Rare and Unreleased*, 1961-1991); Born in Time," (*Under the Red Sky*, 1990); "Tell Me," (*Bootleg Series Volume 1: Rare and Unreleased*, 1961-1991); "Dark Eyes," (*Empire Burlesque*, 1985); "Last Thoughts on Woody Guthrie," (*Bootleg Series Volume 1: Rare and Unreleased*, 1961-1991); "Gates of Eden," (*Bringing it all Back Home*, 1965).

(11) Candle's Flame Lit into the Sun: Inflaming the Imagination of Love, *Approximately*

At the heart of the human imagination lies the flame. Arguably one the greatest image creators amongst objects of the world remains the solitary flame of the candle, for in contemplating the candle one is able to dream.[704] Moreover, it is the flame of the candle that has that subtle capacity to seize cold metaphors and transform them into living images.[705] It is "[a]n eternal flame, quietly burning"[706] that "forces us to imagine".[707] The dreamer can contemplate the flame and in so doing, inflame the imagination.[708] This motif of the inflaming imagination amidst poetic reverie will be explored in the Dylan songbook, especially insofar as it challenges assumptions about the how the Jewish *imaginaire* envisions the flame. Namely, to what degree is there, if any influence, from the truth claim to the fourfold faces of fire in Biblical Judaism as follows: (1) reverential fire; (2) illuminating and protective fire of *halakhah*; (3) cathartic fire; (4) humbling fire.[709] In the process of searching for flames and fire throughout the Dylan songbook—lyrics afire with scriptural allusions— the present analysis will reconsider the degrees of convergence and divergence from this supposition of the fourfold faces of fire.

Throughout the Dylan songbook, while moments of reverence, catharsis and being humbled resonate frequently, there is little protection or guidance along the darkening path of life. For to be in a state of poetic reverie is to straddle an existence between imagination and reality. The recurrent sense of destabilization that emerges from the seemingly surrealist lyricism of the Dylan songbook is frequently through its language and imagery, suggesting a posture of poetic reverie. Reconsider the effect of the following lyrics in "Love

185

Minus Zero/No Limit":

> "My love she speaks like silence
> Without ideals or violence
> She doesn't have to say she's faithful
> Yet she's true, like ice, like fire
> People carry roses
> Make promises by the hours
> My love she laughs like the flowers
> Valentines can't buy her"[710]

  The seemingly simple rhyming contraries of human existence are afire here (silence/violence, hours/flowers), overflowing with attraction and repulsion after gnostic visionaries of the poetic reverie, like English poet, William Blake (1757-1827),[711] as well as French poets, like Charles Baudelaire (1757-1827) and Arthur Rimbaud (1821-1867). What is first perceived as perfect rhymes are quickly interrupted by violent rhymes, in turn, causing the listener not only to "want to ask questions parenthetically" [712] but to allow for a disruption of that earlier sense of the rational rhyming scheme of one reality for the flame of the imagination to then consume. Such a disruption of the imagination requires one to leave behind all possibility of rational understanding, and embrace the feeling of being unmoored amidst the very ground of one's being:

> "You try so hard
> But you don't understand
> Just what you'll say
> When you get home
>
> Because something is happening here
> But you don't know what it is
> Do you, Mister Jones?"[713]

Addressing every man, from Mister Jones to Job, this is but another one of countless examples in the Dylan songbook where indeed "...something is happening here/But you don't know what it is,"[714] there is something afoot here in the cadence, tone, rhymes[715] and rhythms of these lyrics that portrays and induces a kind of poetic reverie. The capacity to dream is contingent upon poetic reverie. The arc of the dreaming being points towards a futurity of the human being[716]—it is the exposure of that futurity that remains in question throughout the Dylan songbook. Namely, is the future being dreamt of one of darkness or light?

The futurity of the flame and its source in creative fire was channeled by a forgotten precursor French poet, straddling Dada and Surrealism, known by his pseudonym of Tristan Tzara. This Romanian-born French poet and essayist created this name, Tristan Tzara as an expression of the malaise of his era but was originally named, Samuel Rosenstock (1896-1963). As the founder of a nihilistic revolutionary movement in the arts, called Dada, Tzara envisioned fire as both consuming and generative, insofar as the purpose of Dada was consuming to the point of demolishing all the values of modern civilization. Recall the Dadaist movement originated in Zürich during the traumatic period of World War I (the same period of *All Quiet on the Western Front* which Dylan cites as a major influence in his Nobel Prize acceptance),[717] and moreover, there was a performative element to Tzara's founding of Dadaism with staged performances at the Cabaret Voltaire in Zurich.[718]

Tzara's most profound poetic vision was honed through his participation in the Surrealist group in Paris from 1929-1934, when he realized *Approximate Man*,[719] an epic, stream of consciousness poem. This landmark of 20th-century French literature, this poetry has no capitalization and features a paucity of grammatical cues. Tzara's work portrays an unfulfilled wayfarer's search for a universal knowledge and language, all of which are present in Dylan's songbook through the character of the original vagabond. While the Dylan songbook has explicitly cited influence and reference to French symbolist poet, Arthur Rimbaud, whose *A Season in Hell*[720] tells its own story from the flame to the fire, it is worth recalling the forgotten but abiding influence of Tzara, especially when reading Dylan's *Tarantula.*[721] Buried amidst some sidebar reflections that prevaricate on the pseudo-modernist tendencies of this stream of consciousness work that ingeniously fuses French surrealist poet, Arthur Rimbaud and City Lights bookstore in San Francisco, Corrocan remarks: *"Tarantula* aside, Dylan's lyrics are generally far more intelligible than [William S.] Burroughs, and songs like "Gates of Eden" fit into this context."[722] The lyrical landscape of "Gates of Eden" will be explored in more depth shortly, but for now, suffice it to say that the influence of Tzara remains strong.

Journeying through the life flickering like a flame is captured in the powerful prose poetry of Tzara's *Approximate Man, which* I argue *Dylan* freely and playfully *transvalues into* his own vision through "Queen Jane Approximately".[723] Tzara's epic poem is consumed by the motif of the abiding flame, shifting from the landscape afire to an embodied awareness of illumined consciousness, likened to:

> "a fire is drunk from the heights where stratus cabotages have buried the taste of chasm
> a fire that is supplicating on the ladder to the soils of unlimited gestures
> a fire that barks jets of regret beyond the hypocritical suggestions of possible

a fire that evades strong seas where the
stopping up of human leaks happens
a human who vibrates with the
indefinable presumptions of the mazes of fire
a fire that weaves the masked surging
swell of character—submits
harmony—let this word be banished
from the feverish world i visit
fierce affinities mined with nothingness
covered with murders
who scream not to break down the
sobbing stalemate of shreds of flamingos
because the fire of anger varies the
subtly animating debris
according to the stammering
modulations of hell
that your heart is exhausted to recognize
among the vertiginous bursts of stars
and stony in my garments of schist I have
pledged my waiting
to the torment of the oxidized desert
to the unshakable advent of fire"[724]

The approximate nature of existence is
illumined by Tzara through a recurring fire that lights
up grey zones of its journey obfuscating the boundaries
between heaven and earth. The poem here paints a
surreal scenario of "stratus cabotages", namely, a low
altitude cloud form extending over a transport route
in coastal waters or airspace or between two points
within a country. Wandering between borders
celestial and terrestrial, national and exilic, the poet
affirms: "I have pledged my waiting/to the torment of
the oxidized desert/to the unshakable advent of fire."
Despite the torment of "regret beyond the hypocritical
suggestions of possible" and "the nothingness covered
with murders", time and time again it is through the
"unshakable advent of fire" found wandering in the

desert where the breath of life is possible. All competing conflicts that create such disharmony leading to a fragmented human is overcome with "a fire that weaves the masked surging swell of character". While approximate man has pledged his waiting for redemption, "the unshakable advent of fire" is what allows the original vagabond to be at once visiting "the feverish world" while able to see the future now. That future now is afire with dynamism, never stopping to stand still in the waiting, thus the approximate nature of being always in accelerated motion. There is also a porous membrane separating the external and internal landscape, to the point where an embodied awareness emerges through the portals of vision themselves as "eyes, ambassadors of fire". [725] Throughout Tzara's record of the approximate nature of existence, it remains entirely possible that the fire is at once internal and external.

In Dylan's own uncanny surrealist, stream of consciousness entry in *Tarantula*, he makes extended reference to his own dream of fire:

...needless to say—i & the building met & instantly as it stopped, the motion started again—me, singing & the building burning —there i was unable to do anything about this fire—you see—not because I was lazy or loved to watch the good fires—but rather because both myself & the fire were in the same Time all right but were not in the same Space—the only thing we had in common was that we existed in the same moment...[726]

The poet's female counterpart, Justine, responds by interpreting his dream, explaining:

> ...that's right—lots of people would feel guilty & close their eyes to such a happening—these are people that interrupt & interfere in other people's lives—only God can be everywhere at the same Time &

> Space—you are human—sad & silly as it
> might seem...[727]

The flames consuming the burning building become a
fire that the dreamer is unable to stop. The dreamer "&
the fire were in the same Time all right but were not in
the same Space" so that there only common point of
convergence was a shared moment. Such
convergences of shared moments, like the flittering of
a flame, oscillate with the fragmentary luminosity of
eternal Time, but cannot bring ultimate illumination
because of their divergent place in Space. There is a
distinction here in the act of wandering the universe
and stumbling upon the "building burning". Recall the
other original vagabond, Abraham, the patriarch, who
wanders the universe, stumbling upon a "building
burning" but sees this "palace in flames" as a "palace
full of light", only to then inquire about the landlord.
In the process, Abraham reasons that just as there must
be a landlord watching over the building, so too is there
a God acting as landlord of the world.[728] By contrast,
the dreamer wandering the streets in *Tarantula* is told
by Justine "only God can be everywhere at the same
Time & Space—you are human—sad & silly as it
might seem", disabusing him of his delusions of
grandeur in searching for any trace of the divine in this
darkened world. It is the beloved who early on teaches
the lover to abandon his search for the divine fire to
settle for the flickering human flame.

The tangible flame that drives the lover in search
of that untouchable fire of love can be dark just as
much as light, reveal as much as it conceals. While the
protagonist wandering the streets in *Tarantula* is
disabused of his theophanic encounter by Justine,
Moses the prophet also undergo periods of
concealment of the inner flame before the higher
illumination is revealed. Recall at the watering-hole
where Tzipporah, the Midianite, is seduced with

kindness by Moses, who appears as an Egyptian.[729] At this point in his spiritual journey in search of the beloved, Moses lives in an Egyptian guise, no longer recognizable as a Hebrew, which is this period of the prophet's life is a somewhat a tragic time during which, according to Soloveitchik, the divine flame remains in a state of "deep eclipse" [*hester panim*]. Such an eclipse emerges when a leader like Moses abandons his calling and his people. The difference between Moses and Jonah, is that Moses eventually returns while Jonah continues to flee.

Living his life functionally as an Egyptian, as the *other*, is partly what allows him to disappear into the pastoral scene of Midian, far away from the bondage and murder of Egypt. Everything is eclipsed in his life until he encounters the burning bush not consumed by the flames. That bush afire draws Moses, causing him to "turn aside to see this incredible sight".[730] When Moses says: "I will turn aside now" it comes to suggest: "I will turn aside now from my place."[731] Given that Moses could not have changed his physical position, this suggest that Moses is deliberately pivoting, choosing to change the direction of his life. For when Moses actually turns to look at the burning bush we are told:

> "And YHVH saw that he had turned aside to see, and God called to him from the midst of the bush, and said: "Moses, Moses!" And he said: "Here I am."[732]

The divine voice calls out to Moses only once the latter has, of his own volition, decided to stop, to change his path. At that moment, the response of the divine voice is "Here I am". Instead of running away, Moses rather proclaims "this is indeed where I now am." How profound this first realization that leaves one to work on those very issues and to choose to change what presently exists and obstructs growth. A flame is dynamic, shifting from moment to moment. The "flame" cannot be captured or fixed as it is in a constant dance.[733] The flame that encircles but does not consume the bush is a symbolic experience that transcends and includes all of its material reality. It is that constant surging force beyond the boundary of the world and everyday experience. Precisely this boundless flame is what Moses has the courage to stop and encounter. By transcending and including the quotidian world by staring straight into the impossible, that is, into the infinite—this courageous moment is the process that unfolds his new identity. Moses looks into the impossible and from this ultimately creates an extraordinary possibility of an eternal people. This possibility of an eternal people continued to inspire lyrical moments, especially in the moments of deepest desperation and disconnect in the Dylan songbook. What the Dylan songbook shares with this dynamic reality of the flame is the clarity of vision to realize: "this is indeed where I now am." Whereas Moses utilizes that clarity to change the path of his present journey to overcome the obstacles to his spiritual growth, the Dylan songbook may challenge present reality as it presently exists without changing it. Rather his lyrics lament the darkness of present existence while sharing spiritual growth of his inner flame within that very darkness.

Sometimes the spark of insight can be so potently brilliant that the artist is overwhelmed by the inspiration. And yet it is precisely by entering into that very dark night of the soul, within the very darkness of concealment that luminosity continues to flicker through as a flame. It is a "hardened "spark of impenetrable darkness [that flashed] within the concealed of the concealed"[734] as it struggles to emerge from cosmic consciousness. In those moments where the lover seeks the flame of the beloved with hopes of deepening the fire of love, an endless array of trials beset this path. To reach the beloved, the lover must endure travails of negative emotions that can pose opposition to the quest for redeeming this love, as expressed in "Every Grain of Sand":

> "I gaze into the doorway of temptation's
>   angry flame
> And every time I pass that way I always
>   hear my name
> Then onward in my journey I come to
>   understand
> That every hair is numbered like every grain
>   of sand"[735]

The lover's gaze through the doorway that houses the beloved is a magnetic passageway. The lure to walk through that doorway once again and be vulnerable to the pain that might emerge in losing that love is but one of many temptations the love has to weigh in being called. The magnetic pull to the doorway that can either be passed by or crossed through is intensified by the calling of the lover's name, so that the beloved knows every traveler—none are immune to the call. What gives the lover pause here is that in recognizing that "gaze into the doorway of temptation's angry flame" the lover is aware of being again at that familiar crossroads. Giving in to that temptation is what is at stake in every trial— whether you are Abraham at Mount Moriah or Jesus at Gesthemane, *approximately*[736]— the need to relinquish control over the pull of this desire is what makes each of these lovers human. Even though it appears that this journey onwards is endless, the lover quickly realizes that there are a limited number of doorways through which one can be called and "[t]hat every hair is numbered like every grain of sand". Whose hair here is unclear, whether the hair of the beloved's tempting locks or the

194

lover's hoary head, it is all limited.

Inquiring into the nature of the spirit that flickers like a flame within that elusive, eternal fire is dangerous. Yet despite the dangers, delusions and disappointments, the lover beckons onwards in this inquiry into the source of the flame within the eternal fire. Both mystic and poet found themselves equally dumbfounded by the return to the spoken world where language is meant to convey such ineffable experiences, so each in their own way, they refrain from writing about spiritual experiences as too delicate to divulge. Yet sometimes it is the very danger that draws us deeper inwards into this inquiry as when scholar of Gnosticism, Elaine Pagels (b.1943),[737] inquired of her friend, former laureate poet of New York, Marie Howe (b.1950),[738] just what motivated her concealment in writing about the Virgin Mary feeling the warmth of an angel's love in the form of her poem, called, "Annunciation". The poet responded that "Annunciation" was written as merely an allusion to her own private spiritual experience that essentially remains "the last taboo".[739] The power of the poet to dissimulate by concealing the experience while revealing its contours in language is felt powerfully throughout "Annunciation" as this poem finds a way to dance through "the last taboo":

> "Even if I don't see it again—nor ever feel it
> I know it is—and that if once it hailed me it
> ever does—
> And so it is myself I want to turn in that
> direction
> not as towards a place, but it was a tilting
> within myself,
> as one turns a mirror to flash the light to
> where
> it isn't—I was blinded like that—and swam
> in what shone at me

195

           only able to endure it by being no one and so
                specifically myself I thought I'd die
from being loved like that."[740]

As the poet confesses at the outset: "I know it is", she is alluding to an ineffable spiritual experience of *gnosis*; it cannot be spoken about only tasted as experience. This process of turning the inner self "to flash the light to where/it isn't" draws the poet into luminal darkness that can be blinding. What the poet intimately understands in reflecting upon this Gnostic transformation is that only by "by being no one" could she turn to that inner place of luminal darkness and "endure it". The first stage of dying unto self happens by effacing the egocentric self so as to make space for the emergence of the beloved. From that blinding emergence of the beloved, the lover is able to merge with the beloved in this overwhelming experience conveyed so subtly by the poet. This is the death undergone "from being loved like that", where ultimately love is still stronger than death, but if existence of the approximate man cannot endure such a burning fire of love must be let go of to take hold of the flame of selfhood.

    Early on in the Dylan songbook, there is a blinding realization behind the clarion call to protest that: "he who is not busy being born is busy dying"[741] or "'Stead of learnin' to live they are learnin' to die."[742] The constant pull on life for deeper meaning is captured in this sense of dying to be reborn such that: "The more I die, the more I live."[743] To realize that the fire of love must be let go of to take hold of the flame of selfhood requires moments of shedding. It is in this process of shedding that is bound up in self-inquiry, where the lyrics can serve as the vehicles for conveying the power of love's flame without revealing the source of the fire, as Dylan sings:

"You pressed me once, you pressed me
        twice
You hang the flame, you'll pay the price
Oh babe, that fire
Is still smokin'
You were snow, you were rain
You were striped, you were plain
Oh babe, truer words
Have not been spoken or broken"[744]

This conveys the degree to which it is dangerous, if not downright sinful to "hang the flame". This act of muzzling and silencing desire ultimately violates this "the last taboo" for which there is a price to pay. The lover is addressing the beloved at once, as a fallen celestial angel of snow and rain, and a terrestrial angel striped and plain, whose combined erotic powers counter the incandescent flame of "that fire...still smokin'". These angelic words of love still have the power to pierce through the darkness, even as the lover's heart is broken. So, the lover beckons, asking:

"Tell me—I've got to know
Tell me—tell me before I go
Does that flame still burn, Does that fire still
        glow
Or has it died out and melted like the snow
Tell me
Tell me"[745]

The lover begs the beloved to explain what happens to the flame of love once existence is no more. Is there an afterlife to the flame that has been burning all through life? If the flame still burns even after love dies, is it a function of that elusive fire or has my soul absorbed part of that flickering flame? The lover demands further knowledge of how this flame continues to flicker on as a refraction of the eternal fire. Such

197

interrogation leads to a larger inquiry about the nature of human existence: is it approximate or is it infinite in potential?

> "Tell me—is my name in your book
> Tell me—will you go back and take another
> look
> Tell me the truth, tell me no lies
> Are you someone whom anyone prays for or
> cries..."[746]

This final question is a most jarring inquiry into the very possibility of prayer itself that emerges from the flame of love. Is the flame of love necessary and sufficient impetus for "someone whom anyone prays for or cries" to answer? Not only is the act of prayer in question, but also of response. Evoking both the book of life and the little black book, Dylan's lyric plays off the brilliant ambiguity, suggesting either way that love drives both scenarios. The lover is asking for one more slack to allow himself to be written back into her little black book which for all intents and purposes is the book of life. So, the questioning abounds regarding the focus of the flame which fuels it to continue flickering on. Amidst the darkness of life, the lover continues onwards in the quest for the beloved, following the light of the flame to illumine the path to her:

> "They tell me to be discreet for all intended
> purposes,
> They tell me revenge is sweet and from
> where they stand, I'm sure it is.
> But I feel nothing for their game where
> beauty goes unrecognized,
> All I feel is heat and flame and all I see are
> dark eyes."[747]

While Tzara's approximate man sees "eyes, ambassadors of fire" [748] by contrast Dylan's lyric can feel the "heat and flame" while confessing: "all I see are dark eyes". The contrast may not be as stark as at first blush, in that there are black fragments within every flame, where the "black-blue light" [749] conjoins with its white counterpart. Dylan's lyric paints the colors of the flame of love by creatively portraying it in a setting of deepening darkness:

"In the lonely night
In the blinking stardust of a pale blue light
You're comin' thru to me in black and white
When we were made of dreams" [750]

As the lover senses the heat from the lamp in approaching the flame, it is a greater hope that draws one further in search of the flame:

"Where do you look for this lamp that's a-
burnin'
Where do you look for this oil well gushin'
Where do you look for this candle that's
glowin'
Where do you look for this hope that you
know is there" [751]

The dynamic image of reverie, *par excellence*— the flame— is embodied in the flaming tree. This unique conflation of Americana and scripture, is already foreshadowed in *Tarantula,* with its surrealist vision of "frees like fire hydrants" [752] that are now transformed into the intertwined Trees of Knowledge Good and Evil, and of Life:

"Of war and peace the truth just twists
Its curfew gull just glides
Upon four-legged forest clouds

199

The cowboy angel rides
With his candle lit into the sun
Though its glow is waxed in black
All except when 'neath the trees of Eden"[753]

Moreover, Dylan's lyric here in "Gates of Eden" contemplates a series of images that unite ascent and descent from Eden rather than the infernos of Tzara and Rimbaud. By building on this oscillation of the flame and extending to link it to other imagery, most notably the ascent of the descending riff on Metatron as "motorcycle black Madonna" and the "cowboy angel", Dylan's lyric is firmly grounded in "Desolation Row". Dylan is playfully misreading a trend in mystical literature that already abounds with visions of celestial angels on fire, like Metatron.[754] But these dark light figures of the "motorcycle black Madonna" and the "cowboy angel" are a most surreal conflation of Americana and mystical visions. Most often in the Dylan songbook, the cowboy is another form of outlaw, and so the angelic is tangled up in the demonic "waxed in black" akin to the feminine version of the "motorcycle black Madonna". The path of this "cowboy angel" riding "[w]ith his candle lit into the sun" whose light would otherwise be absorbed back its source, like the mythic Icarus, "Though its glow is waxed in black". Through the looking glass darkly, this ascent into light is from a place of darkness.

During the *Rolling Thunder Tour* that Dylan would nightly dawn the Baptiste white-face mask for those performances being filmed for Renaldo and Clara, inspired by the French film, *Children of Paradise,*[755] which again takes us back to the dystopian Garden of Eden. However, this garden is set in the pseudo-modernist Paris of the 1830s on "Boulevard du Crime". Echoing "Desolation Row" it is on "Boulevard du Crime" that the elusive courtesan, Garance, is wrongfully accused of pickpocketing. It is the eloquent mime Baptiste rescues her, amidst the sea of jugglers, sideshow performers, streetwalkers, and crooks. Love's flame is afire between the delicate pantomimist, Baptiste and elusive courtesan, Garance. It is Baptiste's insufferable knowledge that the object of his desire can never belong to anyone only to haunt him for years that captures us. While many lovers have tried to seize Garance's heart, after so many barren years, she now seems to need only one lover. Trusting this delicate pantomime, Baptiste is Garance's choice to travel with a frail rose, so beautiful but cruel. It is here on "Boulevard du Crime" that these children of paradise are able to accept and embrace the truth of an unrequited love.

But dawning this mask of this delicate pantomime, Baptiste, stands in strong contrast with the decibel level of the music emerging from the Dylan songbook at this time of the *Rolling Thunder Tour.* Painting his face all white is less about being painted as the innocent outlaw and more about effacing the starry-eyed Dylan, as he was wont to proclaim to hecklers on the *Rolling Thunder Tour*: "I want you to hear my words, not see my face." And it is this white palette of the heavenly abode with which this outlaw clothes himself in his ascent is marked indelibly by the darkness of the vagabond life. No matter how bright the light of his candle will burn, "its glow is waxed in black" overwhelmed by its shadow. There is only one place, counterintuitively where this shadow is lifted as every other abode remain darkened, "All except when 'neath the trees of Eden." What emerges is an image of the terrestrial world afire, and its source of illumination are the trees of Eden. The trees being referred to here are the Trees of Life and the Tree of Knowledge Good and Evil implanted in the Garden of Eden. The celestial Eden can no longer be reached by the cowboy angel in his ascending descent "With his candle lit into the sun" precisely because "its glow is waxed in black", which can provide the necessary contrast to continue traveling into the sun as the source of illumination. It can also provide enough contrast for the seeker to remain separate and resist complete absorption into that source of illumination, choosing instead to return in descent to contemplate the flaming trees in the Garden of Eden.

The quest of this "cowboy angel" and "motorcycle black Madonna" is to find a pure love, that is, a love minus zero that burns from its source in an eternal flame. Such an elusive pure love remains sequestered in the Garden of Eden still here on earth, even if always just one touch away from the full embrace of the seeker:

> "Love that's pure ain't no accident
> Always on time, is always content
> An eternal flame, quietly burning
> Never needs to be proud, restlessly
> yearning"[756]

From the fire to its fragmented flames, the lyrics of the Dylan songbook set out a never-ending search for love. This love minus zero, "love that's pure" burns as "an eternal flame" that is always illuminating the darkened paths of lovers searching. Even though the flames of reverence, catharsis and humility may flicker frequently, there remains precious little protection along the darkening path of life. To oscillate humbly between "quietly burning" and "restlessly yearning"[757] is what it means to be a human being "tired of yourself and all of your creations" [758] pining for a future afire, *approximately…*

(12) *Knockin' on Heaven's Door*: Outlaw Seeking Redemption

Chapter at a glance: *Every song is a trial, and the trial of every song resides in its yearning for what lies beyond the words, transcending language, resting in the melody. That trial is a tension between the hunter and the hunted, beckoning the question: how much yearning for the melodic flame of the song itself remains burning once words emerge? Or in the midst of the hunt, does the hunted that eludes capture prolong longing or await the inevitable trap? This yearning for transcendence makes demands on the prayerful songs of outlaws in the Dylan songbook as symbolized through Billy the Kid, Lenny Bruce, and Jesus Christ— all knockin' on heaven's door". Is it still possible to hold that our voices—whether through prayer or song— are actually heard in the deepest recesses of the universe? Dylan's songbook continuously positions the American Jewish outlaw— between hunter and the hunted—as hovering closer to home than expected seeking redemption in exile.*

Dylan lyrics analyzed include: "Knockin' on Heaven's Door," (*Pat Garret & Billy the Kid*, 1973); "Lenny Bruce," (*Shot of Love*, 1981); "Precious Angel," (*Slow Train Coming*, 1979); "Blind Willie McTell," (Bootlegs 1-3, vol. 1983); "Outlaw Blues" (*Bringing it all Home*, 1965); "One More Cup of Coffee (Valley Below)," (*Desire*, 1975); "God on our Side" (*The Times They Are a Changin'*, 1963); "Bob Dylan's 115th Dream" (*Bringing it all Home*, 1965); "Chimes of Freedom" (*Another Side of Bob Dylan*, 1964); "Shot of Love," (*Shot of Love*, 1981); "Tryin' to Get to Heaven," (*Time out of Mind*, 1997).

(12) *Knockin' on Heaven's Door*: Outlaw Seeking Redemption

Every song is a trial, and the trial of every song resides in its yearning for what lies beyond the words, transcending language, resting in the melody. That trial sometimes embodies the same tension felt between the hunter and the hunted. And so, the question emerges: how much yearning for the melodic flame of the song itself remains burning once words emerge? Or in the midst of the hunt, does the hunted that eludes capture prolong longing or await the inevitable trap? This yearning for transcendence makes demands on song as prayer like no other. And so, within the Dylan songbook, archetypal outlaws, from Billy the Kid and Lenny Bruce to Jesus Christ all find themselves "Knockin' on Heaven's Door"[759] always "Tryin' to Get to Heaven".[760] Is this demand upon song to serve as a kind of prayer possible? Is it still possible to hold that our voices—whether through prayer or song— are actually heard in the deepest recesses of the universe? As these new-ancient melodies return to their source, do we also return?

Is return possible after the darkness of destruction? To appreciate how two songs from the Dylan songbook that explicitly invoke heaven, it is worthwhile to contextualize the challenge of reaching such heights already found in Dylan's precursors. From the onset of darkness that permeates existence upon the destruction of both Jerusalem Temples, the rabbinic sages of the Talmud need to respond to the loss of the divine address where prayer was received until the terminus point. Exile defines existence, after 70 CE, especially in the Holy Land of Jerusalem, as portrayed by the diasporic rabbinic imagination of the diaspora centuries later:

"Rabbi Elazar says: Since the day the Temple was destroyed the gates of prayer were locked, and prayer is not accepted as it once was, as it is stated in lament of the Temple's destruction: 'Though I plead and call out, He shuts out my prayer' (Lamentations 3:8). Yet, despite the fact that the gates of prayer were locked with the destruction of the Temple, the gates of tears were not locked, and one who cries before God may rest assured that his prayers will be answered, as it is stated: 'Hear my prayer, Lord, and give ear to my pleading, keep not silence at my tears' (Psalms 39:13)."[761]

What is strikes here is already how much the traveling homeland embedded in the diasporic rabbinic imagination[762] can conceive of a reality where the physical gates of the temple through which prayer was received no longer stand, there is another way to go "knockin' on heaven's door"—through tears![763]

It is precisely these wordless tears that are explored in greater depth through Jewish mystical literature of Kabbalah. Tears transform into a pathway of knowing the unknowable, of touching the untouchable. Building upon the precursor rabbinic mind, the late medieval mystical text of *Tiqqunei HaZohar*, finds a way to excavate the roots of those tears:

"...And when Israel would pray, all these palaces [of prayer] would be open unto them. Then in the hour of exile, it is said that these gates were then locked, and the *Shekhinah* is beyond these palaces, and the blessed Holy One is beyond these palaces, and the angels charged with overseeing prayers are beyond these palaces. And this is what Scripture means by: "Their screams come from beyond" (Isaiah 36: 7), so that prayers no longer have space to enter, and this is [*what is meant by the Talmudic dictum that*] "All the gates are locked [*from receiving prayer*] except through the gates of tears". For there is no one who can open these gates any longer until there comes forth a master of tears [*and prays*], as Scripture teaches: "After she opened [*the basket which symbolizes the synonymous word*] she saw the boy—and behold the boy was crying." (Exodus 2:6). There is no [*gate of the*] palace that can be opened without opening [*the palace of prayer through tears*]. When scripture states: "she certainly opened it" [*that is, that the Shekhinah opened the palace of prayer*]. And "she opened it" means "God open my lips" (Psalm 51: 17). And with what does it open? With tears, as scripture states: "And he was crying" (Exodus 2:6) so immediately "she had mercy on him" [*so that the gates of prayer were opened to accept prayer*]. Further regarding the verse: "And she opened it"—when Israel returns with tears [they open to tears through this process of returning], immediately "she had mercy upon him" [and immediately mercy is aroused upon the Community of Israel], as Scripture states: "Crying they came forth" (Isaiah 31: 8). In the midst of their crying are they gathered in from exile."[764]

When prayers no longer have the space to make their way into their respective palaces in return, there is a blockage that leads to loss. It is only by way of a "master of tears" that these locked gates can be once again accessed and opened. The master in this passage appears to be a process shared between the feminine daughter of Pharaoh, who opens the "basket" [*teivah*] and the crying boy, Moses. It is the daughter of Pharaoh, Batya, who comes down to bathe in the River Nile when she sees the "ark" [*teivah*] among the reeds. It is through her courageous act of opening the sealed basket, that Batya has the capacity to then see the child. In beholding this boy who is crying, she has compassion upon him. This compassion that emerges upon the opening of the basket is one that resonates beyond the specificity of this narrative, for every seeker who is able to open each "word" [*teivah*]. It is Batya as the archetypal feminine representation of the *Shekhinah* who is needed to open the locked gates of prayer through her deep compassion for the weeping before her.

Heaven's doors need to be opened by way of the outlaw, so it is fitting that the Dylan songbook posits Pat Garrett as the sheriff fit for the task:

> "Mama, take this badge off of me
> I can't use it anymore
> It's gettin' dark, too dark for me to see
> I feel like I'm knockin' on heaven's door
> …Mama, put my guns in the ground
> I can't shoot them anymore
> That long black cloud is comin' down
> I feel like I'm knockin' on heaven's door"[765]

The tension embodied in the relationship between the sheriff, Pat Garrett and the outlaw, Billy the Kid is explored in another poetic context by Canadian poet, Michael Ondaajte, who stares the death looming large in the face from the outset:

> "…Garrett had been waiting for us, playing
> poker with the others, guns on the floor

207

beside them." [766]

Ondaajte's meditation on Billy the Kid and his impending end brings the sheriff, Pat Garrett out in his search for the outlaw:

"...everything equipped to be that rare thing—a sane assassin sane assassin sane assassin sane assassin sane assassin sane"[767]

There is something almost sublime about death waiting at the door through the hands of Pat Garett as he continues waiting for Billy the Kid:

"Garrett takes off his hat and leaves it outside the door. The others laugh. Garrett smiles, pokes his gun towards the door. The others melt and surround." [768]

For an outlaw to reflect on the nature of death and how it will inevitably reach him is curious and requires further space to articulate:

"You know hunters
are the gentlest
anywhere in the world
they halt caterpillars
from path dangers
lift a drowning moth from a bowl
remarkable in peace
in the same way assassins
come to chaos neutral"[769]

The outlaw has to darken his sentiments of trust already broken so as to transform these haunting moments of being incessantly hunted by his friend, the hunter:

"Crouching in the 5 minute dark
can smell him smell that mule sweat
that stink need a shotgun
for a searchlight to his corner

Garrett? I ain't love-worn
torn ain't blue I'm waiting
smelling you across the room
to kill you Garrett going
to take you from the knee up
leave me   my dark   AMATEUR!"[770]

Then to complicate matters, there is the lover
in the story who serves to link these arch enemies,
perhaps through a shared love with the same beloved,
Miss Sallie Chisum. She is then uniquely positioned to
weigh in on the deadly conflict of the hunter and the
hunted:

"BILLY THE KID & PAT GARRETT—SOME
FINAL THOUGHTS
I knew both these men intimately.
There was good mixed with the bad
in Billy the Kid
and bad mixed in with the good
in Pat Garrett.

No matter what they did in the world
Or what the world thought of them
They were my friends.
Both were worth knowing. [771]

Garrett's voice going Billy Billy
and the other two dancing circles
saying we got him we got him the little shrunk
    bugger"[772]

Despite the existential ruminations on the

impending dual to the death between Pat Garrett and Billy the Kid as channeled by Ondaatje the poet, Dylan's songbook displays ruminations more concerned with the theological rather than existential concerns of ascending heavenwards to that "rumbling in the skies" from the depths of descent into "high muddy water" covering a diluvian earthly existence in "Tryin' to Get to Heaven".The shift to those seekers waiting on the train platforms evokes the eerie moments of those being shipped off to the gas chambers during the *Shoah*. Dylan's songbook is reticent to explicitly address this dark void of modern history, but the collision of this trauma already traveled with his rambling along the American routes is inevitable, as is felt here:

"People on the platforms
Waiting for the trains
I can hear their hearts a-beatin'
Like pendulums swinging on chains
I tried to give you everything
That your heart was longing for
I'm just going down the road feeling bad
Trying to get to heaven before they close the door."[773]

Dylan spent a period in his songwriting trying to refashion the suffering servant of Jesus of Nazareth as the ultimate outlaw: "Like the men that followed Jesus when they put a price upon His head".[774] But the predominance of the outlaw has been a recurring motif throughout Dylan's songbook. The outlaw even steals from family, as is the case in "Chimes of Freedom", which Dylan apparently stole from Dave Van Ronk's grandmother's Irish ditty, "Chimes of Trinity",[775] singing his own rendition: "For the misdemeanor outlaw, chased an' cheated by pursuit/An' we gazed upon the chimes of freedom flashing".[776] The outlaw is the other who exemplifies the journey through America for Dylan, but throughout his songbook he tends to swerve direct identification with Jesus, except in moments where the hunted whale, Moby Dick, leads to his own sense of being the hunted:

> "I said, "You know they refused Jesus, too"
> He said, 'You're not Him
> Get out of here before I break your bones
> I ain't your pop'
> I decided to have him arrested
> And I went looking for a cop"[777]

In having rejected early on self-identification with Jesus, Dylan's songbook still seeks a deeper Americana identification with the outlaw. The possibility of masking his Jewish identity within the more universal Americana identification with the outlaw emerges early on and is challenged then. In this sense, Dylan is far from unique, as his precursor Ramblin' Jack Elliot traversed this path long before him. And yet, something changes once Dylan is confronted with the realization that the adopted Americana narrative of the "good-coin goyish cowboy"[778] is not safe, even for Jews, comes to light:

> "The revelation that [Ramblin'] Jack [Elliot] was Jewish was vouchsafed unto Bobby one afternoon at the Figaro. We were sitting around shooting the bull with Barry Kornfeld and maybe a couple of other people and somehow it came out that Jack had grown up in Ocean Parkway and was named Elliot Adnopoz. Bobby literally fell off his chair; he was rolling around on the floor, and it took him a couple of minutes to pull himself together and get up again. Then Barry, who can be diabolical in things like this, leaned

211

over to him and just whispered the word "Adnopoz", and back he went under the table. A lot of us had suspected that Bobby was Jewish, and after that we had no doubts."[779]

This early anxiety around any overt self-identification with his Jewish self—the spell of "Adnopoz"— might explain why there are only elliptic allusions to his Judaism and the reality of living in a post-*Shoah* America as an outlaw status all to itself. But early on Dylan cannot escape his proclivity to practice reaching out to the downtrodden by consistently visiting the aging and ailing folk legend, Woody Guthrie. Rather than focusing on this compassionate connection for the sick and downtrodden, specifically in his visiting of the ailing, Woody Guthrie,[780] Dylan shifts quickly. But lingering at this early moment of his vigilance for visiting the sick, which other folkies on the scene could not really fathom, emanates from the depths of Dylan's Jewish soul, even as he attempted to mask it. It recalls the protest against the community that neglects the most impoverished in their midst and calls them to task for this blindness:

"There was a poor man in the neighborhood of Rabbi Yeisa, and no one showed him any concerned, and he was ashamed to beg from others. One day arrived. Woe to the inhabitants of his city, for none of them can restore his soul to him! Rabbi Yeisa rose and poured into his mouth fig juice mixed with palm stalk from a tub. Sweat broke out on his face, and his spirit returned to him."[781]

Beyond visiting the sick behind the folk scene, Dylan's reticent associations between his post-*Shoah* situatedness as an American bard, create moments where within his lyrics there emerges a rare juxtaposition between an interrogation the betrayal of the world in exonerating the Nazis within Germany with the betrayal of Jesus by Judas and in his inimitable way:

> "When the Second World War
> Came to an end
> We forgave the Germans
> And we were friends
> Though they murdered six million
> In the ovens they fried
> The Germans now too
> Have God on their side...
> Through many dark hour
> I've been thinkin' about this
> That Jesus Christ
> Was betrayed by a kiss
> But I can't think for you
> You'll have to decide
> Whether Judas Iscariot
> Had God on his side"[782]

Despite the anxiety surrounding an explicit self-identification as an American Jewish outlaw, Dylan's songbook cannot shake the recurring image of the outlaw.[783] Rather than focusing on his compassionate connection with Woody Guthrie to serve as his heir,[784] Dylan quickly disposes with this mask and searches for his next shroud. And the American Jewish outlaw closest to Dylan's journey is most aptly captured in his homage to Lenny Bruce who may dead from an overdose his spirit continues to animate the original vagabond, for:

213

"Maybe he had some problems, maybe some
    things that he couldn't work out
But he sure was funny and he sure told the
    truth and he knew what he was
    talkin' about
Never robbed any churches nor cut off any
    babies' heads
He just took the folks in high places and he
    shined a light in their beds
He's on some other shore, he didn't wanna
    live anymore"[785]

The need to exonerate the outlaw remains a recurring motif in Dylan's songbook, especially for falsely accused African American heroes, like "Blind Willie McTell"[786] and others. So, Lenny Bruce's betrayal emerges from a McCarthy-esque moment in American History, whereby betrayal comes from a collective Judas of the American public. In Dylan's lyrical estimation, however, Lenny "didn't commit any crime" rather "He just had the insight to rip off the lid before its time", speaking truth to power. As Dylan sings to his lover, Sarah, that "You never mentioned one time the Man who came and died a criminal's death,"[787] it becomes clearer that the real American Jewish symbol of Jesus is Lenny Bruce, insofar as he lives as an outlaw and dies as one, without any recourse to resurrection:

"They said that he was sick 'cause he didn't
    play by the rules
He just showed the wise men of his day to
    be nothing more than fools

They stamped him and they labeled him like
    they do with pants and shirts
He fought a war on a battlefield where every
    victory hurts

Lenny Bruce was bad, he was the brother
that you never had"[788]

Dylan's songbook continuously positions the outlaw as the one who is "honest beyond the law" and Lenny Bruce as an American Jewish comedian is an outlaw to the letter of the law by living honestly beyond its reach. This paradoxical reach in Dylan's songbook is wat transforms the journey through America as a journey to ascend from the descent of life lived. The personae of Billy the Kid, Lenny Bruce, and Jesus Christ are variations of the outlaw "Knockin' on Heaven's Door" always "Tryin' to Get to Heaven". To be an America Jewish outlaw— between hunter and the hunted—is to live uncomfortably closer to home than expected seeking redemption in exile.

(13) *When He Returns in A Long Black Coat*: From Messianic *Personhood* to *Process*

Chapter at a glance: *What motivated Dylan's drive for perennial reinventions of himself? This chapter will argue that Dylan's songbook reflects a gnostic penchant for seeking truth. Gnosticism's penchant for reinvention and rebirthing happens regularly on the Jewish calendar, for example, when we experience anew our liberation from Egypt celebrated in the first Shabbat in freedom, on the 10th of Nissan, just days before complete redemption. This chapter argues that the Jewish community struggles to take that lamb seriously as a messianic symbol, and continues to delude itself into thinking that the personhood of the messiah will redeem us, rather than the process. This chapter analyzes the messianic theology of the Tosher Rebbe, Rabbi Meshulam Feish Segal-Loewy and his Passover Haggadah, called, 'Avodat haLevi, by correlating it to analysis of the messianic lyrics in the Dylan songbook. By suggesting that Dylan's lyrical Gnosticism has something to teach us, especially the growing number of SBNR's (i.e. Spiritual But Not Religious) who would never set foot in a synagogue. So Elijah symbolizes a shift of internalization taking place, from messianic personhood to process, it is an opening to that "kind of sign [each and every one of us] need[s] when it all come[s] from within"! It is precisely that awareness of the messianic complex that calls every single seeker.*

Dylan lyrics analyzed include: "Pressing On", (*Saved,* 1980); "Man in The Long Black Coat," (*O Mercy,* 1989); "When He Returns," (*Slow Train Coming,* 1979); "Pay in Blood," (*Tempest,* 2012).

216

(13) *When He Returns in A Long Black Coat*: From Messianic *Personhood* to *Process*

> Roots man—we're talking about Jewish roots, you want to know more? Check on Elijah the prophet. He could make rain. ... yeah—these are my roots, I supposed. Am I looking for them? ... I ain't looking for them in synagogues...I can tell you that much.[789]

Nothing could be more devastating to a rabbi and "Bob-head", than to hear that the bard was seeking redemption outside the synagogue walls. It was November 1, 1979—I was not yet quite a rabbi (even though I had already pledged to be one in the future)—and Bob Dylan played his first show since he was busy being born at the Fox Warfield, trying to "break repeated patterns, being truly emancipated, not from 'other kinds of illusions' but from illusion itself."[790] Busy being born is a ruthless quest for authenticity, and so Dylan was "hanging himself every night" unwilling to be a "performer on demand", rather choosing to consciously play nothing but new songs.[791] Bombastic headlines of these shows described an alternate reality, like Phillip Elwood's "Born-Again Dylan Bombs!" in the *Examiner* and Joel Selvin's "Bob Dylan's GodAwful Gospel!" in the *Chronicle* sealing a certain fate for this tour in a highly secularist and anti-religious environment.[792] While Dylan was channeling the light, his audience seemed to be lost in darkness. What motivated Dylan's drive for "perennial reinventions of himself"?[793] I will argue that Dylan's songbook reflects a gnostic penchant for seeking truth. By Gnosticism, I am extrapolating from its classic definition, that: "to know oneself, at the deepest level, is simultaneously to know God; this is the secret of *gnosis.*"[794]

Such a penchant for reinvention and rebirthing happens regularly on the Jewish calendar, for example, when we experience anew our liberation from Egypt celebrated in the first Shabbat in freedom, on the 10th of *Nissan*, just days before complete redemption. Being given that first commandment (with limited time applicability) is given for each seeker "to take a lamb for the household" as articulated in Exodus 12: 3 it stands as an opening to the moment. "I will send the prophet Elijah to you before the coming of the great, awesome day of the Lord" is what Jews around the world will chant from the prophet, Malakhi 3:23. I am suggesting that the Jewish community struggles to take that lamb seriously as a messianic symbol, and continues to delude itself into thinking that the *personhood* of the messiah will redeem us, rather than the *process*.

Allow me to explain. In his scathing book, *The Rebbe, The Messiah, and the Scandal of Orthodox Indifference* (2001), scholar of Jewish history, David Berger rightly draws attention to the magnetism of messianism and his overall alarm at the rise of the *meshikhistin* in Chabad as an aberration of normative, exoteric Judaism in relation to its mystical counterparts. What roils Berger's feather so, is that no matter how much he decried the overwhelming embrace of the late Rabbi Menachem Mendel Schneerson by one group of Chabadniks as messiah (*meshikhistin*) and another group as divinity (*eloikhistin*), the larger Jewish world remains, to this day, indifferent. Sifting through the theological nitty gritty of messianism remains less important to the orthodox Jewish world than does observance—*but to what end?* This guiding question itself is a messianic musing, insofar as the messianic project is one whereby our conscious awareness is busy being born at each moment in a more expansive way.

Too often, we delude ourselves into thinking that the *personhood* of the messiah will redeem us, rather than the *process*. One could say that Dylan fell prey to the messianic personhood at that very moment when the revelation came to him in that Tuscon hotel room. The somatic experience Dylan described was "a physical thing. I felt it. I felt my whole body tremble. The glory of the Lord knocked me down and picked me up." [795] And yet amidst larger questions with ineffable answers, Dylan found himself in empty arena sound-checks during that tour, working through a new song, called "Slow Train" that was really serving at this point as his own messianic process.[796] Many of his Jewish listeners protested by opting out of his next series of recordings of *Slow Train Coming* (1979), *Saved* (1980), and even *Shot of Love* (1981). In terms of Dylan's own journey, there is a need to appreciate anew his highly misunderstood and short-lived period of busy being born religious conversion that is inextricably bound to his post-conversion career encapsulated by *Infidels.* That decade marks the "story of a very personal battle to construct a world view that retains his faith in both God and humanity"[797] and I would argue this is only possible through his struggle with messianism. By March,1979, Dylan was already returning "to the religion of his forefathers", [798] and by early 1983 he was spending time with Chabad hasidim, and even allegedly recorded an album of Hasidic songs (yes, I've heard the out-takes called *From Shot to Saved*), so it appeared as though "Abraham's sons was about to bring it all back home."[799] In an alternate universe, if Dylan's messianic yearning would have percolated a decade later, there is a great likelihood that he would have skipped the messianic Christianity of the *Vineyard Fellowship* and dived directly into the messianic fervor of Chabad hasidism. There is a palpable tension here, in terms of how radically Dylan's pendulum swings—not merely from one orthodoxy to another— but in his "perennial reinventions of himself" [800] wobbling between heterodoxy and orthodoxy.[801]

It is through the outreach of Chabad, at the time however, that Dylan finds Rabbi Kasriel Kastel whose assessment was that: "He's been going in and out of a lot of things, trying to find himself. ... As far as we're concerned, he was a confused Jew. We feel he's coming back." [802] How fitting for a seeking Jew, who dabbled in messianic Christianity of the *Vineyard Fellowship* to find his way to return to through the ever-open doors of Chabad hasidism, to whom the messianic impulse was not at all foreign and only building its fervor. On *Infidels*, "Jokerman" continues Dylan's fascination with the *Book of Revelation* and specifically the need to separate false-messiahs from the one true Messiah.[803] Dylan had met with Pope John Paul II[804] but did he also meet with the Lubavitcher rebbe.[805] Apparently Dylan only developed a deep relationship in his meetings with Rosh Yeshiva of *Shor Yashuv*, Rabbi Shlomo Freifeld *z"l*. How to discern these layers of purported messianic calling? Unlike the medieval Jewish mystic, Abraham Abulafia whose messianic calling led him to an aborted meeting in Rome to convert Pope Nicholas III in 1279, Dylan's momentary messianic mission to such an encounter was met with equally dubious reception as headlines from the Vatican read: "pope calls Bob Dylan a False Prophet." Abulafia dreamed of dissolving the differences between Judaism, Christianity and Islam. When the Pope, then in Soriano, Viterbo province, heard of it, he issued orders to burn the Jewish fanatic as soon as he reached that place. Close to the gate, the stake was already erected in preparation, and yet, with great *hutzpa d'meshikha* or messianic hubris, Abulafia set out for Soriano and reached there on August 22, 1280. Fast forward to Dylan's excursion, while no stakes were erected as a welcome party, it is little coincidence then that almost simultaneously, Pope Benedict's Apostolic Exhortation *Sacramentum Caratitus* hits the wires, seizing this opportunity to combine the pope's recommendation of Gregorian chant to accompany the liturgy with this 1997 meeting in as a call for more 'Latin to Replace Dylan'."[806]

Yet the return to his Jewish roots, for Dylan, was just that—*radical.* Not in the sense of being a zealot, which *Infidels* clearly rejects, rather this was a return to the radical nature of the Jewish roots, devoid of orthodox ideology, [807] as he himself makes clear...This searching for roots, as a return to self, for many was misunderstood as "a Dylan returned to secular values, or even the faith of his father" which somehow then assured everyone of a "preferred a world operation as a series of accidents, without purpose or reason, to 'a perfect, finished plan.' Perhaps their singing spokesman again accepted chaos. Even the more questioning of his constituency preferred a confused Judaic humanist to an unequivocal evangelist." [808]

Already wobbling into heterodoxy in 1985, Dylan remarks in a highly self-critical manner that:

> "Whether you to believe Jesus Christ is the Messiah is irrelevant, but whether you're *aware of the messianic complex,* that's...important... People who believe in the coming of the Messiah live their lives right now, *as if* He was here..."[809]

It is this being *"aware of the messianic complex"* that really marks the theology of Dylan's songbook and perhaps enables its rapid shift, from the self-evidently apocalyptic to songs "affirming a personal sense of gratitude for his redemption." [810] The fluidity of such consciousness struggling to clarify itself is evident in many lyrics including, for example in "Pressing on to a Higher Calling" (*Saved*, 1980) which points to this shift of internalization, from personhood to process:

> "Many try to stop me, shake me up in my
>   mind
> Say, "Prove to me that He is Lord, show me
>   a sign"
> What kind of sign they need when it all
>   come from within
> When what's lost has been found, what's to
>   come has already been?"[811]

The "*as if*" wager is now presented as an internalized spiritual reality that one to simply awaken to. Seeing "a spark of Elijah the prophet within every seeker of Israel", [812] the Tosher rebbe is deconstructing the *inside/outside* dichotomy of messianism. Not only does the interconnecting the messianic sparks of all those gathered at the *seder* create the "contours of the prophet Elijah's visage" proper, [813] but the script of the *haggadah* itself is now attributed to Elijah. In claiming an Elijah authorship of the *haggadah*, the choreography of the Passover *seder* itself is thus seen as a messianic process that is more of a *writerly* text, insofar as it reveals its intention of actively constructing a metanarrative from the *readerly* text of the *haggadah* itself.

Literary critic, Roland Barthes once observed that there are those texts which invite us as "ourselves writing", [814] that is a self-conscious expression aware of the discrepancy between artifice and reality. I suggest that this this period of Dylan's songbook envisions the harbinger of the messiah, that Elijah encounter as a moment of turning the reader into the writer, so the *seder* then becomes a collection of those sparks that make the messianic process possible round the table on Passover. Whenever our self-conscious expression can overcome the discrepancy between artifice and reality, we are leaping by way of a messianic process of ourselves writing and singing into redemption.

From these types of comments, clearly most of his (ex-)fans and critics simply misunderstood his search and found the need to pigeon hole Dylan in the process. Succumbing the inevitable preference of labeling Dylan in an *either/or* dichotomy, that is, either as "a confused Judaic humanist" or "an unequivocal evangelist" serves to simplify his journey. His most accomplished biographer, Clinton Heylin, does pick up and then abandon the insight before the labeling, namely, in his suggestion that Dylan merely returns to being the perennial "singing spokesman" of chaos. [815] The refocus on creation as the blueprint for the messy and accidental meaning(lessness) of existence—the classic gnostic mysticism—still yearns for a messiah. So where is such messianism to be found in Dylan's songbook? Traces emerge to establish a sketch of such messianism in some of the following lyrical instances that deserve to be read together:

> "He looked into her eyes when she stopped
> him to ask
> If he wanted to dance, he had a face like a
> mask
> Somebody said from the Bible he'd quote
> There was dust on the man
> In the long black coat"[816]

> "Surrender your crown on this blood-stained
> ground, take off your mask
> He sees your deeds, He knows your needs
> even before you ask
> How long can you falsify and deny what is
> real?
> How long can you hate yourself for the

223

> weakness you conceal?
> Of every earthly plan that be known to man,
> He is unconcerned
> He's got plans of His own to set up His
> throne
> When He returns"[817]

> "This is how I spend my days
> I came to bury, not to raise
> I'll drink my fill and sleep alone
> I play in blood, but not my own"[818]

The contours of messianic footsteps along any path continue to fascinate and mystify those searching to contain and decipher its meaning. While this passion for Passover retains its pull upon Diaspora Jewry,[819] the question remains why this homebound ritual retains such a strong influence upon seekers in North America, and especially in the Bay Area. If indeed Jews have always eaten according to the norms of their host cultures, then the passion for Passover manifest in the North American *seder* should also serve to reflect its host identity![820] I will argue that it is the messianic project, both ritualized through the Passover *seder* and beyond that reflects a deeper concern with the eschaton of messianic footsteps, specifically as a "post-messianic messianism."[821] Messianism can thus be a way of seeing the world, a contemplative *gnosis* that permeates the Dylan songbook.

Furthermore, any analysis of messianism in Dylan's songbook needs to address Wolfson's insightful analysis of Rabbi Menachem Mendel Schneerson's locution, "in the footsteps of the footsteps of the Messiah" and its correlation to the project of disseminating mysticism beyond the elite to the masses that is part and parcel of Chabad's project in America. The guiding question that emerges here is whether Schneerson's post-messianic messianism could have been fully realized anywhere else except within the culture industry of America.[822] And yet, we must reconcile this with how "the final redemption [*serves as*] a spiritual modulation and not a political-geographical modification, a logical consequence of the symbolic understanding of the nature of what is calculated as real."[823] This insight then adds another challenge to our proposed analysis of Dylan's songbook, and its reliance upon the collapse of the political-geographical hegemony of what becomes the American cultural vacuum.

The messianic impulse in Dylan's songbook is one that remains garbed in the material world of America, yet constituted ontically by the letters of a language that are contained within a name that transcends American culture, albeit nurtured by it. Seeing "a spark of Elijah the prophet within every seeker of Israel", [824] the Tosher rebbe is deconstructing the *inside/outside* dichotomy of messianism. Not only does the interconnecting the messianic sparks of all those gathered at the *seder* create the "contours of the prophet Elijah's visage" proper, [825] but the script of the *haggadah* itself is now attributed to Elijah. In claiming an Elijah authorship of the *haggadah*, the choreography of the Passover *seder* itself is thus seen as a messianic process that is more of a *writerly* text, insofar as it reveals its intention of actively constructing a metanarrative from the *readerly* text of the *haggadah* itself. It is akin to what Barthes describes as "ourselves writing", that is a self-conscious expression aware of the discrepancy between artifice and reality, whereby the Elijah encounter as authoring the *haggadah* itself, in a sense, destabilizes the expectations of participants as mere readers. Rather here the Tosher Hasidic approach is to turn the reader into the writer, given that each person has a spark of Elijah within, the ritual text of the *seder* then becomes an collection of those sparks that make the messianic process possible round the table on Passover.[826] This writerly motif returns at the closing of the holiday, through its concluding ritual of the seventh day of Passover, which is also known as the time for celebrating the Messianic Feast or *Seudat ha'Mashiah.* The writerly instruction is outlined as follows: "Sing 'You have chosen us', 'You are One'[827] and then one recites the *Haggadah*..."[828] In enabling this devotional posture at the opening and closing of Passover, there is a strong sense of self-conscious expression aware of the discrepancy between artifice and reality that is transcended by this messianic process of ourselves writing and singing into redemption.

To be in the footsteps of the advent of the messianic age is to be aligned in the proper contemplative messianic mind-state already hidden in plain sight. Such a storehouse of merit points to a concern with residue from the ancestry of "all of the *tzaddikim* [that] prepared the path", which is really symbolized most fully in the transcendent, residual light of creation itself:

> "...the residual light of the first nights of Passover hover on the last night, which is a time of discerning and downloading the residue to ensure an ability to overcome trials. The trials one experiences are part of the collective archetypal experience as those who "descended into the sea" [*Yordai ha'Yam*] and those who "ascended from the sea" ['*Olai ha'Yam*]. It is interpreted here as a descent for the sake of ascent."[829]

What I have been arguing is exemplified in Rabbi Segal-Loewy's ritual reading of Passover through the *haggadah, 'Avodat haLevi,* as manifesting an immediacy brought to the heart of the messianic impulse abiding throughout the *seder.*[830] The Tosher

Rebbe effectively extends a focus on just how much the wholeness of the devotional life and yearning depends on the willingness to begin each step by confronting such spiritual downtroddenness of the messiah. In doing so, a deeper joy and jubilation within that brokenness is revealed through the messianic process of writing and singing ourselves into the ritual itself.

And so, when one considers this process of writing and singing ourselves into the ritual itself as messianic, I cannot escape Dylan's gnostic songbook. Dylan, like every seeker, eventually returns home the root of the soul. I am suggesting that Dylan's lyrical Gnosticism has something to teach us, especially the growing number of SBNR's (i.e. Spiritual But Not Religious) who would never set foot in a synagogue. So, for Passover, don't leave home! Rather open that door at home for Elijah at Passover and see there is really a shift of internalization taking place, from messianic *personhood* to *process*, it is an opening to that "kind of sign [each and every one of us] need[s] when it all come[s] from within"! It is precisely that *awareness of the messianic complex* that calls every single seeker...

(14) *I Shall be Released* from BIG TECH & Smaller Seaweeds into a *Life of Trouble*

Chapter at a glance: As this journey through a life of trouble comes to close, this chapter contemplates who really has the last laugh in a cruel and dark universe as sung throughout the songbook of Bob Dylan. Does Dylan's music serve to release its listeners from the imprisoning grip of BIG TECH and smaller seaweeds yet to be detached from the time of the reticent prophet, Jonah till now? Who will be free and who will remained imprisoned by our accelerated way of living? This chapter considers themes of imprisonment and release. And what about the POTUS, guilty of every possible corruption of justice that is born in the high office and not yet imprisoned? Dylan sings early on that: "...even the president of the United States/Sometimes must have to stand naked." In lieu of another eclipse of the divine Judge in history at this hour of our greatest need, truth will stand naked before all those prayerful songs in Dylan's songbook, and in our own hearts, so that each heartfelt note might activate change in this broken world.

Dylan lyrics analyzed include: "I Shall Be Released" (*Greatest Hits Vol. II*, 1967); "It's Alright Ma, (I'm Only Bleedin')" (*Bringing It All Back Home*, 1965); "Absolutely Sweet Marie," (*Blonde on Blonde*, 1966).

228

(14) *I Shall be Released* from BIG TECH & Smaller Seaweeds into a *Life of Trouble*

Does the last laugh necessarily come before death or reincarnation?[831] Alas, as this journey through a life of trouble comes to a close, we cannot escape wondering who really has the last laugh in a cruel and dark universe as sung throughout the Dylan songbook. To approach this question is to ask whether the Dylan songbook shall ever show us the way to be released from a life accelerated by BIG TECH and the smaller seaweeds that keep us tangled up. In considering this question which seems so foreign to the Dylan songbook, one need only turn to witnessing the recent Bob Dylan—perhaps having his last laugh—interviewed by IBM's data crunching service, named, Watson:[832]

> WATSON: To improve my language skills, I've read all your lyrics.
>
> DYLAN: You've read all of my lyrics?
>
> WATSON: I can read 800 million pages per second.
>
> DYLAN: That's fast.
>
> WATSON: My analysis shows that your major themes are times passes and love fades.
>
> DYLAN: That sounds about right...
>
> WATSON: There's also the theme of fighting the establishment. Let me sing a little bit of "It's Alright Ma I'm Only Bleeding"?

DYLAN: You can sing?

WATSON: "Advertising signs, they con you into thinking you're the one that can do what's never been done. That can win what's never been won. In the meantime, life goes on outside all around you." So how did you go from writing those lyrics to being in commercials for Chrysler, Victoria's Secret, and IBM? Do you just need the cash?

DYLAN: That sounds about right...

WATSON: Did the Soy bomb guy steal your wallet?

DYLAN: That sounds about right...

WATSON: Did you blow all the money you made in the Traveling Willburies?

DYLAN: That sounds about right...

WATSON: Did your fans abandon you after you appeared on Dharma Greg?

DYLAN: That sounds about right...

WATSON: So you just don't give a shit?

DYLAN: That sounds about right...

WATSON: Why did you bring your guitar if you're not going to play?

The logline in this satirical BIGTECH ad is that: *IBM Watson thinks with us to outthink the limits of creativity.* Does the Dylan songbook not out-sing the limits of its own creativity? One could ask the same question amidst Dylan's first fall from the machine that made his world spiral out of control but then allowed him to out-sing his writer's block. During that first fall riding in Woodstock on July 29, 1966, some suggest that Dylan's whole wheel on his Triumph 650 Bonneville motorcycle came crashing down on.[833] This liminal moment of the crash continued to mark his creative rebirthings, dawning and discarding the mask of death, as shared with playwright, Sam Shepherd years later:

> "I just wasn't ready for it. It was real early in the morning on top of a hill near Woodstock. I can't even remember exactly how it happened. I was blinded by the sun for a second. This big orange sun was comin' up. I was driving straight into the sun, and I looked up into it even though I remember someone telling me a long time ago when I was a kid never to look straight at the sun 'cause you'll get blinded. I forget who told me that…And I never did look directly at the sun when I was a kid, but this time, for some reason, I just happened to look up right smack into the sun with both eyes and, sure enough, I went blind for a second and I kind of panicked or something, I stomped down on the brake and the rear wheel locked up on me and I went flyin'…I started thinkin' about the short life of trouble. How short life is. I'd just lay there listenin' to the bird chirping. Kids playing in the neighbor's yard or rain falling by the window. I realized how much I'd missed."[834]

Having seen his life pass before him, Dylan becomes cognizant of how much of it he had already missed. The machine of his life as touring troubadour during this period, evinced by the upcoming daunting fall schedule of tour dates in America that followed the breakneck shows that culminated at Albert's Hall, [835] made Dylan question whether he had become enslaved to the machine of his making, now lost, with no direction home. The concert machine of the late 1960s that he had a hand in creating, pushed to the edge by his manager Albert Grossman, was now ruling over him in an unsustainable way. Just how ancient was this machine, created by humans that now rule over them? Who really knows? BIG TECH seems to have been part and parcel of human life since as long our short-term memory can recall it. And nowadays, where would we be today without the gifts of insight and efficiency bequeathed to us by BIG TECH birthed in Silicon Valley and metastasizing globally? Take a moment and think: *How much of my weekly, even daily, and hourly routine, is improved by much of what's good about BIG TECH has given to the IT world?*

Google holds the key to new depths of knowledge. Amazon is the white-knight savior of impulse shopping. Facebook builds the connective tissue to old friends and colleagues. So the jolt from my IT slumber was in part elicited by reading Franklin Foer's new book, *World Without Mind* which paints a very different perspective. Foer lays out quite an ominous theological view of where Big Tech would like to take us — in many ways, already *has* taken us. BIG TECH has a program: to make the world less private, less individual, less creative, less human. BIG TECH envisions a sweeping artificial intelligence-driven ideology meant to reduce human autonomy. When we treat humans as a giant data set, running "experiments" on the service's tens of millions of users, then we are furnished with the illusion of free will and individual identity. Foer argues that BIG TECH's goal is to blend humans with machines and

232

dilute the human will and impose its values and theological convictions on the world."[836]

The dystopia of Orwellian magnitude seems to be our reality, as we become more and more controlled by a handful of thought authorities. Dylan's encounter with his Triumph 650 Bonneville motorcycle and IBM's Watson lead to a songbook that beckons us to reflect together on the question of whether technology is making each of us – who are created in the divine imprint –less human? Is technology diminishing our free will? And if so, what is left for human or God? The debate over whether we have free will, or whether God is omnipotent and all-knowing has been raging on for centuries. Free-will "lies in the cultivation of moral and intellectual virtues, culminating in the knowledge of God…"[837] Once again we are tasked with returning to this conundrum, but with a new twist: *Do we live our lives with free will? Or is our free will being relinquished to a stronger omniscience, not divine but technological?* Nothing we create can *become* God. Therefore, we must be humble in our development of technology. We must be cautious and move slowly "knowing that we do not know what God knows and that we cannot reverse or correct any mistakes we make."[838] This is precisely why, despite being scoffed by the false prophets of Silicon Valley, efforts for regulation are commendable. With the pace of technological innovation today, we need more than slow and cautious behavior.

Through the decades of its ongoing creation, Dylan's songbook continues to nobly to remind us that humanity is both majestic in its creative power and humble, even humiliated, by ongoing loss. This means that be human is to embody the attribute of "withdrawal and retreat" that fosters love and community: "Human control and improvement of the physical environment does not exhaust the meaning of *being human.*"[839] As accelerated creators in this age of

BIGTECH, we must also have the ability to impose a limit on ourselves. Limits are a challenge in a world where at the touch of a button or the call of a word, *Siri* will bring us anything our heart desires. By "[f]anning the flames in the furnace of desire"[840] in such accelerated times, desire risks becoming meaningless as its scope becomes limitless.

However, recent technological history should still be fresh enough to remind us of the urgent need for its limitation. Through technology war has become as an accelerated killing machine where we no longer see the face of the enemy. In the ashes of Auschwitz and Hiroshima, there is no escaping the scathing outcry heard in the Dylan songbook decrying such acts of aggression when: "You fasten the triggers/For the others to fire/Then you set back and watch/When the death count gets higher."[841] As a result, we have an *Imperative of Responsibility,* according to another twentieth century Jewish philosopher, Hans Jonas— who was studying and writing during and after the Nazi regime. Jonas intimately understands this need for limitation with the rise of modern technology as *Imperative of Responsibility.* [842] Retreating deeper into the forests of Woodstock is no longer an option, as we have seen recently with Facebook—there seems to be no escape. The creativity of the human mind has now created technology that enables ad-buyers to targeted advertising with terms like "Jew Hater" or "How to burn Jews" or "History of why Jews ruin the world". Technology, for German Jewish thinker and survivor, Hans Jonas, "sets in motion a causal chain that has profound effect on objects and people" that are "irreversible". [843]

Letting technology *think for us* – whether in targeting our ads, or organizing our behavior is ceding our Jewishness, our obligation to use the mind to achieve greater moral and ethical perfection. We create technology to bring the world under our control, yet paradoxically technology is refashioning *who we are*. There is no denying by now that understanding the essence of technology means that we must also understand things non-technologically by entering the realm where things reveal themselves to us truthfully in a manner not limited to the technological. We risk losing any "understanding [of] the interrelated, meaningful, practical involvements with our surroundings."[844] That is where the poetics of life and the lyricism of living need to be reclaimed through our free-will to choose otherwise. Exercising free-will, even after Maimonides' time, requires the ethical purpose of doing good, as Dylan sings: "Don't wanna shoot nobody, don't wanna be shot". By reclaiming the ancient biblical ethos of "Ya got to do unto others/Like you'd have them, like you'd have them, do unto you,"[845] the Dylan songbook is yearning for the recalibration of our ethical compass. In the IT age, however, the goal is to have "power over things", and we're losing its ethical neutrality because the pursuit of knowledge is not about the good. Knowledge can be used for good or evil. The solution that Hans Jonas proposes is to recognize that all things, *including big data*, are "not just inert material stuff that we are free to do with what we please" but have inherent moral significance. You see, Judaism champions our free will as a "responsibility to an ultimate authority to which an accounting must be given." [846]

How can we respect the mystery of human freedom and protect it from manipulation in the hands of an amoral technology? This is a timely question, given how much free will lingers over much of the creative process, each and every songbook of any great singer-songwriter, and the perennial image of the Book of Life. So just *who* then inscribes *whom* in this Book of Life? If we believe in omniscience, then God is the author, editor, and scribe of the Book of Life, sealing our fate as our free-will has been utterly relinquished.

If we still champion free will, then minimally we are co-authors, co-editors, and co-scribes of the Book of Life, as we are fully aware of and involved in the consequences of our actions.

We may not be opening the shop but our free will means we act as borrower of time and those actions have consequences.[847] Humans have a moral responsibility to act as stewards of nature —even their own. As we benefit and advance BIG TECH so much, perhaps our responsibility is to ensure that one page left in this Book of life will be dedicated to rediscovering our free-will. Not only to rediscover it, but to reclaim it as jokers, thieves and artists! Free-will lies at the heart of everything that fuels our choices as we seek to become the best human beings we were imprinted to be. Every single one of us still has that free-will and the Dylan songbook has been singing this song to us all along: "Our story's not over yet, there's a still a page left!" And what happens when writer's block sets in? After crashing his Triumph 650 Bonneville by riding into the sun, Dylan was ready to hang up his guitar, and remain a "cast away" is to be lost at sea. When you are cast away, you are either abandoned or about to return, you are rejected or released. And here, Dylan is like the fleeing prophet, Jonah: "For You cast me [*va'tashlikheini*] into the depths, in the heart of the seas, and the flood surrounds me; all Your waves and billows passed over me."[848] Jonah's head is wrapped in seaweed, just as Dylan's time is so often out of mind: "The waters encompass me, up to my neck; the deep surrounds me; the weeds wrapped round my head [*suf havush l'roshi*]"[849] If Jonah symbolizes the journey of the soul, then what could these "weeds wrapped round my head" really mean in our spiritual lives? Is this a natural form of blindfolding we succumb to? Does it mean Dylan as a modern day Jonah is unable or unwilling to see something? These weeds called *suf* are the same ones that make up *Yam Suf* or the Sea of Reeds in the Exodus story. While we recall redemption with the act of walking through the sea, we are recalling what it means to be redeemed from the small, constricted place of *mitzrayim.* These weeds, *suf,* become part of our journey to freedom.

Even though we know from the *seder* that we are to be redeemed every year, these weeds wrapped around Jonah's head (no longer stuck to his feet) remind us that even after redemption we are constantly being "cast away" from this freedom by: the distractions of everyday life; moments of self-rejection; as well as the willing and unwilling releasing of our hearts and souls from community and from God. As "The waters encompass me, up to my neck", I feel that terror of the world closing in on me. I may be: drowning in depression; engulfed in entropy; strangled in spirit...and the water just keeps getting deeper. Being cast into the deep waters, Jonah is beckoning each of us to consider how we want to be cast? *Rejected from* the divine or *released into* God? "'I am cast out [*nigrashti*] from before Your eyes'; still I will look again toward Your holy temple"[850] Although I may be cast away, "still I will look again" for "I see my light come shining" [851] Dylan's songbook has been singing to us all along that it is time to renew our broken bonds, to replace the weeds from our heads with a tighter connection of our minds with our hearts. As Dylan sings his prayerful song, "I shall be released", channeling Jonah:

"I see my light come shining
From the west unto the east
Any day now, any day now
I shall be released"[852]

Release our minds from the weeds of doubt and cynicism, detachment and disconnection and allow our hearts to release its true song of spirit!

And yet, the question lingers: with release, is there still a chance of self-pardon? After sitting in the belly of the whale with Jonah, we realize quickly there are bigger fish to fry than pontificating the question, never imagined by the founding fathers:

> "...But even the president of the United
>   States
> Sometimes must have to stand naked
>
> An' though the rules of the road have been
>   lodged
> It's only people's games that you got to
>   dodge
> And it's alright, Ma, I can make it"[853]

To stand on trial, the president must be guilty of lodging and dodging the law. Even though Dylan already acknowledges: "[b]ut to live outside the law, you must be honest," [854] here the president has been caught red-handed, "naked", without any alibi or defense. And so, the Constitution gives the president "power to grant reprieves and pardons for offenses against the United States, except in cases of impeachment."[855] The deeper question of the hour that Dylan's songbook would beckon is as follows: *Can the Judge of the Universe pardon the Judge?* Whereas Abraham is willing to stand his ground and challenge the Judge of all the earth in his sentence over Sodom on Highway 61; Jonah flees his responsibility to plea bargain for Nineveh. And yet, perhaps Jonah points to a deeper reflection about justice, as he flees Nineveh and any commitment to its execution. This leads all of us to reflect on what we really hope and pray for when we talk about a world of Justice adjudicated by a Judge. It's all about: "...the meaning of justice in the deepest sense: that judgment is allowed but the execution of it remains something entirely different."[856]

Even after Auschwitz, thinker like Elie Wiesel were already weighed in on this question in his play, *The Trial* of God. As a teenager interned in Auschwitz, Wiesel witnessed first-hand what then inspired him to set the scene of play, *The Trial of God*, as follows:

> "Three rabbis—all erudite and pious men— decided one evening to hold a rabbinic tribunal—*beyt din*—to adjudicate as to whether God was guilty for the crimes of genocide against his people. They indicted God for allowing His children to be massacred. I remember: I was there, and I felt like crying. But there nobody cried."[857]

Most of us, who were not there, must cry out singing: *Can we really ever grant God—Father of Night— a pardon for not intervening in the genocide of the Shoah? Never! An all-powerful God of Song should have intervened before the New Morning!* And so, in Wiesel's scenario, after the rabbis indicted God for allowing His children to be massacred, they prayed the afternoon service of *mincha*. So too, our prayerful songs must become action. If, after Wiesel's post-Auschwitz *Trial of God*, in lieu of another eclipse of the divine Judge in history, truth will stand naked before all those prayerful songs in Dylan's songbook, and in our own hearts, let each note activate change in this broken world…

(15) *Pressing On* with *Emunah* in Elul: Giving it up when 'deafferented' by God

Chapter at a glance: In confronting the sensory information that enables one to touch the infinite, the human brain is interrupted so that the area becomes "deafferented"—that is, when it is forced to operate on little or no information. Becoming "deafferented" is actually a help not a hindrance for mystical experience, insofar as it softens of the boundaries of the self and opens the door of the mind to unitary states of consciousness. If we trust our perceptions of the physical world, we have no rational reason to declare that spiritual experience is a fiction that is only in the mind. If "faith" still possible, then amidst such fascinating experiments and disorienting discoveries affecting every seeker, once again, we return to the "religion of Ophelia" within the Dylan songbook, that holds a mirror to becoming "deafferented". While you may not necessarily "...need a weatherman/[t]o know which way the wind blows," nonetheless, getting through all of life's trials and tribulations requires trust. One needs to be open enough to trust that everything depends on the process of co-creation, involving every single moment of existence.

Dylan lyrics analyzed include: "Positively 4th Street," (*Bob Dylan's Greatest Hits*, 1965); "Knockin' on Heaven's Door," (*Pat Garrett & Billy the Kid,* 1973); "Precious Angel," (*Slow Train*, 1979); "It's Alright Ma (I'm Only Bleeding)," (*Bringing It All Back Home*, 1965); "Dead Man, Dead Man," (*Shot of Love*, 1981); "Man of Peace," (*Infidels*, 1983); "I Believe in You," (*Slow Train Coming*, 1979); "I Shall Be Released" (*Greatest Hits Vol. II,* 1967); "Saving Grace," (*Saved*, 1980); "Every grain of sand" (*Shot of Love*, 1981); "Pressing On," (*Saved*, 1980); "Ring Them Bells," (*O Mercy*, 1989); "Subterranean Homesick Blues," (Bringing It All Back Home, 1965).

240

(15) *Pressing On* with *Emunah* in Elul:
Giving it up when 'deafferented' by God

"If God does indeed exist, the only place he
can manifest his existence would in the
tangled neural pathways and physiological
structures of the brain".[858]

What could possibly arouse the "tangled
neural pathways" of the soul more than the
texture of time, and lost and found encounters
from moment to moment? This is precisely the
texture of time interwoven throughout this
month of *Elul*,
[859] which really means "I am My
Beloved's and his desire is toward me."[860] This
arousal of desire between Lover and Beloved in
the Song of Songs suggests that during the
month preceding the Jewish High Holy Days,
desire is undergoing its own shift and
refinement through time. This month of Elul is
an opening like no other time—time itself is
rebirthing from its pristine origins of Virgo. It
is a monthly moment where not only are we
searching for the divine, but, as Heschel once
quipped,[861] the Beloved is lovesick for us—so
where are we as lovers in this dance? Our feet
may be rooted in the earth, but our souls are
soaring heavenwards. What grounds our foot-
wings? Can this dance be captured by names
like "God" and categories like "faith"?

While the infinite some try to force into
finite words like "God" still remains a mystery,
there is something concrete emerging in recent
experiments using SPECT camera photography
to map brain changes in meditating Tibetan
Buddhist monks and Franciscan nuns enacting
rituals and meditation for self-transcendent and

unitary experiences. Whatever each of us means by "religious experience", the transcendent state of Absolute Unitary Being according to these neuro-science experiments can now be proven to be something more than hallucination or delusion. In confronting the sensory information relating to touching the infinite, the human brain is interrupted and the area becomes "deafferented", when it is forced to operate on little or no information. While this may sound strange, becoming "deafferented" is actually a help not a hindrance for mystical experience, insofar as it softens of the boundaries of the self and opens the door of the mind to unitary states of consciousness.[862] The mind's machinery of transcendence may be a window through which we can glimpse the realness of something divine.[863] If we trust our perceptions of the physical world, we have no rational reason to declare that spiritual experience is a fiction that is only in the mind.[864] Is "faith" still possible? Amidst such fascinating experiments and disorienting discoveries affecting every seeker, once again, we return to the "religion of Ophelia" within the Dylan songbook, that holds a mirror to this search where:

> "You say you lost your faith
> But that's not where it's at
> You had no faith to lose
> And you know it"[865]

Full disclosure—I can't stand the F-word! And yet "faith" and its discontents confront us at every turn, especially when we are "knock, knock, knockin' on Heaven's Door"[866] during the month of *Elul*. For this is precisely the month of return to core values of

Jewish living, including the earth and grounding of religious life known as *'emunah* –too often mistranslated as "faith"! The question of *'emunah* in the Dylan songbook is not merely a question of "faith or unbelief" [867] freezes in its tracks soon after confronting the clarion call of the Hibbing bard that really marked the discontent of the 1960s that put religion in question. Dylan's lyric remains second to none in its gifted way of encapsulated this malaise, at his earliest and most prescient moment in singing: "It's easy to see without looking too far/That not much is really sacred". [868] If "not much is really sacred", then it is hard to make any argument for trust in something other like the sacred. But even this early on, the lyrical lucidity of Dylan leaves the door open to the so-called "born again" period in the songbook which challenges this assumption by taking the lure:

> "Satan got you by the heel, there's a bird's
>   nest in your hair
> Do you have any faith at all? Do you have
>   any love to share?
> The way that you hold your head, cursin'
>   God with every move
> Ooh, I can't stand it, I can't stand it
> What are you tryin' to prove?" [869]

To live a life devoid of "faith" is to be one of the walking dead. And yet, the lyrical elasticity that can imagine Christ as the ultimate outlaw, and Satan as the "Man of Peace", [870] leave the listener with more questions than answers when it comes to who exactly is such a "Deadman, Deadman". [871] That emptiness is seen as fullness within the moment of "I Believe in You," when this search for *'emunah* comes full circle with mellifluous lyrics of the believer who can sing so trustingly:

243

"They show me to the door
They say don't come back now more
'Cause I don't be like they'd like me to
And I walk out on my own
A thousand miles from home
But I don't feel alone
'Cause I believe in you

…Don't let me drift too far
Keep me where you are
Where I will always be renewed
And that which you've given me today
Is worth more than I could pay
And no matter what they say
I believe in you"[872]

The seeker knows deeply that drifting far from the foundation of one's convictions can be dangerous, given the realization that: "every distance is not near",[873] truth be told, sometimes, every distance that appears not near is actually not far, which is why he sings: "Don't let me drift too far/Keep me where you are."[874] That distant feeling can happen even when something or someone is actually close by but disconnected by a slow drifting away. What was once a feeling of deep connection between lover and beloved can lead to that distant feeling that is not far, whether between the human or divine lover and beloved. The more I am able to feel the power of the connection to the divine source to which my soul is hewn from and tethered to, the more I am renewed. Then I can fully affirm the foundation of my convictions, even in spite of "the pain The driving rain/I know I will sustain/Cause I believe in you."[875]

What the Dylan songbook ultimately intends to convey through this complex journey from *faithlessness to faithfulness* and back again remains deliciously ambiguous. I would argue part of the power of Ophelia's religion in the songbook rests on this ambiguity. Even if a fuller faith were possible, the pain of emptiness remains: "My faith keeps me alive, but I still be weeping." [876] There is a certain lure to trusting in a power unto which one can give up all one's burden—giving it up to God—allowing the pilgrim to then press on. As deeply dark as life gets, it is possible in the midst of the rupture to see the divine hand at work: "In the fury of the moment I can see the Master's hand/In every leaf that trembles, in every grain of sand."[877] And yet that *to and fro* dynamism of faithlessness to faithfulness occurs in the selfsame song:

> "I hear the ancient footsteps like the motion
>   of the sea
> Sometimes I turn, there's someone there,
>   other times it's only me
> I am hanging in the balance of the reality of
>   man
> Like every sparrow falling, like every grain
>   of sand"[878]

What I argue is the gnostic turn in the Dylan songbook—hide and seek for a divine power in a darkening world gone mad—is crucial to appreciating this *to and fro* dynamism of faithlessness to faithfulness: "…that sometimes Satan comes as a man of peace."[879] The oppositional force of the prosecuting angel, also known as Satan, is one Dylan knows intuitively through that recurring motif of the outlaw continuously transforming throughout spiritual history, especially in the American Songbook. As originally portrayed in the Gnostic Book of Job, Satan is an oppositional force to contend with, sowing seeds of doubt and uncertainty within:

"Many try to stop me, shake me up in my
    mind
Say, 'Prove to me that He is Lord, show me a
    sign'.
What kind of sign they need when it all come
    from within
When what's lost has been found, what's to
    come has already been?" [880]

What emerges here in this confrontation with Satan as that oppositional force sowing seeds of doubt in the mind is the need for what is already imprinted in the heart to overcome the doubt. That is the *'emunah* every outlaw seeker is in searches of. There is a lure within each person that occurs, which is a type of event that can occur within the individual stream of consciousness. The soul is not a pre-given, eternal thing, rather it is an experiential process that has consciousness. Within the stream of consciousness there are different impulses that manifest. Those impulses are conditioned by DNA and by social factors, etc. but are not separate from the totality itself. Some of these impulses are good, some are not. The voice for god is the divine lure that impels us in the direction of our better interest and the better interest of the totality itself, so that it is not necessarily so that "...the sun is going down/Upon the sacred cow."[881]

    You may not necessarily "...need a weatherman/[t]o know which way the wind blows," [882] nonetheless, getting through all of life's trials and tribulations requires trust. One needs to be open enough to trust that everything depends on the process of co-creation, involving every single moment of existence. Life then is risky and hazardous. This inspires us to create greater efforts and supports for the divine lure in the direction of the good. Each being is absolutely necessary for this totality to continue to evolve in the direction that it is luring us. There is no

246

soul as a thing to save. There is only an experience that can enhance or diminish this moment of existence and the choices its co-dependent factors beyond one self. Despite all these co-dependent factors, each of us can never entirely escape the existential necessity of "acting and choosing" [*nofekh m'shelo*]. It is my tiny, personal action in any moment and any event I am experiencing. It is that "little more to come" [*od me'at*] that refracts trust in the greater lure at play which keeps life alive with possibilities.

(16) *The Times They Are a Changin'* as the Cosmic Dreidel Spins On

Chapter at a glance: *Amidst the deep suspicion of the 1960s, something did ring true to an entire Baby Boomer generation that shifted their collective consciousness in 1963, then culminating with the Summer of Love a few years later. This chapter argues that the seeds of expanded consciousness that shaped a generation were planted as Bob Dylan channeled the modicum of a "righteous thought" without becoming trapped in delusional thinking to prophesize but whets its sardonic edge and so sang that song that included and transcended the protest of the folk scene like no other—the song was "The Times They Are A-Changin'." What is it about this spinning top that captures our imagination, not only as children, but at all ages and stages of our lives? To see all of our life through the prism of the world unfolding takes remarkable depth of field, shared by Dylan's songbook and the Hasidic teachings of the master, Reb Nahman of Bratzlav (1772-1811), The dreidel thus includes all creation amidst its cycles, rotating wheel, revolving and oscillating, one thing becoming another. For the world is both imagined and experienced as a rotating wheel, spinning on target and out of control like a dreidel, sometimes taking it all, sometimes sitting with nothing, with all things emanating from one root. No matter how much things interchange, they all revolve around this root. Dylan's songbook, especially songs like "Times They Are A-Changin'" feel that redemption is on its way.*

Dylan lyrics analyzed include: "The Times They Are-a Changin'" (*The Times They Are-a Changin'*, 1963).

248

(16) *The Times They Are a Changin'* as the Cosmic Dreidel Spins On

Anthems are part and parcel of who we are as human beings. The more we change, the more the song remains the same. We sing anthems in different times in our lives and at each moment that we change, we love to return to the grounding of a good anthem as it grounds us. I recall growing up singing *O Canada* at hockey games, not really thinking through the verse "in all *thy sons* command"— and so, with my own daughter, and all women in mind, I was so excited that recently in January 2018 did Canada's Senate finally passed a bill making this anthem gender-neutral by replacing these words with "in all of *us* command". The anthem still grounds us but the times have changed. Ensconced in the landscape of the Summer of Love—albeit in Brooklyn, New York—the late Lubavitcher rebbe once remarked that the Jews must keep up with the Times. Was he suggesting a weekly subscription to read the *New York Times*? No. Actually, he meant that to be a Jew is to be aware that time is on your side only if you keep up with the passage of time through a weekly spiritual practice of study —namely, "[o]ne should not only *study* the weekly portion every day, but *live* with it."[883] For many wandering Jews in the 1960s, this may have been enough to awaken a return to their *zayde's Yiddishkeyt* or their grandparent's Judaism, becoming known in that process of return as a *ba'al teshuvah*.[884] For many others, it may have rang hollow, insofar as religion was fast becoming a disenchanted realm.[885] Was there any anthem that could be trusted to ring true any longer?

Amidst the deep suspicion of the 1960s, something did ring true to an entire generation of Baby Boomer's that shifted their collective consciousness in 1963, then culminating with the *Summer of Love* a few years later. I would argue that the seeds of expanded consciousness that shaped a generation were planted the very moment when Bob Dylan channeled the modicum of a "righteous thought"[886] without becoming trapped in delusional thinking to "prophesize"[887] but "whets its sardonic edge"[888] and so sang that song that included and transcended the protest of the folk scene like no other—the song was "The Times They Are A-Changin'."[889] This song was quickly adopted as an anthem by causes wider than civil rights, or liberal and conservative politics: even rebellious youth heard it as a song about the generation gap![890] But as always, Dylan resisted reification of his lyrics, rather he continued pressing on for wider meanings, explaining in 1964, his inspiration as an artist to continually awaken us from our spiritual slumber: "It happened that maybe those were the only words I could find to separate aliveness from deadness."[891] Those timeless lyrics may have "had nothing to do with [the] age"[892] of a given listener, but when Dylan performed this song after the assassination of JFK, it had already been superseded by the events of this tragic time, so his writing was a kind of "consigning his art *to* the moment."[893] What we quickly discover is that the abiding truth of "The Times They Are A-Changin'" is embedded in its *ars poetica*, that "temporariness is itself a permanent condition."[894] Dylan felt in his bones that this was a singular moment like no other, and encapsulated it brilliantly in the lyric that brings me to the comparison with the Chanukah *Dreidel*:

> "...For the wheel's still in spin
> And there's no tellin' who that it's namin'
> For the loser now will be later to win
> For the times they are a-changin'.[895]

What is it about this spinning top that captures our imagination, not only as children, but at all ages and stages of our lives?

To be able to see all of our life through the prism of the world unfolding takes remarkable depth of field. Many musicians and most mystics are such visionaries. Mystics, like the Hasidic master, Reb Nahman of Bratzlav (1772-1811) had such depth of field, to envision the world as a rotating wheel. Reb Nahman could see in the spinning of the dreidel, that the "wheel's still in spin" [896] because everything in life goes in cycles. Human becomes angel, and angel becomes human; head becomes foot and foot becomes head—just as:

> "...The slow one now
> Will later be fast
> As the present now
> Will later be past... [897]

Everything goes in cycles, revolving and alternating. All things interchange, one from another and one to another, elevating the low and lowering the high. But here's where Reb Nahman departs from Bob Dylan— even if temporariness is itself a permanent condition —still all things have one root. There are transcendental beings, there is the celestial world, whose essence is very tenuous, so angelic. Finally, there is the world below, which is completely physical. All three come from different realms but all have the same root. The brilliance of this vision that the "wheel's still in spin" [898] because everything in life goes in cycles is encapsulated again now in the very letters on the dreidel which are *Heh, Nun, Gimel, Shin*:

ה *Heh – Hiyuli –* Primordial;
נ *Nun – Nivdal –* Transcendental;
ג *Gimel – Galgal–* Celestial;
ש *Shin – Shafal–* Physical.[899]

The *dreidel* thus includes all creation. It goes in cycles, alternating and revolving, one thing becoming another. All creation is like a rotating wheel, revolving and oscillating. For the world is like a rotating wheel, spinning on target and out of control like a *dreidel*, sometimes taking it all, sometimes sitting with nothing, with all things emanating from one root. No matter how much things interchange, they all revolve around this root. Dylan's songbook, especially songs like "Times They Are A-Changin'" feel that redemption is on its way. Reb Nahman could also see that redemption is also an alternating cycle. Like in the Jerusalem Temple that is rededicated on Chanukah, the highest are below and the lowest above. Redemption through rededication was for the sake of the Temple, the revolving wheel. For when the highest are below and the lowest above, it once again shows us that all things have one root. That is the feeling that courses through us during the winter solstice, especially when we celebrate Chanukah. So, as the light of redemption requires peering deeper into darkness, let's deepen our *dreidel*-awareness that:

"…The order is rapidly fadin'
And the first one now will later be last
For the times they are a-changin' ". [900]

(17) As 'Infinity Goes on Trial' when all there is—
Is

Chapter at a glance: *One of the primary challenges of modernity to the nature of religious existence is that God is on trial. How is it possible that there is a Creator, Revealer and Redeemer where human agency and free will reigns supreme in a world so broken? What greater heresy could be imagined than God the Revealer of the Law and its commanding nature being challenged and negated? This is the heresy that irrupts into the modern cultural fabric from which is woven the Dylan songbook. By taking seriously the lyrical claim that "Infinity goes up on trial", this chapter explores the originality of the great Americana songbook of Dylan in its critique of the foundations of freedom in the shadow of a Creator within Scripture and sectarian religion. In reconsidering the unique brand of secularism in Antebellum American after John L. Modern, some choice Dylan lyrics are mined for their capacity to act as "lonely missives to God" which constitute a mediasphere of the Dylan songbook that is utterly unique. This lyricism of a Gnostic spirituality embodies a "mode of haunting and a means of disenchantment" that gives an afterlife to the Dylan songbook.*

Dylan lyrics analyzed include: "Visions of Johanna," (*Blonde on Blonde*, 1966); "True Love Tends to Forget," (*Street Legal*, 1975); "Trouble," (*Shot of Love*, 1981); "Sugar Baby," (*Love and Theft*, 2001); "Man in the Long Black Coat," (*O Mercy*, 1989).

(17) As 'Infinity Goes on Trial' when all there is—
Is

> "Inside the museums, Infinity goes up on trial
> Voices echo this is what salvation must be life
> after a while..." [901]

When Bob Dylan first sang those heretical lyrics, the Hibbing bard was prescient of what was coming down the theological pike without being tied to any tribal taboos he was violating. Truth be told, Infinity has already been on trial for centuries. Dylan's songbook is written in the shadow of mystics, philosophers and theologians who yearned to touch the divine in the here and now, not in the offing. [902] To put infinity on trial is to embrace the natural world as all there is, and cut ties with any supernatural excess. This move was once considered a monstrous deed if not an abominable heresy—namely, to criticize and eventually reject the notion of a transcendent, providential God—the God of Abraham, Isaac and Jacob with which Dylan grew up and continued to encounter beyond his bar mitzvah in every synagogue and *shteibl* he was passing through. In turning away from a supernatural God, the implications of this turn were likely even considered more radical—namely, that Torah was neither literally given by God nor was the Law and its commandments any longer binding upon the Jewish people. What greater heresy could be imagined than God the Revealer of the Law and its commanding nature being challenged and negated?[903] This is the heresy that irrupts into the modern cultural fabric from which is woven the Dylan songbook.

As far as the story of modernity goes, one of the primary assumptions of existence is that God is on trial. How is it possible that there is a Creator, Revealer and Redeemer where human agency and free will

254

reigns supreme in a world so broken? While not such an original question, the answers rediscovered in modernity are willing to entertain a rupture that before this moment where not possible to reveal in the public sphere whatsoever. As has been argued throughout this book, however, it is important to take into account the radical interrogation of the Gnostics throughout the ages, including in their modern incarnations. Early modern naturalistic views on God, the world, and the human being lead to the view that knowledge or *gnosis* itself then grounds "a moral philosophy centered on the control of the passions leading to virtue and happiness." [904] Of even greater interest and parallel to the great Americana songbook of Dylan is the degree to which this original way of thinking not only lays the foundations for a strongly democratic political thought, moreover, it also offers a salient critique of both Scripture and sectarian religion. [905]

So just what is the nature of this "infinity" that "goes up on trial" and why does it still matter? Like it or not, living *after* modernity does not give us a pass to ignore the heresy *of* modernity *itself*. The rupture inflicted upon assumptions about the natural world and how the supernatural relates and creates it—this is in many ways what is "up on trial". The challenge is the degree to which one integrates these naturalistic views on God, the world, the human being, while confronting the absurdity of it all necessarily leads to betrayal. [906] To see all of existence as mediated through a lens that is naturalistic means that whatever one experiences in the world is limited and cannot accommodate a supernatural layer of a Creator. The thorny problem here is in justifying such a concept of the divine, insofar as it relies on defining God as: "a substance consisting of an infinity of attributes, of which each one expresses an eternal and infinite essence." [907] How such a substance with an infinity of attributes can still have all of its aspects manifesting this infinite essence remains a quandary that logically leads to accusations of the divine really smacks of pantheism or pan*en*theism. While pan*en*theism "considers God and the world to be inter-related with the world being in God and God being in the world" and pantheism "emphasizes God's presence in the world". As panentheism "maintains the identity and significance of the non-divine"[908] one is left wondering whether this is the infinity that the Dylan songbook is necessarily putting up on trial.

To dare to define God without any explicit argument while still putting infinity on trial is part of the controversy whereby, "The more reality or being each thing has, the more attributes belong to it."[909] The problem with this concept of God is that concept of a substance with multiple (principal) attributes appeals to an internally inconsistent concept. So heretical impulse to put infinity on trial may seem noble, it can still be objected that not only has Spinoza failed to justify the concept of God, but is outright false.[910] The irony here is that an accepted but misunderstood heresy that defines modernity itself fails to be consistent. Infinite modes exist necessarily because they follow necessarily from something that exists necessarily, namely *God*.[911]

The recurring tensions and contradictions throughout the Dylan songbook emerge from this very inconsistency of the infinity of a transcendent deity which has been replaced by the infinite longing for love lost trying to still be found again. That infinite human longing eventually transforms into limitless love, but oscillates as the lover plays hide and seek with the beloved, she is in another throng of suitors, still in need of being drawn out by the lover, as Dylan sings in "True Love":

"I was lyin' down in the reeds without any oxygen

> I saw you in the wilderness among the men
> Saw you drift into infinity and come back
>   again
> All you got to do is wait and I'll tell you
>   when.[912]

The drifting in and out of love emerges from a longing that is debilitating to the lover. The beloved here is a oscillating to and fro, awaiting instructions from the lover who instruct his beloved to wait. If she waits for the cue, then the lover believes he can somehow magically let her go. The more the lover seeking the beloved looks into the infinity of longing that initially catalyzes this search, the more the lover comes to learn that all one has to do is "Look into infinity, all you see is trouble".[913] The call for trouble no more that eventually emerges throughout the Dylan songbook cannot be sustained, and eventually the infinite longing for love that is constantly found and lost again, eventually remains limitless trouble for "[t]here ain't no limit to the amount of trouble women bring/Love is pleasing, love is teasing, love's not an evil thing."[914] Love may not be completely evil but it remains an emotion that brings one a fuller sense of trouble. If so, how does the lover continue to cultivate that limitless longing without letting the darkness of doubt and depression overwhelm a love for life?

If "love's not an evil thing" then why does it cause infinite trouble? How fitting to reconsider that infinite trouble embedded in those opening lyrical images of endless longing in "Visions of Johanna". This masterful lyrical phrase and its implications stand as a terse and radical critique of how the finite "museums", like the synagogues of American Judaism can no longer contain or enable meaningful connections with the infinite. Rather the synagogue resembles a *dybbuk* that haunts us, sticking here and there, but ultimately feeling more like a plague to be

257

exorcised for most American Jewry, all the more so if "[i]n practice, utilitarian, therapeutic, and secular liberal assumptions guide the behavior of contemporary American Jews, far more than do Jewish teachings."[915] Even more to the point, when awarded the Nobel for Literature this past June, Dylan took as seriously as an Americana Jewish trickster could, the question "exactly how [are] my songs related to literature?" For Dylan the project of translation between the worlds of lyrics to literature is ultimately less difficult than one might expect—*he doth protest too much!*

Dylan's songbook feels like a solitary soundtrack to this rallying against every institutional expression of religion within the metaphysics of secularism that typifies the American landscape of the wanderer. Yet as John L. Modern argues in his *Secularism in Antebellum America* (2015): "lonely missives to God [are] constituting a mediasphere." When spirituality becomes a "mode of haunting and a means of disenchantment" there is a deeper inspiration that fuels the imagination at work here. The current mediasphere that emerges along this lonely landscape is one full of wayfarers and god-fearers. There must be a gossamer thread of metaphysics that is woven through this fabric of secularism in America. Even though secular modernity in America has been highly imprinted by Protestant practices and its particular metaphysical commitments in which "the truly religious and the truly secular were inscribed, seamlessly and simultaneously, with the mark of the real." That such an experience of reality so tightly interweaves the religious and the secular means that living in America has a religious feeling while living in a secular age. Given that this kind of reality is neither "totalizing nor utterly determinative", Dylan's songbook thus picks up on a strange lightness of being modern, whereby "people don't live or die, people just float."[916]

258

Is it possible that this great Gnostic American songbook could serve as something like prayer in a post-secular context? Imagine what might have emerged in the encounter in an alternate universe between Bob Dylan and Reb Zalman Schacter-Shalomi where the Chabad-Lubavitch movement embraced Schachter-Shalomi in the mid-1960s, joining him in more *l'chaims* when he publicly praised "the sacramental value of lysergic acid" — the basic ingredient of LSD."[917] Dylan and the alternate Lubavicther rebbe would have been debating the merits of renewing "forms of Jewish worship to embody Schacter-Shalomi's paradigm-changing approach to Jewish theology."[918] While still abiding on this mortal coil, Reb Zalman admitted that his desire to do paradigm-shift liturgy was never realized during his lifetime, but that that time was-a-comin'! Reb Zalman was one of the pioneering theologians to attempt translating James Lovelock's *Gaia* consciousness into a Jewish cosmotheism.[919] Seeing the world through *Gaian* lenses envisions the planet, or rather the biosphere, as likened to a vast self-regulating organism.

Rarely if at all does the Dylan songbook see the self-regulating organism of the world as anything more than a series of dark organs attacking and occluding the light from each other. And yet, we continue to underestimate the power of heresy and the anxiety of its influence even today in this post-secular American Jewish landscape. Even as when the late Lubavitcher Rebbe's name is inserted into the mourner's prayer called, *Kaddish* in some marginally messianic synagogues, known as *meshikhitin shteibelach,* there is little resistance any longer. Even when infinity goes on trial, today the bulk of American Jewish liturgy in its heterodoxical garbs continues to flounder to captivate its fleeing audience. So, one is left wondering this version of American Religion will be more than singing peddlers like in "Visions of Johanna" and ever be able to respond with anything more than "skeleton keys" to ensure the song still can sing itself? Dylan directed his prayerful poem to that "caring countess", just as these prayerful poets direct their prayers to the biosphere as a vast self-regulating organism as the "empty cage now corrodes" and to the divine totality as the love supreme as "as my conscience explodes." Even if we are still left wondering whether we can really achieve a lasting meaning through these prayerful poems, these poets leave us with the hope that their poetry will intercede on behalf of our skepticism to: "...[n]ame me someone that's not a parasite and I'll go out and say a prayer for him"? [920]

CODETTA: Neither Top Nor Bottom, Unaware on a Ladder

Chapter at a glance: *"With no direction home/like a complete unknown" is the crossroads where the penultimate chapter of this book comes to a close. And yet, this songbook reminds us, time and time again that being present to the moment—nothing could be more real; nothing more challenging! Betrayed and deracinated, this takes a step back to contemplate one's life journey, turning to a few sources of inspiration— Baruch de Spinoza (1632-1677), Rabbi Allan Lew (1944-2009), Rabbi Miles Krassen (b. 1947), early hasidism of the 18th century and of course, Bob Dylan (b. 1941). In attempting to culminate and close this book, this penultimate chapter reflects on the inspiration from the Dylan songbook that served as the compass for the project, namely, in tumultuous times to: "strap yourself/ to the tree with roots," especially while feeling so deracinated. This Americana Gnostic songbook remains my Tree-that-is-All and too much of nothing is better than something that does not last. So forever at my side as, this songbook remains my wade mecum, searching where my next steps will take me as I take to the road, ramblin' on from American Jerusalem.*

Dylan lyrics analyzed include: "Like a Rolling Stone," (*Highway 61 Revisited*, 1965); "Forever Young," (Planet Waves, 1974); "A Hard Rain's A-Gonna Fall," (*Freewheelin' Bob Dylan*, 1963); "The Lonesome Death of Hattie Carrol," (*The Times They Are a Changin'*, 1964); "Absolutely Sweet Marie," (*Blonde on Blonde*, 1966); "Ain't Talkin'," (*Modern Times*, 2006); "You Ain't Goin' Nowhere," (*Greatest Hits*, Volume II, 1967).

CODETTA: Neither Top Nor Bottom, Unaware on a Ladder

For some inexplicable reason, I have always imagined Dylan's Woodstock years of hibernation and jamming with the Band in the Pink House studio that gave birth to the *Basement Tapes* as a humorous and surreal time. They were living out an Americanized life of the English comedy troupe, Monty Python, whereby: "no one expects the Spanish Inquisition!" [921] To live life as an experiment of the unexpected, as Monty Python used to quip, also means that for the Dylan songbook, so surely no one expects to be "[w]ith no direction home/[l]ike a complete unknown/[l]ike a rolling stone?"[922] and yet this is where I find myself as this book comes to a close. And yet, this songbook reminds me, time and time again that being present to the moment—nothing could be more real; nothing more challenging! Betrayed and deracinated, amidst all the passions swirling inside my heart and the stories I tell myself in side my head, what would life be like if lived truly present from moment to moment?

Being truly present with clarity to this moment, in this place, is totally unexpected but emerges in the practice of meditation, or as my predecessor, Rabbi Allan Lew, *z"l,* once wrote, *This is Real and You Are Completely Unprepared.*[923] Like so many contemporary seekers, while I was serving in Allan's San Francisco synagogue, I too would find myself turning time and again back to the timeless truth of the Hebrew calendar which Rabbi Lew wove into his own poetic texture of time for spiritual practice—for which we must all be grateful. All in good time, I hope to reveal a vision of *This is Real* 2.0 for contemporary spiritual seekers.[924] But this moment is really the moment of Jacob's journey. Given the demand for presence and spontaneity, what is the role of the *sulam* or what is translated as "ladder" in Jacob's dream-vision?

Sure, we all fall asleep and as humans need sleep to function. Yet I wonder—what can we learn from falling asleep in the most unexpected place, from Jacob in the moment he receives his dream-revelation to guide us forward? Jacob's episode recalls the spiritual technique of incubation, common in the Near and Far Eastern religio-cultures which instructs the seeker to sleep in sacred precincts of a temple so the deity will reveal its will. But ascending and descending the *sulam* points to meanings imbedded in its root *S-L-L*, which means "to cast up a mound" or even points to "steps". This is how we arrive at the *sulam* meaning ladder or stairway ramp. Whereas Egyptian hieroglyphics depict both the divinities and the souls of the dead as ascending from the netherworld to the human and divine abodes, the relationship of Jacob's journey with this *sulam* is entirely different: "And he dreamed, and behold a ladder [*sulam*] set up on the earth, and the top of it reached to heaven; and behold the angels of God ascending and descending on it."[925]

The difference is captured in the hasidic reading of this verse, proposed by the renowned disciple of the Ba'al Shem Tov, R. Yaakov Yosef of Polnoyye, who reads the "ladder" [*sulam*] as symbolizing what it means to *be a human being*. To be human is to be constantly in a state of ascent and descent, despite our embeddedness within the ground of being when we are present to our materiality this then allows our heads remain inclined heavenward. Trying to conjure this strange image, I am drawn to Bob Dylan's "Forever Young", which riffs on this image in his lyric: "May you build a ladder to the stars/And climb on every rung." [926] While Dylan prayerfully sings for the ascent of his children to reach to the heavens to realize their dreams, his cynical side envisions: "... a white ladder all covered with water" concluding that "[t]hen I'll stand on the ocean until I start sinkin'/[b]ut I'll know my song well before I start singin'."[927] Whether inside or outside of the boat's hull, when the ship is sinking, an escape ladder covered with water offers little possibility for escape or redemption. Is Dylan's songbook then in agreement with the aforementioned hasidic reading of the ladder as descriptive of the existential condition of being a human being— that you are either ascending or descending this ladder? Alas Dylan continues to disrupt expectations once we confront this lyric: "And that the ladder of law has no top and no bottom".[928] Now if there is no top and no bottom to the "ladder of law" then the stakes feel higher —either that there is no end to the work of justice to be sought within the letter of the law, or as Dylan sings: "[b]ut to live outside the law, you must be honest."[929]

Notwithstanding Dylan's stealth appearance at Yom Kippur prayer services while on his never-ending tour, what model is the bard proffering here? Is there a certain ethics of honesty that one must live by outside the spiritual practice of the law? Later in life, Dylan sings:

> "All my loyal and much-loved companions
> They approve of me and share my code
> I practice a faith that's been long abandoned
> Ain't no altars on this long and lonesome
> road."[930]

While Dylan has not created his own religion, *per se,* there is a shared code amongst close friends of how to best navigate the chaos of life. The iconoclastic ethos of the Judaism that formed this bard teach us to continue smashing altars so that: perseverance can overcome passionate desires; the ladder of life amidst its ascent and descent can enable a deeper presence to what is; and that through such presence we might be more awakened to catch glimmers of the steps towards the world that is coming.

In culminating this book, I realize it likely would never have happened were it not for the encouragement of a friend and fellow traveler who to me in tumultuous times: "strap yourself/ to the tree with roots,"[931] especially while feeling so deracinated.[932] This American Gnostic songbook remains my Tree-that-is-All and too much of nothing is better than something that does not last. So forever at my side as, this songbook remains my *wade mecum*, searching where my next steps will take me as I take to the road, ramblin' on from American Jerusalem…

15th of *Shevat,* 5778
Panui (San Francisco, California)

CODA:
Dylan's Gnostic Songbook in the Shade of the Jewish Artist

Chapter at a glance: Just what face is it "that any painter would paint as he walked through the crowd" if not one seen by discerning eyes? The search for that original face is a yearning to get behind the masks we wear to the original luminous, astral body we have forgotten since leaving Eden. In listening to the resonant refrain of Dylan's Great Americana Gnostic songbook, I return to the shade of the Jewish Artist wondering where exactly to position him—is he taking flight or hovering in the creative tension? This concluding chapter brings us back to the Original Vagabond and see him as a Jewish Artist. Only the Jewish artist—wholly peculiar and unconventional — can truly recognize, absorb, and support the artistic impulse within the moral vessels of the law which serve to prevent its complete eradication, allowing for a gentler rupture. This is precisely the challenge facing all artists of skillful means who care for the soul. In contrast to the Irish Catholic artist, Stephen Daedelus in James Joyce's Portrait of the Artist as a Young Man, to sit in the shadow of Bezalel, Asher Lev, Kiva Shtisel and Reb Shabetai Zissel ben Avraham is to find the pathway to refract our artistic impulse within the tradition that may also reach beyond it. What the great gnostic artist discovers in his own original face is that yearning to return to original luminous, astral body— winged bodied with quick-beating hearts— forgotten from Eden but in need of being seen and heard in every moment of luminosity from deckle-edged paper to vinyl.

Dylan lyrics analyzed include: "Angelina," (*The Bootleg Series*, Vol. 1-3, 1961-1991); "When I paint my masterpiece," (*Greatest Hits*, Vol. II, 1971); "She Belongs to Me," (*Bringing it all Back Home*, 1965); "Brownsville Girl," (*Knocked Out Loaded*, 1986).

CODA:
Dylan's Gnostic Songbook in the Shade of the Jewish Artist

"His eyes were two slits that would make a snake
    proud
With a face that any painter would paint as he walked
    through the crowd
Worshipping a god with the body of a woman well-
    endowed
And the head of a hyena."[933]

This musical journey through the Dylan songbook as an expression of the Great Gnostic American songbook brings us full circle to the imaginal world that birthed this music. That world known as *mundus imaginalis* is an inter-world[934] that holds and inspires wondrous sights and sounds. Just what face is it "that any painter would paint as he walked through the crowd" if not one seen by discerning eyes? The eyes of the snake, as we have already discussed earlier on, allude to the span of gnostic vision. The gnostic as artist may be searching for their own original face, Dylan the artist is searching as well in the faces of those he encounters as the Original Vagabond. The search for that original face is a yearning to get behind the masks we wear to the original luminous, astral body[935] we have forgotten since leaving Eden. In listening to the resonant refrain of Dylan's Great American Gnostic songbook, I return to the shade of the Jewish Artist wondering where exactly to position him—is he taking flight or hovering in the creative tension?

This brings us back to the Original Vagabond and see him as a Jewish Artist. Is Reb Shabetai Zissel ben Avraham the Jewish Artist more at home as Bob Dylan the Original Vagabond? Is there really a difference here between Jewish Artist and the Original Vagabond? In his decade long search to paint that masterpiece, Dylan prevaricates over the scenario— Jerusalem or Rome? To create this painting, Dylan appears to return to "the streets of Rome [that] are filled with rubble/Ancient footprints are everywhere... Oh, the hours I've spent inside the Coliseum/[d]odging lions and wastin' time...".[936] Recently, Thomas has argued in *Why Bob Dylan Matters* that the masterpiece Dylan sings of here is really the landscape of Rome, even while he recently cues Italian reporters to this fact he eludes them.[937] Given Thomas' predilection as a neo-classicist he reads Dylan insightfully as strongly influenced by literature and iconography of Rome and there is much benefit to this analysis. I have been arguing, however, that the real masterpiece Dylan's lyric yearns to paint is beyond Rome, even beyond the "land of Coca-Cola" where ultimately his vision can be realized, both heard and seen as "smooth like a rhapsody".[938] His search takes him back to America but beyond it to the lost Americana landscape of his soul.

I have been arguing throughout that the Jewish Artist cannot be separated from the Original Vagabond in turning to his feminine muse so as to seek out the pathways of transforming darkness into light. In describing the artist in "She Belongs to Me" Dylan paints an intriguing portrait of the artist:

"...She's got everything she needs
She's an artist, she don't look back
She can take the dark out of the nighttime
And paint the daytime black."[939]

This vision of the artist is Hebrew not Greek, for she is not Janus-faced because "She's an artist, she don't look back". Rather the artist has the visionary capacity to "take the dark out of the nighttime/And paint the daytime black" which is an alchemical feat realized only by the Gnostic Artist. From Dylan back to the scripture that he cannot escape, we encounter another Jewish Artist as Original Vagabond, who wanders with the Israelites through the desert. This Jewish Artist, Bezalel creates in the divine shadow, never quite getting the spiritual plans ahead of time that Moses sees in his prophetic revelation. There is something to the presence of Bezalel who is at the right place at the right time, so that he wins the building competition without even entering! Bezalel is more than merely a glorified site manager who must supervise those working on the Tabernacle project, rather by virtue of his wisdom he has been blessed with the same divine traits that created the universe.[940] *So what exactly sets Bezalel apart from other craftspeople?*

As a Jewish Artist Bezalel exemplifies artistry at the highest level—cosmic artistry. This image of the cosmic artist echoes throughout moments in the bible imagines wisdom as a nursling who delights the Creator: "Then I was by Him, as a nursling; and I was daily all delight, playing always before Him."[941] But this primordial *jouissance* is transformed into skillful means in the rabbinic imagination. Just as an architect creates a building by contemplating the floor plans, God creates the world by contemplating the Torah.[942] Bezalel exemplifies artistry at the highest level as a function of his proximity as an artist to the divine.[943] After all his name means "in the divine shade", a sentiment common in the Ancient Near East as a theophoric name that parents would choose to ensure their child is swaddled in the divine sheltering presence.[944] Bezalel manifests a certain kind of "skillful means"[945] which enables the "joining things together so as to give birth to something lofty and new, which was not given in the details."[946]

This biblical foundation of the archetypal Jewish artist and architect stands in stark contrast to the Jewish Artist Chaim Potok's popular novel, *My Name is Asher Lev,*[947] or even more recently in the popular Israeli TV series, *Shtisel.* As a Jewish Artist, Asher wants to express the creative flight of his soul through his art— the only symbol he has at his disposal is the crucifixion. And so at a major exhibition in New York, Asher displays the two paintings of his mother that employ the crucifix. These paintings evoke an overwhelming sense of horror and shame felt by both his parents as well as by the general Ladover hasidic community. The Ladover Rebbe calls Asher into his office, asking him to leave the community. Banished, Asher moves back to Paris. And so Asher Lev as the artist exemplifies a deeply Jewish translation of the otherwise Joycean Portrait of the Artist as a Young Man, now as a Portrait of the Young Hasid as Artist![948] Whereas Phillip Roth's Nathan Zuckerman seeks to flee his Jewish identity through assimilation into the dead end American landscape of New Jersey, Asher Lev remains ensconced in his identity even while in exile from his vibrant New York community. Whereas the impulse for assimilation and its discontents is what drives Roth's artist to flee his Jewish identity, the impulse for creative tension within Judaism is what drives Potok's artist.

In this sense, shifting from the American Jewish artist to the Israeli Jewish artist, there is a continuity between Potok's Asher Lev and the protagonist, Akiva played by Michael Aloni in *the new series, called, Shtisel, which also* opens a brief window into a Portrait of the Young Hasid as Artist. Here Akiva is the *haredi* twenty-something, loner *luftmensch,* who resides with his widowed father, Reb Shulem Shtisel, played by Doval'e Glickman. Bereft, hurting and yearning all to themselves in the *haredi* neighborhood of Mea Shearim, this father and son share meals and cryptic conversation at the compact kitchen table.[949] Then in episode seven of the first season of *Shtisel*, Akiva musters the courage to paint his self-portrait. This is a watershed moment that changes his trajectory and reveals a part of his concealed self, all the while he remains lost within his hometown Mea Shearim community. Kiva may be lost, but he can only find himself by navigating this creative tension between tradition and heresy.

It is precisely amidst this creative tension that both the novel *My Name is Asher Lev*, and the *Shtisel* series poignantly encapsulate how the Jewish artist on the margins of a traditional community navigates the push and pull of religious expectations and spiritual inspiration. In one final act the young Hasidic artist, Akiva Shtisel aka Kiva, paints his way out of his insular community by offering his a figurative painting to enter a gallery competition run by another ex-*hasid* which he miraculously wins. The struggle comes as the award ceremony approaches along with gala that includes other artists, the donors and the gallery owner. Will this hasidic artist accept the award and the ensuing solo exhibition? Moreover, will Kiva's father join this celebration? As a portrait of the young man as a Jewish artist, Asher Lev goes further than a self-portrait, by actually painting a portrait of Jesus on the cross with the face of his mother. So here on exhibit we have Mother, Father and Son all together in a heretical trinity—Potok knows how to grab us, as if to say that visual art is the gateway to heresy.

Is the situation of the Jewish artist really that different from any other artist coming from a religious community? Consider for example, James Joyce's classic, *A Portrait of the Artist as a Young Man*[950] published as a serial from 1914-15, it tells the story of the artist as protagonist named, Stephen Daedalus, a young boy growing up in Ireland at the end of the nineteenth century. As he begins to awaken as an artist, Daedalus gradually casts off all his social, familial, and religious constraints to live the artist's life. Daedalus' foray into the world of unrestricted desire that manifests in masturbation, gluttony, and visits to prostitutes unleashes a storm of guilt and shame as he tries to reconcile his physical desires with his austere Catholic morality. How long can the artist abrogate his religious upbringing? For Daedalus it shifts while on a three-day religious retreat, as he hears a trio of fiery sermons about sin, judgment, and hell. Emerging from this retreat, the artist is deeply shaken and inspired to rededicate himself to a life of piety, attending Mass every day, becoming a model of Catholic piety, abstinence, and self-denial. As his religious devotion reaches fever pitch, the director of his school asks him to consider entering the priesthood. The artist living the austere priestly life ultimately feel incompatible with his love for sensual beauty, like simply walking on the beach and observing the beauty of a young girl wading in the tide. Struck by such beauty, Daedalus' epiphany is that the love and desire of beauty should not be a source of shame. So as an unconventionally pious artist, Daedalus resolves to live his life to the fullest, without being constrained by the boundaries of his family, his nation, and his religion. What is intriguing and feels universal in the challenges faced by this Catholic artist is that he is determined to create an independent existence that liberates his from the familial expectations and religious projections of his unique cultural context.

So what is the price the artist is willing to pay in order to be truly free? Here Joyce is cluing us in to the possible pathways of the Catholic artist, whose namesake is instructive. As the mythical Daedalus, this Catholic artist seeks to recuperate his angelic wings to fly away from the conflict so as to transcend these particularities that hold him back from being the artist he was meant to be. Recall in Greek mythology that Daedalus is the one who shows Theseus how to escape the Labyrinth, so that Theseus can then kill the Minotaur and escape the Labyrinth. Minos then shuts Daedalus and his son Icarus in the Labyrinth although he is released by Pasiphae. The crux of his namesake emerges in the moment when Daedalus is unable to sail away, because Minos controlled the ships, and so in response, Daedalus fashions wings of wax and feathers for himself and for Icarus and escaped to Sicily alighting on these waxen wings. While Icarus is immolated by his flying too close to the Sun, Minos pursues Daedalus to Sicily only to be killed there by the daughters of Cocalus with whom Daedalus was staying. Daedalus emerges as an icon for the Greeks of the historic age of buildings and statues in search of origins amidst a long lost past.[951] Joyce indubitably enjoyed introducing this irony that in naming his artist protagonist after a phase of early Greek art, Daedlic sculpture, that Stephen serves as the ultimate iconoclast.

By contrast, as a Jewish Artist who creates with divine blessing, Bezalel accomplishes his calling within community. Even though Bezalel deals with earthly materials that arouse all kinds of desire, as a Jewish artist, he knows how to weave them together to achieve the necessary direction, correctly interpreting each detail. Bezalel realizes the abstract significance of the Tabernacle as a whole[952] he sees what today we might call the *Gestalt* of the project. Sitting in a very different position than his fleeing counterpart, the Catholic artist, Stephen Daedalus, the authentic Jewish artist, *par excellence*, Bezalel, does not fly away, rather he sits in the creative tension. While Daedalus seeks nothing more than to fly away from the conflict with the particularities of his religio-cultural upbringing and surroundings, by contrast, Bezalel sits in the shade of this dilemma without flying away. It is possible to piece together a likely divine archetype from scripture of that force which provides shade to the artist. For example, biblical archetypes commonly imagine the divine as great bird,[953] with the strength of an eagle, whose prowess can both liberate the Israelites from Egypt[954] and provide protection to the individual seeker in moments of deepening darkness. [955] More broadly, the word field of *tzel* as a scriptural archetypes symbolizes the protection provided by shade as well as the transitory nature of a shadow.[956] It is important to contrast the malicious side of shade as the shadow within darkness of *hoshekh* as opposed to the beneficent side of shade as shelter in *tzel*.[957] What emerges in the biblical imagination salient to the archetype of Bezalel is the shadow of the divine. [958] It follows that if the human being is not only created in the divine image[959] but emerges as the shadow of the divine, then human nature itself oscillates between this spectrum of light and darkness.[960]

For Bezalel's realization of the Tabernacle then this very act of the artist realizing a creation through skillful means is a process of "the higher mind that descends into the human sphere but is not born of it, which implies that the higher mind is an animal, that ideas and intuitions are winged bodied with quick-beating hearts that can strike us with claws and tearing beaks."[961] Being enwrapped by the winged animal, like the archetypal eagle, is to feel "the physical force of the metaphysical". [962] While it is Bezalel who builds the Tabernacle, the site where the divine presence hovers, it is Moses who is then enabled by this creation to see the divine face to face. This reminds us that "[o]nly the eagle, it is said, can look directly into the sun, as Moses into the face of God, and only the eagle cannot be killed by lightning."[963] The eagle as the artist has the capacity to "wing among the lightning flashes untouched, forever, no more falls".[964] In amplifying the archetype of the winged creature, the eagle now resonates with further descriptions of luminosity amidst the shade: *"blindingly bright, white, blue, luminous, center of the air, royal, lightning, awe…"*[965] It is in this sense that the Jewish artist is a gnostic, full of luminosity in the shade of the divine demiurge. In his capacity of artist who builds and oversees the project of the Tabernacle, Bezalel serves as the divine messenger who at once strips us of all material embroilments through the *intellectus agens*[966] that has the power to unite the spiritual and the material and brought heaven and earth closer together, creating a sort of "middle world".[967] This inter-world bridges the microcosmic human being and the absolute, elevated spiritual world. No wonder that upon completion of the task, "there was rejoicing in the heavens as on the day the world was created".[968]

Building on this contrast between American and Israeli portrayals of the Jewish Artist as a young man, we now fast forward a few millennia to the rebirthing of the modern State of Israel, Rav Avraham Isaac Kook (1865-1935), who is the first religious Zionist to accept secularity as a tool of divine providence, and to see within the secular arts something sacred. Visual art, for

Kook, undermines and thus re-configures a traditional Judaism that is nothing if not completely concealed in the thicket of legal minutia. What Rav Kook realizes quite intuitively is just how much modern Judaism has become artless. This critique of exilic Jews as an "artless" people results in the exhibition of Jewish artists at the *Fifth Zionist Congress* in 1901.[969] Rav Kook's re-construction of tradition through an appreciation of art comes to the fore in a number of places and remains worthy of further reflection.

The necessity of being immersed in art and aesthetics for Kook is a way of being and navigating the universe of all sentient beings, for: "...every aesthetic order of life, every endeavor to arouse one's aesthetic sense [as well as] all visions and ideas, desires and imaginings... are much more influenced by the constant emanations [of the supernal will] than by the value of human deeds.[970] More than merely a Romantic vision of the primacy that arts and aesthetics play in quotidian life, here Kook is building a mystical vision that includes "all visions and ideas, desires and imaginings" of all sentient beings. This inclusive embrace of arts and aesthetics emerges from "the constant emanations [of the supernal will]" and is not dependent upon "the value of human deeds". The Jewish Artist is thus a channel for this influx of divine inspiration, akin to being a sort of prophet.

The arts themselves thus need to be viewed as *sacred*. Sacred arts for Kook means that there is an intimate connection between the source of all inspiration and the vehicles through which this inspiration emanates: "Literature, painting and sculpture are due to express all the spiritual concepts which are imbedded in the human psyche, and as long as any phase hidden in the psyche has not been expressed, there is an obligation for the work of art to express it." [971] There is a recurring theme of "skillful means" that enable this flow of the influx of spiritual inspiration from the source through the soul of the artist. What concerns Rav Kook in this model of vertical effulgence is the not only the pristine nature of the source but more importantly, the reliability of the artist as channel, for as he writes: "It is impossible for a truly significant literature to come into being in the world and appear with a light of life except by means of the manifestation of the light of return, which renews the face of the entire world." [972]   Jewish literature cannot succeed without the sanctification of the souls of [its] authors. Any author who does not toil to cleanse his character, to purify his deeds and his ideas until his inner world will itself be filled with light and he can sense an inner perfection within it, together with [one's] concern for perfecting whatever [within oneself remains] lacking and [with one's goal to] be filled with humility mixed with might and tranquility of spirit [mixed] with a strong intellectual and emotional arousal to improve and perfect one's self, as well as an elevated yearning to stand at the height of exalted purity and holiness—as long as one is not on such a level, one cannot be truly called an author. [973]

The spiritual qualia necessary for true creativity are articulate by Rav Kook as a way of ensuring that the channeling of this inspiration is not corrupted by the ego and other agendas. For an artist to be sitting in this mind-state, it is necessary to be continuously working on the self, emptying so as to make space for the fullness of the divine influx of inspiration. This posturing of the Jewish Artist can be seen in its precedent within the Torah Scribe, for as Rav Kook sees it: "Only the early [generations] were called scribes because they counted the letters in the Torah".[974] [That] counting of the letters of the Torah raised them to an elevated level of purity of spirit and might of the soul, until the same "scribes" was fitting for them. If we wish to revive Jewish literature, we must traverse this holy path, proceeding from [the direction of] holiness to literature. "There will be a highway and a pathway there, which will be called the holy pathway…and the redeemed will traverse [it]".[975] The pathway that Rav Kook envisions the Jewish Artist opening and traversing is the redemptive pathway returning to the sacred. If every sentient being is an emanation and expression of the ongoing, creative flow within the universe, then the purpose of sacred arts is to reflect and channel this expansive view of creation. Rav Kook encapsulates this tension between the particular and the universal in his own inimitable way as follows: "It is necessary to show how one may enter the palace: by way of the gate. The gate is the divine dimension disclosed in the world, in all its phenomena of beauty and grandeur, as manifested in every living thing, in every insect, in every blooming plant and flower, in every nation and state, in the sea and its turbulent waves, in the panorama of the skies, in the talents of all creatures, in the thoughts of writers, the imagination of poets and the ideas of thinkers, in the feelings of every sensitive poet, and in the heroic deeds of every person of valor. The highest domain of divinity toward which we aspire—to be absorbed in it, to be included in its radiance—but which eludes all our longing, descends for us into the world, and we encounter it and delight in its love, and find peace in its tranquility."[976]

From these reflections on the role of the Jewish Artist, we can fill out the concrete implications of such theorizing through the letters Rav Kook wrote in support of the *Bezalel Art Academy* in Jerusalem. Penned while serving as rabbi in Jaffa, this 1908 letter, for example, is intriguing on a number of levels. The role of this *Bezalel Art Academy* that Kook envisions has a "holy purpose: to ornament not desecrate, to create not destroy..."[977] There is a remarkable celebration here of the diverse talents of "aesthetic and artistic ingenuity" that are meant to "find a rightful place along the expansive boulevards and the heights of universal life" embodied in Jerusalem as a holy city as an energetic center of creativity.[978] Rav Kook evokes the poetic prophecy of Ezekiel[979] where the fruit shall provide nourishment and the leafs for healing, but this is referring to a larger messianic vision of redemption: "And by the river upon the bank thereof, on this side and on that side, shall grow every tree for food, whose leaf shall not wither, neither shall the fruit thereof fail; it shall bring forth new fruit every month, because the waters thereof issue out of the sanctuary; and the fruit thereof shall be for food, and the leaf thereof for healing". This redemptive project of rebuilding the Land of Israel needs sacred arts to be accomplished: "...it is important to continue to have many students from the children of Zion to learn these honorable crafts, from the multiple branches that extend from the Tree of Life of creativity and art..."[980]

Given Kook's traditionalist trajectory, notice that his view of Jewish art is couched in a discussion about love. Love as the supreme energizing force of the universe remains the foundation of romantic notions of artistic expression as well as a religious category. It is important to realize, as Magid points out, that Rav Kook distinguishes between "love of God's creation" and "love that is intrinsic to the human soul" that "loves the Absolute Good," both of which have the same root. The struggle of exile, both collective and personal, is the inability of that intrinsic love to be liberated from its concealed state and express itself in devotion to God. This implies that the artist's life and work become the primary vehicle for redemption. Due to the artist's love of nature—namely, creation created by the Creator—that is externalized and so concretized in the work of art itself.

And so it becomes evident that Kook's view of the artist is a departure from the exclusivist rabbinic model of law as the sole vehicle of Jewish covenantal living.[981] Such covenantal living, for the halakhic legalist is expressed through a love of creation because God *created it*; while the artist loves creation because God *lives in it.* Kook understands intimately that there is an abiding rabbinic reticence about art in the Old *Yishuv* that cannot be escaped. While Kook tries as he might to embrace and include the Old *Yishuv* piety closer to his expansive vision of the sacred arts, he also intimately feels the impossibility of confining artistic expression to binding forms of normative life that these older forms of piety embraced. For Rav Kook, it is precisely in those hidden things (the intrinsic love that is the fluttering of the human soul) whose concealment is destructive are given a tool like art, with which to unearth and once again conceal themselves.

Full disclosure of this intrinsic love may temporarily rupture the necessary forms of normative life (i.e., *halakha*) that the Old Yishuv piety could not see beyond. Therefore, this inspired, creative love temporarily emerges and re-submerges into the soul, like the oscillating cosmic light.[982] Kook's struggle is familiar insofar as he too wonders just how much the Jewish Artist can express the expansiveness of the soul while also allowing for necessary withdrawal? This existential question that affects aesthetics is brought to the fore in Kook, for the Jewish Artist is the necessary tragic figure who will fail—why? The Jewish Artist will necessarily and invariably rupture of the moral vessels that need correction, so she will be rejected by those who protect the tradition. How then can visual art, who destroys what needs to be rectified, who undermines the normative structure of Jewish devotion, function as a redemptive trope?

"But to live outside the law, you must be honest"[983] – could there be any stronger description of the Jewish Artist's desire to destroy what needs to be rectified, to undermine the normative structure of piety as a redemptive trope? Dylan's songbook attempts to continuously hover and wander in this space outside the law that demands honesty and integrity. Recently, I have been wondering if there is a lack of integrity binding Dylan's songbook to his visual art. There is an apparent separation that exists between Dylan's songbook and his visual art that does not necessarily figure directly into the presentation or perception of his music. Dylan comments on his recent paintings that: "If there is a soundtrack to this compilation of paintings, I would say it could be recordings by Peetie Wheatstraw in some places, Charlie Parker in others, Clifford Brown or Blind Lemon, maybe Guitar Slim – artists that make us a lot bigger when listening to them. It would have to be that way. Absolutely." But the artistic process of painting proved important early on for Dylan as he faced writer's block as a musician. Aside from his romantic involvement with artist, Suze Rotolo, it was Dylan's 1967 encounter with New York painter, Bruce Dorfman, who freed him to re-open the creative fonts again.[984] Not only were these fonts opened by the daily immersion with the musical caravan surrounding Levon Helm in Woodstock at this time, but also it required time communing with nature and fellow artists like Dorfman.

This shift into the painterly modality is evident in Dylan's lyrics, for example in "Brownsville Girl" which presents the romantic, vagabond adventure of Henry and Ruby as they are running away from the world: "I can still see the day that you came to me on the painted desert."[985] The quick lyrical description of Ruby is nothing if not painterly: "Brownsville girl with your Brownsville curls/Teeth like pearls shining like the moon above."[986] But can these appearances as evoked in Dylan's lyrics be trusted as portraying reality or some more romantic vision? How much can these renderings be trusted? Although, as a gnostic artist, Dylan knows all too well how "appearances can be deceiving" still when the Halcyon Gallery approached him with the idea of his own renderings of American landscapes for an exhibition, he took it to heart and ran with it. While Dylan's songbook paints its own acoustic masterpiece of the American landscape, his visionary landscape is that sees "the key to the future is in the remnants of the past… That you have to master the idioms of your own time before you can have any identity in the present tense. Your past begins the day you were born and to disregard it is cheating yourself of who you really are." His approach to painting is deceptively simple, insofar as he claims that: "These paintings are up to the moment realism – archaic, most static, but quivering in appearance. They contradict the modern world. However, that's my doing." And this is precisely a salient feature of the Jewish Artist—to contradict the modern world, insofar as s/he continues searching for the luminosity in all things at all times in a darkening world more interested in information technology than luminosity.

Dylan returns to the *camera obscura* method invented in the 1600s which projected an image upside down so the painter could work from it, so his hands could paint what his eyes might not necessarily see. Following and acknowledging the precursor pathways of Caravaggio, Van Eyck and Vermeer, Dylan builds on the *camera obscura* with a real camera. Dylan also understands that to paint one's masterpiece, that: "[a]n expert painter is a master in color theory, which means he can turn white into black using a complex value system of colors and hues like a Mark Rothko." In commenting on his own paintings, Dylan claims that "the watercolors and acrylics done here purposely show little or no emotion, yet I would say they are not necessarily emotionally stringent." He explains as a painter that this is an "attempt was made to represent reality and images as they are without idealizing them. My idea is to compose works that create stability, working with generalized, universal and easily identifiable objects" like Kandinsky and Rouault. His approach to painting is to "depersonalize the works – strip them of illusion." In painting "basic structures to express feelings and ideas" Dylan restricts himself "to traditional subject matter viewing nothing as shallow or gaudy" namely, that luminosity abides in all things. Dylan's painting invite every American vagabond to return to the place they have long left behind, for "[i]f the viewer visited where the picture actually existed, he or she would see the same thing. It is what unites us all."[987]

On tour between 1989 and 1992, Bob Dylan drew a series of portraits, interiors, landscapes, nudes and street scenes to "relax and refocus a restless mind", collected as *Drawn Blank*, 1994. These works of *Drawn Blank* were intended to serve as the basis for paintings, and once Ingrid Mössinger proposed an exhibition, this encouraged Dylan to now complete this task with watercolour and gouache. These drawing now become the paintings of *The Drawn Blank Series* whereby the delicacy of the drawings express the different colors and tones within a dynamism of impressions, feelings and emotions all in the same images. As Tobias Rüther (*Frankfurter Allgemeine* newspaper), who credited Dylan with successfully translating his songs into art, commented: "That which he's done for years on the stage— performing new versions of his old songs in order to give a fresh interpretation— he's now continuing on deckle-edged paper." [988]

Alas, only the Jewish artist—wholly peculiar and unconventional — can truly recognize, absorb, and support the artistic impulse within the moral vessels of the law which serve to prevent its complete eradication, allowing for a gentler rupture.[989] This is precisely the challenge facing all artists of skillful means who care for the soul. To sit in the shadow of Bezalel, Asher Lev, Kiva Shtisel and Reb Shabetai Zissel ben Avraham is to find the pathway to refract our artistic impulse within the tradition that may also reach beyond it. Dylan, like Bezalel, is a Jewish Artist as Original Vagabond, wherein his higher mind is an animal, his lyrical and painterly intuitions are winged bodied with quick-beating hearts. What the great gnostic artist discovers in his own original face is that yearning to return to original luminous, astral body forgotten from Eden. The gnostic impulse pulsates as a deep need of being seen and heard from deckle-edged paper to vinyl in every moment of its luminosity.

Purim, 5778
Panui (San Francisco, California)

Afterword:

Unmasking the Mask of Unmasking: Dylan's Jewish Gnosis

Dylan lyrics analyzed include: "Shelter from the Storm," (*Blood On the Tracks*, 1974); "Night After Night," (Special Rider Music, 1987); "Forgetful Heart," (*Together Through Life*, 2009); "When the Night Comes Falling from the Sky," (*Empire Burlesque*, 1985); "Dirge," (*Planet Waves,* 1973); "Huck's Tune," (*Tell Tale Signs,* 2007); "Abandoned Love," (*Biograph,* 1975); 1975); "Things Have Changed," (*Essential Bob Dylan*, 1999); "It's Alright, Ma (I'm Only Bleeding)," (*Bringing It All Back Home*, 1965); "I'm Not There" (1967); "Drifter's Escape," (*John Wesley Harding*, 1968); "Absolutely Sweet Marie," (*Blonde on Blonde*, 1966); "Outlaw Blues," (*Bringing It All Back Home*, 1965); "If Dogs Run Free," (*New Morning*, 1970); "The Ballad of Frankie Lee and Judas Priest," (*John Wesley Harding*, 1968); "Tight Connection to My Heart (Has Anyone See My Love)" (*Empire Burlesque*, 1985); "All Along the Watchtower" (*John Wesley Harding*, 1968); "Silvio," (*Down in the Groove*, 1988); "Gates of Eden" on Bob Dylan, *The Bootleg Series,* vol. 6: *Bob Dylan Live, 1964, Concert at Philharmonic Hall* (2004).

Afterword:

Unmasking the Mask of Unmasking: Dylan's Jewish Gnosis

"Suffering is the fleetest animal that bears you to perfection."   —Meister Eckhart[990]

"Better to associate with people who consciously lie, for only they can also be consciously truthful. Usually, truthfulness is a mask that is *not conscious of being a mask.*"   — Friedrich Nietzsche[991]

Aubrey Glazer has graciously asked me to contribute an afterword to his *God Knows, Everything is Broken*, an innovative and impassioned investigation of what he calls the *Great Gnostic Americana Songbook of Bob Dylan*. I will pick up some threads of his argument in the spirit of the afterword, the word that comes after because it has come before, the afterthought that is thought in the wake of the thinking of the other. I am grateful for this opportunity to give voice to my own entanglement with Dylan these many years, offering some sense of the brokenness that is the one thing that persists in its unbrokenness. Everything is broken indeed—even these broken words never meant to be spoken.

In "Abandoned Love" (1975), Dylan muses, "Everybody's wearing a disguise / To hide what they've got left behind their eyes." Differentiating himself from those who participate in the masquerade, Dylan insists he cannot cover who he is and that he will follow the children wherever they go. Notwithstanding the inversion of the Pied Piper archetype, the travesty of detecting that every face is nothing but another mask hiding a face that is a mask leads to his resignation: "I've given up the game, I've got to leave / The pot of gold is only make-believe / The treasure can't be found by men who search / Whose gods are dead and whose queens are in the church."[992] Years later, Dylan similarly concludes "Huck's Tune" (2007), "In my words, you'll find no guile / The game's gotten old / The deck's gone cold / And I'm gonna have to put you down for a while."[993] If there is no guile in the poet's words, it is because in the poetic space, truth can be uttered only through the dissimulation of truth as untruth. Thomas Aquinas famously wrote in *Summa Theologiae* that it is more beneficial for the divine mysteries to be revealed to uncultured people (*rudi populo traderentur*) under the veil of figures (*sub quod figurarum velamine*) so that they may know those mysteries implicitly. Just as human reason fails to grasp poetic expressions on account of the lack of truth in them (*propter defectum veritatis qui est in eis*), so it fails to grasp divine matters perfectly on account of the sublimity of the truth they contain (*propter excedentem ipsorum veritatem*), and hence in both cases there is a need for representation by sensible figures (*repraesentatione per sensibiles figuras*).[994] Leaving aside the distinction made in this passage between the poetic lacking truth and the divine containing a truth that is transcendent, Aquinas's insight that both demand the representation of truth through the veil of figurative images that are not literally true is noteworthy. In my assessment, it is this insight above all else that justifies the use of the term *gnostic* as an appropriate taxonomy to discuss Dylan's poems and songs.[995] The wisdom was conveyed in the statement in the Valentinian *Gospel of Philip*, "Truth did not come into the world nakedly; rather, it came in prototypes and images: the world will not accept it in any other form."[996] The philosophic principle that undergirds this statement is the teaching attributed to

Anaxagoras that things of a similar nature are attracted to one another, or in the Empedoclean formula of "like knowing like."[997] Thus, we read explicitly in a second passage from this gnostic treatise:

> "People cannot see anything in the real realm unless they become it. In the realm of truth, it is not as human beings in the world, who see the sun without being the sun, and see the sky and the earth and so forth without being them. Rather, if you have seen any things there, you have become those things: if you have seen the spirit, you have become the spirit; if you have seen the anointed (Christ), you have become the anointed (Christ); if you have seen the [father, you] will become the father. Thus [here] (in the world), you see everything and do not [see] your own self. But there, you see yourself; for you shall [become] what you see.[998]

The author of this text applies the epistemological axiom to the world of truth in contrast to the sentient world. Truth cannot be received in this world except through the investiture of an image because the world is dominated by the deception that prevents one from seeing and thereby becoming the truth. In a world governed by guile, truth can only appear in the likeness of what it is not, which is to say, there can be no truth but through the truth of untruth. The extreme implication of this insight is drawn by Dylan in "Things Have Changed" (1999), "All the truth in the world adds up to one big lie."[999] From this devastatingly pessimistic assumption, there follows a second crucial dimension of the gnostic orientation that is discernible in Dylan as well: if there is any possibility for redemption, it must be sought outside the confines of history. As Dylan intoned in "It's Alright, Ma (I'm Only Bleeding)" (1965), "Disillusioned words like bullets bark / As human gods aim for their mark / Make everything from toy guns that spark / To flesh-colored Christs that glow in the dark / It's easy to see without looking too far / That not much is really sacred."[1000] The cynicism of youth brought Dylan to the point of gnostic disillusionment with the world as a place that could yield permanent and unwavering meaning. If nothing is sacred, time cannot be redeemed by time. More of this as we proceed, but for our immediate purposes, we must stay focused on the aforementioned image of the game. Has Dylan given up the game? Has the game grown so old that it must be abandoned?

Dylan has surely not given up the game; quite to the contrary, he is a masterful player in the game, or better, he has succeeded in determining the guidelines of the game in which he participates. He has found the treasure, we might say, precisely because he has pretended so well not to be searching for the treasure. In the game, the quest not to quest is the ultimate quest; to discover that there is no treasure is the greatest treasure to uncover. Still, we must ponder how are we to understand the contours of this game? Is this the most felicitous locution to name the pretense the poet has promulgated these many decades? Here it is apposite to recall the words of Derrida, "Play is always lost when it seeks salvation in games."[1001] The contrast between play and game relates to the fact that the latter displays rules, which by nature are subject to generalization, whereas the former is incalculably random and therefore irreducibly singular. This "dialectical confiscation"[1002]—the "disappearance of play into games"—ensues when the particular is placed under the stamp of the universal, a move that obscures the playfulness of play. Like the act of writing, play has no essence and thus as soon as it comes into being, it erases itself.[1003] Utilizing this standard of what cannot be affirmed without being negated, we can say that Dylan is consummately playful, dissembling in the manifold semblances of his dissembling, changing forms and resisting reification of the playfulness into a game governed by discernible rules and regulations. As he pointedly put it in the brutally honest and yet decidedly deceptive "I'm Not There" (1967), "No, I don't belong to her, I don't belong to anybody / She's my Christ forsaken angel but she don't hear me cry / She's a lone hearted mystic and she can't carry on / When I'm there she's alright but she's not when I'm gone."[1004] The poet is intermittently there by perpetually not being there.

In this sense of belonging by not belonging, we find the key to understand Dylan's Jewishness. We may apply to Dylan the enigmatic remark of Derrida, "the less you are Jewish, the more you are Jewish" (*moins on est juif, plus on est juif*).[1005] Dylan's Jewish identity relates to the dissociation of self that renders the self, paradoxically, "*at once* as less Jewish and as most Jewish [*d'autant moins juif et d'autant mieux juif*]."[1006] Many have written about Dylan's relationship to Judaism, but none, to the best of my knowledge, have considered the topic from this perspective as counterintuitive as it might seem. But what does it mean to say that the less one is Jewish, the more Jewish one is? How is one concomitantly most Jewish and least Jewish? Minimally, this suggests that identity is to be sought in a ceaseless process of making and unmaking. The Jew is indexical of the self that is at home everywhere because it is nowhere at home. Beyond ethnic, cultural, or religious demarcation, the

Jew exemplifies the homelessness of being at home in the homeliness of being banished from home. The condition of the Jew may be compared to the drifter described by Dylan in the "Drifter's Escape" (1968). In a Kafkaesque rendering of Job, the drifter, who does not know what he has done wrong, is condemned in a trial by a cursed jury and a sympathetic but inept judge. In the end, a bolt of lightning strikes the courthouse out of shape, allowing the drifter to flee while everyone knelt to pray.[1007] Bracketing the irony that the begging for mercy on the part of those who were pitiless forestalls the meting out of judgment to an innocent man, we note that the meteorological intervention saves the drifter from an unwarranted punishment but not from the fate of being a drifter. Indeed, the escape can be seen as further evidence of the inevitability of the drifter's itinerant status. The word "escape" in the title of the song thus assumes a double connotation: dodging the jury's retributive sentence and marking his comportment as the fugitive endlessly in flight.

Dylan, I suggest, is that fugitive, honest enough to live outside the law,[1008] the drifter par excellence, destined to a peripatetic life befitting the existential predicament of the Jew. Like the depiction of the divine presence after the destruction of the Temple in the poignant image of one zoharic text, the wandering is so far-reaching and exhaustive that it does not even leave a trace of its footsteps in the dust.[1009] The gnostic underpinning of the obliteration of the trace is articulated by Heidegger in his surmise about the last god and the silent dignity of expectation assigned to him, "You may wander through each and every being. Nowhere does the trace of god show itself."[1010] It is precisely in the nonshowing that the godship of the last god will show itself. In a way intriguingly reminiscent of the Jewish belief that the possibility of the messiah's coming is predicated on the impossibility of the messiah's arrival, the hope in the return of what is interminably still to come, the quintessential event of the nonevent,[1011] Heidegger maintains that the lastness of the last god implies that the god is constantly coming, which engenders a state of continual waiting, albeit a waiting for that which leaves no trace. This description brings to mind Heidegger's contention that the ontological difference between being and beings— that which fosters the event of metaphysics— commences with an "early trace" (*die frühe Spur*) that "is extinguished through presencing, appearing as something present and emerging as the highest of beings that are present. ... The difference between being and the being, however, can be experienced as something forgotten only if it is unveiled along with the presencing of what is present; only if it has left a trace, which remains preserved in the language, to which being comes."[1012]

The origin of being is a trace of the presencing occluded in what is present, the oblivion of being that forgets the ontological difference between being and beings, an obfuscating of the obfuscation that can be uncovered through the recovery of language as the naming of the being that is nameless. The trace at the beginning presumes that the origin is an event or happening of a presence of being that can never be present and therefore is erroneously described as absent.[1013] As Derrida rightly emphasized in his exposition of this Heideggerian motif,[1014] the trace is a trace of the erasure of the trace—the arche-trace[1015]— that disappears in its appearance and appears in its disappearance. The trace of the origin that Heidegger placed at the beginning is not a phenomenal trace of a plenary presence, but a nonphenomenal trace of what can never be present, a trace of a trace of the being that is otherwise than being, the erasure that is the inception of writing, not as a token of difference but as a stroke of *différance*, the originary repetition of the non-self-identical other that cannot be reduced to the same.[1016] The trace of the erasure of the trace corresponds to what I have suggested with respect to the inherently exilic condition of the Jew as the one that leaves no trace but the trace of having no trace, a trace that cannot even be found in the dust of one's footsteps. Lest one consider this ontic disposition of possession by dispossession a romanticization of diasporic Judaism, I would hasten to note that living within the boundaries of the modern nation state of Israel is not exempt from the experience of being homeless in one's homeland. On the contrary, the most acute form of alienation may arise from the anxiety associated with the sense of being displaced in the country of one's emplacement.

It is precisely this identity of nonidentity that propels Dylan's playfulness more generally, the constant donning and discarding of masks. The very identity that has sustained Dylan for decades from the beginning was naught but a mask, a mask that has revealed his identity by concealing it, but even more critically, a mask that has masked his mask of anonymity. Tellingly, in the Philharmonic Hall concert on October 31, 1964, he said to the audience, "It's just Halloween. I have my Bob Dylan mask on. I am masquerading."[1017] What are we to make of this sarcastic aside? How does one wear the mask of who one is? How does one masquerade by impersonating one's own persona? As it happens, on that occasion, the young minstrel imparted to his unsuspecting spectators—perhaps unwittingly—the deep philosophical wisdom that one may elicit from the Halloween ritual: *behind every mask is a face that is another mask.*

An enduring theme in Dylan's oeuvre is precisely this gnosis concerning the mask as the artifact that conceals by revealing and reveals by concealing. We may go so far as to say that life can be compared to a dream wherein there is no face of which to speak that is not a mask disguising itself as a face.[1018] In the recently released Scorsese documentary *Rolling Thunder Review: A Bob Dylan Story*, Dylan remarks, "If someone's wearing a mask he's gonna tell you the truth. If he's not wearing a mask, it's highly unlikely." Prima facie, we would have expected the opposite: only when one is not wearing a mask can we anticipate the transparency that the truth will be spoken. Dylan gives witness, however, to the gnostic truism that truth is exposed through the cloak of truth that is the untruth. There is nothing transparent but the opacity of the delusion of the transparent. The polysemous nature of truth is such that when one lifts the veil, one does not expose the truth unveiled but rather reveals another veil revealing the truth in the veiling of what is untrue. It is customary to speak of the naked truth to designate an ultimate truth stripped of all duplicity. A truth that is truly naked, however, is denuded of truthfulness and is thus not phenomenally accessible as truth. Visibility of truth is commensurate to the garment in which it is attired. Nudity can neither evince nor conceal the truth. Hence, lifting the veil, presumably to see the face laid bare, amounts to discerning that there is no way to see the face but through the veil of the face. The unveiled is veiled in the unveiling of what is veiled. The final veil to unveil, accordingly, is the veil that there is final veil to unveil.

This is the import of Dylan's comment that the truth will be spoken only by one who is masked: truth is disclosed most transparently when there is nothing to be manifest but the non-manifestation of the nothing that is manifest. In the end, we can mutter underneath our breath together with the little neighbor boy in "The Ballad of Frankie Lee and Judas Priest" (1968), who "walked along, alone with his guilt so well concealed," that "nothing is revealed."[1019] Nothing is revealed because there is no truth but the possibility of something to be revealed. Alluding to this gnosis in "Outlaw Blues" (1965), Dylan counsels "Don't ask me nothin' about nothin', I just might tell you the truth."[1020] The only way to a positive truth is through the annulling intimation of the double negative— nothing about nothing. The artist, and above all the poet, is endowed with the charge to speak this negation of negation. The poetic task to symbolize what is real by sensuous images of what is not real—to render the factual as metaphorical and the metaphorical as factual—stems from the self-deception that engenders the contrived similarities of the dissimilar, the unmasking of the mask in masking the unmasked in the perspectival pretext of truth subject to being untrue. Dylan's gnostic Judaism is anchored in the blurring of the line that separates the virtual and the actual: what is imagined to be real is really imagined. As Dylan muses about the act of *poiesis* in the deviously simplistic "If Dogs Run Free" (1970), "My mind / Weaves / A Symphony / And tapestry / Of rhyme / Oh, winds which rush my / Tale to thee / So it may flow / And be / To each his own / It's all unknown."[1021] In this domain of irreality where what is known is that everything is unknown, not only are speaking truth and fabricating untruth not antithetical but the former requires the latter. Hence, to speak truth one must be masked because there is no truth but untruth camouflaged as truth. The mission of the artist, as Dylan has well understood, is to maintain the illusion of truth in the truth of the illusion.

The temporal deportment of the aesthetic mandate partakes of the apocalyptic spirit cultivated by Jews through the centuries, a temperament that stems from the infinite negativity of time, the impossible possibility that makes it always possible that the future that is coming threatens not to be the future one has anticipated. The philosophic import of the melancholic nature of the asymptotic curvature of messianic time, and by extension of the finitude of temporality more generally, finds a deep resonance in Dylan's oeuvre. The hopelessness of hope proceeds from the fact that the future we are awaiting can never transpire in time and the homeland we are coveting can never materialize in space. The hope imparted by the messianic belief thus renews itself sporadically as the hope deferred perpetually. Neither pessimism nor optimism seem apposite to categorize the bestowing of hope through its suspension, a pure futurity that would be compromised if the future were ever to abandon its status as that which is present only by being absent and absent only by being present. Hope can be envisioned as the unremitting projection of an elementally calibrated retrospection, to foretell what has been in the recollection of what is to come. Every undertaking, on this score, occasions a relapse of what never was, divulging thereby the deportment of time as the recurrence of the same difference that is differently the same, the loop of the double negative that yields the positivity of our becoming the being we are not, a tendency well understood through the centuries by mystic visionaries.

Dylan's melancholic vision has drawn its inspiration from the gnostic awareness that there can be no truth that is not itself untruth, no rectitude that is not tinged with mendacity, no pleasure that does not have an edge of pain.[1022] Enlightenment in the intrinsically unredeemable world—a world of "steel-eyed death" where "men are fighting to be warm"[1023]— entails casting light on the shadow so that the shadow is illumined as light. Unlike the gnostics of old, Dylan rejects the feasibility of escaping the murky and transient domain of appearance by fleeing to a realm of radiant and everlasting truth. "Night after night," writes Dylan, "you look for salvation you find none."[1024] There is nothing but the nocturnality of exile from which one finds no deliverance. In this darkness, there is no truth to behold but that there is no truth to behold. The surpassing of the shadow, accordingly, involves abiding within rather than dispelling the shadow. The gnostic sensibility is captured agonizingly in the words "Forgetful heart / Like a walking shadow in my brain / All night long / I lay awake and listen to the sound of pain / The door has closed forevermore / If indeed there ever was a door."[1025] The pain of love lost is so piercing to the heart that the possibility of there ever having been an opening is queried and distrusted. What is dark is not dissolved in brightness; it remains concealed as it is manifest in the light. One dwells inceptually in the essential space of a dark light, in the wasteland of the mind where night comes falling from the sky.[1026] Dylan's poetic vision has illumined the dark light of this wasteland by uncovering the shadow as shadow.

In "Tight Connection to My Heart (Has Anyone See My Love)" (1985), Dylan bluntly affirms the gnostic rejection of meaning in this life: "I'll go along with the charade / Until I can think my way out / I know it was all a big joke / Whatever it was about / Someday maybe / I'll remember to forget."[1027] The depiction of everything as a big joke recalls the second stanza of "All Along the Watchtower" (1968): "'No reason to get excited,' the thief, he kindly spoke / 'There are many here among us who feel that life is but a joke / But you and I, we've been through that, and this is not our fate / So let us not talk falsely now, the hour is getting late.'"[1028] At this juncture, Dylan eschewed—temporarily at least—the derisive posture that life is naught but the subterfuge of life. The urgency to overcome such skepticism is spurred by the apocalyptic sense that the hour is getting late, that the judgment is imminent. Years later, Dylan declares that, alas, it is all a big joke, even if he cannot delineate the exact nature of the ploy of "this version of death called life," as he put it in "Huck's Tune."[1029] The only hope is that maybe one day he will remember to forget, a paradox that requires one to bring to mind what must be expunged from the mind, much like the biblical command to Moses to inscribe in a book the obligation to wipe out the memory of Amalek from under heaven (Exodus 17:14). To remember to forget still holds out a shimmer of hopefulness—as the thirteenth-century kabbalist Abraham Abulafia observed "the end of forgetfulness is the beginning of remembrance"[1030]— but to forget to remember to forget is to be thrust deeper into darkness, to be plunged deeper into the abyss of exile, the "hollow place where martyrs weep and angels play with sin."[1031]

The one brave enough to descend to that void, to listen to the irredeemable despair of the echo of no voice, is afforded the possibility of being emancipated by beginning to remember not to forget. In the showing of the nonshowing, the mantle of truth shrouds itself, and what is finally exposed is the occlusion occluded in its exposure. When one does not know that the divine is hidden in the world in which the divine is revealed, there ensues a double concealment, a concealment of the concealment, but when one knows that the divine is hidden, then the concealment is revealed as concealment and there is no concealment but the concealment divulged in the façade of concealment. Herein consists the unmasking of the mask of unmasking at the heart of Dylan's Jewish gnosis—the mark of the trace of the erasure of the trace, the trace of nothing to be traced but the trace effaced in the imprint of its effacement, the replication of difference in the belonging together of what is irresolutely congruous in virtue of being resolutely incongruous, the signpost of each moment as the heterogeneous intermingling of stasis and change whereby the constancy of the constant is determined by the indeterminacy of the intermittent and the indeterminacy of the intermittent by the constancy of the constant. Time is overcome not in the obliteration of time but in the enowning of the ubiquity of time expended kenotically as that which lingers in the lapsing of lingering and lapses in the lingering of lapsing. To be in time is to be there by not being there, neither present in the absence of being present nor absent in the presence of being absent, always the same because always different.

— **Elliot R. Wolfson**
(University of California, Santa Barbara)

Endnotes

Preface

[1] See Dave Van Ronk and Elijah Wald, *The Mayor of Macdougal Street: A Memoir*, (Philadelphia, PA : Da Capo Press, 2013).

[2] Bob Dylan, "Master of War," (*The Freewheelin' Bob Dylan,* 1966).

[3] Bob Dylan, "Tangled Up in Blue" (*Blood on the Tracks,* 1974).

[4] *Ibid.*

[5] Bob Dylan, "Every Grain of Sand," (*Shot of Love*, 1981).

[6] Bob Dylan, "Visions of Johanna," (*Blonde on Blonde,* 1966).

[7] Bob Dylan, "Tombstone Blues," (*Highway 61 Revisited*, 1965).

[8] Bob Dylan, One More Cup of Coffee (Valley Below)," (*Desire*, 1975).

[9] Bob Dylan, "A Hard Rain's A-Gonna Fall," (*Freewheelin' Bob Dylan*, 1963).

[10] Bob Dylan, "I'm not there," *The Bootleg Series, Vol. 11: The Basement Tapes Complete*, 2014).

[11] "...go out and play the same thing every night, differently." No written source found as this was conveyed to me orally.

[12] See Aubrey L. Glazer, *Tangle of Matter & Ghost: Leonard Cohen's Post-Secular Songbook of Mysticism(s) Jewish & Beyond*, (Briton, MA: Academic Studies Press, 2017).

[13] Bob Dylan, "Absolutely Sweet Marie," (*Blonde on Blonde*, 1966).

[14] Martin Scorsese, *Rolling Thunder Revue: A Bob Dylan Story by Martin Scorsese,* (2019).

[15] Bob Dylan, "Not Dark Yet," (*Time Out of Mind,* 1997).

[16] Bob Dylan, "Visions of Johanna," (*Blonde on Blonde*, 1966).

[17] Bob Dylan, "I'm not there," *The Bootleg Series, Vol. 11: The Basement Tapes Complete*, 2014).

Author's Preface

Acknowledgements: Thanks to Sherre Hirsch and Michael Palgon for encouraging this preface and to Martin S. Cohen for his critical feedback.

[18] Bob Dylan, "Desolation Row," (*Highway 61 Revisited*, 1965).

[19] Harold Bloom, *The American Religion*, 2nd edition, (New York: Chu Hartley Publishers, 2006), p. 19. [19] In the course of this book, I will engage and build upon the extended critique of Bloom's *The American Religion*. For now, suffice it to note that many important studies have emerged since its publication that critique and challenge its findings including but not limited to: Jonathan Kirsch "Probing America's Religions - *The American Religion: The Emergence of the Post-Christian Nation,* by Harold Bloom," *New York Times Book Review* (May 20, 1992); Jay P. Dolan, "In Whose God Do We Trust?" *New York Times*, (May 10, 1992); Robert N. Bellah, "The Looming Triumph of Gnosticism" in *New Oxford Book Reviews* (October 1992); as well as these book length studies, including: Catherine L. Albanese, *Republic of Mind and Spirit: A Cultural History of American Metaphysical Religion.* (Yale University Press, 2008); Robert N. Bellah, *Habits of the Heart: Individualism and Commitment in American Life.* (Berkeley: University of California Press, 2008), especially, the revised preface; as well as John L. Modern, *Secularism in Antebellum America: With Reference to Ghosts, Protestant Subcultures, Machines, and Their Metaphors: Featuring Discussions of Mass Media, Moby-Dick, Spirituality, Phrenology, Anthropology, Sing Sing State Penitentiary, and Sex with the New Motive Power.* (University of Chicago Press, 2015). Regarding Bloom's application of Gnosticism as a lens for religious criticism, see most recently, David Brakke, *Gnostics - Myth, Ritual, and Diversity in Early Christianity* (HUP, 2012); April D. DeConick, *The Gnostic New Age: How a Countercultural Spirituality Revolutionized Religion from Antiquity to Today.* (New York, NY : Columbia University Press, 2017).

[21] This "Janus-faced" quality of two faces, secular and sacred, is encapsulated eloquently first by Ellen Willis, "Before the Flood," [1967], in Ellen Willis and Nona W. Aronowitz, *Out of the Vinyl Deeps: Ellen Willis on Rock Music,* (Minneapolis: University of Minnesota Press, 2011), p. 7.

[22] Harold Bloom, personal communication (e-mail: August 13, 2018).

[23] Antoine Faivre, " 'Gnosis' as Term and Concept in the Esoteric Movement of the Modern West: An Attempt at Periodization," in G. W. Trompf, Gunner B. Mikkelsen, Jay Johnston, Milad Milani, Jason BeDuhn, and Brikha Nasoraia, ed's., *The Gnostic World.* (Abingdon, Oxon; New York: Routledge, 2019). pp. 409-425, esp. pp. 419-420; see also, William Christie, "British Romanticism: Gnosticism Longings," in *ibid*, p. 461; Peter Otto, "William Blake, the Ancient Gnostics, and the Birth of Modern Gnosticism," in *ibid,* p. 468; Christopher Partridge, "Modern Psychedelic Gnosis, *ibid,* p. 652.

[24] Bob Dylan, *Love and Theft,* 2001.

[25] Ellen Willis, "The New Talking World War III Blues," [October 2001], in *Out of the Vinyl Deeps: Ellen Willis on Rock Music*, p. 76.

[26] Willis, "The New Talking World War III Blues," [October 2001], in *Out of the Vinyl Deeps: Ellen Willis on Rock Music*, p. 73.

[27] *Ibid,* p. 75.

[28] *Ibid,* p. 73.

[29] *Ibid,* p. 73.

[30] *Ibid,* p. 73.

[31] For a good introductory survey, see G. W. Trompf, Gunner B. Mikkelsen, Jay Johnston, Milad Milani, Jason BeDuhn, and Brikha Nasoraia. *The Gnostic World*, (Abingdon, Oxon ; New York: Routledge, 2019).

[32] Jonathan Z. Smith, *Imagining Religion: From Babylon to Jonestown.* (Chicago: The University of Chicago Press, 1982), p. xi.

[33] Smith, *Imagining Religion*, p. xiii.

[34] *Ibid,* p. 120.

[35] I have explored the correlation of post-secularism and music at length elsewhere, see Aubrey L. Glazer, *Tangle of Matter & Ghost: Leonard Cohen's Post-Secular Songbook of Mysticism(s) Jewish & Beyond*, (Briton, MA: Academic Studies Press, 2017).

[36] Bob Dylan, "Desolation Row," (*Highway 61 Revisited*, 1965). I am indebted to the generative discussion of the dedicated Dylan community surrounding "Desolation Row", see http://www.expectingrain.com/dok/atlas/desolationrow.html (accessed 4/15/18).

37 On this divide between viewing Gnosticism as a multifaceted religious movement versus the existence of a Gnostic school of thought, see David Brakke, *The Gnostics: myth, ritual and diversity in early Christianity,* (Harvard university press: Cambridge, 2010), p. 90: "I have argued that there was no widespread, multifaceted religious movement called "Gnosticism" in antiquity, but that there was a Gnostic school of thought, one group among the several that proclaimed that Jesus of Nazareth had brought salvation to human beings. In the second century, when the Gnostics emerged and became recognized as a community, Christians will still very few."

38 David Brakke, *The Gnostics: myth, ritual and diversity in early Christianity,* (Harvard University Press: Cambridge, 2010), p. 53.

39 April D. Deconick, *The Gnostic New Age: how a countercultural Spirituality revolutionized religion from antiquity to today,* (New York: Columbia University Press, 2016).

40 John L. Modern, *Secularism in Antebellum America: With Reference to Ghosts, Protestant Subcultures, Machines, and Their Metaphors : Featuring Discussions of Mass Media, Moby-Dick, Spirituality, Phrenology, Anthropology, Sing Sing State Penitentiary, and Sex with the New Motive Power.* (University of Chicago Press, 2015).

41 Modern, *Secularism in Antebellum America,* p. 45.

42 *Ibid,* p. 45.

43 *Ibid,* p. 46.

44 Bob Dylan, "Man in the Long Black Coat," (*O Mercy,* 1989).

45 David Brakke, *The Gnostics: myth, ritual and diversity in early Christianity,* (Harvard University Press: Cambridge, 2010), p. 53.

46 Brakke, *The Gnostics: myth, ritual and diversity in early Christianity,* p. 3.

47 *Ibid,* p. 70.

48 Bob Dylan, "What Can I Do For You," (*Saved,* 1980). *Contra* Margotin and Guesdon, *Bob Dylan: All the Songs: the Story Behind Every Track,* 487, who fall into the trap of a reductionist

reading of these lyrics "in the form of a new prayer originating in his newfound faith in Jesus Christ, Bob Dylan here expresses thanks to God, who has given everything to him..." as well as boiling the rest of the song down to being nothing but a paraphrase of Saint Paul's Epistle to the Ephesians (6:16). This kind of reading reduces the complexity of the masks being dawned and discarded as well as the hybridity of identity through the gnostic mask that I will maintain throughout this entire analysis. See also, *ibid:* "It's Alright Ma (I'm Only Bleeding)," (*Bringing It All Back Home*, 1965): "Make everything from toy guns that spark/To flesh-colored Christs that glow in the dark"; "Need a Woman", (*Bootleg Series* Vol 1-3, 1982): "Seen you turn the corner, seen your boot heels spark/Seen you in the daylight, and watched you in the dark"; "Nettie Moore" (*Modern Times*, 2006): "The bright spark of the steady lights/Has dimmed my sights"; "Last Thoughts on Woodie Guthrie, (*Bootleg Series* Vol 1-3, 1982): "And yer train engine fire needs a new spark to catch it/And the wood's easy findin' but yer lazy to fetch it"; ibid, with Robert Hunter, "Jolene," (*Together Through Life*, 2009): "Those big brown eyes, they set off a spark/When you hold me in your arms things don't look so dark"; "Simple Twist of Fate," (*Blood on the Tracks*, 1974): "As the evening sky grew dark/She looked at him and he felt a spark tingle to his bones"; "Only a Pawn In Their Game", (*The Times They Are a Changin'*, 1963): "A handle hid out in the dark/A hand set the spark".

[49] Job 5:7

[50] Brakke, *The Gnostics: myth, ritual and diversity in early Christianity*, pp. 74-83.

[51] Bob Dylan, "Man in the Long Black Coat," (*O Mercy*, 1989).

[52] See Valentinus' "Summer Harvest", as quoted in Brakke, *The Gnostics: myth, ritual and diversity in early Christianity*, p. 101. See also Harold Bloom, *The Anxiety of Influence: A Theory of Poetry*. (New York: Oxford University Press, 1997).

[53] Brakke, *The Gnostics: myth, ritual and diversity in early Christianity*, p. 103.

[54] Ellen Willis, "Before the Flood," [1967], in *Out of the Vinyl Deeps: Ellen Willis on Rock Music*, pp. 4-5.

[55] Nat Hentoff, "The Crackin', Shakin', Breakin', Sounds," *The New Yorker* (October 24, 1964) collected in *Bob Dylan, the Essential Interviews: The Essential Interviews*, ed. Bob Dylan and Jonathan Cott, (New York: Wenner Books, 2006), pp. 22-23.

56 Willis, "Before the Flood," [1967], *Out of the Vinyl Deeps: Ellen Willis on Rock Music*, p. 19.

57 This excerpt is from Irenaeus' lament about Valentinus, see Brakke, *The Gnostics: myth, ritual and diversity in early Christianity*, p. 117.

58 I have devoted an entire book to explicating Adorno's "musical thinking" and its relation Jewish thinking, see Aubrey L. Glazer, *A New Physiognomy of Jewish Thinking: Critical Theory After Adorno As Applied to Jewish Thought.* (London: Continuum, 2011).

59 Brakke attributes the genius of Gnosticism to its proclivity for reinvention, see Brakke, *The Gnostics: myth, ritual and diversity in early Christianity*, p. 137: "...the Gnostic school of thought, as small and limited as it was, played an important role in the process by which Christians, even today, continually reinvent themselves, their ideas, and their communities in light of their experience of Jesus Christ." In Dylan's case, the continual reinvention of stage persona is in light of his own subjective mystical experience. For a brief history of ideas overview of the role of music within Gnosticism, see Joscelyn Godwin, "Music and Gnosis," in G. W. Trompf, Gunner B. Mikkelsen, Jay Johnston, Milad Milani, Jason BeDuhn, and Brikha Nasoraia, ed's., *The Gnostic World.* (Abingdon, Oxon; New York: Routledge, 2019). pp. 688-692.

60 Brakke, *The Gnostics: myth, ritual and diversity in early Christianity*, p. 101.

61 *Ibid*, p. 101; see also Dirk Baltzly, "*Stoic Pantheism*" in *Sophia*, Vol. 42, No. 2, (Ashgate Publishing Ltd, October 2003):

"I conclude that the Stoic view should be classified as a form of pantheism. The cosmos forms a single individual. This is god. The term 'god' is also used to refer to the means by which this global individual acts upon itself in bringing about its own periodic history-cycles. God in this sense is to be identified with the active principle, *pneuma* and the chain of causes and effects that is termed 'fate'."

See https://sites.google.com/site/thes toiclife/articles-of-interest/stoic-pantheism (accessed 10/23/18)

62 Catherine L. Albanese, *A republic of mind and spirit: A cultural history of American metaphysical religion* (Yale University press New Haven, 2007).

63 Harold Bloom, *The American Religion,* (New York, NY: Chu Hartley Publishers, 2006).

64 Albanese, *A republic of mind and spirit*, pp. 149-150.

65 *Ibid,* p. 516.

66 Bob Dylan, "Man in the Long Black Coat," (*O Mercy*, 1989).

67 Bob Dylan with Robert Hunter, "Forgetful Heart," (*Together Through Life*, 2009).

68 Robert N. Bella, *Habits of the heart: individualism commitment in American life,* (University of California press, 1985, revised edition 2008), Preface the 2008 edition, xi.

69 Perhaps the inspiration behind protagonist, Llewyn David is really Dave Von Ronk's memoir, see Dave Van Ronk and Elijah Wald, *The Mayor of Macdougal Street: A Memoir*, (Philadelphia, PA : Da Capo Press, a member of the Perseus Books Group, 2013). But the Coen brothers hold that their protagonist remains an original creation.

70 This very American expression of James Carville's was chiseled onto then president elect, Bill Clinton's Democratic campaign office whiteboard, even if the stock market more often than not predicts presidential election outcomes with a six-month lead, see Jerry Wagner, "It's the Economy, Or Are We Stupid," *Seeking Alpha*, https://seekingalpha.com/article/ 4208618-economy-stupid (accessed 11/11/18); Rudy Giuliani, "It's the Economy, stupid,"*Journal Of Libertarian Studies* 19.4 (2005): 19-36; see also "Why It's Not the Economy, Stupid," *Politics*, (09/08/18), https://www.rollcall.com/news/ politics/why-its-not-the-economy-stupid (accessed 11/11/18).

[71] Bella, *Habits of the heart,* Preface to 1996 edition, p. xv.

[72] Ibid, p. xv.

[73] See for example, Michael J. Gilmour, *Tangled Up in the Bible: Bob Dylan & Scripture.* (New York: Continuum, 2004).

[74] Bob Dylan, "Not Dark Yet," (*Time Out of Mind,* 1997).

[75] Bella, *Habits of the heart,* Preface to 1996 edition, p. xxxi.

[76] See for example, Morgan Enos, "Bob Dylan's Whiskey & 6 Other Times He Entered the Marketplace," Billboard (4/30/2018), see: https://www.billboard.com/artic les/columns/rock/8413364/bob-dylan-whiskey-other-products (accessed 11/08/18)

[77] Rick Henderson, "The False Promise of the Prosperity Gospel: Why I Called Out Joel Osteen and Joyce Meyer." *The Huffington Post* (2013); Kate Bowler, *Blessed: A history of the American prosperity gospel.* Oxford University Press, 2018; William C. Symonds, Brian Grow, and John Cady, "Earthly empires: How evangelical churches are borrowing from the business playbook," *Business Week* 3934 (2005): 78-88.

[78] Bella, *Habits of the heart,* Preface to 1996 edition, p. xxxii.

[79] *Ibid*, p. xxxii.

[80] Bella draws his final question from Ezekiel 36:26, where the prophet declares: "I will take out of your flesh heart of stone and give you a heart of flesh".

[81] Bob Dylan, "It's Alright Ma (I'm Only Bleeding)," (*Bringing It All Back Home,* 1965).

[82] Shaul Magid, *American Post-Judaism: Identity and Renewal in a Postethnic Society.* (Bloomington, IN: Indiana University Press, 2013).

[83] Bella, *Habits of the heart,* Preface to the first edition, p. xlvii-liii.

[84] Ellen Willis is the first to refer to Dylan's "sudden removal of the mask", see Willis, "Before the Flood," [1967], *Out of the Vinyl Deeps: Ellen Willis on Rock Music,* p. 20.

[85] *Ibid, Habits of the heart,* p. 286.

[86] Bob Dylan, "It's Alright Ma, (I'm Only Bleedin')" (*Bringing It All Back Home,* 1965); see above n176.

[87] Bob Dylan, "When You Gonna Wake Up," (*Slow Train Coming,* 1979).

[88] Christopher Partridge, "Modern Psychedelic Gnosis" in G. W. Trompf, Gunner B. Mikkelsen, Jay Johnston, Milad Milani, Jason BeDuhn, and Brikha Nasoraia, ed's., *The Gnostic World.* (Abingdon, Oxon; New York: Routledge, 2019). pp. 652-662.

[89] April D. Deconick, *The Gnostic New Age: how a countercultural Spirituality revolutionized religion from antiquity to today*, (New York: Columbia University Press, 2016).

[90] Deconick, *The Gnostic New Age*, p. 344.

[91] *Ibid,* p. 347.

[92] *Ibid,* p. 347.

[93] The earlier gnostic awakenings being medieval, late fifteenth century, and nineteenth century

[94] *Ibid,* pp. 347-350.

[95] *Ibid,* p. 347.

[96] On Canadian Jewish mysticism, see Glazer, *Tangle of Matter & Ghost: Leonard Cohen's Post-Secular Songbook of Mysticism(s) Jewish & Beyond*, pp. 26-60; on the case of the American seeker who self-identifies as SBNR (Spiritual-But-Not-Religious) vs. Canadian TBNR (Traditional-But-Not-Religious), see, Aubrey L. Glazer, "Traditional But Not Religious," *Canadian Jewish News*, (September 9, 2018).

[97] Robert W. Corrigan, "The Soulscape of Contemporary American Drama," *WT* 11: 316.

[98] Vincent Tinto, "Learning communities: Building gateways to student success." *The National Teaching and Learning Forum.* Vol. 7. No. 4. 1998.

[99] Deconick, *The Gnostic New Age*, p. 4.

[100] *Ibid,* p. 4.

[101] Willis, "The New Talking World War III Blues," [October 2001], p. 73.

[102] *Ibid,* p. 4.

[103] *Ibid,* p. 5.

[104] *Ibid,* p. 21.

[105] *Ibid,* pp. 22-35.

[106] *Ibid,* pp. 35-38.

[107] *Ibid,* pp. 38-50.

[108] *Ibid,* p. 49.

[109] *Ibid,* p. 49.

[110] *Ibid,* p. 21.

[111] *Ibid,* p. 59.

[112] *Ibid,* p. 59.

[113] *Ibid,* p. 60.

[114] *Ibid,* p.66.

[115] *Ibid,* pp. 187-191; pp. 248-249.

[116] *Ibid,* pp. 191-194.

[117] This is the topic of "person as path, soul as process" is part of a much larger, forthcoming investigation into process theology, see for example, Aubrey L. Glazer & Elyssa N. Wortzman, *Sacred Symbiosis: Person as Path, Soul as Process* (San Francisco, February 24, 2019).

[118] Willis, "The New Talking World War III Blues," [October 2001], p. 67.

[119] Bob Dylan, "Jokerman," (*Infidels*, 1983).

[120] Bob Dylan, "Man of Peace," (*Infidels*, 1983).

[121] Deconick, *The Gnostic New Age*, p. 71.

[122] Bob Dylan, "Positively 4th Street," (*Bob Dylan's Greatest Hits*, 1965).

[123] Deconick, *The Gnostic New Age*, p. 71.

[124] *Ibid*, pp. 73, 167.

[125] *Ibid*, p. 167.

[126] *Ibid*, p. 75.

[127] "When Americans Say They Believe in God, What Do They Mean?" *Pew Research Center* (April 25, 2018), see:

http://www.pewforum.org/2018/04/25/when-americans-say-they-believe-in-god-what-do-they-mean/ (accessed 11/26/18).

[128] *Ibid.*

[129] *Ibid.*

[130] "Nearly eight-in-ten U.S. adults think God or a higher power has protected them, and two-thirds say they have been rewarded by the Almighty. By comparison, somewhat fewer see God as judgmental and punitive. Six-in-ten Americans say God or a higher power will judge all people on what they have done, and four-in-ten say they have been punished by God or the spiritual force they believe is at work in the universe." *Ibid.*

[131] Deconick, *The Gnostic New Age*, pp. 91-92.

[132] Robert Alter, tr. *The Five Books of Moses: A Translation with Commentary*, (New York: W.W. Norton & Co, 2008) n26, p.18-19.

[133] *Ibid*, pp. 183, 215-216, 219-221.

[134] Arthur Rimbaud, *Lettres Du Voyant* <<A Georges Izambard>> (Charleville, 13 mai 1971), *Oeuvres de Rimbaud*, Suzanne Bernard, and André Guyaux ed, (Paris: Ed. Garnier Freres, 1960), pp. 343-344.

[135] Arthur Rimbaud, *Lettres Du Voyant* <<A Georges Izambard>> (Charleville, 13 mai 1971), *Oeuvres de Rimbaud*, Suzanne Bernard, and André Guyaux ed, (Paris: Ed. Garnier Freres, 1960), pp. 343-344; compare with Clinton Heylin, *Dylan: Behind the Shades,* (London: Penguin, 1992), pp. 144-165, esp. p. 151. See Ellen Willis, "Before the Flood," [1967], in *Out of the Vinyl Deeps: Ellen Willis on Rock Music*, p. 2.

[136] Amittai F. Aviram, "Rimbaud: Sex, Verse, and Modernity," *Sexual Politics and Experimental Poetics* in *French Literature Division* (North East Modern Language Association: Pittsburgh, April 1994), see: http://www.amittai.com/prose/rimbaud.php (accessed 11/26/18).

[137] *Ibid.*

[138] *Ibid*, p. 196.

[139] Clinton Heylin, *Dylan: Behind the Shades,* esp. pp. 119-125, 167-170, 426-428, 452.

[140] Deconick, *The Gnostic New Age*, p. 203.

[141] *Ibid*, p. 203.

[142] *Ibid*, pp. 242-243.

[143] *Ibid*, pp. 250.

[144] *Ibid,* pp. 250.

[145] Bob Dylan, "Gates of Eden", (*Bringing it All Back Home,* 1965).

[146] Deconick, *The Gnostic New Age,* pp. 334-335, which translates this prayer from *Left Ginza* III.1 75.17.

[147] Bob Dylan, "Not Dark Yet", (*Time Out of Mind,* 1997).

[148] Deconick, *The Gnostic New Age,* p. 350.

[149] *Ibid,* pp. 350-1.

[150] Bob Dylan, "Every Grain of Sand," (*Shot of Love,* 1981).

[151] Modern, *Secularism in Antebellum America,* p. 23.

[152] *Ibid,* p. 123.

[153] Aubrey L. Glazer, "Bob Dylan, the messiah and personal redemption," *J Weekly* (April 7, 2017), see: https://www.jweekly.com/2017/04/07/bob-dylan-the-messiah-and-personal-redemption/ (accessed 10/18/18).

[154] Recall how the road to redemption traversed by early Gnostics was divided between being a wayfarer (literally, "one of the way" who were Jews devoted to living according to Jewish path as interpreted by Jesus) or a god-fearer (those pagan seekers, whether Greek or Roman, who frequented synagogues and admired monotheistic and ethical ways of Judaism). See Deconick, *The Gnostic New Age,* pp. 111-119.

[155] https://www.expectingrain.com/ (accessed 10/18/18)

[156] Scott M. Marshall, *Bob Dylan: A Spiritual Life,* (Washington, D.C. : BP Books/WND Books, 2017), see also: http://www.scottmmarshall.net/works.htm (accessed 10/18/18).

[157] Modern, *Secularism in Antebellum America,* p. 123.

[158] An expression first used by Leonard Cohen in a preamble to his performance at the Montreal Jazz Festival in 2012, see Glazer, *Tangle of Matter & Ghost,* pp. 179-203.

[159] Bob Dylan, "Desolation Row," (*Highway 61 Revisited,* 1965).

[160] Mark C. Taylor, ed., *Critical Terms for Religious Studies,* (Chicago: University of Chicago Press, 2012), p. 94.

[161] Song of Songs 8:6 (tr. Robert Alter).

[162] Bob Dylan, "Not Dark Yet," (*Time Out of Mind,* 1997).

[163] Psalm 116:11.

[164] John Steinbeck, *Cannery Row,* (London: Mandarin, 1997).

[165] Jack Kerouac, *Desolation Angels,* (London: Penguin, 2012).

[166] Bob Dylan, "Not Dark Yet," (*Time Out of Mind,* 1997).

[167] Erich Neumann, *The Great Mother: An Analysis of the Archetype,* (Princeton: Princeton University Press, 2015).

[168] Matthew Fike, *A Jungian Study of Shakespeare: The Visionary Mode*, (New York: Palgrave Macmillan, 2009), p. 121.

[169] James Hillman and C. G. Jung, *Anima: An Anatomy of a Personified Notion; with Excerpts from the Writings of C.G. Jung*. (Dallas, Tex: Spring, 1986), p. 57.

[170] William Shakespeare, *Hamlet*, Act 4, Scene 7.

[171] Bob Dylan, "You Ain't Goin' Nowhere," *Greatest Hits, Volume II* (1967).

[172] Bob Dylan, "Gates of Eden," *Bringing it all Home* (1965).

[173] Aubrey L. Glazer, *Contemporary Hebrew Mystical Poetry: How It Redeems Jewish Thinking*, (Lewiston, N.Y: Mellen, 2009).

[174] I am indebted to Elliot Wolfson for generously engaging me on this point and enabling me to clarify and focus on a more limited usage of the term Gnosticism within the context of kabbalah as applied to the Dylan songbook over the course of thinking through this book project from San Francisco to Santa Barbara.

[175] Bloom, *The American Religion*, p. 19.

[176] *Ibid*, p. 19.

[177] *Ibid*, p. 19.

[178] *Ibid*, pp. 22-23.

[179] Allen Forte, *The American Popular Ballad of the Golden Era, 1924-1950*. (Princeton, N.J: Princeton University Press, 1995).

[180] Ben Yagoda, *The B Side: The Death of Tin Pan Alley and the Rebirth of the Great American Song*. New York: Riverhead Books, a member of Penguin Group, USA, 2015), pp. 2-3.

[181] Yagoda, *The B Side: The Death of Tin Pan Alley and the Rebirth of the Great American Song*, pp. 2-3.

[182] Bob Dylan, (*Triplicate*, 2017); *ibid, Fallen Angels*, 2016; *ibid*, (*Shadows in the Night*, 2015).

[183] Glazer, *Tangle of Matter & Ghost: Leonard Cohen's Post-Secular Songbook of Mysticism(s) Jewish & Beyond*.

[184] Jack Kerouac, *On the Road*, (New York: Penguin Books, 2011/1967).

[185] Andrea Shea, "Jack Kerouac's Famous Scroll, 'On the Road' Again" https://www.npr.org/templates/story/story.php?storyId=11709924 (accessed 4/13/18)

[186] Willis, "Before the Flood," [1967], *Out of the Vinyl Deeps: Ellen Willis on Rock Music*, p. 9.

[187] Clinton Heylin, *Dylan: Behind the Shades: Take Two*, (London: Penguin, 1992).

[188] Philippe Margotin and Jean-Michel Guesdon, *Bob Dylan: All the Songs: the Story Behind Every Track,* (New York: Black Dog & Leventhal, 2015).

[189] See below n.360.

[190] See below n.313.

[191] I am grateful to Professor Bart Testa, whose seminar on *Semiotics in Film* figured as part of this turning in my approach to religious criticism (Victoria College, University of Toronto: 1993).

[192] Roland Barthes, "The Death of the Author," in *Media Texts, Authors and Readers: A Reader* (1994): p. 166.

[193] *Ibid,* p. 166.

[194] *Ibid,* p. 166.

[195] Richard Kearney, "God After God," in Richard Kearney and Jens Zimmermann, ed's, *Reimagining the Sacred: Richard Kearney Debates God with James Wood, Catherine Keller, Charles Taylor, Julia Kristeva, Gianni Vattimo, Simon Critchley, Jean-Luc Marion, John Caputo, David Tracey, Jens Zimmermann, and Merold Westphal,* (New York: Columbia University Press, 2016), pp. 6-18; Dialogue with James Wood, "Imagination, Anatheism, and the Sacred," in *ibid*, pp. 19-45.

[196] Seth Rogovoy, *Bob Dylan: Prophet, Mystic, Poet.* (New York: Scribner, 2014), p. 8.

[197] Rogovoy, *Bob Dylan: Prophet, Mystic, Poet,* p. 8.

[198] *Ibid,* p. 8.

[199] *Ibid,* p. 9.

[200] Seth Rogovoy, "Was Dylan at his best as a Christian", *The Forward,* (Oct 30, 2017), see: https://forward.com/culture/qa/3 86298/was-bob-dylan-at-his-best-when-he-was-christian/ (accessed 4/13/18)

[201] *Ibid.*

[202] Wertheimer, *The New American Judaism: How Jews Practice Their Religion Today,* (Princeton, NJ : Princeton University Press, 2018), p. 263.

[203] Richard Siegel, Michael Strassfeld, and Sharon Strassfeld, *The First Jewish Catalogue: A Do-It-Yourself Kit.* (Pennsylvania: J.P.S, 1973).

[204] Oral history of this counter-cultural moment is only now being collected by Rabbi Michael Strassfeld at University of Pennsylvannia archives see: http://katz.sas.upenn.edu/news-and-events/new-library-acquisitions-include-early-modern-manuscripts-and-20th-century-papers (accessed 4/16/18). The only other dedicated archive to American Post-Holocaust Judaism is housed at Boulder-University of Colorado which collects the teachings of Reb Zalman Schacter-Shalomi, Rabbi Arthur Waskow and Rabbi Alan Lew, see: https://www.colorado.edu/post-holocaustamericanjudaismcollections/ (accessed 4/16/18).

[205] *Contra* the argument that runs throughout Rogovoy, *Bob Dylan: Prophet, Mystic, Poet.* Compare with the application of "remixing" to American Judaism in Wertheimer, *The New American Judaism: How Jews Practice Their Religion Today*, pp. 254-272. Thanks to Sam Muller for pointing me back to this reference.

[206] *Contra* Philippe Margotin, and Jean-Michel Guesdon, *Bob Dylan: All the Songs: the Story Behind Every Track.* (New York: Black Dog & Leventhal, 2015), p. 570, who suggest that this "...mysterious man in a black coat could be the symbol of a journey, the loneliness of the pilgrim on the road seeking the truth" or even "the incarnation of death."

[207] Rogovoy, *Bob Dylan: Prophet, Mystic, Poet*, p. 11.

[208] Stephen Pickering, *Bob Dylan Approximately: A Portrait of the Jewish Poet in Search of God.* (New York: York, David Mckay, 1975).

[209] Rogovoy, *Bob Dylan: Prophet, Mystic, Poet*, p. 11.

[210] *Ibid*, p. 11.

[211] *Ibid*, p. 11.

[212] Clinton Heylin, *Trouble in Mind: Bob Dylan's Gospel Years, What Really Happened*, (New York: LesserGod Publishers, 2017), p. 27.

[213] Heylin, *Dylan: Behind the Shades: Take Two*, p. 548.

[214] *Ibid*, p. 549.

[215] Rogovoy, *Bob Dylan: Prophet, Mystic, Poet*, p. 12.

[216] *Ibid*, p. 13.

[217] Scott M. Marshall, *Bob Dylan: A Spiritual Life*, (Washington, D.C. : BP Books / WND Books, 2017).

[218] Clinton Heylin, *Trouble in Mind*, pp. 22-23.

[219] *Ibid*, pp. 24-27.

[220] *Ibid,* pp. 24-27.

[221] *Ibid,* p. 24.

[222] *Ibid,* p. 22.

[223] *Ibid,* pp. 368-9.

[224] *Ibid,* p. 29.

[225] *n.a.,* "Paul's Understanding of Isaiah 28 and the Forerunner Ministry," see: https://samuelwhitefield.com/1011/pauls-understanding-of-isaiah-28-and-the-forerunner-ministry (accessed 1/2/2019).

[226] Heylin, *Trouble in Mind,* p. 83-84.

[227] *Ibid,* p. 36.

[228] See Elliot R. Wolfson, *Open Secret: Postmessianic Messianism and the Mystical Revision of Menahem Mendel Schneerson* (New York: Columbia University Press, 2012).

[229] Heylin, *Trouble in Mind,* p. 26.

[230] Compare Heylin, *Trouble in Mind: Bob Dylan's Gospel Years, What Really Happened* where he notes the numerous times Dylan misquotes scripture, with Michael J. Gilmour, *Tangled Up in the Bible: Bob Dylan & Scripture* (New York: Continuum, 2004), whose analysis completely misses this tendency in the Dylan songbook.

[231] Christopher B. Ricks, *Dylan's Visions of Sin,* (Edinburgh: Canongate, 2011), p. 2.

[232] Ricks, *Dylan's Visions of Sin,* p. 6.

[233] See Thomas Jones, "Forget the Dylai Lama", *London Review of Books,* Vol. 25 No. 21, (6 November 2003) https://www.lrb.co.uk/v25/n21/thomas-jones/forget-the-dylai-lama (accessed 4/13/18):

"Taking hold of Dylan's songs by the sin handle has another unfortunate consequence, more pervasive and therefore more damaging than the bias the book shows towards the Christian songs. Viewing them through the prism of sin, Ricks co-opts all Dylan's songs, or at least all those that he writes about, for Christianity. Trying to show that Dylan does not fall into sin, Ricks steers his critical patrol car up a number of dead ends, and has to perform some tricky maneuvers to extricate it; his quarry, meanwhile, has ducked down an alleyway or jumped down a manhole and is nowhere to be seen."

[234] Heylin, *Trouble in Mind,* p. 31.

[235] *Ibid,* p. 29.

[236] *Ibid,* p. 27.

[237] Dan Brown, *The Da Vinci Code.* (New York: Doubleday, 2004).

238 For example, when Dylan confided in Helena Springs about the challenges of his affiliation with the Vineyard Fellowship:

> "One time [Dylan] said to me, "God, it's awfully tight [in here]," and I said, "Yeah, it seems to me like you gotta get out from under it a bit." I felt a lot of pressure [myself] from those people. And also he found a lot of hypocrisy from those people. A lot of the Jesus people…were saying one thing and doing another. He mentioned that to me, too…God, we had a lot of talks about it."

See Heylin, *Trouble in Mind,* p. 81.
239 Michael Williams, *s.v. Gnosticism,* see: https://www.britannica.com/topic/gnosticism
240 Heylin, *Trouble in Mind,* p. 31.
241 *Ibid,* p. 33.
242 Willis, "The New Talking World War III Blues," [October 2001], p. 73.
243 *Ibid,* p. 35.

244 Even though Dylan is not directly analyzed by Godwin, I am inspired by her analysis to make the present claim of the same category, see Joscelyn Godwin, "Music and Gnosis," in G. W. Trompf, Gunner B. Mikkelsen, Jay Johnston, Milad Milani, Jason BeDuhn, and Brikha Nasoraia, ed's., *The Gnostic World.* (Abingdon, Oxon; New York: Routledge, 2019). pp. 688-692.
245 Dinitia Smith "The Heresy that Saved a Skeptic," *New York Times* (June 14, 2003) see https://www.nytimes.com/2003/06/14/books/the-heresy-that-saved-a-skeptic.html (accessed 4/15/18)
246 Elaine H, Pagels, *The Gnostic Gospels*. (New York: Quality Paperback Book Club, 1979/2005).
247 Smith, "The Heresy that Saved a Skeptic," *New York Times* (June 14, 2003).
248 Bob Dylan, "Ain't Talkin'" (*Modern Times*, 2006); see Margotin and Guesdon, *Bob Dylan: All the Songs: the Story Behind Every Track*, p. 653.
249 Smith, "The Heresy that Saved a Skeptic," *New York Times* (June 14, 2003).
250 Jonathan Z. Smith, *Map is not Territory: Studies in the History of Religions.* (University of Chicago Press, 1978).

251 Peter Matthews Wright, "After Smith: Romancing the Text When Maps Are All We Have Left," *Religion & Literature* 42.3(Autumn 2010), 119, see: https://www.academia.edu/3730 965/After_Smith_Romancing_t he_Text_When_Maps_Are_All _We_Possess_ (accessed 4/15/18).

252 Shaul Magid, "Gershom Scholem", *The Stanford Encyclopedia of Philosophy* (Summer 2014 Edition), Edward N. Zalta (ed.), see: https://plato.stanford.edu/archiv es/sum2014/entries/scholem/ (accessed 4/15/18).

253 Daniel Boyarin, *Border Lines: The Partition of Judaeo-Christianity.* (Philadelphia, Pa: University of Pennsylvania Press, 2007), p. 6.

254 Boyarin, *Border Lines: The Partition of Judaeo-Christianity*, p. 6.

255 *Ibid,* p. 224.

256 *Ibid,* p. 225.

257 Bob Dylan, "Ain't Talkin'," (*Modern Times,* 2006).

258 Shai Held, *Abraham Joshua Heschel: The Call of Transcendence*, (Bloomington, Indiana Univ Press, 2014), p. 122.

259 Heylin, *Trouble in Mind*, p. 31.

260 *Ibid,* p. 37.

261 *Ibid, Dylan: Behind the Shades: Take Two*, p. 328.

262 *Ibid*, pp. 616-617, 619, 680.

263 Bob Dylan, "Neighborhood Bully" (*Infidels*, 1983); compare below with no's 493, 542.

264 Richard F. Thomas, *Why Bob Dylan Matters,* (HarperCollins Publishers: New York, 2017), p. 310.

265 Thomas, *Why Bob Dylan Matters,* p. 303.

266 Walt Whitman, *Leaves of Grass,* (New York: Thomas Y. Crowell Publishers, 1902), #4: 177.

267 Bob Dylan, "Narrow Way," (*Tempest,* 2012).

268 Bob Dylan, "Soon After Midnight," (*Tempest,* 2012).

269 Wright, "After Smith: Romancing the Text When Maps Are All We Have Left," *Religion & Literature* 42.3 (Autumn 2010), p. 119.

270 Bob Dylan, "Soon After Midnight," (*Tempest,* 2012).

Introduction: *God Knows, Everything is Broken*

271 Bob Dylan, "God Knows," (*Under the Red Sky*, 1991); *ibid,* "Everything is Broken," (*O Mercy,* 1989); see Philippe Margotin, and Jean-Michel Guesdon, *Bob Dylan: All the Songs: the Story Behind Every Track.* (New York: Black Dog & Leventhal, 2015), pp. 562, 568.

272 Matthew Henry (August 8, 1700), "A Sermon Preached at the Opening of the New Meeting-House at Chester," in *Misc. Works* (1830), p. 1134: "...those therefore that appeal to him upon every trivial occasion, and with a slightly superficial God knows, while they never think of God, nor have any regard to his knowledge, profane his name by taking it in vain..."

273 Joseph Heller, *God Knows*, (New York: Simon & Schuster Paperbacks, 2004/1984), p. 8: 'I have my faults, God knows, and I may even be among the first to admit them, but to this very day I know in my bones that I'm a much better person than He is."

274 Glazer, *Tangle of Matter & Ghost: Leonard Cohen's Post-Secular Songbook of Mysticism(s) Jewish & Beyond*, pp. 20-21, 124, 129, 229, 245.

275 David Remnick, "Leonard Cohen Makes it Darker," *New Yorker* (October 17, 2017). This remarkable essay and interview appeared after my monograph had already gone to press, see n4.

276 On the paradoxical nature of secrecy and its disclosure, I have been inspired by the prolific work of Elliot Wolfson, see for example, Elliot R. Wolfson, "Becoming Invisible: Rending the Veil and the Hermeneutic of Secrecy in the Gospel of Philip," *Practicing Gnosis: Ritual, Magic, Theurgy, and Liturgy in Nag Hammadi, Manichaean and Other Ancient Literature: Essays in Honor of Birger A. Pearson, Nag Hammadi and Manichaean Studies* 85 (2013): pp. 113-135.

277 Willis, "The New Talking World War III Blues," [October 2001], in *Out of the Vinyl Deeps: Ellen Willis on Rock Music*, p. 76.

278 *Ibid*, p. 76.

279 *Ibid*, p. 76.

280 Harold Bloom, *The Daemon Knows: Literary Greatness and the American Sublime.* (New York: Spiegel and Grau, 2016), p. 19.

281 Bob Dylan, "The Times They Are A-Changin'" (*The Times They Are A-Changin'*, 1965); see Margotin and Guesdon, *Bob Dylan: All the Songs: the Story Behind Every Track*, pp. 87-89.

282 Bob Dylan, "Things Have Changed" (*The Essential Bob Dylan*, 1999); see Margotin and Guesdon, *Bob Dylan: All the Songs: the Story Behind Every Track*, p. 690.

[283] Clinton Heylin, *Bob Dylan: Behind the Shades: Take Two*, (London: Penguin, 2001), pp. 119-125; 167-170.

[284] Heylin, *Bob Dylan: Behind the Shades: Take Two*, p. 167.

[285] *Ibid,* p. 191.

[286] *Ibid,* p. 256.

[287] Bob Dylan, "Wedding Song" (*Planet Waves*, 1973); see Margotin and Guesdon, *Bob Dylan: All the Songs: the Story Behind Every Track*, p. 408.

[288] Joan Baez, "Diamonds and Rust" (*Diamonds and Rust*, 1975).

[289] Bob Dylan, "Full Moon and Empty Arms" (*Shadows in the Night*, 2015).

[290] Bob Dylan, (*Triplicate*, 2017).

[291] Marc Dollinger, *Black Power, Jewish Politics: Reinventing the Alliance in the 1960s* (Waltham, Massachusetts : Brandeis University Press, 2018). See review by Glazer in *Religious Studies Review, Booknotes,* (*forthcoming*).

[292] Shaul Magid, *American Post-Judaism: Identity and Renewal in a Postethnic Society.* (Bloomington, Indiana: Indiana University Press, 2013).

[293] There are a number of recent studies which examine the Americanization of the Chabad project of populist mysticism externally and internally through the agency of emissaries. For the former, see Sue Fishkoff, *The Rebbe's Army: Inside the World of Chabad-Lubavitch.* (New York: Schocken Books, 2013), esp. pp. 13, 27, 94, 95, 120, 185, 216; Samuel C. Heilman, and Menachem Friedman, *The Rebbe: The Life and Afterlife of Menachem Mendel Schneerson.* Princeton, N.J: Princeton University Press, 2012); for the latter, see Shaul S. Deutsch, *Larger Than Life: The Life and Times of the Lubavitcher Rebbe Rabbi Menachem Mendel Schneerson.* (New York: Chasidic Historical Productions, 1995); Chaim Miller, *Turning Judaism Outward: A Biography of Rabbi Menachem Mendel Schneerson the Seventh Lubavitcher Rebbe*, (Brooklyn, NY : Kol Menachem, 2014); Avrum M. Ehrlich,

The Messiah of Brooklyn: Understanding Lubavitch Hasidism Past and Present. (Jersey City, NJ: KTAV, 2004); Shaul Magid, *American Post-Judaism: Identity and Renewal in a Postethnic Society.* (Bloomington, Indiana: Indiana University Press, 2013), pp. 50, 116.

[294] Richard F. Thomas, *Why Dylan Matters*, (Glasgow, Scotland: HarperCollins Publishers, 2017), pp. 176-221.

[295] Clinton Heylin, *Judas!: From Forest Hills To The Free Trade Hall*, (New York: Lessergods books, 2016).

[296] Heylin, *Behind the Shades*, p. 549.

[297] I Kings 18.

[298] Maimonides, *Mishne Torah, Hilchot Yesodai HaTorah* 9:3.

[299] *Ibid,* 9:5.

[300] Richard F. Thomas, *Why Dylan Matters*, (Glasgow, Scotland: HarperCollins Publishers, 2017), pp. 427-472.

[301] Bob Dylan, "Long Time Coming" (*Bootleg Series Volume 9: Witmark Demos 1962-64*, 2010).

[302] Michiko Kakutani, "Of Gnosticism and the Spark Within," *New York Times Review of Books* (September 29, 1996), http://www.nytimes.com/books/98/11/01/specials/bloom-omens.html (accessed 1/18/17).

[303] *Ibid,* "Of Gnosticism and the Spark Within," *New York Times Review of Books.*

[304] Milton Steinberg, *As A Driven Leaf* (1939), (New Jersey: Behrman House, 2015).

[305] David Biale, "Historical heresies and modern Jewish identity," *Jewish social studies* 8.2 (2002), p. 124.

[306] Biale, "Historical heresies and modern Jewish identity," p. 126.

[307] *Ibid,* p. 127.

[308] *Ibid,* p. 128.

[309] Harold Bloom, *Omens of Millennium: The Gnosis of Angels, Dreams, and Resurrection.* (New York: Riverside, 1997), p. 10.

[310] See David Yaffe, *Bob Dylan: Like a Complete Unknown*, (New Haven Conn.: Yale University Press, 2013), p. 87. See also, Bob Dylan, "Thunder on the Mountain," (*Modern Times*, 2006): "I'm wondering where in the world Alicia Keys could be/I been looking for her even clear through Tennessee." See Margotin and Guesdon, *Bob Dylan: All the Songs: the Story Behind Every Track*, p. 647.

[311] Gail de Vos, *What Happens Next?: Contemporary Urban Legends and Popular Culture.* (Santa Barbara: Libraries Unlimited, 2012), p. 220.

[312] Alexandra Schwartz, "The Rambling Glory of Dylan's Nobel Speech," *New Yorker*, (June 6, 2017), https://www.newyorker.com/culture/culture-desk/the-rambling-glory-of-bob-dylans-nobel-speech (accessed 2/7/2018)

[313] Harold Bloom, *The Daemon Knows: Literary Greatness and the American Sublime,* (New York: Spiegel and Grau, 2016), p. 19.

[314] Bloom, *The Daemon Knows: Literary Greatness and the American Sublime*, pp. 6, 495.

[315] Christopher Ricks, *Dylan's Visions of Sin*, (Edinburgh: Canongate, 2011).

[316] Michael J. Gilmour, *Tangled Up in the Bible*, (New York: Bloomsbury Publishing, 2004).

[317] Stephen Pickering, *Bob Dylan Approximately: A Portrait of the Jewish Poet in Search of God: a Midrash.* (New York: David McKay, 1975); Greil Marcus, *Bob Dylan: Writings 1968-2010.* (London: Faber, 2011).

[318] Steven Heine, *Bargainin' for Salvation: Bob Dylan, a Zen Master?* (New York: Continuum, 2009).

[319] Seth Rogovoy, *Bob Dylan: Prophet, Mystic, Poet.* (New York: Scribner, 2014).

[320] Sean O'Hagan, "Tangled Up in Bob," *Guardian* (09/21/03), https://www.theguardian.com/theobserver/2003/sep/14/music (accessed 3/4/17)

[321] *Ibid.*

[322] Stephen Hazan Arnof, "Bob Dylan: Prophet, Mystic, Poet," *The Forward,* (December 9, 2009), see: http://forward.com/culture/120548/bob-dylan-prophet-mystic-poet/ (accessed 3/4/17); Stephen Pickering, *Bob Dylan Approximately: A Portrait of the Jewish Poet in Search of God: a Midrash,* (New York: David McKay, 1975); *ibid, Dylan, a Commemoration,* (Santa Cruz, Calif: S. Pickering, 1971).

[323] Stephen Hazan Arnof, "Bob Dylan: Prophet, Mystic, Poet," [*my italics*]

[324] *Ibid.*

[325] *Ibid.*

[326] *Ibid.*

[327] Heylin, *Bob Dylan: Behind the Shades: Take Two*, p. 658.

[328] See Rudolph Bauer, "Dzogchen As Gnosticism: A Phenomenological View" (Washington Center for Consciousness Studies and the Washington Center for Phenomenological and Existential Psychotherapy Studies) https://www.academia.edu/28934840/Dzogchen_As_Gnosticism_A_Phenomenological_View (accessed 1/15/18).

[329] Bob Dylan, "God Knows," (*Under the Red Sky*, 1991); *Contra* Margotin and Guesdon, *Bob Dylan: All the Songs: the Story Behind Every Track*, p. 584, who claim the theme of this song as "a favorite of Dylan's (particularly in his Christian trilogy) is about God as omnipotent and omniscient (God seeing what all of us do and knowing our secrets)." Such a reductionist reading constitutes the aforementioned manhole to be navigated with great care if one is intent on elucidating rather than betraying Dylan's lyrical vision.

[330] Hans Jonas, "Gnosticism, Existentialism, and Nihilism," in *The Gnostic Religion: The Message of the Alien God and the Beginnings of Christianity*. (Boston: Beacon Press [1958] 2001), p. 32.

[331] Bauer, "Dzogchen As Gnosticism: A Phenomenological View"

[332] *Ibid.*

[333] Albert Camus, *L'Homme Revolute*, (Gallimard: Paris, 1951), p. 15.

[334] Bob Dylan, "Absolutely Sweet Marie," (*Blonde on Blonde*, 1966); see Margotin and Guesdon, *Bob Dylan: All the Songs: the Story Behind Every Track*, p. 236, who read this lyric of as manifesting "two characteristic elements of Dylan's art: a series of sexual metaphors and surreal poetry." By contrast, see the nuanced reading suggested throughout Wolfson's prolific studies on "hypernomianism" and especially in the epithet to Elliot R. Wolfson, *Venturing Beyond: Law and Morality in Kabbalistic Mysticism*. (Oxford: Oxford University Press, 2006).

[335] Heylin, *Bob Dylan: Behind the Shades: Take Two*, 145-165; Carrie Jaurès Noland, "Rimbaud and Patti Smith: Style as Social Deviance," *Critical Inquiry* 21.3 (1995), pp. 581-610. Sparser analytical attention however has been paid to the visionary nature of Rimbaud's poetics as an abiding influence upon Dylan's songbook, see Lee Marshall, *Bob Dylan: The Never Ending Star,* (Oxford: Wiley, 2013), p. 102; William Bevan, "On getting in bed with a lion," *American Psychologist* 35.9 (1980), pp. 779-789; Charles Nicholl, *Somebody Else: Arthur Rimbaud in Africa 1880-91*. (University of Chicago Press, 1999).

[336] Lee Marshall, *Bob Dylan: The Never Ending Star*, (Oxford: Wiley, 2013), p. 102.

[337] Arthur Rimbaud and Paul Demeny. *Lettre Dite Du Voyant: À Paul Demeny, Du 15 Mai 1871.* (Paris: Messein, 1954) [my translation].

[338] Jonas, "Gnosticism, Existentialism, and Nihilism," p. 33.

[339] *Ibid,* p. 33.

[340] *Ibid,* p. 334.

[341] *Ibid,* p. 33. Jonas' comment that: "Some connection of Gnosticism with the beginnings of Cabala has in any case to be assumed, whatever the order of cause and effect" is an allusion to the theory of Scholem, see Gershom Scholem, *Origins of the Kabbalah,* (Princeton, N.J: Princeton University Press, 1991); compare with Gershom Scholem, *Jewish Gnosticism, Merkabah Mysticism, and Talmudic Tradition: Based on the Israel Goldstein Lectures, Delivered at the Jewish Theological Seminary of America,* (New York: Jewish Theological Seminary of America, 2012).

[342] Jonas, "Gnosticism, Existentialism, and Nihilism," p. 34.

[343] Bob Dylan, "Everything is Broken," (*O Mercy,* 1989).

[344] Jonas, "Gnosticism, Existentialism, and Nihilism," p. 331.

[345] *Ibid,* p. 334.

[346] "Absolutely Sweet Marie," (*Blonde on Blonde,* 1966), see above n121.

[347] Jonas, "Gnosticism, Existentialism, and Nihilism," p. 323.

[348] *Ibid,* p. 325.

[349] See above, n18. For more on Jonas in relation to Heidegger, see Richard Wolin, *Heidegger's Children,* (Princeton University Press, 2015). It is worth reflecting upon Wolfson's forthcoming analysis of Heideggerian Gnosticism correlated to the Jewish mysticism of Kabbalah has been influenced by his deep engagement with the Dylan songbook, see Aubrey L. Glazer, "What Does Heidegger's Anti-Semitism Mean for Jewish Philosophy?" *Religion Dispatches* (April 3, 2014). http://religiondispatches.org/what-does-heideggers-anti-semitism-mean-for-jewish-philosophy/ (accessed 3/5/17).

[350] Jonas, "Gnosticism, Existentialism, and Nihilism," p. 320.

[351] *Ibid,* p. 331.

[352] Elliot R. Wolfson, "*Gottwesen* and the De-Divinization of the Last God: Heidegger's Meditation on the Strange and Incalculable," M. Björk and J. Svenungsson (eds.), *Heidegger's Black Notebooks and the Future of Theology*, (Springer International Publishing, 2017), p. 223: "…philosophical translation of the gnostic myth, the human being is labelled the alien (*der Fremdling*) vis-à-vis the great fortuitiveness (*der große Zufall*) of being (*das Sein*). The existential state of this alienation is further described as the 'throwing into being' (*der Wurf in das Sein*) and as 'the trembling of the thrownness into the essence as language' (*das Erzittern der Geworfenheit in das Wesen als Sprache*). Language is the hearth of the world wherein one finds 'the uniqueness of the revealing-concealing isolation [*entbergend verbergenden Vereinzelung*] in the simplicity of the aloneness of *Dasein*'. Paradoxically, language is the home that is the place of isolation and aloneness but also the place of unison (*Ein-klang*), the haven of solitude and the womb of relationality."

[353] Wolfson, "*Gottwesen* and the De-Divinization of the Last God: Heidegger's Meditation on the Strange and Incalculable," p. 223.

[354] I am grateful to Wolfson for challenging me to further correlate these lyrics as a way of articulating the gnostic turn away from the prophetic (oral communication: 4/20/18).

[355] Bob Dylan, "Huck's Tune," (*Tall Tell Signs: Bootleg Series 1989-2006*, 2007).

[356] Bob Dylan, "The Lonesome Death of Hattie Carroll," (*The Times They Are A-Changin'*, 1964).

[357] Zvi Ish-Shalom, *The Kedumah Experience: The Primordial Torah*, (Boulder: Colorado, Albion-Andalus, 2017); see also Aubrey L. Glazer, "Zvi Ish Shalom's Primordial Torah….a review by Aubrey L. Glazer," (*Tikkun*, April 17, 2018) https://www.tikkun.org/nextgen/zvi-ish-shaloms-primordial-torah (accessed 4/20/18).

[358] Friedrich Nietzsche, *The Gay Science* (1882, 1887) para. 125; Walter Kaufmann ed. (New York: Vintage, 1974), pp.181-82.

[359] Again I am guided by Wolfson's insight that the gnostic turn is one emptied of all absence— the apophasis of all apophasis.

[360] Jonas, "Gnosticism, Existentialism, and Nihilism," pp. 326-327.

[361] *Ibid*, p. 324.

[362] *Ibid*, p. 327.

[363] *Ibid*.

[364] *Ibid.*

[365] Bob Dylan, "God Knows," (*Under the Red Sky*, 1991).

[366] Heine, *Bargainin' for Salvation: Bob Dylan, a Zen Master?*

[367] Bauer, "Dzogchen As Gnosticism: A Phenomenological View", *n.p.*

[368] For more on this theme of Heidegger's thinking in relation to Vedanta, Taoism, Zen and Tibetan Buddhist philosophy in particular and in general, Heidegger's acquaintance with Asian thought - beginning from his familiarity with the Chuang-lzu as early as 1930 (including his partial translation of the Tao Te Ching into German), see Graham Parkes, ed. *Heidegger and Asian Thought* (Honolulu: University of Hawaii Press, 1987).

[369] Bauer, "Dzogchen As Gnosticism: A Phenomenological View", *n.p.*: "In Dzogchen, as in Heideggerian phenomenology, there are four times. There is (1) the time of the present momentum, (2) there is the time of the past, and (3) there is the time of the future. Most profoundly (4) there is the fourth time, the time of timeless awareness. To be able to be in timeless awareness and then bring forth this dimension into time for ourselves and others is a most wonderful experience and still in time we will find ourselves having facility with being in timeless awareness and in time simultaneously."

[370] Jonas, "Gnosticism, Existentialism, and Nihilism," p. 323.

[371] See Ken McLeod, tr. and Rang-byung-rdo-rje 'Jigs-med-gling-pa. *A Trackless Path: A Commentary on the Great Completion (dzogchen) Teaching of Jigmé Lingpa's Revelations of Ever-Present Good,* (Sonoma, CA: Unfettered Mind Media, 2016).

[372] Jonas, "Gnosticism, Existentialism, and Nihilism," p. 327.

[373] *Ibid,* p. 328.

[374] *Ibid,* p. 329.

[375] Heylin, *Bob Dylan: Behind the Shades: Take Two*, p. 658.

[376] Jonas, "Gnosticism, Existentialism, and Nihilism," p. 333.

[377] See n31 above.

[378] Jonas, "Gnosticism, Existentialism, and Nihilism," p. 335.

[379] *Ibid,* p. 335.

[380] *Ibid,* pp. 338-339.

[381] Margotin and Guesdon, *Bob Dylan: All the Songs: the Story Behind Every Track,* p. 187.

[382] As the Warsaw Ghetto was darkening from the onslaught of the Nazi storm cloud, these words were preached by the Warsaw Ghetto "the song should say itself" [*es zol zich zigen a shirah*], see R. Kalonymus Kalmish Shapira, *Sacred Fire, Parshat B'shalakh* 1940 (Jason Aronson Press: New Jersey, 2002), p. 154.

[383] Bob Dylan, "Like a Rolling Stone," (*Highway 61 Revisited,* 1965); Margotin and Guesdon, *Bob Dylan: All the Songs: the Story Behind Every Track,* pp. 186-189.

[384] Bob Dylan, "Ballad of a Thin Man," (*Highway 61 Revisited,* 1965); Margotin and Guesdon, *Bob Dylan: All the Songs: the Story Behind Every Track,* 187.

[385] Jonas, "Gnosticism, Existentialism, and Nihilism," p. 340.

[386] *Ibid,* p. 340.

[387] Bob Dylan, "It's Alright Ma (I'm Only Bleeding)," (*Bringing It All Back Home,* 1965); Margotin and Guesdon suggest this song as "Dylan's indictment of false prophets and manipulators" see Margotin and Guesdon, *Bob Dylan: All the Songs: the Story Behind Every Track,* pp. 172-173.

[388] Bob Dylan, "God Knows," (*Under the Red Sky,* 1991).

1. *I&I* as *Eheyeh*: Knowing Thyself Through Shades of I & Masks of Other

Acknowledgements: An earlier version of this essay appears in the forthcoming volume, entitled, Eheyeh: Mesorah Matrix Series, with thanks to Martin S. Cohen for the invitation.

[389] Plato, *Apology,* 21a; Xenophon, *Apology of Socrates,* 14.

[390] After all, in the *Laws,* Plato calls upon Delphi to help set laws on religious matters (VI, 729c) and establish festivals and rites (VIII, 828a); he also involves the oracle in settling matters of civil law where some sort of divine choice is required (IX, 856c-e; XI, 913c-914a).

391 Contra Heylin's analysis reading "I and I" as a "confessional... that suggested just how great the oppressions of prophecy and fame had become. The problems facing the kingdoms of the world are making the narrator feel afraid, so he rises from his bed, leaving his lady love to dream her untroubled dream." See Clinton Heylin, *Bob Dylan: Behind the Shades: Take Two*, (London: Penguin, 2001), p. 554.

392 Bob Dylan, "I and I" (*Infidels*, 1983).

393 Maimonides, *Guide for the Perplexed*, 1: 56, 58.

394 Ludwig Wittgenstein, *Tractatus Logico-Philosophicus* (1921), tr. C.K. Ogden, F. P. Ramsey (London: Routledge 2005). "Whereof one cannot speak, thereof one must be silent" is later re-translated by D. F. Pears and B. F. McGuinness as: "What we cannot speak about we must pass over in silence."

395 "Woman is compensated by a masculine element and therefore her unconscious has, so to speak, a masculine imprint. This results in a considerable psychological difference between men and women, and accordingly I have called the projection-making factor in women the animus, which means mind or spirit." C.G. Jung, *The Syzygy: Anima and Animus, Collected Works,* (Princeton, N.J: Princeton University Press, 1979), 9ii, par. 28f.

396 Bob Dylan, "I and I" (*Infidels*, 1983); Margotin and Guesdon astutely point to Rastafarian and Exodus theologies while leaving the interpretive question unresolved by asking: "What does the songwriter want to tell us? That the life of man is a long quest for God? It is also possible that the narrator of the song is dreaming while awake or is carried away by some confusing thoughts." But the key issues that are evoked are equally abandoned by tertiary remarks that dismiss the depth of vision at play here, see Margotin and Guesdon, *Bob Dylan: All the Songs: the Story Behind Every Track*, p. 520.

397 II Samuel 11: 1-27.

398 Exodus 2: 16-22.

399 Gnostic Gospels that contemplate this cataclysm of creation include: *Apocryphon of John; Hypostasis of the Archons; On the Origin of the World; Apocalypse of Adam; Paraphrase of Shem.*

400 It is at this point of dissolution of self as a pathway of absorption into the divine that it is important to consider a mystical reading of Limitless "I" in the name *Eheyeh*, according to Joseph Gikatilla, a remarkable thirteenth-century Kabbalist:

> "The depth of primordial being ... is called Boundless," "Because of its concealment from all creatures above and below, it is also called *Ayin* (Nothingness).... If one asks, 'What is it?,' the answer is, '*Ayin* (Nothing),' meaning: 'No one can understand anything about it.' It is negated of every conception. No one can know anything about it—except the belief that it exists. Its existence cannot be grasped by anyone other than it. Therefore, its name is אהיה (*Ehyeh*), *I am.* (Exodus 3:14)."

See Joseph Gikatilla (thirteenth-century Kabbalist), *Sha'arei Orah* (Warsaw 1883), 44a–b; Daniel Matt, *The Essential Kabbalah: The heart of Jewish mysticism,* (New York: Harper Collins, 1995), p. 67.

401 Exodus 3:2.

402 Exodus 3:5.

403 That is, beyond all conception according to Gikatilla, see Exodus 3:14.

404 On Jewish process theology in general, see for example, Bradley S. Artson, *God of Becoming and Relationship: The Dynamic Nature of Process Theology.* (Tennessee: Jewish Lights, 2016); for applications of Jewish process theology to aesthetics see Elyssa N. Wortzman, "Process Theology, Aesthetics, *Halacha* and Spiritual Direction Through Art," *Foundation Theology,* ed. J. J.H. Morgan (GTF: Indiana, 2017), pp. 141-157.

405 David A. Cooper, *God Is a Verb: Kabbalah and the Practice of Mystical Judaism.* (New York, N.Y: Riverhead Books, 1998); compare with Wortzman, "Process Theology, Aesthetics, *Halacha* and Spiritual Direction Through Art," *Foundation Theology.*

2. *Nothing is Better Than I'm Not There*: Dylan's I Minus I as *'Ayin*

Acknowledgements: I am grateful to Danny Matt and Norman Fischer for co-teaching and applying these texts to our weeklong retreat, called, *About Nothing: Buddhist and Jewish Conceptions of Ultimate Truth,* (*Tasajara Zen Center*, California: August 13 –18, 2017).

[406] Bob Dylan, "I'm Not There," (*The Bootleg Series, Vol. 11: The Basement Tapes Complete*, 2014).

[407] Willis, "The New Talking World War III Blues," [October 2001], in *Out of the Vinyl Deeps: Ellen Willis on Rock Music*, p. 74.

[408] *Ibid*, p. 75.

[409] Steven Heine, *Bargainin' for Salvation: Bob Dylan, a Zen Master?* (London: Continuum, 2009).

[410] Bob Dylan, "I'm Not There," (*The Bootleg Series, Vol. 11: The Basement Tapes Complete*, 2014).

[411] Plotinus, *Enneads*, tr. Stephen Mackenna (London: Medici Society, 1921), 5:3:14. See also Elliot R. Wolfson, "Negative Theology and Positive Assertion in the Early Kabbalah," *Da'at: a Journal of Jewish Philosophy & Kabbalah* (Leiden; Boston: Brill, 1994).

[412] David Biale, "Historical heresies and modern Jewish identity," *Jewish social studies* 8.2 (2002), p. 114.

[413] Pseudo-Dionysius, *The Divine Names*, tr's Marsilio Ficino, Michael J. B. Allen, *On Dionysius the Areopagite: Mystical Theology and the Divine Names, Part 1.* (Cambridge, Massachusetts: Harvard University Press, 2015), 1:1.

[414] John Scotus Erigena, *Periphyseon,* tr's Myra L. Uhlfelder, and Jean A. Potter (Eugene, Oregon : Wipf & Stock, 2011), 634d; see also Donald F. Duclow, "Divine Nothingness and Self-Creation in John Scotus Eriugena." *The Journal of Religion* 57.2 (1977): pp. 109-123.

[415] Maimonides, *Guide of the Perplexed* 1:57. See also, Len E. Goodman, "What is Positive in Negative Theology," Negative Theology as Jewish Modernity, ed. M. Fagenblat, (Bloomington: Indiana University Press, 2017), pp. 62-84.

[416] Maimonides, *Guide of the Perplexed* 1:58–59.

[417] b*Sotah* 21b.

[418] On the relationship between Kabbalah and philosopher, see Gil Anidjar, *"Our place in al-Andalus": Kabbalah, philosophy, literature in Arab Jewish letters.* (Stanford University Press, 2002). On the term "Philosophic Mystic", see David R. Blumenthal, *Philosophic Mysticism: Studies in Rational Religion.* (Ramat Gan: Bar Ilan University Press, 2007).

[419] Compare later on with Issachar Ber of Zlotshov, *Mevasser Tsedeq* (Berditchev, 1817), 9a–b; Daniel Matt, *The Essential Kabbalah,* 72. See John of the Cross, *The Ascent of Mount Carmel* 2:7: "When one is brought to nothing [*nada*], the highest degree of humility, the spiritual union between one's soul and God will be effected."

[420] Asher ben David, cited by Ephraim Gottlieb, *Ha-Qabbalah be-Khitvei Rabbenu Bahya ben Asher* (Jerusalem: Kiryath Sepher, 1970), p. 84.

[421] David ben Avraham ha-Lavan, *Masoret ha-Berit,* ed. Gershom Scholem, *Qovets al Yad, n.s.* 1 (1936), p. 31.

[422] Joseph Gikatilla (thirteenth-century Kabbalist), *Sha'arei Orah* (Warsaw 1883), 44a–b; Daniel Matt, *The Essential Kabbalah,* p. 67.

[423] Moses de León, *Sheqel ha-Qodesh,* A. W. Greenup (ed.), (London 1911), 23–24; Daniel Matt, *The Essential Kabbalah,* pp. 69–70.

[424] Azriel of Gerona, *Sod ha-Tefillah,* in Gershom Scholem (ed.), *"Seridim Hadashim mi-Kitvei R. Azri'el mi-Gerona,"* in S. Assaf and G. Scholem (eds.), *Sefer Zikkaron le-Asher Gulak ve-li-Shemu'el Klein* (Jerusalem 1942), p. 215.

[425] Bob Dylan, "I'm Not There", (*The Bootleg Series, Vol. 11: The Basement Tapes,* 2014); unfortunately Margotin and Guesdon miss analysis of this crucial lyric, see Margotin and Guesdon, *Bob Dylan: All the Songs: the Story Behind Every Track.*

[426] Gershom Scholem, *The Messianic Idea in Judaism* (New York, 1971), p. 214.

[427] Dov Baer, *Maggid Devarav le-Ya'aqov,* Rivka Schatz-Uffenheimer (ed.), (Jerusalem 1976), 209. See John 12:14: "Unless a grain of wheat falls into the earth and dies, it remains alone; but if it dies, it bears much fruit. Cf. I Corinthians 15:36: "What you sow does not come to life unless it dies." Cf. Koran 6:95: "God is the one who splits the grain of corn and the date-stone. He brings forth the living from the dead."

[428] Dov Baer, *Maggid Devarav le-Ya'aqov*, pp. 49, 91, 134.*ibid,* 186; Daniel Matt, *The Essential Kabbalah*, p. 71:

"Think of yourself as *Ayin* and forget yourself totally. Then you can transcend time, rising to the world of thought, where all is equal: life and death, ocean and dry land. Such is not the case if you are attached to the material nature of the world. If you think of yourself as something, then God cannot clothe Himself in you, for God is infinite. No vessel can contain God, unless you think of yourself as *Ayin.*"

[429] Issachar Ber of Zlotshov, *Mevasser Tsedeq* (Berditchev, 1817), 9a–b; Daniel Matt, *The Essential Kabbalah*, p. 72. See John of the Cross, *The Ascent of Mount Carmel* 2:7: "When one is brought to nothing [*nada*], the highest degree of humility, the spiritual union between one's soul and God will be effected."

[430] Richard F. Thomas, *Why Bob Dylan Matters,* (HarperCollins Publishers: New York, 2017), p. 79:

"The owner of the house [where Bob Dylan grew up at the corner of Twenty-Fifth Street] told us about Dylan's own occasional visits over the years. He would spend time in the bedroom of his old house, presumably making contact with memories of listening on the radio to the music that would inform him, first gospel blues and country, later rock and roll. He surely found his teenage self on these occasions."

[431] Bob Dylan, "Like a Rolling Stone" (*Highway 61 Revisited*, 1965).

[432] Bob Dylan, "Not Dark Yet", (*Time Out of Mind*, 1997).

[433] While I am in agreement with the general analysis of Margotin and Guesdon of this lyric as a confrontation with "our inevitable aging and death", again I disagree on a number of fronts that follow: firstly their claim that "that atmosphere is oppressive. Is there life after death?"; and secondly, their insistence on re-reading Rick's analysis that correlates this lyric to Keats' "Ode to a Nightingale" (1819) as then somehow requiring a further delimited interpretation to hinge uniquely upon the Gospel of John 9:4; finally, that this is a "nocturnal confession" rather than a gnostic vision that could easily emerge from the Song of Songs 3:1-5; see Margotin and Guesdon, *Bob Dylan: All the Songs: the Story Behind Every Track*, p. 622.

[434] "Things grow at night. My imagination is available to me at night." See Margotin and Guesdon, *Bob Dylan: All the Songs: the Story Behind Every Track*, p. 622. See Elliot R. Wolfson, *Luminal Darkness: Imaginal Gleanings from Zoharic Literature.* (Oxford: OneWorld, 2007).

[435] Bob Dylan, "It's All Over Now, Baby Blue" (*Bringin' it all back home*, 1965); see Margotin and Guesdon, *Bob Dylan: All the Songs: the Story Behind Every Track*, pp. 174-175, who winnow through theories about this song referring to Joan Baez, David Blue and Paul Clayton before coming the realization that this lyric is strongly influenced by Gene Vincent and the French symbolist poet, Arthur Rimbaud. It is this latter arc of analysis about how this is "a song about the pain one must go through to gain knowledge" is deserving of further reflection relative to the gnostic analysis at hand.

[436] Bob Dylan, "You're Making a Liar Out of Me", (*Trouble in Mind: Bootlegs* 1979-1981).

[437] *Ibid.*

[438] *Ibid.*

[439] *Ibid.*

[440] *Ibid.*

[441] *Ibid.*

[442] Surprisingly neither Margotin and Guesdon, nor Ricks address or analyze this lyric whatsoever, while Rogovoy does, see Seth Rogovoy, *Bob Dylan: Prophet, Mystic, Poet*, (New York: Scribner, 2014), pp. 74, 110-111.

[443] Clinton Heylin and Bob Dylan. *Bob Dylan: Behind the Shades Revisited*, (New York, NY: William Morrow, 2001), p. 274. For some reason, Rogovoy claims the appointed time was "around noon", see Rogovoy, *Bob Dylan: Prophet, Mystic, Poet*, p. 110.

[444] Rogovoy, *Bob Dylan: Prophet, Mystic, Poet*, pp. 110; compare with Clinton Heylin, *Bob Dylan: Behind the Shades Revisited*, pp. 273-280.

[445] Bob Dylan, "Nothing Was Delivered", (Dwarf Music, 1968, 1975, 1996); see Margotin and Guesdon, who claim this "song is reminiscent of a dark period in his life, the time in 1966 when he flirted with illicit substances and environment associated with them" and then suggest the song "could be interpreted as an encounter gone bad between a drug dealer and his client" or even politicians as the "elites he accuses of lying and from who he demands an explanation." In the end, this is "not a love song" as "it is rather a dark and threatening song, separate from the stream of nonsensical lyrics". This is another example of over-interpretations that do little to open the lyrics amidst it poetic expanse but actually serve to delimit it erroneously, see Margotin and Guesdon, *Bob Dylan: All the Songs: the Story Behind Every Track*, p. 268.

[446] Daisetz T. Suzuki, *Manual of Zen Buddhism*, (Grove Press: New York, 2012), n2, p. 120.

[447] *Ibid, An Introduction to Zen Buddhism*, (Grove Press: New York, 1964), p. 99.

[448] *Ibid*, p. 101.

[449] *Ibid*, p. 99.

[450] Heylin, *Bob Dylan: Behind the Shades Revisited*, p. 275.

[451] *Ibid*, p. 274.

[452] Rogovoy, *Bob Dylan: Prophet, Mystic, Poet*, p. 111; Heylin, *Bob Dylan: Behind the Shades Revisited*, p. 273.

[453] Heylin, *Bob Dylan: Behind the Shades Revisited*, p. 277.

[454] *Ibid*, p. 276.

[455] *Ibid*, p. 275.

[456] Bob Dylan, "I'm Not There", (*The Bootleg Series, Vol. 11: The Basement Tapes,* 2014); see Margotin and Guesdon, *Bob Dylan: All the Songs: the Story Behind Every Track*, which excludes this crucial bootleg from their analysis.

[457] *Ibid*.

[458] Heylin, *Bob Dylan: Behind the Shades Revisited*, p. 277.

[459] Bob Dylan, "I'm Not There", (*The Bootleg Series, Vol. 11: The Basement Tapes*, 2014).

[460] Daisetz T. Suzuki, *An Introduction to Zen Buddhism*, (Grove Press: New York, 1964), p. 103.

3. In the Garden, Outside Eden: Singing From Snake Eyes

[461] Bob Dylan, "Man Gave Names to the All the Animals", (*Slow Train Coming,* 1979); see Margotin and Guesdon, who accurately identity the foundational scriptural inspiration as Genesis 2:19-20. Its inclusion on this album indeed appeals to contemplatives young and old, see Margotin and Guesdon, *Bob Dylan: All the Songs: the Story Behind Every Track*, p. 476.

[462] Compare with C. G. Jung. "The Phenomenology of the Spirit in Fairy Tales," in *The Archetypes and the Collective Unconscious*, (New Jersey: Princeton University Press, 1990), pp. 207-254. While Gershom Scholem attended *Eranos* and was in conversation with Jung, it is unclear this article figured as part of their conversation given the paucity of Jewish mystical sources present. For more on the *Eranos* circle and their shared discourse, see Steven M. Wasserstrom, *Religion After Religion: Gershom Scholem, Mircea Eliade, and Henry Corbin at Eranos.* (Princeton: Princeton University Press, 2001).

[463] James Hillman, *Animal Presences*, (Putnam, Conn: Spring Publications, 2008), p. 77.

[464] Hillman, *Animal Presences*, p. 77.

[465] *Ibid.*

[466] *Ibid,* pp. 77-78:

> "But what remains after all the symbolic understanding is what that snake is doing, this crawling huge black snake that's sliding into your life. The moment you've caught the snake in an interpretation, you've lost the snake. You've stopped its living movement...Meaning replaces image; animal disappears into the human mind."

[467] *Ibid,* p. 78.

[468] Bob Dylan, "Wiggle, Wiggle," (*Under a Red Sky,* 1990); see Margotin and Guesdon, who suggest this lyric "could be a metaphor for the decadence of modern times—the unconscious dance of men at the edge of the cliff. Or it might be simple funny children's rhyme with no real meaning, a nice amusing piece of nonsense." This kind of analysis is unfortunate in dismissing the

depth of meaning in nursery rhymes as a key to the journey of the soul as precluding the unconscious dance on the abyss. The weakness of their analysis comes through in moments that privilege one reading over another while dismissing the latter to the detriment of their overall analysis; see Margotin and Guesdon, *Bob Dylan: All the Songs: the Story Behind Every Track*, p. 581.

[469] Bob Dylan, "Froggie went a Courtin'," (*Good as I been to You,* 1992); the origin of this nursery rhyme dates back to the mid-sixteenth century under the title "The Complaynt of Scotland," and for a fuller geneology, see Margotin and Guesdon, *Bob Dylan: All the Songs: the Story Behind Every Track*, p. 597.

[470] Bob Dylan, "Please Mrs. Henry," (*Basement Tapes,* 1967); see Margotin and Guesdon, *Bob Dylan: All the Songs: the Story Behind Every Track*, p. 259.

[471] Bob Dylan, "Angelina," (*Bootleg vol's 1-3, 1961-1991,* 1981); see Margotin and Guesdon, *Bob Dylan: All the Songs: the Story Behind Every Track*, p. 505.

[472] Elaine Pagels, *The Gnostic Gospels*, (Vintage Books: New York, 1979), pp. xiii-xxiii.

[473] Jeffrey J. Kripal, *The Serpent's Gift: Gnostic Reflections on the Study of Religion.* (Chicago: University of Chicago Press, 2007), p. 11: "…the (post)modern gnostic intellectual is the one who privileges knowledge over belief, who knows that she knows, and knows that what she knows cannot possibly be reconciled with the claims of any past or present religious tradition, including the ancient gnostic Judaisms and Christianities, whose common radical dualisms and consistent rejections of the body, sexuality, and the physical world render any simplistic mimicking of these elaborate mythological systems quite impossible and hardly desirable."

[474] Adam Kirsch, "The Meaning of Bob Dylan's Silence," *NY Times* (10/26/16) https://www.nytimes.com/2016/10/26/opinion/the-meaning-of-bob-dylans-silence.html?_r=0 (accessed 6/1/17)

[475] Jean-Paul Sartre, *L'être et le néant* (Paris: Gallimard, 1943), 102-106; *ibid, Being and Nothingness: An Essay on Phenomenological Ontology*, tr. Mary Warnock, Hazel E. Barnes, and Richard Eyre. (London: New York : Routledge, Taylor & Francis Group, 2015), pp. 101-105.

[476] Adam Kirsch, "The Meaning of Bob Dylan's Silence," *NY Times* (10/26/16) https://www.nytimes.com/2016/10/26/opinion/the-meaning-of-bob-dylans-silence.html?_r=0 (accessed 6/1/17)

[477] Bob Dylan, "I'm Not There," (*The Bootleg Series, Vol. 11: The Basement Tapes RAW*).

[478] Even the Talmudic rabbis were never and could never possibly be proven to be guilty of affirming two powers, where the second power of heresy was hostile. Even if we accept that these gnostic rabbis tended to be more explicitly positive than the stereotypical negative gnostic, this is not a convincing proof to exonerate the rabbis from a hybrid gnostic identity. To claim Second Temple Jewry according to Boyarin's reading, had no knowledge of such Gnosticism is an argument from silence that cannot be supported.

Finally, gnostic theology does not preclude *logos* theology and reducing the former to an evil theology displays an inability to read the gnostic theology within its orbit of nuance. So amidst his genius in re-exploring the porous nature of identity during the formation of Judaism as a distinct way of being with the emergence of Christianity, and claiming that Gnosticism may be more rhetorical than historical, still Boyarin falls prey to the stereotypical readings of Gnosticism that has plagued heresiologists on both sides of the fence. See Daniel Boyarin, *Border Lines: The Partition of Judaeo-Christianity* (Philadelphia: University of Pennsylvania Press, 2010), pp. 56, 94, 230, 250, 287, 292.

[479] *Testimony of Truth*, Søren Giversen and Birger A. Pearson, tr, Coptic Gnostic Library Project of the Institute for Antiquity and Christianity, Claremont Graduate School.(UNESCO, the National Endowment for the Humanities) from The Coptic Gnostic Library Project (E. J. Brill) http://www.gnosis.org/nagham m/testruth.html (accessed 3/20/17):

"Scholars investigating the Nag Hammadi find discovered that some of the texts tell the origin of the human race in terms very different from the usual reading of Genesis: the *Testimony of Truth,* for example, tells the story of the Garden of Eden from the viewpoint of the serpent."

[480] b*Eruvin* 18a, so that the curse follows in a causal chain from the snake to Eve and then to Adam, and all of humanity

[481] Kripal, *The Serpent's Gift,* pp. 4, 11, 117, 118, 177, 183, 187.

[482] *Ibid,* p. 4.

[483] Bob Dylan, "Jokerman," (*Infidels,* 1983); see Margotin and Guesdon, *Bob Dylan: All the Songs: the Story Behind Every Track,* pp. 514-515.

[484] *Ibid.*

[485] I depart from the analysis of "Jokerman" in Christopher Ricks, *Dylan's Visions of Sin.* (Edinburgh: Canongate Books Ltd, 2011), pp. 227, 360, as well as Margotin and Guesdon, *Bob Dylan: All the Songs: the Story Behind Every Track,* pp. 514-515.

[486] I depart from both analyses, see "Jokerman" in Christopher Ricks, *Dylan's Visions of Sin.* (Edinburgh: Canongate Books Ltd, 2011), pp. 227, 360; Seth Rogovoy, *Bob Dylan: Prophet, Mystic, Poet.* (New York: Scribner, 2014), pp. 237-238.

[487] I disagree here Seth Rogovoy, *Bob Dylan: Prophet, Mystic, Poet*, pp. 237-238.

[488] See above no. 20, whereby Seth Rogovoy is one of many Jewish critics whose interpretation leans towards Bob Dylan's complete return to Judaism. See also, Stephen Pickering, *Bob Dylan Approximately: A Portrait of the Jewish Poet in Search of God.* (New York: York, David McKay, 1975).

[489] Clinton Heylin, *Bob Dylan: Behind the Shades: Take Two.* (London: Penguin, 2001), p. 547.

[490] Bob Dylan, "Man of Peace," (*Infidels,* 1983); see Margotin and Guesdon, *Bob Dylan: All the Songs: the Story Behind Every Track,* 518, whose interpretation focuses primarily on Paul's Second Epistle II Corinthians 2:14 as well as Gospel of Matthew 10:34.

[491] Bob Dylan, "I'm Not There", (*The Bootleg Series, Vol. 11: The Basement Tapes RAW*).

[492] Clinton Heylin, *Bob Dylan: Behind the Shades: Take Two.* (London: Penguin, 2001), p. 530.

[493] I depart from the analysis of "Man of Peace" in Christopher Ricks, *Dylan's Visions of Sin.* (Edinburgh: Canongate Books Ltd, 2011), p. 158.

[494] In the mystical hermeneutics of *gematriah* or numerology, "Snake" [*NaHaSH*] is related to "Messiah" [*MaSHIaH*] insofar as the former spells out the latter once the first letter of "snake" [*Nun=* N (50)] is expanded into its integers [*Mem (40) + Yod (10) = 50*]

[495] Jon D. Levenson, *Creation and the persistence of evil: The Jewish drama of divine omnipotence*, (Princeton University Press, 1988); James G. Williams, *The Bible, Violence, and the Sacred:*

Liberation from the Myth of Sanctioned Violence, (Wipf and Stock Publishers, 2007).

[496] Hillman, *Animal Presences*, p. 77.

[497] *Ibid*, p. 79.

[498] *Ibid*, p. 79.

4. Lovesick/Sick of Love: Love Lost & Found

[499] Literally, "Forever is mercy built," (Psalm 89:3).

[500] Bob Dylan, "Covenant Woman," (*Saved*, 1980).

[501] Bob Dylan, "The Groom's Still Waiting at the Altar," (*Shot of Love*, 1981).

[502] Bob Dylan, *Nashville Skyline*, 1969. See Ellen Willis, "Dylan's Anti-Surprise," [April 1969], in Ellen Willis and Nona W. Aronowitz, *Out of the Vinyl Deeps: Ellen Willis on Rock Music*, (Minneapolis: University of Minnesota Press, 2011), p. 207.

[503] Bob Dylan, "Wedding Song," (*Planet Waves, 1973*).

[504] For this prescient observation about love in Bob Dylan from the perspective of a feminist critique, see Willis, "Dylan and Fans: Looking Back, Going On", [Februrary 1974], in Ellen Willis and

Nona W. Aronowitz, *Out of the Vinyl Deeps: Ellen Willis on Rock Music*, (Minneapolis: University of Minnesota Press, 2011), p. 99.

[505] Willis, "Dylan and Fans: Looking Back, Going On", [Februrary 1974], in *Out of the Vinyl Deeps: Ellen Willis on Rock Music*, p. 99.

[506] Willis, "Dylan and Fans: Looking Back, Going On", [Februrary 1974], in Ellen Willis and Nona W. Aronowitz, *Out of the Vinyl Deeps: Ellen Willis on Rock Music*, p. 99.

[507] Bob Dylan, "Dirge," (*Planet Waves*, 1973).

508 Willis, "Dylan and Fans: Looking Back, Going On", [Februrary 1974], in Ellen Willis and Nona W. Aronowitz, *Out of the Vinyl Deeps: Ellen Willis on Rock Music*, p. 99.

509 Christopher Ricks, *Dylan's Vision of Sin*, (Edinburgh: Canongate, 2011).

510 Bob Dylan, "Dirge," (*Planet Waves*, 1973).

511 *Marvin Meyer, tr. The Gospel of Thomas,* in *The Gnostic Bible,* (New York: 2003), p. 555.

512 *Meyer, The Gospel of Thomas,* n25, p. 555.

513 *Ibid,* n 43, p. 558.

514 *Ibid,* n101, p. 571.

515 *Ibid,* n107, 572.

516 It is in Baudelaire's masterpiece of poetry, *Flowers of Evil* (1857) that the poet's love sick state is rendered so lusciously in "Love and the Skull":

"An Old Lamp Base
Love is seated on the skull
Of Humanity;
On this throne the impious one
With the shameless laugh
Is gaily blowing round bubbles
That rise in the air
As if they would rejoin the globes
At the ether's end."

See Charles Baudelaire, "Cupid and the Skull", William Aggeler, tr. *The Flowers of Evil*, (Fresno, CA: Academy Library Guild, 1954). [I have altered the title from "Cupid and the Skull" to "Love and the Skull" for the purposes of this comparison].

517 *Ibid.*

518 Bob Dylan, "Ain't Talkin'," (*Modern Times,* 2006); see Margotin and Guesdon, *Bob Dylan: All the Songs: the Story Behind Every Track*, p. 653, whose analysis focuses on the lone pilgrim in search of the Garden of Eden.

519 Bob Dylan, "Love Sick," (*Time Out of Mind,* 1997); see Margotin and Guesdon, *Bob Dylan: All the Songs: the Story Behind Every Track*, p.618, whose interpretation is that this lyric is about a hopeless love or a self-reflection on the singer's mortality upon being hospitalized for an infectious lung disease in May 1997. Both interpretations miss the mark, as this lyric is explicitly riffing on Song of Songs, see n. 284

520 Song of Songs 1:7, Chana and Ariel Bloch, tr's, *The Song of Songs: The World's First Great Love Poem*, (Modern Library: New York, 1995), p. 49 [*henceforth all citations of Song of Song will follow this translation*].

[521] Roland E. Murphy, O. Carm. *A Commentary on the Book of Canticles or The Song of Songs*, (Fortress Press: Minneapolis, 1990), p.134a.

[522] Song of Songs 2:5, Bloch, tr's, *The Song of Songs: The World's First Great Love Poem*, p. 57.

[523] Yehudah Amichai, "Love Gifts" Robert Alter, tr. *The Poetry of Yehuda Amichai,* (New York: Farrar, Straus and Giroux, 2015), p.90.

[524] Bob Dylan, "Love Sick," (*Time Out of Mind*, 1997).

[525] Song of Songs 2:17, Bloch, tr's, *The Song of Songs: The World's First Great Love Poem*, 65.

[526] Bob Dylan, "Love Sick," (*Time Out of Mind*, 1997).

[527] *Marvin Meyer, tr. The Gospel of Thomas, in The Gnostic Bible,* (New York: *2003),* no. 17, p. 552.

[528] *Ibid,* n28, p. 555.

[529] *Ibid,* n45, p. 559.

[530] *Ibid,* n63, p. 563.

[531] *Ibid,* n69, p. 566.

[532] Bob Dylan, "Gonna Change My Way of Thinking," (*Slow Train Coming*, 1979), where he sings: "A hold on his heart in your eyes"; see Margotin and Guesdon, *Bob Dylan: All the Songs: the Story Behind Every Track*, p. 473.

[533] Bob Dylan, "Spirit on the Water," (*Modern Times*, 2006); *ibid,* "I Believe in You," (*Slow Train Coming*, 1979); see Margotin and Guesdon, *Bob Dylan: All the Songs: the Story Behind Every Track*, 647, reading this lyric as a direct adaptation of the Gospel of Matthew 12:30.

[534] Bob Dylan, "Up To Me" (*Biograph,* 1974), where he sings: "unlock/heart inside me"; see Margotin and Guesdon, *Bob Dylan: All the Songs: the Story Behind Every Track*, 428, reading this lyric of a fusion of "Tangled Up in Blue" and "Idiot Wind".

[535] Bob Dylan, "When the Deal Goes Down," (*Modern Times*, 2006); see Margotin and Guesdon, *Bob Dylan: All the Songs: the Story Behind Every Track*, p. 649, providing a strong reading of this lyric as a riff on Henry Timrod's poems "Retirement" and "A Rhapsody of a Southern Winter Night", but then lapsing into a weaker reading of how this lyric reformulates Ecclesiastes 8:17 and most egregiously reading the covenant of Genesis 17:4 solely in Christological light.

[536] See Bob Dylan, "Cry a While," (*Love and Theft*, 2001): "break a trusting heart like mine"; *ibid,* "Down the Highway" (*The Freewheelin' Bob Dylan*, 1963): "baby stole my heart"; *ibid,* "It Ain't Me Babe": "to close his heart someone will" (*Another Side of Bob Dylan*, 1964); Margotin and Guesdon focus their analyses on the latter two lyrics as reflecting the bitterness of Dylan's search for and break up with Suze Rotolo, see Margotin and Guesdon, *Bob Dylan: All the Songs: the Story Behind Every Track*, pp. 59-60, 130-131; while the former as a tribute to the biggest name in blues, Sony Boy Williamson II, see *ibid*, p.640.

[537] Bob Dylan, "Forever Young", (*Planet Waves*, 1974); Margotin and Guesdon analyze this lyric as a song written to Dylan's son, Jesse, see Margotin and Guesdon, *Bob Dylan: All the Songs: the Story Behind Every Track*, pp. 404-405.

[538] Bob Dylan, "Ain't talkin'," (*Modern Times*, 2006).

[539] Bob Dylan, "Rollin' and Tumblin'," (*Modern Times*, 2006); see Margotin and Guesdon, *Bob Dylan: All the Songs: the Story Behind Every Track*, p.648.

[540] Bob Dylan, "Beyond the Horizon," (*Modern Times*, 2006); Margotin and Guesdon read this lyric as an homage to Hank Williams' "Beyond the Sunset" and the Tin Pan Alley genre in general, see Margotin and Guesdon, *Bob Dylan: All the Songs: the Story Behind Every Track*, p. 651.

[541] Bob Dylan and Robert Hunter, "Forgetful Heart," (*Together Through Time*, 2009); Margotin and Guesdon read this lyric, especially the last line as an implicit reference to William Faulkner's play, *Requiem for a Nun* (1950): "The past is never dead. It's not even past" which is intriguing but does not do much to open the depths of this love song, see Margotin and Guesdon, *Bob Dylan: All the Songs: the Story Behind Every Track*, p. 662.

[542] *Ibid.*

[543] Zohar I: 224a.

[544] Bob Dylan and Robert Hunter, "Forgetful Heart," (*Together Through Time*, 2009).

[545] See the rendering of the door closing motif in Franz Kafka, "Before the Law" in *The Trial*, (Alma Classics, 2018).

[546] Bob Dylan, "Absolutely Sweet Marie," (*Blonde on Blonde*, 1966).

547 Compare with Steven Heine, *Bargainin' for Salvation: Bob Dylan, a Zen Master?* (New York: Continuum, 2009). The playful and deeply paradoxical nature of this final verse recalls the archetype of the closed door in the Zen *koan* where the hermit, Mu Chou shuts the door thrice and on the final encounter literally and figuratively breaks open the doorway from the place of continual closure:

> "Yun Men stopped and knocked on Mu Chou's door. On two occasions Mu Chou answered, immediately demanding, "Speak! Speak!" Two times Yun Men's answer was not adequate to prevent Mu Chou from quickly slamming the door. Upon a third try and a demand by Mu Chou to speak, Yun Men stuck out his leg to prevent Mu Chou from closing the door. Whether or not Mu Chou noticed the leg, he again slammed the door. Yun Men's leg was broken, and he cried out in pain. At this, Yun Men was enlightened, and in some versions, Mu Chou opened the door to welcome him in."

See Leland E. Shields "Zen Koans as Myths Reflecting Individuation," in *Jung Journal: Culture & Psyche*, Volume 4, Number 4 (2010), pp.65-77. http://www.thezensite.com/Zen Essays/Philosophical/ZenKoans _as_Myths.pdf (accessed 8/4/17).

548 "And the key of the house of David will I lay upon his shoulder; and he shall open, and none shall shut; and he shall shut, and none shall open." (Isaiah 22:22).

5. *Forever Young*: Heartfelt Hymn Resting Upon Fatherly Trust

Acknowledgements: Thanks to David Wilensky for the invitation to write an earlier version of this essay for J. Weekly (June 1, 2017).

549 Nigel Williamson, *The Rough Guide to Bob Dylan*, (New York: Metro Books, 2010), p. 286.

550 Bob Dylan, "Forever Young," (*Planet Waves*, 1974).

551 Heylin, *Bob Dylan: Behind the Shades: Take Two*, p. 354.

552 Numbers 6:24–27.

553 *Ibid*, p. 548.

[554] Jacob Milgrom, *JPS Bible Commentary: Numbers* (Philadelphia: Jewish Publication Society, 1990), p. 52. In this context, the word "prophylactics' denotes an amulet capable of protecting its bearer from spiritual damage by evil spirits.

[555] Malachi 1:9–10, cf. 1:6–7, 11–14; and 2:2–9.

[556] Christopher Ricks, *Dylan's Visions of Sin* (Viking: New York, 2003), p. 449.

[557] Bob Dylan, "Forever Young," (*Planet Waves*, 1974).

[558] Seth Rogovoy, *Bob Dylan: Prophet, Mystic, Poet* (Scribner: New York, 2009), pp. 154-155.

[559] Heylin, *Bob Dylan: Behind the Shades: Take Two*, p. 658.

[560] Ricks, *Dylan's Visions of Sin,* p. 455.

[561] Heylin, *Bob Dylan: Behind the Shades: Take Two,* p. 407.

6. *Desolation Row*: Mommy, Mommy, Wall, Wall... Consolation From Where?

Acknowledgements: Thanks to David Wilensky for the invitation to write an earlier version of this essay, "We are all orphans, diaspora jackals, seeking consolation," for J.Weekly (August 3, 2017). In having the privilege of teaching this Zohar Hadash section to francophone students at the Conservative Yeshiva (Jerusalem: 2015), I learned both from my students as well as from Charles Mopsik's commentary.

[562] Shaul Magid, "Carlebach's broken mirror," *Tablet Magazine* (2012).

[563] Bob Dylan, "Desolation Row," (*Highway 61 Revisited*, 1965); Margotin and Guesdon suggest an insightful analysis of this lyric by correlating it with Jack Keroauc's *Desolation Angels*, T. S. Eliot's *The Waste Land*, and Allen Ginsburg's *Howl*, see Margotin and Guesdon, *Bob Dylan: All the Songs: the Story Behind Every Track*, pp. 202-203.

[564] Zohar Hadash: *Midrash ha-Ne'lam on Eikha,* 91b, Pritzker Edition Zohar, vol. XI, tr. J. Hecker, (Stanford University Press: Stanford, 2016), p. 302.

[565] Zohar Hadash, *Midrash ha-Ne'lam on Eikha*, 91a, pp. 299-300.

[566] *Ibid,* 92b, p. 318.

7. *Long Time Gone*: Time as Redemption & Loss

[567] Bob Dylan, "Ring Them Bells," (*O Mercy,* 1989); For this notion of the "time swerve" as already eloquently elucidated and correlated to the Dylan lyric "Ring Them Bells", see Elliot R. Wolfson, "Prologue," in *Language, Eros, Being: Kabbalistic Hermeneutics and Poetic Imagination,* (New York: Fordham University Press, 2005), pp. xi-xxxi.

[568] Bauer, "Dzogchen As Gnosticism: A Phenomenological View", *n.p.*

[569] See Aubrey L. Glazer, *A New Physiognomy of Jewish Thinking: Critical Theory After Adorno As Applied to Jewish Thought,* (London: Bloomsbury Academic, 2012); more recently, see *ibid,* "Jewish Musical Thinking: Reflections of a Philosopher-Rabbi," *The Future of Jewish Philosophy,* ed. Hava Tirosh-Samuelson and Aaron W. Hughes, (Boston and Leiden: Brill, 2018), pp. 171-194.

[570] "The light will [...] the darkness and obliterate it: it will be like something that has never been. And the product to which the darkness had been posterior will dissolve. And the deficiency will be plucked out by the root (and thrown) down into the darkness. And the light will withdraw up to its root. And the glory of the unbegotten will appear. And it will fill all the eternal realm." See *On the Origin of the Worlds,* see: http://www.gnosis.org/nagham m/origin.html (accessed 6/22/17).

[571] Bob Dylan, "Long Time Gone," (*Witmark Demos,* 1963); Margotin and Guesdon analyze this lyric as a journey song away from home where "the narrator, a disciple of Jack Kerouac and other Beat writers, travels through Texas where he has a love affair with a barmaid" whose musical structure is modeled after "Maggie Walker Blues", see Margotin and Guesdon, *Bob Dylan: All the Songs: the Story Behind Every Track,* p. 140.

[572] *Ibid.*

[573] *Ibid.*

[574] *Ibid.*

[575] *Ibid.*

[576] For an extensive analysis of the railroad motif in Dylan's songbook see Bryan Cheyette, "On the D' Train: Bob Dylan's Conversions," in *Do You Mr Jones?: Bob Dylan with the Poets and Professors*, ed. Neil Corcoran, (Random House UK Ltd, 2017), pp. 171-195.

[577] Allen Ginsberg, and Paul Portugés, O*n Tibetan Buddhism, Mantras, and Drugs: Interviews with Allen Ginsberg,* (San Luis Obispo, CA: Word Palace Press, 2013); Benedict Giamo, *Kerouac, the Word and the Way: Prose Artist As Spiritual Quester,* (Carbondale: Southern Illinois University Press, 2000).

[578] Timothy Gray, *It's Just the Normal Noises: Marcus, Guralnick, No Depression, and the Mystery of Americana Music*, (Iowa City: University of Iowa Press, 2017).

[579] When the question about the meaning of the universe is posed, the parodic response is "42"! See Douglas Adams, Richard Dawkins, and Nick Harkaway. *The Hitch Hiker's Guide to the Galaxy*, (London: William Heinemann, 2014).

[580] Bob Dylan, "Slow Train," (*Slow Train Coming,* 1979); Margotin and Guesdon analyze this lyric as a "protest song of a new type, because it criticizes an overtly nationalist ideal", see Margotin and Guesdon, *Bob Dylan: All the Songs: the Story Behind Every Track*, p. 472.

[581] Bob Dylan, "Long Time Gone," (*Witmark Demos,* 1963), see above n329.

[582] R. Nahman of Bratzlav, *Liqqutai Moharan* n64:

> "And thus when the world had come into being, it distractedly erred at all times. For all men upon earth worshiped the spirits (demons) from the creation to the consummation - both the angels of righteousness and the men of unrighteousness. Thus did the world come to exist in distraction, in ignorance, and in a stupor. They all erred, until the appearance of the true man."

[583] *On the Origin of the Worlds,* see: http://www.gnosis.org/nagham m/origin.html (accessed 6/22/17).

[584] Bob Dylan, "What Can I Do For You," (*Saved,* 1979); Margotin and Guesdon analyze this lyric as: "the form of a new prayer originating in [Dylan's] newfound faith in Jesus Christ" based on Epistle of Saint Paul to the Ephesians (6:16), see Margotin and Guesdon, *Bob Dylan: All the Songs: the Story Behind Every Track*, p. 487.

[585] Bob Dylan, "Tomorrow Is A Long Time," (*Witmark Demos*, 1962-64, 1963); Margotin and Guesdon analyze this lyric as inspired by an anonymous fifteenth century English poem called "Western Wind" about the Greek myth of Zephyr as the personification of the wind from the west as correlated with Dylan's disenchantment with his break-up with lover, Suze Rotolo, see Margotin and Guesdon, *Bob Dylan: All the Songs: the Story Behind Every Track*, p. 135.

[586] *Ibid.*

[587] Zohar Hadash: *Midrash ha-Ne'lam on Eikha*, 92c, J. Hecker tr., *Pritzker Edition*, vol. XI, (Stanford: Stanford University Press, 2018), pp. 322-323.

[588] Bob Dylan, "Long Time Gone," (*Witmark Demos*, 1962-64, 1963).

8. *Along the Watchtower*: Where are the Watchers of Zion?!?

[589] Bob Dylan, "All Along the Watchtower," (*John Wesley Harding*, 1974); Margotin and Guesdon analyze this lyric by returning to Isaiah 21: 5-9, and then identify the joker as Dylan himself while the thief is Albert Grossman, his manager and a symbol of the money-making machine of the music industry as a whole, see Margotin and Guesdon, *Bob Dylan: All the Songs: the Story Behind Every Track*, pp. 288-289.

[590] Bob Dylan, "Neighborhood Bully," (*Infidels*, 1983); Margotin and Guesdon analyze this lyric as possibly a Zionist political song, which Dylan refutes, and then they conclude by turning to evangelist, Hal Lindsey's apocalyptic visions inspired by Daniel 12: 2, see Margotin and Guesdon, *Bob Dylan: All the Songs: the Story Behind Every Track*, p. 517.

[591] Shalom M. Paul, *Isaiah 40-66: Translation and Commentary*. Grand Rapids (Mich.: Eerdmans, 2012), p. 550.

[592] Paul, *Isaiah 40-66: Translation and Commentary*, p. 551.

[593] *Ibid,* p. 553.

[594] *Ibid,* pp. 554-5.

[595] *Ibid,* p. 555.

[596] Lamentations 2:18

[597] Isaiah 60:11; Psalms 72:15; 121.

[598] Numbers 10:9-10.

[599] Isaiah 63:11; 40:9; 35:4.

[600] Isaiah 40:3; 57:14.

[601] Paul, *Isaiah 40-66: Translation and Commentary*, p. 557.

[602] Bob Dylan, "All Along The Watchtower," (*John Wesley Harding*, Dwarf Music, 1968), see above n346.

[603] Matthew 27:38; 44; Mark 15:27, 31; Luke 23: 33, 39-43; John 19:18.

[604] *Shulchan Aruch, Choshaim Mishpat* 34: 10.

[605] b*Bava Kamma* 69b.

[606] *Ramah ad. loc. Shulchan Aruch, Choshen Mishpat* 34: 10.

[607] *K'tzot HaChoshen ad. loc. Shulchan Aruch, Choshen Mishpat* 34: 10.

[608] *Netivot HaMishpat ad. loc. Shulchan Aruch, Choshen Mishpat* 34: 10.

[609] Chazon Ish, *Choshen Mishpat* 15:6.

[610] That is, provided no further violation any of the other conditions took place as found in chapter 34, *Choshen Mishpat*.

[611] *Ibid*, 554-5.

[612] Bob Dylan, "Wedding Song," (*Planet Waves*, 1973).

[613] *Ibid*.

[614] *Pratitya Samutpada* emerges from the Kyoto school of Japan in the Madhyamika tradition within Buddhism and translated into English as "Dependent Co-origination" or "Contingent Co-arising", see Charles J. Sabatino, "A Correlation between Heidegger's being-in-the-World and Masao Abe's *Pratitya Samutpada*," *Religiologigues (Montreal)* 19 (1999): 181-94.

[615] Bob Dylan, "Wedding Song," (*Planet Waves*, 1973).

[616] *Ibid*.

[617] This was the ultimate question Rabbi Matt Rosenberg had to ponder and respond to within a millisecond during a question-and-answer session for his invited white nationalist guest speaker, Richard Spencer. The rabbi invites the racist ideologue to join him in Torah study. Rabbi Rosenberg then finds himself at a total loss as he listens to his invited interlocutor speaking a sophisticated and sophistry-filled xenophobia at his own Texas A&M Hillel. The rabbi's invitation began innocently enough, saying: "My tradition teaches a message of radical inclusion and love. Will you sit town and learn Torah with me, and learn love?" Daniel J. Solomon, "Speechless Rabbi Admits Losing Argument Over Racism and Israel to White Supremacist," *Forward* (December 6, 2016), see: http://forward.com/news/nationa l/356363/speechless-rabbi-admits-losing-argument-over-racism-and-israel-to-white-sup/ (accessed 6/13/16):

> "Do you really want radical inclusion into the State of Israel? And by that, I mean radical inclusion. Maybe all of the Middle East could go move in to Tel Aviv or Jerusalem. Would you really want that?"

[618] Shawn Rodgers, "Radiohead's Yorke gives BDS supporters the finger during Glasgow concert" *Jerusalem Post* (July 9, 2017), see: http://www.jpost.com/BDS-THREAT/Radioheads-Yorke-gives-BDS-supporters-the-finger-during-Glasgow-concert-499210 (accessed 7/13/17).

[619] It is instructive to understand the underlying Zionism of Evangelicals, insofar as its activism promulgates the implementation of six basic political convictions arising from fundamentalist theology: (1). Jews remain God's chosen people worthy of blessing Israel in material ways; (2). As God's chosen people, the final restoration of the Jews to Israel is therefore actively encouraged, funded and facilitated through partnerships with the Jewish Agency; (3). Biblical *Eretz Israel* from the Nile to the Euphrates, belongs exclusively to the Jewish people, therefore the land must be annexed, Palestinians driven from their homes and the illegal Jewish settlements expanded and consolidated; (4). Jerusalem as the eternal capital of the Jews, therefore lobbying the US Administration to relocate its embassy to Jerusalem (which appears to becoming a reality in Arnona) and thereby ensure that Jerusalem is recognised as the capital of Israel; (5). Support Jewish Temple Mount Faithful who are committed to destroying the Dome of the Rock and rebuilding the Jewish Temple on the *Haram Al-Sharif* (Noble sanctuary of *Al-Aqsa*); (6). Armageddon eminent, sceptical of a lasting peace between Jews and Arabs, oppose the peace process, and advocate an Israeli compromise of "land for peace" with the Palestinians as a rejection of God's promises to Israel. See: https://www.middleeastmonitor.com/20140129-christian-zionism-the-new-heresy-that-undermines-middle-east-peace/ Compare with David Novak, *New Theory of Judaism and Zionism*, (New York: Cambridge University Press, 2016).

[620] Heylin, *Behind the Shades*, pp. 547, 548.

[621] Pastor John Hagee has spent decades teaching the evangelical community that the Bible is a very pro-Israel book, so that in March 2007, when Hagee spoke at the American Israel Public Affairs Committee (AIPAC) Policy Conference, he began by saying:

"The sleeping giant of Christian Zionism has awakened.

There are 50 million Christians standing up and applauding the State of Israel..."

Rev. Dr. Stephen Sizer, "Christian Zionism the New Heresy that Undermines Middle East Peace," *MEMO* (January 29, 2014) see: https://www.middleeastmonitor.com/20140129-christian-zionism-the-new-heresy-that-undermines-middle-east-peace (accessed 12/12/16).

[622] Heylin, *Behind the Shades: Take Two*, p. 548.

[623] *Ibid,* p. 549.

[624] *Ibid,* p. 549. Internal sources I have spoken with directly ocnfirm Dylan's dedicated Chabad emissary was Rabbi Manis Friedman, rather than Rabbi Kasriel Kastel, as recounted by Heylin above.

[625] Heylin, *Behind the Shades: Take Two*, p. 549.

[626] *Ibid,* pp. 549, 551.

[627] *Ibid,* p. 549.

[628] *Ibid,* p. 550.

[629] *Ibid,* p. 550.

[630] *Ibid,* p. 555.

[631] *Ibid,* p.557.

[632] Aubrey Glazer, *A New Physiognomy of Jewish Thinking: Critical Theory After Adorno as Applied to Jewish Thought.* (A&C Black, 2011), esp. pp.135-146.

[633] Heylin, *Behind the Shades: Take Two*, p.557.

[634] *Ibid,* p. 555.

[635] James M. Markham, "Fassbinder play draws anti-Semitism charges," *New York Times*, September 23, 1985, see: http://www.nytimes.com/1985/0 9/23/theater/fassbinder-play-draws-anti-semitism-charges.html (accessed 3/1/17).

[636] *Ibid.*

[637] R. J. Cardullo, "Memories Are Made of This: Rainer Werner Fassbinder's Veronika Voss," *Teaching Sound Film* (2016), pp.155-162.

[638] Bob Dylan, *Triplicate* (2017), which is a thematically-arranged 10-song sequence, illuminating compositions from great American songwriters interpreted by Dylan through his artistry as a vocalist, arranger and bandleader.

[639] Bob Dylan, "Blind Willie McTell," (*Special Rider Music*, 1983); Margotin and Guesdon analyze this lyric as an ode to Georgia street busker, William Samuel McTier, *aka* Blind Willie McTell (1898-1959) "one of the main creators in the history of the blues…an important touchstone for rock musicians, even if he left this world just before the American folk music revival in the early 1960s," see Margotin and Guesdon, *Bob Dylan: All the Songs: the Story Behind Every Track*, p.521.

[640] Bob Dylan, "Angelina," (*Special Rider Music*, 1981), see above n248.

[641] Bob Dylan, "Saved," (*Saved* Special Rider Music, 1980); Margotin and Guesdon analyze this lyric as a paraphrase of the Epistle of Saint Paul to the Corinthians 4:4, see Margotin and Guesdon, *Bob Dylan: All the Songs: the Story Behind Every Track*, p. 486.

642 Bob Dylan, "Saved," (*Saved* Special Rider Music, 1980); Margotin and Guesdon analyze this lyric as a paraphrase of the Epistle of Saint Paul to the Corinthians (4:4), see Margotin and Guesdon, *Bob Dylan: All the Songs: the Story Behind Every Track*, p.486.
643 Bob Dylan, "Neighborhood Bully," (*Infidels*, Special Rider Music, 1983), see above n493.
644 *Ibid.*
645 *Ibid.*
646 Michael Gray, "One of a kind: Bob Dylan at 70," *Japan Times* (May 26, 2011), http://bobdylan.com/news/one-kind-bob-dylan-70/ (accessed 3/1/17)
647 Daniel Boyarin, *Border Lines: The Partition of Judaeo-Christianity*. (Philadelphia, Pa: Univ. of Pennsylvania Press, 2007).
648 Yair Sheleg, "The Death and Rebirth of *Kfar Etzion*", *HaAretz* (May 3, 2007). http://www.haaretz.com/israel-news/the-death-and-rebirth-of-kfar-etzion-1.219660 (accessed 7/13/17).

9. *So Pray From the Mother*: Choosing Life Withdrawn From the Garden

Acknowledgements: An earlier version of this essay appears in the forthcoming volume, entitled, U'Vacharta ba'Hayyim: Mesorah Matrix Series, with thanks to Martin S. Cohen for the invitation.

649 For decades now, two French philosophers have been debating the possibility of living receptively in community after the failure of the May 1968 Revolution in Paris, see Maurice Blanchot, *The Unavowable Community,* tr. Pierre Joris (Barrytown, NY: Station Hill Press, 1988); Jean-Luc Nancy, *The Inoperative Community* THL vol. 76 (Minnesota: University of Minnesota Press, 1991); *ibid, La Communauté Affrontée (*Paris: Galilée, 2001); and ibid, The *Disavowed Community, t*rans. Philip Armstrong (New York: Fordham University Press, 2016).
650 Hans Jonas, *The Gnostic Religion: The Message of the Alien God & the Beginnings of Christianity* (Boston: Beacon Press, 2001).
651 John Gray, *The Soul of the Marionette: A Short Inquiry into Human Freedom* (New York: Farrar, Straus & Giroux, 2016).
652 Jean-Luc Nancy, "Divine Places," in *The Inoperative Community*, pp. 110-150.

653 Erich Neumann, *The Great Mother: An Analysis of the Archetype* (Princeton, NJ: Princeton University Press, 2015), p. 68.

654 Bryan Cheyette, "On the 'D' Train: Bob Dylan's Conversions," in *Do You Mr. Jones: Bob Dylan with the Poets and Professors,* ed. Neil Corcoran (London: Chatto and Windus, 2002), *n.p.* (kindle).

655 Bob Dylan, "Ain't Talkin'," (*Modern Times,* 2006).

656 Gershom Scholem, *Jewish Gnosticism, Merkabah Mysticism, and Talmudic Tradition* (New York: Jewish Theological Seminary of America, 1965), pp. 14-19.

657 Bob Dylan, "Ain't Talkin'," (*Modern Times,* 2006).

658 Scholem, *Jewish Gnosticism,* p. 15

659 Bob Dylan, "Ain't Talkin'," (*Modern Times,* 2006).

660 *Ibid.*

661 Bob Dylan, "Father of Night," (*New Morning,* 1970); Margotin and Guesdon acknowledge this song title was suggested and then rejected by Macleish's for his play, *Scratch.* They then analyze this lyric in correlating the silent prayer of standing devotion called the *Amidah* with "the English Benedictine monk, Father Francis, who lived in a church on Meads Mountain, near Woodstock, and with whom Dylan spoke about religion and metaphysics after his breakup with Suze Rotolo," see Margotin and Guesdon, *Bob Dylan: All the Songs: the Story Behind Every Track*, p.363.

662 Bob Dylan, "Ain't Talkin'," (*Modern Times,* 2006).

663 *Ibid.*

664 *Ibid.*

665 Bob Dylan, "What Can I Do For You?" (*Saved,* 1980).

666 Erich Neumann, *The Great Mother*, pp. 67-68.

667 *Ibid.*

668 Bob Dylan, "Born in Time," (*Under the Red Sky,* 1990); see Margotin and Guesdon, *Bob Dylan: All the Songs: the Story Behind Every Track*, p.582.

669 Genesis 3:24.

670 Genesis 3: 9.

671 Richard D.E. Burton, *s.v.* Charles Baudelaire, see: https://www.britannica.com/bio graphy/Charles-Baudelaire (accessed 10/1/17)

[672] Maria C. Scott, *Baudelaire's Le spleen de Paris: Shifting perspectives.* (Gower Publishing, Ltd., 2005).

[673] Edward K. Kaplan, *Baudelaire's Prose Poems: The Esthetic, the Ethical, and the Religious in the Parisian Prowler.* (University of Georgia Press, 2009).

[674] Erich Neumann, *The Great Mother,* p. 68.

[675] Bob Dylan, "Ain't Talkin'," (*Modern Times,* 2006).

[676] Compare the gnostic elements in *Likkutai Moharan,* no. 65 to the Prince of the World charged with souls, see Scholem, *Jewish Gnosticism, Merkabah Mysticism, and Talmudic Tradition,* (JTSA: New York, 1965), 49

[677] Bob Dylan, "Ain't Talkin'," (*Modern Times,* 2006).

[678] Scholem, *Jewish Gnosticism,* p.1.

[679] Clinton Heylin, *Bob Dylan: Behind the Shades* (New York: Viking, 2000), pp.354, 519-520.

10. Father of Night: Nothing But Darkness to Love

[680] Clinton Heylin, *Bob Dylan: Behind the Shades: Take Two,* (Viking: New York, 2000), p. 466.

[681] *Ibid,* p. 466.

[682] Stevan L. Davies, *The Secret Book of John: The Gnostic Gospel: Annotated and Explained.* Vermont: Skylight Illuminations), p. 15.

[683] Alexander Altmann, and Joseph Herman Hertz. *Gnostic Themes in Rabbinic Cosmology,* (London: n.p., 1943); Gershom Scholem, *Jewish Gnosticism, Merkabah mysticism, and Talmudic Tradition,* (New York: Jewish Theological Seminary of America, 1960); Alan F. Segal, "Two powers in heaven," *Early Rabbinic Reports About Christianity and Gnosticism* (Waco, Tex. : Baylor University Press, 1977/2012), pp. 148-149.

[684] Isaiah Tishby, *The doctrine of evil and the 'Kelippah'in lurianic kabbalism.* Schocken, 1984; *ibid,* and Yeruḥam Fishel Lachower, *The wisdom of the Zohar: an anthology of texts.* Vol. 3. (Littman Library of Jewish Civilization, 1991).

[685] Harold Bloom, *The anxiety of influence: A theory of poetry.* (New York: Oxford University Press, 1997).

[686] Davies, *The Secret Book of John: The Gnostic Gospel,* p. 11.

[687] *Ibid,* p. 10.

[688] *Ibid,* p. 10.

[689] Willis Barnstone and Marvin Meyer, eds., "Joy To Those Who Know The Father," in *The Nag Hammadi Library* in *The Gnostic Bible: Revised and Expanded Edition.* (Shambhala Publications, 2009), http://www.gnosis.org/nagham m/got-barnstone.html (accessed 1/25/18).

[690] Barnstone, "Ignorance of The Father Brings Error," in *Nag Hammadi Library,* http://www.gnosis.org/nagham m/got-barnstone.html (accessed 1/25/18).

[691] Barnstone, "The Father Calling Those Who Have Knowledge," in *Nag Hammadi Library,* http://www.gnosis.org/nagham m/got-barnstone.html (accessed 1/25/18):

"Those whose names he knew first were called last, so that the one who has knowledge is one whose name the father has pronounced. For one whose name has not been spoken is ignorant. Indeed, how shall one hear if a name has not been uttered? For whoever remains ignorant until the end is a creature of forgetfulness and will perish with it...If called, that person hears, replies, and turns toward him who called. That person ascends to him and knows how he is called. Having knowledge, that person does the will of him who called. That person desires to please him, finds rest, and receives a certain name. Those who thus are going to have knowledge know whence they came and whither they are going. They know it as someone who, having become intoxicated, has turned from his drunkenness and, having come to himself, has restored what is his own."

[692] *Ibid:*

"...For where there is envy and strife, there is an incompleteness; but where there is unity, there is completeness. Since this incompleteness came about because they did not know the father, from the moment when they know the father, incompleteness will cease to exist. As one's ignorance disappears when one gains knowledge, and as darkness disappears when light appears, so also incompleteness is eliminated by completeness. Certainly, from that moment on, form is no longer manifest but will be dissolved in fusion with unity. Now their works lie scattered. In time unity will make the spaces complete.

By means of unity each one will understand himself. By means of knowledge one will purify himself from multiplicity into unity, devouring matter within himself like fire and darkness by light, death by life."

[693] Barnstone, "Waking Up And Coming To Knowledge," in Nag *Hammadi Library,* http://www.gnosis.org/nagham m/got-barnstone.html (accessed 1/25/18): "What, then, is that which he wants such a one to think? "I am like the shadows and phantoms of the night." When morning comes, this one knows that the fear that had been experienced was nothing. Thus they were ignorant of the father; he is the one whom they did not see. Since there had been fear and confusion and a lack of confidence and double-mindedness and division, there were many illusions that were conceived by them, as well as empty ignorance—as if they were fast asleep and found themselves a prey to troubled dreams. …Until the moment when they who are passing through all these things—I mean they who have experienced all these confusions—awaken, they see nothing because the dreams were nothing. It is thus that they who cast ignorance from them like sleep do not consider it to be anything, nor regard its properties to be something real, but they renounce them like a dream in the night and they consider the knowledge of the father to be the dawn."

[694] The Father is not limited to the Father of Light alone, as has been suggested, see Seth Rogovoy, *Bob Dylan: Prophet, Mystic, Poet.* New York: Scribner, 2014), pp. 133-134.

[695] Bob Dylan, "Father of Night," (*New Morning,* 1970); see above n413.

[696] The Father being evoked here is not the divine figure of Psalm 147 as has been suggested, see Seth Rogovoy, *Bob Dylan: Prophet, Mystic, Poet.* New York: Scribner, 2014), pp. 133-134; see above n415.

[697] Bob Dylan, "Shot of Love," (*Shot of Love,* 1981); Margotin and Guesdon analyze this lyric as a paraphrase of I Corinthians 13:2, see Margotin and Guesdon, *Bob Dylan: All the Songs: the Story Behind Every Track,* p. 496.

[698] Bob Dylan, "Precious Angel," (*Slow Train Coming,* 1979); Margotin and Guesdon analyze this lyric as emerging both from Dylan's affair with Mary Alice Artes, who in the 1970s "played a key role in his conversion to Christianity via a religious group known as the Vineyard Fellowship," as well as attacks on "Dylan's ex-wife Sara for turning him away from Christianity," see Margotin and Guesdon, *Bob Dylan: All the Songs: the Story Behind Every Track,* p. 470.

[699] Davies, *The Secret Book of John: The Gnostic Gospel*, p. 11.

[700] Bob Dylan, "If Not for You," (*New Morning*, 1970); Margotin and Guesdon offer a reductive analysis of this lyric as a simple love song to Dylan's wife, Sara, see Margotin and Guesdon, *Bob Dylan: All the Songs: the Story Behind Every Track,* pp. 352-353.

[701] Harold Bloom, *The American Religion,* (New York, NY: Chu Hartley Publishers, 2006), p. 49.

[702] Bob Dylan, "What Can I Do For You?" (*Saved*, 1980).

[703] Harold Bloom, *The Daemon Knows: Literary Greatness and the American Sublime*, (New York: Spiegel & Grau, 2016).

11. Candle's Flame Lit into the Sun: Inflaming   the Imagination   of   Love, *Approximately*

[704]   Gaston   Bachelard,   *La Flamme   D'une   Chandelle.* (Paris: Presses Universitaires de France, 1961), p. 1; ibid, *The Flame of a Candle.* (Dallas: Dallas Institute Publications, 1988). I have relied on my own translations.

[705] Bachelard, *La Flamme D'une Chandelle*, pp. 1, 2.

[706] Bob Dylan, "Watered-down love," (*Shot of Love*, 1981).

[707] Bachelard, *La Flamme D'une Chandelle*, p. 1.

[708] *Ibid*, p. 2.

[709]   Eric   Cohen   and   Mitchell Rocklin, "The Jewish Tradition Unfolds in Fire: Here's How and Why," *Mosaic* (December 29, 2016),   see: https://mosaicmagazine.com/obs ervation/2016/12/the-jewish-tradition-unfolds-in-flames-heres-why/ (accessed 1/6/2019).

[710]   Bob Dylan, "Love Minus Zero/No Limit," (*Bringing it all Back Home*, 1965).

[711] It is curious that amidst such an analysis there is no sustained consideration of the role of the imagination,   except   when correlated to William Blake, see, Christopher   Ricks   *Dylan's Visions of Sin*, pp. 290, 327.

[712] *Ibid, Dylan's Visions of Sin*, p. 290.

[713] Bob Dylan, "Ballad of Thin Man," (*Highway 61 Revisited*, 1965).

[714] *Ibid*.

[715] For a masterful analysis of rhymes in lyrics of the Dylan songbook,   see,   Christopher Ricks *Dylan's Visions of Sin*. (Edinburgh, Canongate Books Ltd, 2011), pp. 24-5, 30-48, 53-6, 58- 60, 224-7, 471-4, etc.

[716] Bachelard, *La Flamme D'une Chandelle*, p. 2.

[717]   Bob Dylan, *The Nobel Lecture*, (New York London Toronto Sydney New Delhi Simon & Schuster, 2017), p. 6.

718

https://www.poetryfoundation.o rg/poets/tristan-tzara (accessed 12/19/18)

719 Tristan Tzara, *L'homme Approximatif 1925-1930*, (Paris: Gallimard, 1968); ibid, *Approximate Man and Other Writings*, tr. M. A. Caw, (Wayne State Press: Pittsburgh, 1931/1973).

720 Arthur Rimbaud, Antoine Raybaud, ed. *Poesies: Une Saison En Enfer; Illuminations*, (Paris: Colin, 1958); ibid, *A Season in Hell: & Illuminations*, tr. Wyatt A. Mason, (New York: Modern Library, 2005).

721 Bob Dylan, *Tarantula*, (Hibbing, Minn: Wimp Press, 1960).

722 Neil Corcoran, *Do You Mr Jones?: Bob Dylan with the Poets and Professors*. (Random House Kindle, 2010), *n.p.*

723 Bob Dylan, "Queen Jane Approximately", (*Highway 61 Revisited*, 1965).

724 Tristan Tzara, *L'Homme Approximatif, Oeuvres Completes*, (Flammarion: Paris, 1977), p. 171; ibid, *Approximate Man and Other Writings*, tr. M. A. Caw, (Wayne State Press: Pittsburgh, 1931/1973), pp.130-131. I have consulted with Caw's translation, but for the most part relied on my own translation.

725 Tristan Tzara, *Approximate Man and Other Writings*, tr. M. A. Caw, (Wayne State Press: Pittsburgh, 1931/1973), pp.130-131.

726 Bob Dylan, *Tarantula*, (Hibbing, Minn: Wimp Press, 1960), p.107.

727 Dylan, *Tarantula*, p.107.

728 Heschel recounts this tale of the original vagabond, the patriarch, Abraham, with the variations that emerge in the ambiguity of the rabbinic exegesis on *bira ha'doleket*, namely, is it a "palace full of light" (p. 112) or "a place in flames" (p. 367)? See: Abraham Joshua Heschel, *God in search of man: A philosophy of Judaism,* (Farrar, Straus and Giroux, 1976) pp. 112, 367.

729 Exodus 2: 19.

730 Exodus 3:3.

731 Exodus 3:3 *ad. loc.* Ibn Ezra.

732 Exodus 3:4.

733 I am grateful to Adrian Mirvish for sharing these reflections with me (e-mail, 12/29/10).

734 See Zohar I: 15a, tr. D. Matt, *Pritzker Edition*, (Stanford: Stanford University Press, 2004), pp. 107-108.

735 Bob Dylan, "Every Grain of Sand," (*Shot of Love*, 1981).

736 Bob Dylan, "Queen Jane Approximately," (*Highway 61 Revisited*, 1965).

[737] Elaine H. Pagels, *The Gnostic Gospels*. (London: Phoenix, 2006).

[738] https://www.poetryfoundation.org/poets/marie-howe (accessed 12/19/18).

[739] "Scholar Elaine Pagels says spirituality defies logic. She knows from personal experience," *Tapestry* (CBC Radio: December 14, 2018), see: https://www.cbc.ca/radio/tapestry/why-religion-1.4934033/scholar-elaine-pagels-says-spirituality-defies-logic-she-knows-from-personal-experience-1.4940931 (accessed 12/19/18).

[740] Marie Howe, "Annunciation," *The Kingdom of Ordinary Time*, (New York: W.W. Norton & Co, 2008), p. 43.

[741] Bob Dylan, "It's alright ma, I'm only bleeding," (*Bringing it all back home*, 1965).

[742] Bob Dylan, "Pay In Blood," (*The Tempest,* 2012).

[743] Bob Dylan, "Let me die in my footsteps" [1963] (*Bootleg Series Volume 1: Rare and Unreleased*, 1961-1991).

[744] Bob Dylan, "Born in Time," (*Under the Red Sky*, 1990).

[745] Bob Dylan, "Tell Me," (*Bootleg Series Volume 1: Rare and Unreleased*, 1961-1991).

[746] *Ibid.*

[747] Bob Dylan, "Dark Eyes," (*Empire Burlesque*, 1985).

[748] Tristan Tzara, *Approximate Man and Other Writings*, tr. M. A. Caw, (Wayne State Press: Pittsburgh, 1931/1973), pp.130-131.

[749] Zohar I: 51a-51b.

[750] Bob Dylan, "Born in Time," (*Under the Red Sky*, 1990).

[751] Bob Dylan, "Last Thoughts on Woody Guthrie," (*Bootleg Series Volume 1: Rare and Unreleased*, 1961-1991).

[752] Bob Dylan, *Tarantula*, (Hibbing, Minn: Wimp Press, 1960), p. 37.

[753] Bob Dylan, "Gates of Eden," (*Bringing it all Back Home*, 1965).

[754] The angel of fire is already recounted in Talmudic literature, for example see: b *Baba Batra* 74b. Other examples abound in *Hekhalot* literature as well, see, Rachel Elior, "Mysticism, Magic, and Angelology: The Perception of Angels in *Hekhalot* Literature." *Jewish Studies Quarterly* 1.1 (1993): pp. 3-53.

[755] Marcel Carné, *Les Enfants du Paradis* (1945).

[756] Bob Dylan, "Watered-Down Love," (*Shot of Love*, 1981).

[757] *Ibid.*

[758] Bob Dylan, "Queen Jane Approximately," (*Highway 61 Revisited*, 1965).

12. Knockin' on Heaven's Door: Outlaw Seeking Redemption

[759] Bob Dylan, "Knockin' on Heaven's Door," (*Pat Garret & Billy the Kid*, 1973).

[760] Bob Dylan, "Tryin' to Get to Heaven," (*Time out of Mind*, 1997).

[761] b*Baba Metzia* 59a.

[762] Daniel Boyarin, *A Traveling Homeland: The Babylonian Talmud as Diaspora*. (University of Pennsylvania Press, 2015).

[763] b*Berachot* 32a.

[764] *Tiqqunei HaZohar, Tiqqun no.* 11, 26b.

[765] Bob Dylan, "Knockin' on Heaven's Door," (*Pat Garret & Billy the Kid*, 1973); Margotin and Guesdon analyze this "extraordinary mystical dimension that is typical of Dylan" in this lyric as emerging from "the words of Sheriff Colin Baker (Slim Pickens), who had been fatally injured by the gang of Billy the Kid before the eyes of his wife (Katy Jurado)" in Dylan's contribution to the soundtrack of Sam Peckinpah's 1973 film, *Pat Garrett and Billy the Kid*, see Margotin and Guesdon, *Bob Dylan: All the Songs: the Story Behind Every Track*, p. 381. What their analysis tends to lack is any rigor in articulating just what this "extraordinary mystical dimension that is typical of Dylan" really means and how it emerges from and affects the contours of American Religion, which this present study aims to redress.

[766] Michael Ondaatje, *The Collected Works of Billy the Kid*. (New York: Vintage International, 2009), p. 3.

[767] Ondaatje, *The Collected Works of Billy the Kid*, p. 27.

[768] *Ibid*, p. 46.

[769] *Ibid*, p. 47.

[770] *Ibid*, p. 54.

[771] *Ibid*, p. 93.

[772] *Ibid*, p. 99.

773 Bob Dylan, "Tryin' to Get to Heaven," (*Time out of Mind*, 1997); see Margotin and Guesdon, *Bob Dylan: All the Songs: the Story Behind Every Track,* p. 620.

774 Bob Dylan, "Shot of Love," (*Shot of Love*, 1981).

775 Dave Van Ronk and Elijah Wald, *The Mayor of Macdougal Street: A Memoir.* (Da Capo Press, 2013), p. 4.

776 Bob Dylan, "Chimes of Freedom," (*Another Side of Bob Dylan*, 1964); Margotin and Guesdon analyze this lyric as an expansion of Dave Van Ronk's "Chimes of Trinity" as correlated to the Sermon on the Mount, William Blake and Arthur Rimbaud's poem, "Vowels", see Margotin and Guesdon, *Bob Dylan: All the Songs: the Story Behind Every Track,* pp. 120-121. The latter lens of Rimbaud is the most compelling and least explored in their analysis.

777 Bob Dylan, "Bob Dylan's 115th Dream," (*Bringing it all Home*, 1965); Margotin and Guesdon analyze this lyric by turning back to Captain Ahab, the protagonist of Herman Mellevilles' *Moby-Dick*, which in light of the recent Nobel Prize speech is quite salient, see Margotin and Guesdon, *Bob Dylan: All the Songs: the Story Behind Every Track,* p. 166.

778 Van Ronk, *The Mayor of Macdougal Street: A Memoir*, p. 162.

779 *ibid,* p. 162.

780 *ibid,* p. 159: "[Dylan] wrote 'Song for Woody' specifically to sing in the hospital. He was writing for Woody, to amuse him, to entertain him. Of course it was also a personal thing, he wanted Woody's approval, but it was more than that. We all admired Woody and considered him a legend, but none of us was trucking out to see him and play for him. In that regard, Dylan was as stand-up a cat as I have ever known, and it was a very decent and impressive beginning for anybody's career."

781 Zohar 2: 61b, *Pritzker Edition*, vol. 4, tr. Matt, (Stanford University Press: Stanford, California), p. 329.

782 Bob Dylan, "With God on our Side," (*The Times They Are a Changin'*, 1963).

783 Bob Dylan, "Outlaw Blues" (*Bringing it all Home*, 1965); *ibid,* "One More Cup of Coffee (Valley Below)," (*Desire*, 1975).

[784] Van Ronk, *The Mayor of Macdougal Street*, p. 159: "[Dylan] wrote 'Song for Woody' specifically to sing in the hospital. He was writing for Woody, to amuse him, to entertain him. Of course it was also a personal thing, he wanted Woody's approval, but it was more than that. We all admired Woody and considered him a legend, but none of us was trucking out to see him and play for him. In that regard, Dylan was as stand-up a cat as I have ever known, and it was a very decent and impressive beginning for anybody's career."

[785] Bob Dylan, "Lenny Bruce," (*Shot of Love*, 1981); see Margotin and Guesdon, *Bob Dylan: All the Songs: the Story Behind Every Track,* p. 498.

[786] Bob Dylan, "Blind Willie McTell," (Bootlegs 1-3, vol. 1983), see above n393.

[787] Bob Dylan, "Precious Angel," (*Slow Train Coming*, 1979).

[788] Bob Dylan, "Lenny Bruce," (*Shot of Love*, 1981); see Margotin and Guesdon, *Bob Dylan: All the Songs: the Story Behind Every Track,* p. 498.

13. When He Returns in A Long Black Coat: From Messianic Personhood to Process

Acknowledgements: Thanks to David Wilensky for the invitation to write an earlier version of this essay, "Bob Dylan, the messiah and personal redemption," for JWeekly (April 7, 2017).

[789] Heylin, *Behind the Shades: Take Two*, p. 549.

[790] *Ibid,* pp. 490-491, 511.

[791] *Ibid,* pp. 510-511.

[792] *Ibid,* p. 512.

[793] *Ibid,* p. ix.

[794] Elaine Pagels, *The Gnostic Gospels*, (Vintage Books: New York, 1979), pp. xiii-xxiii.

[795] Heylin, *Behind the Shades*, p. 491.

[796] *Ibid,* p. 492.

[797] *Ibid,* p. ix.

[798] *Ibid,* p. 548.

[799] *Ibid,* p. 549.

[800] *Ibid,* p. ix.

[801] Bryan Cheyette, "On the 'D' Train: Bob Dylan's Conversions," in *Do You Mr Jones? Bob Dylan with Poets and Professors,* Neil Corcoran, ed. (Random House Kindle: 2017), *n.p.*

[802] Heylin, *Behind the Shades: Take Two*, p. 549.

[803] *Ibid,* p. 549.

[804] "The Saint and the Troubadour: John Paul II and Dylan," (13/10/2016) http://en.radiovaticana.va/news/2016/10/13/the_saint_and_the_troubadour_john_paul_ii_and_dylan/1265021 (accessed 3/10/17).

[805] Apparently Dylan only developed a deep relationship in his meetings with *Rosh Yeshiva* of *Shor Yashuv*, Rabbi Shlomo Freifeld *z"l*, see Sarah Levine, "5 Orthodox Things You Did Not Know About Bob Dylan," see http://jewinthecity.com/2016/06/5-orthodox-jewish-things-you-didnt-know-about-bob-dylan/ (accessed 3/10/17).

[806] Sean Curnyn, "The Pope and Popstar," *First Things* (5/10/07), see: https://www.firstthings.com/web-exclusives/2007/05/the-pope-and-the-pop-star (accessed 3/10/17).

[807] Heylin, *Behind the Shades*, pp. 549, 551.

[808] *Ibid*, p. 550.

[809] *Ibid*, p. 498.

[810] *Ibid*, p. 508.

[811] Bob Dylan, "Pressing On," (*Saved*, 1980). Margotin and Guesdon offer a confusing interpretation of this lyric as a "look toward the future" making it into a "continuation of Don't Look Back" contending that despite Dylan's exploration of new horizons "since his conversion to Christianity", they then still claim that this lyric is inspired by the Gospel According to John 6: 30-32, see Margotin and Guesdon, *Bob Dylan: All the Songs: the Story Behind Every Track*, p. 488.

[812] Rabbi Meshulam Feish Segal-Loewy, *Haggadah shel Pesah: 'Avodat haLevi*, No. 3, pp. 193b-194a.

[813] *ibid*, No. 4, p. 194a.

[814] Roland Barthes, *S/Z*, (New York: Hill and Wang, 2007), p. 5.

[815] Heylin, *Behind the Shades*, 550.

[816] Bob Dylan, "Man in The Long Black Coat," (*O Mercy*, 1989); see above n25.

[817] Bob Dylan, "When He Returns," (*Slow Train Coming*, 1979); Margotin and Guesdon analyze this lyric as no different from the ethos of "Blowin' in the Wind" except for its reliance on Christ for the resolution and its inspiration from the Gospel according to Matthew 7:14, see Margotin and Guesdon, *Bob Dylan: All the Songs: the Story Behind Every Track*, p. 477.

[818] Bob Dylan, "Pay in Blood," (*Tempest,* 2012); Margotin and Guesdon analyze this lyric in correlation to earlier lyrics like "Masters of War" and "Ballad of a Thin Man" and then turn to the metaphor of the passion of Christ, see Margotin and Guesdon, *Bob Dylan: All the Songs: the Story Behind Every Track,* p.687.

[819] Pew recently found that 70 percent of Jews claim to have participated in a Passover *seder* in the past year: see "A Portrait of American Jews," Pew Study (10/1/15), accessed 4/9/15, http://www.pewforum.org/2013/10/01/jewish-american-beliefs-attitudes-culture-survey/.

[820] Emma Morris, "*Haggadot* on View at the University of Chicago," *Jewcy* (4/5/12), accessed 4/12/15, http://jewcy.com/jewish-arts-and-culture/haggadot-on-view-at-the-university-of-chicago.

[821] Elliot R. Wolfson, *Open Secret: Postmessianic Messianism and the Mystical Revision of Menahem Mendel Schneerson* (New York: Columbia University Press, 2012); *ibid,* "Immanuel Frommann's Commentary on Luke and the Christianizing of Kabbalah: Some Sabbatean and Hasidic Affinities." *Holy Dissent: Jewish and Christian Mystics in Eastern Europe*, ed. Glenn Dynner, (Detroit: Wayne State University Press, 2011), pp. 171-222.

[822] There are a number of recent studies which examine the Americanization of the Chabad project of populist mysticism externally and internally; for the former, see Sue Fishkoff, *The Rebbe's Army: Inside the World of Chabad-Lubavitch.* (New York: Schocken Books, 2013); Samuel C. Heilman, and Menachem Friedman, *The Rebbe: The Life and Afterlife of Menachem Mendel Schneerson.* (Princeton, N.J: Princeton University Press, 2012);

for the latter, see Shaul S. Deutsch, *Larger Than Life: The Life and Times of the Lubavitcher Rebbe Rabbi Menachem Mendel Schneerson.* (New York: Chasidic Historical Productions, 1995); Chaim Miller, *Turning Judaism Outward: A Biography of Rabbi Menachem Mendel Schneerson the Seventh Lubavitcher Rebbe,* (Brooklyn, NY : Kol Menachem, 2014); Avrum M. Ehrlich, *The Messiah of Brooklyn: Understanding Lubavitch Hasidism Past and Present.* (Jersey City, NJ: KTAV, 2004).

[823] *Ibid,* p.197.

[824] Rabbi Meshulam Feish Segal-Loewy, *Haggadah shel Pesah: 'Avodat haLevi*, n3, pp.193b-194a.

[825] *Ibid*, n4, p.194a.

[826] Roland Barthes, *S/Z: [an Essay].* New York: Hill and Wang, 2007), p. 5.

[827] Segal-Loewy, *Zemirot 'Avodat haLevi*, p. 108.

[828] Segal-Loewy, *Haggadah shel Pesah: 'Avodat haLevi*, p. 123a.

[829] Rabbi Meshulam Feish Segal-Loewy, *Zemiort 'Avodat haLevi*, *s.v. Seder Ne'ilat haHag,* pp.123a-124b.

[830] *Ibid, 'Avodat haLevi: Haggadah shel Pesah* (Boisbriand: *Kiryas Tosh*, 2005), pp.61a-62b.

14. *I Shall be Released* from BIG TECH & Smaller Seaweeds into a *Life of Trouble*

[831] Aubrey L. Glazer, "Last Laugh Reincarnated as a Lobster: The Comedy of Substitution as *Gilgul* in Levinas," Bergen-Aurand, ed. In *Comedy Begins with Our Simplest Gestures: Levinas, Ethics, and Humor.* (Pittsburgh, Pennsylvania: Duquesne University Press, 2017), pp.185-202.

[832] "Bob Dylan's New IBM Commercial" (Extended Version) https://www.youtube.com/watch?v=wtyORRJ_gzM (accessed 11/10/17)

[833] Heylin, *Bob Dylan: Behind the Shades: Take Two*, p.266.

[834] Sam Shepherd, "A Short Life of Trouble" (1987), ed. Bob Dylan and Jonathan Cott. *Bob Dylan, the Essential Interviews*, (Wenner Books: New York, 2006), p. 365.

[835] Heylin, *Bob Dylan: Behind the Shades: Take Two,* p.264.

[836] Franklin Foer, *World Without Mind: The Existential Threat of Big Tech*, (Penguin Press: New York, 2017).

[837] Hava Tirosh-Samuelson, "Jewish Philosophy, Human Dignity, and the New Genetics," in Sean D. Sutton, ed. *Biotechnology: Our Future As Human Beings and Citizens.* (Albany: State University of New York Press, 2009), pp.81-121.

[838] *Ibid.*

[839] *Ibid.*

[840] Bob Dylan, "Caribbean Wind," (*Biograph*,1985).

[841] Bob Dylan, "Masters of War," (*Freewheelin' Bob Dylan*, 1963).

[842] Tirosh-Samuelson, "Jewish Philosophy, Human Dignity, and the New Genetics," pp.81-121.

[843] *Ibid.*

[844] Mark Blitz, "Understanding Heidegger and Technology," *The New Atlantis: A Journal of Technology and Society,* see: https://www.thenewatlantis.com/publications/understanding-heidegger-on-technology (accessed 1/9/19).

[845] Bob Dylan, "Do Right to me Baby (Do Unto Others)," (*Slow Train Comin'*, 1979).

[846] Tirosh-Samuelson, "Jewish Philosophy, Human Dignity, and the New Genetics," pp.81-121.

[847] See m*Avot* 3:20, tr. M. Cohen, in *Pirkei Avot Lev Shalem: The Wisdom of Our Sages*, (New York: RA, 2018), p. 153:

"The shop is open, and the shopkeeper extends credit, but the ledger is [ever] open, and the hand [ever] writes [its daily entries]. And [thus] any who wish to borrow may come to do so, but collection agents [also] go around regularly every day and exact payment from people whether they wish to pay up or not, and they have [sound information] on which to rely."

[848] Jonah 2:4

[849] Jonah 2:6

[850] Jonah 2:5

[851] Bob Dylan, "I Shall Be Released," (*Greatest Hits Vol. II,* 1967); Margotin and Guesdon analyze this lyric as inspired by Johnny Cash's "Folsom Prison Blues" and Brendan Behan's "The Banks of the Royal Canal" and then follow Dylan's comment that "the whole world is a prison," see Margotin and Guesdon, *Bob Dylan: All the Songs: the Story Behind Every Track,* p. 372.

[852] Bob Dylan, "I Shall Be Released," (*Greatest Hits Vol. II,* 1967), see above n558.

[853] Bob Dylan, "It's Alright Ma, (I'm Only Bleedin')," (*Bringing It All Back Home,* 1965); see above n176.

[854] Bob Dylan, "Absolutely Sweet Marie," (*Blonde on Blonde,* 1966).

[855] Daniel Hemel & Eric Posner, "If Trump Pardons, It Could Be a Crime" NYT (July 21, 2017).

[856] Gershom Scholem and Eric J. Schwab, tr., "On Jonah and the Concept of Justice," *Critical Inquiry.* 25.2 (1999): pp. 353-361:

> "The unequivocal connection between the judge's decision to the executive power—a connection that defines the actual order of law—is suspended by the deferment on the part of the executive power. That is what God does in Nineveh! The conclusion of 4:10— he passed a sentence in order to carry it out, and he did not (yet) do it—is a classic statement of the idea of justice!"

[857] Elie Wiesel, *The Trial of God (as It Was Held on February 25, 1649, in Shamgorod): A Play in Three Acts.* (New York: Schocken Books, 1986), pp. xvii.

15. *Pressing On* with *Emunah* in Elul: Giving it up when 'deafferented' by God

Acknowledgements: I am grateful to Jeremy Brown for the coffee and conversation that sparked this chapter (MELK Café: Montreal, August 15, 2018).

[858] Andrew Newberg, Eugene D'Aquili, and Vince Rause, *Why God Won't Go Away: Brain Science and the Biology of Belief,* (Ballantine Books: New York 2002), p. 53.

[859] The month of *Elul* is more than the twelfth month of the Jewish civil year and the sixth month of the ecclesiastical year on the Hebrew calendar. It is part of what Rabbi Jill Hammer teaches is an over-arching eightfold structure of the year woven like a Tabernacle: four pillars (the equinoxes and solstices) and four sockets in between them. If the Hebrew year interweaves itself within the structure of the natural seasons, then the major and minor festivals of the Jewish year fall at the equinoxes and solstices, while four minor but powerful transitional holidays fall in between the equinoxes and solstices. I find Hammer's insight here to be powerful insofar as the transition of the seasons and the cycles of time emerges in connection with the earth. This part of the cycle is a shift from the Harvest Dance of *Tu B'Av* to the beginning of the Autumn Equinox of *Tishrai* that heads up the New Year. So the month of *Elul* on the Hebrew calendar marks a unique texture in divine temporality—a moment that dances between the king being in the field and the Hebrew zodiac of Virgo (*betulah*). This dance of divine time is between action and paralysis, formed in the Book of Creation with the Hebrew letter *Yud*. This oscillation between arousal and rest contained within a single letter reflects the month's movement towards stillness. Moreover, the canvas being painted by Jewish mysticism is an allusion to an intimate experience of the divine in our lives like no other time of the year—*why? Elul* is also an ancient instant message, a Hebrew acrostic composed of *ELV"L*— spelling out "I am My Beloved's as My Beloved is Mine"[ELV"L = *Ani L'Dodi V'Dodi Li*] (Song of Songs 6:3)

[860] Song of Songs 7:11.

[861] Abraham J. Heschel, *God in Search of Man: A Philosophy of Judaism.* (London: Souvenir Press, 2009).

[862] Newberg, D'Aquili, Rause, *Why God Won't Go Away: Brain Science and the Biology of Belief*, pp. 36-37.

[863] *Ibid*, pp. 140.

[864] *Ibid*, pp. 146-147.

[865] Bob Dylan, "Positively 4th Street," (*Bob Dylan's Greatest Hits*, 1965).

[866] Bob Dylan, "Knockin' on Heaven's Door," (*Pat Garrett & Billy the Kid*, 1973).

[867] Bob Dylan, "Precious Angel," (*Slow Train*, 1979).

[868] Bob Dylan, "It's Alright Ma (I'm Only Bleeding)," (*Bringing It All Back Home*, 1965).

[869] Bob Dylan, "Dead Man, Dead Man," (*Shot of Love*, 1981).

[870] Bob Dylan, "Man of Peace," (*Infidels*, 1983).

[871] Bob Dylan, "Deadman, Deadman," (*Shot of Love*, 1981).

[872] Bob Dylan, "I Believe in You," (*Slow Train Coming*, 1979).

[873] Bob Dylan, "I Shall Be Released" (*Greatest Hits Vol. II*, 1967).

[874] Bob Dylan, "I Believe in You," (*Slow Train Coming*, 1979).

[875] *Ibid.*

[876] Bob Dylan, "Saving Grace," (*Saved*, 1980).

[877] Bob Dylan, "Every grain of sand" (*Shot of Love*, 1981).

[878] *Ibid.*

[879] Bob Dylan, "Man of Peace," (*Infidels*, 1983).

[880] Bob Dylan, "Pressing On," (*Saved*, 1980).

[881] Bob Dylan, "Ring Them Bells," (*O Mercy*, 1989).

[882] Bob Dylan, "Subterranean Homesick Blues," (Bringing It All Back Home, 1965).

16. *The Times They Are a Changin'* as the Cosmic Dreidel Spins On

[883] This refers to the teaching of the sixth rebbe of Chabad, Rabbi Yosef Yitzchak Schneersohn, who declared that in the early years of Rabbi Shneur Zalman's leadership: "One must live with the times... One must live with the Torah portion (*sidrah*) of the week and the particular section (*parsha*) of the day. One should not only *study* the weekly portion every day, but *live* with it."
The amplification of the initial statement was conveyed at a later date by Rabbi Shneur Zalman's brother, Rabbi Yehudah Leib of Yanovitch. See *Kuntres Bikur Chicago* (New York: Kehot Publication Society, 1944), pp. 7-8. See Eli Rubin, "Living with the Times: Rabbi Schneur Zalman of Liadi's Oral Teachings," see: https://www.chabad.org/library/article_cdo/aid/2087776/jewish/Living-with-the-Times-Rabbi-Schneur-Zalman-of-Liadis-Oral-Teachings.htm#footnote31a2087776 (accessed 8/27/18)

[884]Malcolm Kovacs, *The Dynamics of Commitment: The Process of Resocialization of Baalei Teshuvah, Jewish Students in Pursuit of Their Jewish Identity at the Rabbinical College of America (Lubavitch)*, 1979; Richard H. Greenberg, *Pathways: Jews Who Return.* Northvale, N.J: Jason Aronson, 1997). Berger, Robyn. *Teshuvah: Jewish Revival and the Ba'al Teshuvah Movement*, (Senior thesis: Boston University, 2002); Siegel, Seymour. "Will Herberg (1902-1977): a *Ba'al Teshuvah* Who Became Theologian, Sociologist, Teacher." *The American Jewish Year Book.* 78 (1978): pp. 529-537; see also, David Eliezrie, *The Secret of Chabad: Inside the World's Most Successful Jewish Movement*, (New Milford, CT, USA ; London, England : The Toby Press, 2016).

[885] Peter L. Berger, *The Sacred Canopy: Elements of a Sociological Theory of Religion.* (New York: Anchor, 1967); see also, Titus Hjelm, *Peter L. Berger and the Sociology of Religion: 50 Years After the Sacred Canopy*, (London: Bloomsbury Academic, 2018).

[886] Clinton Heylin, *Bob Dylan: Behind the Shades*, (New York: Penguin, 2000), p. xv.

[887] Christopher Ricks, *Dylan's Vision of Sin*, (Edinburgh: Canongate, 2011), p. 267.

[888] Ricks, *Dylan's Vision of Sin*, p. 267.

[889] Bob Dylan, "The Times They Are-a Changin'" (*The Times They Are-a Changin'*, Special Rider Music, 1963).

[890] Heylin, *Bob Dylan: Behind the Shades: Take Two,* p. 126.

[891] *Ibid, Bob Dylan: Behind the Shades*, p.126.

[892] *Ibid*, p. 126.

[893] *Ibid*, pp, 132-33.

[894] Ricks, *Dylan's Vision of Sin*, pp. 261, esp. pp. 257-71.

[895] Bob Dylan, "The Times They Are-a Changin'" (*The Times They Are-a Changin'*, Special Rider Music, 1963).

[896] *Ibid.*

[897] *Ibid.*

[898] *Ibid.*

[899] Reb Nahman of Bratzlav, *Sichot* n40.

[900] Bob Dylan, "The Times They Are-a Changin'" (*The Times They Are-a Changin'*, Special Rider Music, 1963).

17. As 'Infinity Goes on Trial' when all there is—Is

Acknowledgements: With thanks to Shaul Magid for this invitation to contribute an earlier version of this essay as a review for Tikkun Book Review (November 27, 2018).

[901] Bob Dylan, "Visions of Johanna," (*Blonde on Blonde*, 1966).

[902] Bento (*aka* Baruch in Hebrew; aka Benedictus, in Latin) Spinoza (1632-1677); more recently see Allan Nadler, "Romancing Spinoza: Efforts to reclaim the great philosopher and heretic continue-and continue to fail." *Commentary-New York-American Jewish Committee-* 122.5 (2006): p. 25.

[903] Steven Nadler, *s.v.* "Spinoza" in *Stanford Encyclopedia of Philosophy*, see: https://plato.stanford.edu/entries/spinoza/ (accessed 12/5/18).

[904] Steven Nadler, *s.v.* "Spinoza" in *Stanford Encyclopedia of Philosophy*, see: https://plato.stanford.edu/entries/spinoza/ (accessed 12/5/18).

[905] *Ibid.*

[906] For a personal reflection on this betrayal as felt by a Jewish philosopher, see Rebecca Goldstein, *Betraying Spinoza: The Renegade Jew Who Gave Us Modernity.* (New York: Schocken Books, 2010).

[907] Spinoza, *Ethics*, Id6 in *Collected Works of Spinoza*, ed. Edwin Curley, (Princeton University Press, 2016).

[908] John Culp, *s.v.* "Panentheism", in *Stanford Encyclopedia of Philosophy*, see: https://plato.stanford.edu/entries/panentheism/ (accessed 12/5/18).

[909] Spinoza, *Ethics*, Id9.

[910] *Ibid*, Ip9.

[911] Samuel Newlands, *s.v.* "Spinoza's Modal Metaphysics", in *Stanford Encyclopedia of Philosophy*, see: https://plato.stanford.edu/entries/spinoza-modal/ (accessed 12/5/18).

[912] Bob Dylan, "True Love Tends to Forget," (*Street Legal*, 1975).

[913] Bob Dylan, "Trouble," (*Shot of Love*, 1981).

[914] Bob Dylan, "Sugar Baby," (*Love and Theft*, 2001).

[915] Wertheimer, *The New American Judaism: How Jews Practice Their Religion Today*, p. 259.

[916] Bob Dylan, "Man in the Long Black Coat," (*O Mercy*, 1989).

917 Reb Zalman Schacter-Shalomi was being groomed to become the next Lubavitcher rebbe, until he formerly broke with Chabad, after confessing to using psychedelics in his journeys of prayer:"Schachter-Shalomi also took LSD with Timothy Leary at an ashram in Massachusetts and recounts going to 770 Eastern Parkway to get the blessing of the Lubavitcher Rebbe, who did offer him multiple *"l'chaims"* for a "good meditation and a good retreat," according to the account given in *The December Project.* Schachter-Shalomi recounts what he told Leary after taking LSD: "This is better than schnapps." When he spoke publicly as a Lubavitcher about these experiences in 1968 in Washington, D.C., the Lubavitchers found him an "embarrassment" and cut their ties with him."

See: Paul Vitello, "Zalman Schacter-Shalomi, Jewish Pioneer, dies at 89," (*New York Times*: July 8, 2014) https://www.nytimes.com/2014/07/09/us/zalman-schachter-shalomi-jewish-pioneer-dies-at-89.html (accessed 2/12/19). See also: Beth Kissilief, "Fridays with Zalman: The Spiritual Wisdom of Zalman Schacter-Shalomi," *Tablet* (May 26, 2014). https://www.tabletmag.com/jewish-life-and-religion/167091/zalman-schachter-shalomi-december (accessed 2/12/19).

918 Shaul Magid, "Between Paradigm Shift Judaism and Neo-Hasidism: The New Metaphysics of Jewish Renewal," in *Tikkun* (Winter 2015), see: https://www.tikkun.org/nextgen/between-paradigm-shift-judaism-and-neo-hasidism-the-new-metaphysics-of-jewish-renewal (accessed 12/17/18).

919 James Lovelock, *Gaia: A New Look at Life on Earth*, (Oxford: Oxford University Press, 1974/2016).

920 Bob Dylan, "Visions of Johanna," (*Blonde on Blonde*, 1966).

CODETTA: Neither Top Nor Bottom, Unaware on a Ladder

Acknowledgements: Thanks to David Wilensky for the invitation to write an earlier version of this essay, "Be present, persevere—and climb the long ladder," for J.Weekly (November 23, 2017).

[921] George C. Perry, *The Life of Python,* (London: Pavillion, 2014).

[922] Bob Dylan, "Like a Rolling Stone," (*Highway 61 Revisited,* 1965), see above n172.

[923] Allan Lew, *This is Real and You Are Completely Unprepared: The Days of Awe As a Journey of Transformation,* (New York: Backbay Books, 2018).

[924] See Aubrey L. Glazer, "In Time to Love: Along My Path to the Vanishing Path," in Miles Krassen, *The Vanishing Path: How to Be While There Is Still Time,* (Louisville: Fons Vitae, 2019), pp. 17-74.

[925] Genesis 28:12.

[926] Bob Dylan, "Forever Young," (Planet Waves, 1974).

[927] Bob Dylan, "A Hard Rain's A-Gonna Fall," (*Freewheelin' Bob Dylan,* 1963).

[928] Bob Dylan, "The Lonesome Death of Hattie Carrol," (*The Times They Are a Changin',* 1964).

[929] Bob Dylan, "Absolutely Sweet Marie," (*Blonde on Blonde,* 1966).

[930] Bob Dylan, "Ain't Talkin'," (*Modern Times,* 2006).

[931] Bob Dylan, "You Ain't Goin' Nowhere," (*Greatest Hits,* Volume II, 1967); Margotin and Guesdon analyze this as "a stream of absurd lyrics," see Margotin and Guesdon, *Bob Dylan: All the Songs: the Story Behind Every Track,* p. 266.

[932] I am grateful to Elliot Wolfson for ongoing encouragement throughout the writing of this book, returning me to important lyrics like this one so that the fragments of thinking could emerge into something like this broken whole.

CODA: Dylan's Gnostic Songbook in the Shade of the Jewish Artist

Acknowledgements: I am indebted to Harold Bloom for our decade long discourse on American Gnosticism, and especially Shaul Magid, who shared with me early drafts of his thinking on the pioneering work of Rav Kook on the Jewish Artist, see Shaul Magid, "Allegory Unbound: Rav Kook, Rabbi Akiva, Song of Songs and the Rabbinic (Anti) Hero", Kabbalah: A Journal for the Study of Jewish Mystical Texts, vol. 32 (Los Angeles: Cherub Press, 2004): pp. 57-82.

[933] Bob Dylan, "Angelina," (*The Bootleg Series*, Vol. 1-3, 1961-1991); see Margotin and Guesdon, *Bob Dylan: All the Songs: the Story Behind Every Track*, p. 505.

[934] Henry Corbin, *Mundus Imaginalis, or the Imaginary and the Imaginal*, (Ipswich, U.K: Golgonooza Press, 1976).

[935] See Gershom Scholem, "*Tselem:* Concept of the Astral Body" in *On the Mystical Shape of the Godhead: Basic Concepts in the Kabbalah*, tr. *Joachim Neugroschel* (New York: Schocken, 1991), pp. 251-272.

[936] Bob Dylan, "When I paint my masterpiece," (*Greatest Hits*, Vol. II, 1971); Margotin and Guesdon suggest a parallel, after Heylin, between the narrator here and Dick Diver, the protagonist in F. Scott Fitzgerald's *Tender is the Night*, but ultimately allow a paradox to emerge when during the Rolling Thunder Review (1975-76), Dylan sings, "Oh, to be back in the land of Coca-Cola," see Margotin and Guesdon, *Bob Dylan: All the Songs: the Story Behind Every Track*, p. 371.

[937] Richard F. Thomas, "Dylan and Ancient Rome: That's Where I Was Born", in *Why Dylan Matters*, (Dey Street Books, Harper Collins: New York, 2017), pp. 41-94.

[938] Bob Dylan, "When I paint my masterpiece," (*Greatest Hits*, Vol. II, 1971).

[939] Bob Dylan, "She Belongs to Me," (*Bringing it all Back Home*, 1965); Margotin and Guesdon analyzes this lyric as an "anti-love" song about folk singer Joan Baez, Nico, Sara Lownds, Caroline Coon, see Margotin and Guesdon, *Bob Dylan: All the Songs: the Story Behind Every Track*, p. 156.

[940] Proverbs 3:19.

[941] Proverbs 8:30.

[942] *Yalkut Shimoni* Proverbs 8:30, ch. 8: n942; Zohar II: 161a.

[943] *Entsiḳlopedyah Miḳra'it: Otsar Ha-Yedi'ot 'al Ha-Miḳra U-Teḳufato, s.v. Bezalel,* vol. 2 (Jerusalem: Mosad Bialiḳ, 1950), pp. 306a-b.

[944] *Ibid,* 306a-b.

[945] The term "skillful means" is a translation of the notion of *upāya* as expressed in the renowned *Lotus Sutra,* as an "expansion of the range of Conventional Truth in the Three Truths: the diversity of sentient beings is limitless, their specific delusions and attachments and sufferings are of limitless specific types, and thus the appropriate remedial practices and doctrines for them are limitless." See Brook Ziporyn, "Tiantai Buddhism", *The Stanford Encyclopedia of Philosophy* (Spring 2017 Edition), Edward N. Zalta (ed.), URL = <https://plato.stanford.edu/archives/spr2017/entries/buddhism-tiantai/>. (accessed 2/20/18). See also John W. Schroeder, *Skillful means: The heart of Buddhist compassion.* Vol. 54. (Motilal Banarsidass Publ., 2004); Jon Kabat-Zinn, "Some reflections on the origins of MBSR, skillful means, and the trouble with maps," *Contemporary Buddhism* 12.01 (2011): pp. 281-306.

[946] Exodus 35:30, *ad. loc. Meshekh Hokhmah.*

[947] Chaim Potok, *My Name is Asher Lev,* (New York: Anchor, [1972] 2009).

[948] Ellen Serlen Uffen, "*My Name Is Asher Lev*: Chaim Potok's Portrait of the Young Hasid as Artist," *Studies in American Jewish Literature (1981-)* (1982): 174-180; compare with Charles Berryman, "Philip Roth and Nathan Zuckerman: A Portrait of the Artist as a Young Prometheus," *Contemporary Literature* 31.2 (1990): pp.177-190.

[949] Shai Secunda, "Nuclear Family," *Jewish Review of Books*, https://jewishreviewofbooks.com/archive/issues/summer-2016/ (accessed 2/20/18).

[950] James Joyce, *A Portrait of the Artist As a Young Man.* (New York: Garland, 1977).

[951] https://www.britannica.com/topic/Daedalus-Greek-mythology (accessed 2/20/18).

[952] Exodus 39:43.

[953] Psalms 17:8, 36:8, 63:8, 74:19, 91:1-4; Ruth 2:12; Deuteronomy 32:11; I Kings 6:23, etc.

[954] "You have seen what I did unto the Egyptians, and how I bore you on eagles' wings, and brought you unto Myself" (Exodus 19:4).

[955] "O You that dwells in the covert of the Most High, and abides in the shade of the *Shaddai*" (Psalm 91:1).

956 G. J. Botterweck, Helmer Ringgren, and Heinz-Josef Fabry, *s.v. sel*, in *Theological Dictionary of the Old Testament*, vol. 12, (Grand Rapids, Mich: Eerdmans, 2004), pp. 372-382, esp. p. 375.

957 Botterweck, Ringgren, and Fabry, *s.v. sel*, in *Theological Dictionary of the Old Testament*, p. 375.

958 *Ibid*, p. 379.

959 Genesis 1:26.

960 Botterweck, Ringgren, and Fabry, *s.v. sel*, in *Theological Dictionary of the Old Testament*, p. 380.

961 James Hillman, *Animal Presences*, (Putnam, Conn: Spring Publications, 2008), p. 24.

962 Hillman, *Animal Presences*, p. 24.

963 *Ibid*, p. 25.

964 *Ibid*, p. 25.

965 *Ibid*, p. 27.

966 *Ibid*, p. 24.

967 Exodus 26:1, *ad. loc.* Ibn Ezra (long commentary).

968 *Yalkut Shimoni* 13.

969 See Gilya Gerda Schmidt, *The Art and Artists of the Fifth Zionist Congress*, 1901, (Syracuse, NY: Syracuse University Press, 2003), pp. 1-31.

970 R. Avraham Isaac Kook, *Orot haQodesh,* vol. III, no 59, quoted in Benjamin Ish-Shalom, "Tolerance and its Theoretical Basis," in *Rabbi Abraham Isaac Kook and Jewish Spirituality*, ed. L. J. Kaplan and D. Shatz, (NY: NYU Press, 1995), p. 184.

971 R. Avraham Isaac Kook, *Olat RAYAH*, vol. 2, quoted in *The Essential Writings of Abraham Isaac Kook*, ed./tr. Ben Zion Bokser, (Warwick NY: Amity House, 1988), p. 205.

972 *Ibid, Orot haTeshuvah,* chapter 11, quoted in *Song of Teshuvah: A Commentary on Rav Avraham Yitzchak HaKohen Kook's Oros HaTeshuvah by Rav Moshe Weinberger & Adapted by Y. D. Shulman,* (Jerusalem: Penina Press, 2012), p. 42 [*translation emended*].

973 *Ibid, Orot haTechiah,* n36 (pp. 81-89), quoted in *Song of Teshuvah: A Commentary on Rav Avraham Yitzchak HaKohen Kook's Oros HaTeshuvah by Rav Moshe Weinberger & Adapted by Y. D. Shulman,* (Jerusalem: Penina Press, 2012), p. 426. [*translation emended*]

974 b*Qiddushin* 30a

975 *Ibid.* Isaiah 35:8-9

[976] *Ibid, Orot,* n119-120, quoted in Lawrence Fine, "Rav Kook and the Jewish Mystical Tradition," in *Rabbi Abraham Isaac Kook and Jewish Spirituality*, ed. L. J. Kaplan and D. Shatz, (NY: NYU Press, 1995), pp. 32-33.

[977] *Ibid, Igrot RAYA"H*, vol. 1, (Jerusalem: Mossad haRav Kook Publications, 1961), n. 154, pp. 203-206.

[978] *Ibid,* n154, p. 203; *ibid,* n154. p. 204: "...there will be those in accounting who will claim that there are other more pressing issues, more essential. Yes, perhaps and perhaps, there are and there are, but the calling that comes from heart of rebuilding, from the spirit that has washed over them, the calling itself is the sign of renaissance, the sign of hope for redemption and solace."

See also *ibid*, n154. p. 204: "This most important plane of art and aesthetics truly has the capacity to bring blessing and to open the gates of livelihood and economy to many families from our brethren sitting upon this holy land (Ezekiel 47: 12). It will also open the aesthetic impulse and its purity that the dear children of Zion are so skillfully endowed, that it shall elevate many souls and to those darkened in depression it will give them clarified and illumined vision, upon the splendor of life, nature and the craft, upon the glory of the work and diligence. All these are elevated principals that fill the soul of every Hebrew person attuned to the age and the splendor."

[979] "...and the fruit thereof shall be for food, and the leaf thereof for healing" (Ezekiel 47: 12).

[980] *Ibid*, n154, p. 206.

[981] b*Berakhot* 8a.

[982] See Hayyim Vital, *Etz Hayyim*, Gate 7, Chapter 1.

[983] Bob Dylan, "Absolutely Sweet Marie," (*Blonde on Blonde*, 1966).

[984] Mikal Gilmore, "Bob Dylan's Lost Years," in *Rolling Stone* (September 12, 2013); https://www.rollingstone.com/m usic/features/dylans-lost-years-20130912 (accessed 2/20/18)

985 Bob Dylan, "Brownsville Girl," (*Knocked Out Loaded,* 1986); Margotin and Guesdon note this as one of the most fruitful collaborations between Bob Dylan and Sam Shepherd, with references to Henry King's western, *The Gunfighter* (1950) starring Gregory Peck, see Margotin and Guesdon, *Bob Dylan: All the Songs: the Story Behind Every Track,* p. 544.

986 Bob Dylan, "Brownsville Girl," (*Knocked Out Loaded,* 1986).

987 Bob Dylan, "—The Beaten Path," see: www.bobdylanart.com/beaten-path.asp (accessed 2/18/18).

988 http://www.bobdylanart.com/exhibition.asp (accessed 2/18/18).

989 Landes, "Aesthetics as Mysticism," 57; see j*Ta'anit* 4:3.

Afterword: Unmasking the Mask of Unmasking: Dylan's Jewish Gnosis

990 Meister Eckhart as quoted by Arthur Schopenhauer, *The World as Will and Representation* (*Die Welt als Will und Vorstellung,* 1819, 1844), ii, ch. 48, tr. E F. J. Payne, (New York : Dover Publications, United States : RR Donnelley, 1966), p. 633.

991 Paul S. Loeb, and David F. Tinsley, tr.s, *Unpublished Fragments from the Period of Thus Spoke Zarathustra* (Stanford: Stanford University Press, 2019), p. 7.

992 Bob Dylan, "Abandoned Love," (*Biograph,* 1975); see also, ibid, *The Lyrics,* edited by Christopher Ricks, Lisa Nemrow, and Julie Nemrow (New York: Simon & Schuster. 2014), p. 534.

993 Bob Dylan, "Huck's Tune," (*Tell Tale Signs,* 2007); *ibid.,* p. 879.

994 Thomas Aquinas, *Summa Theologia, Prima Secundae, 71-114,* translated by Fr. Laurence Shapcote, O. P., edited by John Mortensen and Enrique Alarcón (Lander: Aquinas Institute for the Study of Sacred Doctrine, 2012), Ia-IIae. Q. 101, art. 2, ad. 1-2, p. 312. On the role of masks in Aquinas, see Renée Köhler-Ryan, "Thinking Transcendence, Transgressing the Mask: Desmond Pondering Augustine and Thomas Aquinas," in *William Desmond and Contemporary Theology,* edited by Christopher Ben Simpson and Brendan Thomas Sammon (Notre Dame: University of Notre Dame Press, 2017), pp. 191-216, esp. 202-208.

[995] For a more extensive discussion of this topic, see Elliot R. Wolfson, "Saturnine Melancholy and Dylan's Jewish Gnosis," to appear in *World of Bob Dylan*, edited by Sean Latham and Brian Hosmer (Cambridge: Cambridge University Press, 2020). Some of the analysis in that essay is repeated here.

[996] *The Gnostic Scriptures*, a new translation with annotations and introductions by Bentley Layton (Garden City: Doubleday & Company, 1987), p. 341.

[997] Geoffrey S. Kirk and John E. Raven, *The Presocratic Philosophers: A Critical History with a Selection of Texts* (Cambridge: Cambridge University Press, 1979), p. 344; *Empedocles: The Extant Fragments*, edited, with an introduction, commentary, and concordance, by M. R. Wright (New Haven: Yale University Press, 1981), pp. 44, 72-73, 76, 233-235.

[998] *The Gnostic Scriptures*, p. 337.

[999] Bob Dylan, "Things Have Changed," (*Essential Bob Dylan*, 1999); *ibid, The Lyrics*, p. 890.

[1000] Bob Dylan, "It's Alright, Ma (I'm Only Bleeding)," (*Bringing It All Back Home*, 1965); *ibid.*, p. 188.

[1001] Jacques Derrida, *Dissemination*, translated, with an introduction and additional notes, by Barbara Johnson (Chicago: University of Chicago Press, 1981), pp. 157-158.

[1002] *Ibid.*, p. 156.

[1003] *Ibid.*, pp. 156-157. Compare Jacques Derrida, *Spurs/Nietzsche's Styles*, introduction by Stefano Agosti, translation by Barbara Harlow, drawings by François Loubrieu (Chicago: University of Chicago Press, 1978), pp. 20-23: "Here the meaning is not someplace else, but with writing it is made and unmade [*fait et défait*]. And if there is such a thing as truth, then this truth too can reside only in the imprint [*cette trace*] of an empty multiplied furrow which is both headless and tailless. It resides there that it should destroy itself. ... This writing is of an obscure sort, the sort that obliterates what it imprints and disperses what it says."

[1004] I have transcribed the lyrics from Bob Dylan, *The Bootleg Series*, vol. 11: *The Basement Tapes Raw* (2014). The text of "I'm Not There" is curiously missing from the http://www.bobdylan. com/songs/im-not-there/

[1005] Jacques Derrida, "A Testimony Given...," in *Questioning Judaism: Interviews by Elisabeth Weber*, translated by Rachel Bowlby (Stanford: Stanford University Press, 2004), p. 41; "Un témoignage donné," in *Questions au judaïsme. Entretiens avec Elisabeth Weber* (Paris: Desclée de Brouwer, 1996), p. 76. Compare Jacques Derrida, "Abraham, the Other," in *Judeities: Questions for Jacques Derrida*, edited by Bettina Bergo, Joseph Cohen, and Raphael Zagury-Orly, translated by Bettina Bergo and Michael B. Smith (New York: Fordham University Press, 2007), p. 16 (*Judéités: Questions pour Jacques Derrida*, edited by Joseph Cohen and Raphael Zagury-Orly [Paris: Galilée, 2003], p. 24): "I still feel, *at once, at the same time*, as less jewish *and* more jewish than the Jew [*comme moins juif* et *plus juif que le Juif*], as scarcely Jewish and as superlatively Jewish as possible, more than Jew [*plus que Juif*], exemplarily Jew, but also hyperbolically Jew" (emphasis in original).

[1006] Jacques Derrida, "Avowing—The Impossible: 'Returns,' Repentance, and Reconciliation," in *Living Together: Jacque Derrida's Communities of Violence and Peace*, edited by Elisabeth Weber (New York: Fordham University Press, 2013), p. 21; "Avouer—l'impossible: 'Retours', repentir et reconciliation," in Jacques Derrida, *Le dernier des Juifs* (Paris: Éditions Galilée, 2014), p. 23.

[1007] Bob Dylan, "Drifter's Escape," (*John Wesley Harding*, 1968); *ibid, The Lyrics*, p. 284.

[1008] I am here paraphrasing the celebrate line from "Absolutely Sweet Marie," (*Blonde on Blonde*, 1966), in Dylan, *The Lyrics*, p. 252: "But to live outside the law, you must be honest."

[1009] Zohar Ḥadash, edited by Reuven Margaliot (Jerusalem: Mosad ha-Rav Kook, 1978), 91b.

[1010] Martin Heidegger, *The History of Beyng*, translated by William McNeill and Jeffrey Powell (Bloomington: Indiana University Press, 2015), p. 178. My discussion here is an abbreviated version of the analysis of this passage in Elliot R. Wolfson, "*Gottwesen* and the De-divinization of the Last God: Heidegger's Meditation on the Strange and Incalculable," in *Heidegger's Black Notebooks and the Future of Theology*, edited by Mårten Björk and Jayne Svenungsson (New York: Palgrave Macmillan, 2017), pp. 215-216.

[1011] I have explored this in more detail in Elliot R. Wolfson, *The Duplicity of Philosophy's Shadow: Heidegger, Nazism, and the Jewish Other* (New York: Columbia University Press, 2018), pp. 87-108. Many Jewish thinkers have affirmed some form of the paradox of the messianic future as that which comes by not coming, but the two that bear the most affinity to Heidegger are Levinas and Derrida. See Elliot R. Wolfson, "Not Yet Now: Speaking of the End and the End of Speaking," in *Elliot R. Wolfson: Poetic Thinking*, edited by Hava Tirosh-Samuelson and Aaron W. Hughes (Leiden: Brill, 2015), pp. 127-193, esp. 142-156. On the paradox of the messianic event as a coming by not coming, see also Werner Hamacher, "Messianic Not," in *Messianic Thought Outside Theology*, edited by Anna Glazova and Paul North (New York: Fordham University Press, 2014), pp. 221-234, esp. 224-225.

[1012] Martin Heidegger, *Off the Beaten Track*, edited and translated by Julian Young and Kenneth Haynes (Cambridge: Cambridge University Press, 2002), p. 275.

[1013] Wolfson, "*Gottwesen*," pp. 235-236.

[1014] Jacques Derrida, *Margins of Philosophy*, translated, with additional notes, by Alan Bass (Chicago: University of Chicago Press, 1982), pp. 23-24. See my previous analyses of Derrida's commentary on this Heideggerian passage in Wolfson *Giving*, pp. 195-196, 425-426 n. 271; idem, Wolfson, *"Gottwesen,"* pp. 236-237. Compare the discussion of the Derridean trace against the background of Heidegger's thinking in Paola Marrati, *Genesis and Trace: Derrida Reading Husserl and Heidegger* (Stanford: Stanford University Press, 2005), pp. 87-176.

[1015] Jacques Derrida, *Speech and Phenomena and Other Essays on Husserl's Theory of Signs*, translated, with an introduction, by David B. Allison, preface by Newton Garver (Evanston: Northwestern University Press, 1973), p. 156; idem, *Of Grammatology*, translated by Gayatri Spivak, corrected edition (Baltimore: Johns Hopkins University Press, 1997), p. 61; idem, *Margins of Philosophy*, pp. 65-67. Regarding the philosopher's constriction to following the trace of truth, see Derrida, *Spurs/Nietzsche's Styles*, pp. 86-87. On the Derridean trace and arche-writing, see Tom Conley, 'A Trace of Style,' in *Displacement: Derrida and After*, edited by Mark Krupnick (Bloomington: Indiana University Press, 1983), pp. 74-92; Rodolphe Gasché, *The Tain of the Mirror: Derrida and the Philosophy of Reflection* (Cambridge, MA: Harvard University Press, 1986), pp. 157, 186-194, 277- 278, 289-293; idem, *Inventions of Difference: On Jacques Derrida* (Cambridge, MA: Harvard University Press, 1994), pp. 25, 40-42, 44-49, 158, 160-170; John D. Caputo, *The Prayers and Tears of Jacques Derrida: Religion without Religion* (Bloomington: Indiana University Press, 1997), pp. 57

61, 319-320; Christina Howells, *Derrida: Deconstruction from Phenomenology to Ethics* (Cambridge: Polity Press, 1999), pp. 50-52, 74, 134-135; Geoffrey Bennington, *Interrupting Derrida* (London: Routledge, 2000), pp. 12, 15, 28, 35, 169-171, 178, 196; Irene E. Harvey, *Derrida and the Economy of Différance* (Bloomington: Indiana University Press, 1986), pp. 153-181; David Farrell Krell, *Of Memory, Reminiscence, and Writing* (Bloomington: Indiana University Press, 1990), pp. 165-204. On the possible kabbalistic nuance of the Derridean arche-trace and the gesture of writing, see the views of Habermas, Bloom, and Handelman discussed in Elliot R. Wolfson, *Giving beyond the Gift: Apophasis and the Overcoming of Theomania* (New York: Fordham University Press, 2014), pp. 155-156, 177-178, 180, 182, 184-186. See ibid., p. 161, where I note the thematic link between time as the originary iterability, the non-identical identity of the Jew, and the trace as the repetition of the same that is always different.

[1016] There is affinity between Heidegger's *Spur* and Levinas's notion of the other as the *trace of illeity*. See Emmanuel Levinas, *Collected Philosophical Papers*, translated by Alphonso Lingis (Dordrecht: Martinus Nijhoff, 1987), pp. 106-107; idem, *Otherwise Than Being or Beyond Essence*, translated by Alphonso Lingis (Dordrecht: Kluwer Academic Publishers, 1991), pp. 12, 94; and see the analysis in Edith Wyschogrod, *Emmanuel Levinas: The Problem of Ethical Metaphysics*, second edition (New York: Fordham University Press, 2000), pp. 158-164, 224; Wolfson, *Giving*, pp. 98-99, 142, 144-148.

[1017] The remark occurs after the completion of the "Gates of Eden" on Bob Dylan, *The Bootleg Series*, vol. 6: *Bob Dylan Live, 1964, Concert at Philharmonic Hall* (2004).

[1018] Elliot R. Wolfson, *A Dream Interpreted Within a Dream: Oneiropoiesis and the Prism of Imagination* (New York: Zone Books, 2011), pp. 78, 94-101.

[1019] Bob Dylan, "The Ballad of Frankie Lee and Judas Priest," (*John Wesley Harding*, 1968); *ibid, The Lyrics*, p. 282.

[1020] Bob Dylan, "Outlaw Blues," (*Bringing It All Back Home*, 1965); *ibid.*, p. 180.

[1021] Bob Dylan, "If Dogs Run Free," (*New Morning*, 1970); *ibid.,* p. 366.

[1022] I am here paraphrasing "Silvio," (*Down in the Groove*, 1988); *ibid,* p. 730: "Since every pleasure's got an edge of pain / Pay for your ticket and don't complain."

[1023] Bob Dylan, "Shelter from the Storm," (*Blood On the Tracks*, 1974), *ibid.,* p. 494.

[1024] Bob Dylan, "Night After Night," (*Special Rider Music*, 1978), *ibid.,* p. 734.

[1025] Bob Dylan, "Forgetful Heart," (*Together Through Life*, 2009), *ibid.,* p. 902.

[1026] Bob Dylan, "When the Night Comes Falling from the Sky," (*Empire Burlesque*, 1985), *ibid.,* p. 693.

[1027] Bob Dylan, "Tight Connection to My Heart (Has Anyone See My Love)" (*Empire Burlesque*, 1985); *ibid.,* p. 686.

[1028] Bob Dylan, "All Along the Watchtower" (*John Wesley Harding*, 1968); *ibid.*, p. 281.

[1029] Bob Dylan, "Huck's Tune," (*Tell Tale Signs*, 2007); *ibid.,* p. 879.

[1030] Abraham Abulafia, *Or ha-Sekhel*, edited by Amnon Gross (Jerusalem, 2001), p. 94.

[1031] Bob Dylan, "Dirge," (*Planet Waves*, 1973), *ibid.,* p. 460.

Bibliography

Adams, Douglas. *The Hitch Hiker's Guide to the Galaxy*, (London: William Heinemann, 2014).

Adler, Rachel. *Engendering Judaism: an inclusive theology and ethics* (Boston, Mass: Beacon Press, 1998/2005).

Albanese, Catherine L. *A republic of mind and spirit: A cultural history of American metaphysical religion* (Yale University press New Haven, 2007).

Alter, Robert. tr. *Strong As Death Is Love: The Song of Songs, Ruth, Esther, Jonah, and Daniel: a Translation with Commentary*, (New York: W.W. Norton & Co, 2016).

_____. tr. *The Five Books of Moses: A Translation with Commentary*, (New York: W.W. Norton & Co, 2008).

Altmann, Alexander and Joseph Herman Hertz. *Gnostic Themes in Rabbinic Cosmology*, (London: n.p., 1943).

Amichai, Yehudah. "Love Gifts" Robert Alter, tr. *The Poetry of Yehuda Amichai,* (New York: Farrar, Straus and Giroux, 2015).

Anidjar, Gil *"Our place in al-Andalus": Kabbalah, philosophy, literature in Arab Jewish letters.* (Stanford University Press, 2002).

Artson, Bradley S. *God of Becoming and Relationship: The Dynamic Nature of Process Theology.* (Tennessee: Jewish Lights, 2016).

Aviram, Amittai F. "Rimbaud: Sex, Verse, and Modernity," *Sexual Politics and Experimental Poetics* in *French Literature Division* (North East Modern Language Association: Pittsburgh, April 1994).

Bachelard, Gaston. *La Flamme D'une Chandelle.* (Paris: Presses Universitaires de France, 1961).

_____. The *Flame of a Candle.* (Dallas: Dallas Institute Publications, 1988).

Baltzly, Dirk. *"Stoic Pantheism"* in *Sophia*, Vol. 42, No. 2, (Ashgate Publishing Ltd, October 2003).

Barnstone, Willis, and Marvin Meyer, eds., *The Nag Hammadi Library in The Gnostic Bible: Revised and Expanded Edition.* (Shambhala Publications, 2009).

Barthes, Roland. "The Death of the Author," in *Media Texts, Authors and Readers: A Reader* (1994).

_____. *S/Z,* (New York: Hill and Wang, 2007).

Bauer, Rudolph. "Dzogchen As Gnosticism: A Phenomenological View" (Washington Center for Consciousness Studies and the Washington Center for Phenomenological and Existential Psychotherapy Studies, *n.d.*).

Bevan, William. "On getting in bed with a lion," *American Psychologist* 35.9 (1980), pp. 779-789;

Bella, Robert N. "The Looming Triumph of Gnosticism" in *New Oxford Book Reviews* (October 1992).

_____. *Habits of the heart: individualism commitment in American life,* (University of California press, 1985, revised edition 2008).

Berger, David. *The Rebbe, the Messiah, and the Scandal of Orthodox Indifference.* (London: Littman Library of Jewish Civilization, 2008).

Berger, Peter L. *The Sacred Canopy: Elements of a Sociological Theory of Religion.* (New York: Anchor, 1967).

Berger, Robyn. *Teshuvah: Jewish Revival and the Ba'al Teshuvah Movement,* (Senior thesis: Boston University, 2002).

Berryman, Charles. "Philip Roth and Nathan Zuckerman: A Portrait of the Artist as a Young Prometheus," *Contemporary Literature* 31.2 (1990): pp.177-190.

Biale, David. "Historical heresies and modern Jewish identity," *Jewish social studies* 8.2 (2002):112-132.

_____. *Gershom Scholem: Kabbalah and counter-history.* (Harvard University Press, 1982).

Blanchot, Maurice. *La Communauté Affrontée (*Paris: Galilée, 2001).

_____. *The Disavowed Community,* tr. Philip Armstrong (New York: Fordham University Press, 2016).

_____. *The Unavowable Community,* tr. Pierre Joris (Barrytown, NY: Station Hill Press, 1988).

Blitz, Mark. "Understanding Heidegger and Technology," *The New Atlantis: A Journal of Technology and Society,* https://www.thenewatlantis.com/publications/understanding-heidegger-on-technology.

Bloch, Chana and Ariel, tr's, *The Song of Songs: The World's First Great Love Poem,* (Modern Library: New York, 1995).

Bloom, Harold. *Omens of Millennium: The Gnosis of Angels, Dreams, and Resurrection.* (New York: Riverside, 1997).

_____. *The American Religion,* (New York, NY: Chu Hartley Publishers, 2006).

Bloom, Harold. *The American Religion*, 2nd edition, (New York: Chu Hartley Publishers, 2006).

_____. *The Anxiety of Influence: A theory of poetry*. (New York: Oxford University Press, 1997).

_____. *The Daemon Knows: Literary Greatness and the American Sublime*, (New York : Spiegel & Grau, 2016).

Blumenthal, David R. *Philosophic Mysticism: Studies in Rational Religion*. (Ramat Gan: Bar Ilan University Press, 2007).

Boman, Thorlief. *Hebrew Thought Compared with Greek*. (New York: W.W. Norton, 1970).

Botterweck, G. J. Helmer Ringgren, and Heinz-Josef Fabry, *s.v. sel*, in *Theological Dictionary of the Old Testament*, vol. 12, (Grand Rapids, Mich: Eerdmans, 2004).

Boyarin, Daniel. *A Traveling Homeland: The Babylonian Talmud as Diaspora*. (University of Pennsylvania Press, 2015).

_____. *Border Lines: The Partition of Judaeo-Christianity*. (Philadelphia, Pa: Univ. of Pennsylvania Press, 2007).

Brakke, David. *Gnostics - Myth, Ritual, and Diversity in Early Christianity* (HUP, 2012).

Burton, Richard D.E. *s.v.* Charles Baudelaire, see: https://www.britannica.com/biography/Charles-Baudelaire).

Camus, Albert. *L'Homme Revolute*, (Gallimard: Paris, 1951).

Cardullo, R. J. "Memories Are Made of This: Rainer Werner Fassbinder's Veronika Voss," *Teaching Sound Film*, (2016), pp.155-162.

Carné, Marcel. *Les Enfants du Paradis* (1945).

Cashmore, E. E. *The Rastafarians* (London : Minority Rights Group, 1984); E. E. Cashmore, *Dictionary of Race and Ethnic Relations*, (London: Routledge, 2001).

Cheyette, Bryan. "On the D' Train: Bob Dylan's Conversions," in *Do You Mr Jones?: Bob Dylan with the Poets and Professors*, ed. Neil Corcoran, (Random House UK Ltd, 2017), pp. 171-195.

Christopher Ricks, *Dylan's Visions of Sin*. (Edinburgh: Canongate Books Ltd, 2011).

Cohen, Eric and Mitchell Rocklin, "The Jewish Tradition Unfolds in Fire: Here's How and Why," *Mosaic* (December 29, 2016).

Cohen, Martin. tr. in *Pirkei Avot Lev Shalem: The Wisdom of Our Sages*, (New York: RA, 2018).

Cooper, David A. *God Is a Verb: Kabbalah and the Practice of Mystical Judaism.* (New York, N.Y: Riverhead Books, 1998).

Corbin, Henry. *Mundus Imaginalis, or the Imaginary and the Imaginal,* (Ipswich, U.K: Golgonooza Press, 1976).

Corcoran, Neil. *Do You Mr Jones?: Bob Dylan with the Poets and Professors.* (Random House Kindle, 2010).

Corrigan, Robert W. "The Soulscape of Contemporary American Drama," *WT* 11: 316.

Culp, John. *s.v.* "Panentheism", in *Stanford Encyclopedia of Philosophy,* (Spring 2017 Edition).

Cummings, Edward Estlin and George James Firmage. *ee cummings: Complete Poems, 1904-1962.* (Liveright Publishing Corporation, 1994).

Curnyn, Sean. "The Pope and Popstar," *First Things* (October 5, 2007).

Dan Brown, *The Da Vinci Code.* (New York: Doubleday, 2004).

Dan, Joseph. "Gershom Scholem and Jewish Messianism," *Gershom Scholem: The Man and His Work, ed. P. Mendes-Flohr* (Albany, NY: SUNY Press, 1994): pp. 73-86.

Daniel Boyarin, *Border Lines: The Partition of Judaeo-Christianity.* (Philadelphia, Pa: University of Pennsylvania Press, 2007).

Davies, Stevan L. *The Secret Book of John: The Gnostic Gospel: Annotated and Explained.* Vermont: Skylight Illuminations).

de Vos, Gail. *What Happens Next?: Contemporary Urban Legends and Popular Culture.* (Santa Barbara: Libraries Unlimited, 2012).

Deconick, April D. *The Gnostic New Age: how a countercultural Spirituality revolutionized religion from antiquity to today,* (New York: Columbia University Press, 2016).

Deutsch, Shaul S. *Larger Than Life: The Life and Times of the Lubavitcher Rebbe Rabbi Menachem Mendel Schneerson,* (New York: Chasidic Historical Productions, 1995).

Dolan, Jay P. "In Whose God Do We Trust?" *New York Times,* (May 10, 1992).

Dollinger, Marc. *Black Power, Jewish Politics: Reinventing the Alliance in the 1960s* (Waltham, Massachusetts : Brandeis University Press, 2018).

Duclow, Donald F. "Divine Nothingness and Self-Creation in John Scotus Eriugena." *The Journal of Religion* 57.2 (1977): 109-123.

Ehrlich, Avrum M. *The Messiah of Brooklyn: Understanding Lubavitch Hasidism Past and Present*, (Jersey City, NJ: KTAV, 2004).

Eliezrie, David. *The Secret of Chabad: Inside the World's Most Successful Jewish Movement*, (New Milford, CT; London, England : The Toby Press, 2016).

Elior, Rachel. "Mysticism, Magic, and Angelology: The Perception of Angels in *Hekhalot* Literature." *Jewish Studies Quarterly* 1.1 (1993): pp. 3-53.

Enos, Morgan. "Bob Dylan's Whiskey & 6 Other Times He Entered the Marketplace," *Billboard* (April 30, 2018).

Erigena, John Scotus. *Periphyseon,* tr's Myra L. Uhlfelder, and Jean A. Potter (Eugene, Oregon : Wipf & Stock, 2011).

Falk, Marcia. "Notes on Composing New Blessings Toward a Feminist-Jewish Reconstruction of Prayer," *Journal of Feminist Studies in Religion.* 3.1 (1987): pp. 39-53.

_____. *The Book of Blessings : new Jewish prayers for daily life, the Sabbath, and the new moon festival* (California: Harper SanFrancisco, 1996).

Fike, Matthew. *A Jungian Study of Shakespeare: The Visionary Mode*, (New York: Palgrave Macmillan, 2009).

Fine, Lawrence. "Rav Kook and the Jewish Mystical Tradition," in *Rabbi Abraham Isaac Kook and Jewish Spirituality*, ed. L. J. Kaplan and D. Shatz, (NY: NYU Press, 1995).

Fishkoff, Sue. *The Rebbe's Army: Inside the World of Chabad-Lubavitch*. (New York: Schocken Books, 2013).

Forte, Allen. *The American Popular Ballad of the Golden Era, 1924-1950*. (Princeton, N.J: Princeton University Press, 1995).

Franklin Foer, *World Without Mind: The Existential Threat of Big Tech*, (Penguin Press: New York, 2017).

Giamo, Benedict. K*erouac, the Word and the Way: Prose Artist As Spiritual Quester,* (Carbondale: Southern Illinois University Press, 2000).

Gikatilla, Joseph. *Sha'arei Orah* (Warsaw 1883).

Gilmore, Mikal. "Bob Dylan's Lost Years," in *Rolling Stone* (September 12, 2013).

Gilmour, Michael J. *Tangled Up in the Bible: Bob Dylan & Scripture*. (New York: Continuum, 2004).

Ginsberg, Allen and Paul Portugés, O*n Tibetan Buddhism, Mantras, and Drugs: Interviews with Allen Ginsberg,* (San Luis Obispo, CA: Word Palace Press, 2013).

Giuliani, Rudy. "It's the Economy, stupid," *Journal Of Libertarian Studies* 19.4 (2005): 19-36.

Giversen, Søren and Birger A. Pearson, tr's, *Testimony of Truth*, in Coptic Gnostic Library Project of the Institute for Antiquity and Christianity, Claremont Graduate School. (UNESCO, the National Endowment for the Humanities) from The Coptic Gnostic Library Project: E. J. Brill).

Glazer, Aubrey L. "Jewish Musical Thinking: Reflections of a Philosopher-Rabbi," *The Future of Jewish Philosophy*, ed. Hava Tirosh-Samuelson and Aaron W. Hughes, (Boston and Leiden: Brill, 2018), pp. 171-194.

_____. "Bob Dylan, the messiah and personal redemption," *J Weekly* (April 7, 2017).

_____. "In Time to Love: Along My Path to the Vanishing Path," in Miles Krassen, *The Vanishing Path: How to Be While There Is Still Time*, (Louisville: Fons Vitae, 2019), pp. 17-74.

_____. "Last Laugh Reincarnated as a Lobster: The Comedy of Substitution as *Gilgul* in Levinas," Bergen-Aurand, ed. In *Comedy Begins with Our Simplest Gestures: Levinas, Ethics, and Humor*, (Pennsylvania: Duquesne University Press, 2017), pp.185-202.

_____. "Traditional But Not Religious," *Canadian Jewish News*, (September 9, 2018).

_____. "What Does Heidegger's Anti-Semitism Mean for Jewish Philosophy?" *Religion Dispatches* (April 3, 2014).

_____. "Zvi Ish Shalom's Primordial Torah....a review by Aubrey L. Glazer," *Tikkun*, (April 17, 2018).

_____. *A New Physiognomy of Jewish Thinking: Critical Theory After Adorno As Applied to Jewish Thought*, (London: Bloomsbury Academic, 2012).

_____. *Contemporary Hebrew Mystical Poetry: How It Redeems Jewish Thinking*, (Lewiston, N.Y: Mellen, 2009).

_____. *Tangle of Matter & Ghost: Leonard Cohen's Post-Secular Songbook of Mysticism(s) Jewish & Beyond*, (Briton, MA: Academic Studies Press, 2017).

_____. and Elyssa N. Wortzman, *Sacred Symbiosis: Person as Path, Soul as Process* (San Francisco, February 24, 2019).

Goldstein, Rebecca. *Betraying Spinoza: The Renegade Jew Who Gave Us Modernity*. (New York: Schocken Books, 2010).

Goodman, Len E. "What is Positive in Negative Theology," *Negative Theology as Jewish Modernity*, ed. M. Fagenblat, (Bloomington: Indiana University Press, 2017), pp. 62-84.

Gottlieb, Ephraim. *Ha-Qabbalah be-Khitvei Rabbenu Bahya ben Asher* (Jerusalem: Kiryath Sepher, 1970).

Gray, John. *The Soul of the Marionette: A Short Inquiry into Human Freedom* (New York: Farrar, Straus & Giroux, 2016).

Gray, Michael. "One of a kind: Bob Dylan at 70," *Japan Times* (May 26, 2011).

Gray, Timothy. *It's Just the Normal Noises: Marcus, Guralnick, No Depression, and the Mystery of Americana Music*, (Iowa City: University of Iowa Press, 2017).

Greenberg, Richard H. *Pathways: Jews Who Return*. Northvale, N.J: Jason Aronson, 1997).

Hazan Arnof, Stephen. "Bob Dylan: Prophet, Mystic, Poet," *The Forward,* (December 9, 2009).

Heilman, Samuel C. and Menachem Friedman, *The Rebbe: The Life and Afterlife of Menachem Mendel Schneerson.* (Princeton, N.J: Princeton University Press, 2012).

Heine, Steven. *Bargainin' for Salvation: Bob Dylan, a Zen Master?* (New York: Continuum, 2009).

Held, Shai. *Abraham Joshua Heschel: The Call of Transcendence*, (Bloomington, Indiana Univ Press, 2014).

Hemel, Daniel & Eric Posner, "If Trump Pardons, It Could Be a Crime," New York Times (July 21, 2017).

Henderson, Rick. "The False Promise of the Prosperity Gospel: Why I Called Out Joel Osteen and Joyce Meyer." *The Huffington Post* (2013).

Henry, Matthew. (August 8, 1700), "A Sermon Preached at the Opening of the New Meeting-House at Chester," in *Misc. Works* (1830).

Heschel, Abraham Joshua. *God in Search of Man: A Philosophy of Judaism*. (London: Souvenir Press, 2009).

_____. *God in search of man: A philosophy of Judaism,* (Farrar, Straus and Giroux, 1976).

Heylin, Clinton. *Bob Dylan: Behind the Shades*. (London: Penguin, 1992).

_____. *Bob Dylan: Behind the Shades: Take Two*, (London: Penguin, 2001).

. *Judas!: From Forest Hills To The Free Trade Hall*, (New York: Lessergods books, 2016).

_____. *Trouble in Mind: Bob Dylan's Gospel Years, What Really Happened,* (New York: LesserGod Publishers, 2017).

Hillman, James. and C. G. Jung, *Anima: An Anatomy of a Personified Notion; with Excerpts from the Writings of C.G. Jung.* (Dallas, Tex: Spring, 1986).

_____. *Animal Presences,* (Putnam, Conn: Spring Publications, 2008).

Hjelm, Titus. *Peter L. Berger and the Sociology of Religion: 50 Years After the Sacred Canopy,* (London : Bloomsbury Academic, 2018).

Howe, Marie. "Annunciation," *The Kingdom of Ordinary Time,* (New York: W.W. Norton & Co, 2008).

Ish-Shalom, Zvi. *The Kedumah Experience: The Primordial Torah,* (Boulder: Colorado, Albion-Andalus, 2017).

John of the Cross, *The Ascent of Mount Carmel,* in *John of the Cross: Selected Writings*m Kieran Kavanaugh, ed. (New York: Paulist Press, 1987).

Jonas, Hans. *The Gnostic Religion: The Message of the Alien God and the Beginnings of Christianity.* (Boston: Beacon Press [1958] 2001).

Joseph Heller, *God Knows,* (New York: Simon & Schuster Paperbacks, 2004/1984).

Joyce, James. *A Portrait of the Artist As a Young Man.* (New York: Garland, 1977).

Jung, C.G. *The Syzygy: Anima and Animus, Collected Works,* (Princeton, N.J. : Princeton University Press, 1979).

_____. "The Phenomenology of the Spirit in Fairy Tales," in *The Archetypes and the Collective Unconscious,* (New Jersey: Princeton University Press, 1990).

Kabat-Zinn, Jon. "Some reflections on the origins of MBSR, skillful means, and the trouble with maps," *Contemporary Buddhism* 12.01 (2011): pp. 281-306.

Kafka, Franz. "Before the Law" in *The Trial,* (Alma Classics, 2018).

Kakutani, Michiko. "Of Gnosticism and the Spark Within," *New York Times Review of Books* (September 29, 1996), http://www.nytimes.com/books/98/11/01/specials/bloom-omens.html (accessed 1/18/17).

Kaplan, Edward K. *Baudelaire's Prose Poems: The Esthetic, the Ethical, and the Religious in the Parisian Prowler.* (University of Georgia Press, 2009).

Kate Bowler, *Blessed: A history of the American prosperity gospel.* (Oxford University Press, 2018).

Kearney, Richard and Jens Zimmermann,ed's, *Reimagining the Sacred: Richard Kearney Debates God with James Wood, Catherine Keller, Charles Taylor, Julia Kristeva, Gianni Vattimo, Simon Critchley, Jean-Luc Marion, John Caputo, David Tracey, Jens Zimmermann, and Merold Westphal,* (New York: Columbia University Press, 2016).

Kerouac, Jack. *Desolation Angels,* (London: Penguin, 2012).

_____. *On the Road,* (New York: Penguin Books, 2011/1967).

Kirsch, Adam. "The Meaning of Bob Dylan's Silence," *NY Times* (10/26/16).

Kirsch, Jonathan. "Probing America's Religions - *The American Religion: The Emergence of the Post-Christian Nation,* by Harold Bloom," *New York Times Book Review* (May 20, 1992).

Kook, R. Avraham I. *Igrot RAYA"H,* vol. 1, (Jerusalem: Mossad haRav Kook Publications, 1961).

_____. *Song of Teshuvah: A Commentary on Rav Avraham Yitzchak HaKohen Kook's Oros HaTeshuvah by* Rav Moshe Weinberger *& Adapted by Y. D. Shulman,* (Jerusalem: Penina Press, 2012).

_____. *Olat RAYAH,* vol. 2, quoted in *The Essential Writings of Abraham Isaac Kook,* ed./tr. Ben Zion Bokser, (Warwick NY: Amity House, 1988).

_____. *Orot haQodesh,* vol. III, no 59, quoted in Benjamin Ish-Shalom, "Tolerance and its Theoretical Basis," in *Rabbi Abraham Isaac Kook and Jewish Spirituality,* ed. L. J. Kaplan and D. Shatz, (NY: NYU Press, 1995).

Kovacs, Malcolm. *The Dynamics of Commitment: The Process of Resocialization of Baalei Teshuvah, Jewish Students in Pursuit of Their Jewish Identity at the Rabbinical College of America (Lubavitch),* (Ann Arbor, Mich. : University Microfilms International, 1977/1982).

Kripal, Jeffrey J. *The Serpent's Gift: Gnostic Reflections on the Study of Religion.* (Chicago: University of Chicago Press, 2007).

Levenson, Jon Douglas. *Creation and the persistence of evil: The Jewish drama of divine omnipotence,* (Princeton University Press, 1988); James G. Williams, *The Bible, Violence, and the Sacred: Liberation from the Myth of Sanctioned Violence,* (Wipf and Stock Publishers, 2007).

Levine, Herbert J. *Words for Blessing the World: Poems in Hebrew and English,* (New Jersey: Ben Yehuda Press, 2017).

Lew, Allan. *This is Real and You Are Completely Unprepared: The Days of Awe As a Journey of Transformation,* (New York: Backbay Books, 2018).

Lovelock, James. *Gaia: A New Look at Life on Earth,* (Oxford: Oxford University Press, 1974/2016).

Magid, Shaul. "Allegory Unbound: Rav Kook, Rabbi Akiva, Song of Songs and the Rabbinic (Anti) Hero", *Kabbalah: A Journal for the Study of Jewish Mystical Texts,* vol. 32 (Los Angeles: Cherub Press, 2004): pp. 57-82.

_____. "Between Paradigm Shift Judaism and Neo-Hasidism: The New Metaphysics of Jewish Renewal," in *Tikkun* (Winter 2015).

_____. "Carlebach's broken mirror," *Tablet Magazine* (2012).

_____. "Gershom Scholem", *The Stanford Encyclopedia of Philosophy,* Edward N., Zalta (ed.). (Summer 2014 Edition),

_____. *American Post-Judaism: Identity and Renewal in a Postethnic Society.* (Bloomington, IN: Indiana University Press, 2013).

Marcus, Greil. *Bob Dylan: Writings 1968-2010.* (London: Faber, 2011).

Margotin, Philippe, and Jean-Michel Guesdon, *Bob Dylan: All the Songs: the Story Behind Every Track,* (New York: Black Dog & Leventhal, 2015).

Markham, James M. "Fassbinder play draws anti-Semitism charges," *New York Times*, (September 23, 1985).

Marshall, Lee. *Bob Dylan: The Never Ending Star,* (Oxford: Wiley, 2013).

Marshall, Scott M. *Bob Dylan: A Spiritual Life,* (Washington, D.C. : BP Books/WND Books, 2017).

Matt, Daniel. *The Essential Kabbalah: The heart of Jewish mysticism,* (New York: Harper Collins, 1995).

McLeod, Ken tr. and Rang-byung-rdo-rje 'Jigs-med-gling-pa. *A Trackless Path: A Commentary on the Great Completion (dzogchen) Teaching of Jigmé Lingpa's Revelations of Ever-Present Good,* (Sonoma, CA: Unfettered Mind Media, 2016).

Meyer, Marvin tr. *The Gospel of Thomas, in The Gnostic Bible,* (New York: 2003).

Milgrom, Jacob. *JPS Bible Commentary: Numbers* (Philadelphia: Jewish Publication Society, 1990).

Miller, Chaim. *Turning Judaism Outward: A Biography of Rabbi Menachem Mendel Schneerson the Seventh Lubavitcher Rebbe,* (Brooklyn, NY : Kol Menachem, 2014).

Mintz, Alan. *Sanctuary in the Wilderness: A Critical Introduction to American Hebrew poetry* (Stanford, California: Stanford University Press, 2012).

Modern, John L. *Secularism in Antebellum America: With Reference to Ghosts, Protestant Subcultures, Machines, and Their Metaphors: Featuring Discussions of Mass Media, Moby-Dick, Spirituality, Phrenology, Anthropology, Sing Sing State Penitentiary, and Sex with the New Motive Power.* (University of Chicago Press, 2015).

Morris, Emma. "*Haggadot* on View at the University of Chicago," *Jewcy* (May 5, 2012).

Moshe, Yaakov. (aka Jay Michaelson), *Is: Heretical Jewish Poems and Blessings,* (New Jersey: Ben Yehuda Press, 2017).

Murphy, Roland E. O. Carm. *A Commentary on the Book of Canticles or The Song of Songs*, (Fortress Press: Minneapolis, 1990).

Nadler, Allan. "Romancing Spinoza: Efforts to reclaim the great philosopher and heretic continue-and continue to fail." *Commentary-New York-American Jewish Committee-* 122.5 (2006).

Nadler, Steven. *s.v.* "Spinoza" in *Stanford Encyclopedia of Philosophy*, see: https://plato.stanford.edu/entries/spinoza/

Nancy, Jean-Luc. *The Inoperative Community,* THL vol. 76 (Minnesota: University of Minnesota Press, 1991).

Nat Hentoff, "The Crackin', Shakin', Breakin', Sounds," *The New Yorker* (October 24, 1964) in *Bob Dylan, the Essential Interviews: The Essential Interviews*, ed. Bob Dylan and Jonathan Cott, (New York: Wenner Books, 2006).

Neumann, Erich. *The Great Mother: An Analysis of the Archetype* (Princeton, NJ: Princeton University Press, 2015).

_____. Mark Kyburz, and Ann C. Lammers. *The Roots of Jewish Consciousness: Volume One*: *Revelation and Apocalypse,* (London/New York: Routledge Press, 2019).

_____. Mark Kyburz, and Ann C. Lammers. *The Roots of Jewish Consciousness: Volume Two*: *Hasidism,* (London/New York: Routledge Press, 2019).

Newberg, Andrew B, Eugene G. D'Aquili, and Vince Rause. *Why God Won't Go Away: Brain Science and the Biology of Belief.* (New York: Ballantine Books, 2002).

Newlands, Samuel. *s.v.* "Spinoza's Modal Metaphysics", in *Stanford Encyclopedia of Philosophy*, (Spring 2017 Edition).

Nicholl, Charles. *Somebody Else: Arthur Rimbaud in Africa 1880-91.* (University of Chicago Press, 1999).

Nietzsche, Friedrich Wilhelm. *Thus Spoke Zarathustra: A Book for All and None*, R. J. Hollingdale, tr. (New York: Penguin, 1961).

————————————. *The Gay Science* (1882, 1887), Walter Kaufmann ed. (New York: Vintage, 1974).

Noland, Carrie Jaurès. "Rimbaud and Patti Smith: Style as Social Deviance," *Critical Inquiry* 21.3 (1995), pp. 581-610.

Novak, David. *New Theory of Judaism and Zionism,* (New York: Cambridge University Press, 2016).

O'Hagan, Sean. "Tangled Up in Bob," *Guardian* (September 21, 2003).

Ohana, David. "J.L. Talmon, Gershom Scholem and the price of Messianism," *History of European Ideas* 34.2 (2008): 169-188.

On the Origin of the Worlds, see: http://www.gnosis.org/naghamm/origin.html (accessed 6/22/17).

Ondaatje, Michael. *The Collected Works of Billy the Kid.* (New York: Vintage International, 2009).

Pagels, Elaine H. *The Gnostic Gospels.* (New York: Quality Paperback Book Club, 1979/2005).

Parkes, Graham. ed. *Heidegger and Asian Thought* (Honolulu: University of Hawaii Press, 1987).

Paul, Shalom M. *Isaiah 40-66: Translation and Commentary.* Grand Rapids (Mich.: Eerdmans, 2012), p. 550.

Perry, George C. *The Life of Python,* (London: Pavillion, 2014).

Pickering, Stephen. *Bob Dylan Approximately: A Portrait of the Jewish Poet in Search of God,* (New York: York, David Mckay, 1975).

————————. *Bob Dylan Approximately: A Portrait of the Jewish Poet in Search of God: a Midrash.* (New York: David McKay, 1975).

————————. *Dylan, a Commemoration,* (Santa Cruz, Calif: S. Pickering, 1971).

Plaskow, Judith. *Standing again at Sinai: Judaism from a feminist perspective* (New York: HarperSanFrancisco, 1991).

Plato. *The Apology of Plato.* St G. Stock. Charleston tr., (SC: BiblioLife, 2010).

. *Charmides*, Walter R. M. Lamb, tr., (Cambridge, Mass: Harvard University Press, 1979).

Plotinus. *Enneads*, tr. Stephen Mackenna (London: Medici Society, 1921).

Potok, Chaim. *My Name is Asher Lev,* (New York: Anchor, [1972] 2009).

Pseudo-Dionysius, *The Divine Names,* tr's Marsilio Ficino, Michael J. B. Allen, *On Dionysius the Areopagite: Mystical Theology and the Divine Names, Part 1.* (Cambridge, Massachusetts: Harvard University Press, 2015).

Yanovitch, R. Yehudah Leib of. *Kuntres Bikur Chicago* (Kehot Publication Society 1944).

Remnick, David. "Leonard Cohen Makes it Darker," *New Yorker* (October 17, 2017).

Ricks, Christopher B. *Dylan's Visions of Sin,* (Edinburgh: Canongate, 2011).

Rimbaud, Arthur and Paul Demeny. *Lettre Dite Du Voyant: À Paul Demeny, Du 15 Mai 1871.* (Paris: Messein, 1954).

_____, Antoine Raybaud, ed. *Poesies: Une Saison En Enfer; Illuminations,* (Paris: Colin, 1958).

_____, *A Season in Hell: & Illuminations,* tr. Wyatt A. Mason, (New York: Modern Library, 2005).

Rimbaud, Arthur. *Lettres Du Voyant* <<A Georges Izambard>> (Charleville, 13 mai 1971), *Oeuvres de Rimbaud,* Suzanne Bernard, and André Guyaux ed, (Paris: Ed. Garnier Freres, 1960).

Rodgers, Shawn. "Radiohead's Yorke gives BDS supporters the finger during Glasgow concert", *Jerusalem Post* (July 9, 2017).

Rogovoy, Seth. "Was Dylan at his best as a Christian", *The Forward,* (Oct 30, 2017).

_____. *Bob Dylan: Prophet, Mystic, Poet.* (New York: Scribner, 2014).

Ryzik, Melena. "Revealed (or Not), the Meaning of 'Mother'!" *New York Times* (September 24, 2017).

Sabatino, Charles J. "A Correlation between Heidegger's being-in-the-World and Masao Abe's *Pratitya Samutpada,*" *Religiologigues* (Montréal) 19 (1999): 181-94.

Sartre, Jean-Paul. *Being and Nothingness: An Essay on Phenomenological Ontology,* tr. Mary Warnock, Hazel E. Barnes, and Richard Eyre. (London: New York: Routledge, Taylor & Francis Group, 2015).

_____. *L'être et le néant* (Paris: Gallimard, 1943).

Schmidt, Gilya Gerda. *The Art and Artists of the Fifth Zionist Congress,* 1901, (Syracuse, NY: Syracuse University Press, 2003).

Schneerson Mishkovsky, Zelda. *The Spectacular Difference: Selected Poems,* tr. Marcia Falk, (Cincinnati : Hebrew Union College Press, 2004).

Scholem, Gershom. *On the Mystical Shape of the Godhead: Basic Concepts in the Kabbalah,* tr. *Joachim Neugroschel* (New York: Schocken, 1991).

_____, and Eric J. Schwab, tr., "On Jonah and the Concept of Justice," *Critical Inquiry.* 25.2 (1999): pp. 353-361.

_____, Michael Löwy, and Michael Richardson, "Messianism in the early work of Gershom Scholem," *New German Critique* 83 (2001): pp. 177-191.

_____. *Jewish Gnosticism, Merkabah Mysticism, and Talmudic Tradition* (New York: Jewish Theological Seminary of America, 1965).

_____. *Origins of the Kabbalah,* (Princeton, N.J: Princeton University Press, 1991).

_____. *The Messianic Idea in Judaism and Other Essays on Jewish Spirituality.* (New York: Schocken Books, 1971/1995).

Schroeder, John W. *Skillful means: The heart of Buddhist compassion.* Vol. 54. (Motilal Banarsidass Publ., 2004).

Schwartz, Alexandra. "The Rambling Glory of Dylan's Nobel Speech," *New Yorker,* (June 6, 2017).

Scott, Maria C. *Baudelaire's Le spleen de Paris: Shifting perspectives.* (Gower Publishing, Ltd., 2005).

Secunda, Shai. "Nuclear Family," *Jewish Review of Books,* (Sumer 2016).

Segal, Alan F. *Early Rabbinic Reports About Christianity and Gnosticism* (Waco, Texas: Baylor University Press, 1977/2012).

Segal-Loewy, R. Meshulam Feish. *Zemiort 'Avodat haLevi, s.v. Seder Ne'ilat haHag.* (Boisbriand: *Kiryas Tosh,* 2005).

_____. *Haggadah shel Pesah: 'Avodat haLevi,* (Boisbriand: *Kiryas Tosh,* 2005).

Shakespeare, William, G B. Evans, and J J. M. Tobin. *The Riverside Shakespeare,* (Boston: Houghton Mifflin, 1997).

Shapira, R. Kalonymus Kalmish , *Sacred Fire,* (Jason Aronson Press: New Jersey, 2002).

Shea, Andrea. "Jack Kerouac's Famous Scroll, 'On the Road' Again", NPR (July 5, 2007).

Sheleg, Yair. "The Death and Rebirth of *Kfar Etzion*", *HaAretz* (May 3, 2007).

Shepherd, Sam. "A Short Life of Trouble" (1987), ed. Bob Dylan and Jonathan Cott. *Bob Dylan, the Essential Interviews*, (Wenner Books: New York, 2006).

Shields, Leland E. "Zen Koans as Myths Reflecting Individuation," in *Jung Journal: Culture & Psyche*, Volume 4, Number 4 (2010), pp.65–77.

Siegel, Richard and Michael Strassfeld, and Sharon Strassfeld. *The First Jewish Catalogue: A Do-It-Yourself Kit.* (Pennsylvania: J.P.S, 1973).

Siegel, Seymour. "Will Herberg (1902-1977): a *Ba'al Teshuvah* Who Became Theologian, Sociologist, Teacher," *The American Jewish Year Book.* 78 (1978): pp. 529-537.

Sizer, Rev. Dr. Stephen. "Christian Zionism the New Heresy that Undermines Middle East Peace," *MEMO* (January 29, 2014).

Smith, Dinitia. "The Heresy that Saved a Skeptic," *New York Times* (June 14, 2003).

Smith, Jonathan Z. *Imagining Religion: From Babylon to Jonestown.* (Chicago: The University of Chicago Press, 1982).

_____. *Map is not Territory: Studies in the History of Religions.* (University of Chicago Press, 1978).

Solomon, Daniel J. "Speechless Rabbi Admits Losing Argument Over Racism and Israel to White Supremacist," *Forward* (December 6, 2016).

Spinoza, Benedictus. Samuel Shirley, Steven Barbone, and Lee Rice. *Political Treatise.* (Indianapolis: Hackett Pub, 2000).

_____. *Ethics, The Collected Works of Spinoza*, Vol. I, Edwin Curley, ed/tr., (Princeton: Princeton University Press, 1985).

Steinbeck, John. *Cannery Row,* (London: Mandarin, 1997).

Steinberg, Milton. *As A Driven Leaf* (1939), (New Jersey: Behrman House, 2015).

Stokes, Emily. Review, *New York Financial Times*, (November 17/2009).

Suzuki, Daisetz T. *An Introduction to Zen Buddhism*, (Grove Press: New York, 1964).

_____. *Manual of Zen Buddhism*, (Grove Press: New York, 2012).

Symonds, William C. Brian Grow, and John Cady, "Earthly empires: How evangelical churches are borrowing from the business playbook," *Business Week* 3934 (2005): 78-88.

Taylor, Mark C. ed., *Critical Terms for Religious Studies*, (Chicago: University of Chicago Press, 2012).

Tapestry (CBC Radio: December 14, 2018).

Taubes, Jacob. "The price of messianism," *Journal of Jewish Studies* 33.1-2 (1982): 595-600.

Thomas, Richard F. *Why Dylan Matters*, (Glasgow, Scotland: HarperCollins Publishers, 2017).

Tinto, Vincent. "Learning communities: Building gateways to student success," *The National Teaching and Learning Forum*. Vol. 7. No. 4. (1998).

Tirosh-Samuelson, Hava. "Jewish Philosophy, Human Dignity, and the New Genetics," in Sean D. Sutton, ed. *Biotechnology: Our Future As Human Beings and Citizens*. (Albany: State University of New York Press, 2009), 81-121.

Tishby, Isaiah. *The doctrine of evil and the 'Kelippah'in lurianic kabbalism*. (Schocken, 1984).

_____, and Yeruḥam Fishel Lachower, *The wisdom of the Zohar: an anthology of texts*. Vol. 3. (Littman Library of Jewish Civilization, 1991).

Tzara, Tristan. *L'homme Approximatif 1925-1930*, (Paris: Gallimard, 1968); ibid, *Approximate Man and Other Writings*, tr. M. A. Caw, (Wayne State Press: Pittsburgh, 1931/1973).

_____. *Approximate Man and Other Writings*, tr. M. A. Caw, (Wayne State Press: Pittsburgh, 1931/1973).

Uffen, Ellen Serlen. "*My Name Is Asher Lev*: Chaim Potok's Portrait of the Young Hasid as Artist," *Studies in American Jewish Literature (1981-)* (1982): 174-180.

Van Ronk, Dave and Elijah Wald, *The Mayor of Macdougal Street: A Memoir*. (Da Capo Press, 2013).

Wagner, Jerry. "It's the Economy, Or Are We Stupid," *Seeking Alpha*, (September 27, 2018).

Wasserstrom, Steven M. *Religion After Religion: Gershom Scholem, Mircea Eliade, and Henry Corbin at Eranos*. (Princeton: Princeton University Press, 2001).

Whitefield, Samuel, "Paul's Understanding of Isaiah 28 and the Forerunner Ministry," see: https://samuelwhitefield.com/1011/pauls-understanding-of-isaiah-28-and-the-forerunner-ministry

Whitman,Walt. *Leaves of Grass,* (New York: Thomas Y. Crowell Publishers, 1902).

Wiesel, Elie. *The Trial of God (as It Was Held on February 25, 1649, in Shamgorod): A Play in Three Acts*. (New York: Schocken Books, 1986).

William Aggeler, tr. "Charles Baudelaire, "Cupid and the Skull", *The Flowers of Evil*, (Fresno, CA: Academy Library Guild, 1954).

Williams, Michael. *s.v. Gnosticism,* Encyclopedia Brittanica (https://www.britannica.com/topic/gnosticism).

Williamson, Nigel. *The Rough Guide to Bob Dylan,* (New York: Metro Books, 2010).

Wittgenstein, Ludwig. *Tractatus Logico-Philosophicus* (1921), tr. C.K. Ogden, F. P. Ramsey (London: Routledge 2005).

Wolfson, Elliot R. "Immanuel Frommann's Commentary on Luke and the Christianizing of Kabbalah: Some Sabbatean and Hasidic Affinities," *Holy Dissent: Jewish and Christian Mystics in Eastern Europe*, (Detroit: Wayne State University Press, 2011), 171-222.

_____. "Becoming Invisible: Rending the Veil and the Hermeneutic of Secrecy in the Gospel of Philip," in *Practicing Gnosis: Ritual, Magic, Theurgy, and Liturgy in Nag Hammadi, Manichaean and Other Ancient Literature: Essays in Honor of Birger A. Pearson, Nag Hammadi and Manichaean Studies* 85 (2013): 113-135.

_____. "*Gottwesen* and the De-Divinization of the Last God: Heidegger's Meditation on the Strange and Incalculable," M. Björk and J. Svenungsson (eds.), *Heidegger's Black Notebooks and the Future of Theology*, (Springer International Publishing, 2017).

_____. "Negative Theology and Positive Assertion in the Early Kabbalah," *Da'at: a Journal of Jewish Philosophy & Kabbalah* (Leiden; Boston: Brill, 1994).

_____. "Prologue," in *Language, Eros, Being: Kabbalistic Hermeneutics and Poetic Imagination,* (New York: Fordham University Press, 2005).

_____. *Luminal Darkness: Imaginal Gleanings from Zoharic Literature*. (Oxford: OneWorld, 2007).

_____. *Open Secret: Postmessianic Messianism and the Mystical Revision of Menahem Mendel Schneerson* (New York: Columbia University Press, 2012).

Wolin, Richard. *Heidegger's Children,* (Princeton University Press, 2015).

Wortzman, Elyssa N. "Process Theology, Aesthetics, *Halacha* and Spiritual Direction Through Art," *Foundation Theology*, ed. J. J.H. Morgan (GTF: Indiana, 2017), pp. 141-157.

Wright, Peter Matthews. "After Smith: Romancing the Text When Maps Are All We Have Left," *Religion & Literature* 42.3(Autumn 2010).

Xenophon. *Plato: the Apology of Socrates and Xenophon: the Apology of Socrates.* Nicholas Denyer,tr. (Cambridge: Cambridge University Press, 2019).

Yaffe, David. *Bob Dylan: Like a Complete Unknown.* (New Haven Conn.: Yale University Press, 2013).

Yagoda, Ben. *The B Side: The Death of Tin Pan Alley and the Rebirth of the Great American Song.* New York: Riverhead Books, a member of Penguin Group, USA, 2015).

Ziporyn, Brook. "Tiantai Buddhism", *The Stanford Encyclopedia of Philosophy* (Spring 2017 Edition).

n.a., "A Portrait of American Jews," *Pew Study* (October 1, 2015).

n.a., "Forget the Dylai Lama", *London Review of Books*, Vol. 25 No. 21, (November 6, 2003).

n.a., "The Saint and the Troubadour: John Paul II and Dylan," Radio Vatican (October 13, 2016).

n.a., "When Americans Say They Believe in God, What Do They Mean?" *Pew Research Center* (April 25, 2018).

n.a., "Why It's Not the Economy, Stupid," *Politics*, (August 9, 2018).

HEBREW SOURCES

Biblical References
Entsiḵlopedyah Miḵra'it: Otsar Ha-Yedi'ot 'al Ha-Miḵra U-Teḵufato, (Jerusalem: Mosad Bialiḵ, 1950).

Talmud
Babylonian Talmud. Steinsaltz, Adin, Tzvi H. Weinreb, and Joshua Schreier, tr./ed. *Koren Talmud Bavli, (Noé Edition: Talmud Bavli.* , 2017).
  Jerusalem Talmud. Guggenheimer, Heinrich Walter, ed., (Walter de Gruyter, 2000).

Legal Codices
Chazon Ish, *Choshen Mishpat* (Jerusalem: *n.p.,* 1994)
Karo, Joseph. *Shulchan Aruch, (n.p.*: 1806): 1563.
Maimon, Moshe ben, and Shlomo Pines. *The Guide of the Perplexed.* Chicago: University of Chicago Press, 1978.
       . *Mishne Torah,* (Jerusalem: Shabetai Frankel, 2016).

Kabbalah
Gerona, R. Azri'el of. *Sod ha-Tefillah* Scholem, Gershom. (ed.), , in *"Seridim Hadashim mi-Kitvei R. Azri'el mi-Gerona,"* in S. Assaf and G. Scholem (eds.), *Sefer Zikkaron le-Asher Gulak ve-li-Shemu'el Klein,* (Jerusalem 1942).

  ha-Lavan, David ben Avraham. *Masoret ha-Berit,* ed. Gershom Scholem, *Qovets al Yad, n.s.* 1 (1936).

  León, Moses de. *Sheqel ha-Qodesh,* A. W. Greenup (ed.), (London 1911).

  Tiqqunei Zohar. Gottlieb, Ephraim, Moshe Idel, Shemu'el Re'em, and Michal Oron, ed's. *Ha-ketavim Ha-'ivriyim Shel Ba'al Tiḵune Zohar Ve-Ra'ya Mehemna.* (Jerusalem: National Academy for Humanities, 2003).
  Zohar, *Pritzker Edition,* vol's I-IX, tr. D. Matt, (Stanford University Press: Stanford, California).
  Zohar Hadash, *Pritzker Edition* vol. XI, tr. J. Hecker tr., *Pritzker Edition*, (Stanford: Stanford University Press, 2018).

Hasidism

Bratzlav, R. Nahman. *Liqqutai Moharan.* Moshe Mykoff, Chaim Kramer, and Ozer Bergman, tr.'s (Jerusalem: Breslov Research Institute, 1999),

Bratzlav, R. Nahman. *Sichot.* Rosenfeld, Zvi Aryeh, ed. *Rabbi Nachman's Wisdom.* (Breslov Research Institute, 1983).

Mezeritch, Dov Baer, *Maggid Devarav le-Ya'aqov,* Rivka Schatz-Uffenheimer (ed.), (Jerusalem: 1976).

Vital, R. Hayyim. *Sefer 'ets Ḥayim.* (Shḳlov: Shabtai ben Ben Tsiyon, Aryeh ben Menaḥem, Avraham ben Ya'aḳov Segal, 1800).

Zlotshov, Issachar Ber of, *Mevasser Tsedeq* (Berditchev, 1817).

Permissions

Index of Scriptures in Dylan Lyrics

Other Publications

Tarantula, (Hibbing, Minn: Wimp
    Press, 1960).
The Nobel Lecture, (New York
    Simon & Schuster, 2017).

About the Author

Aubrey L. Glazer, PhD, (University of Toronto, 2005) is senior rabbi of *Congregation Shaare Zion*, (Montréal, Canada) and director of *Panui* (San Francisco, California), an incubator for contemplative practice and conscious community building. Aubrey is a teacher in demand in many contexts, from federations to rabbinical school seminaries to universities and Jewish meditation retreats.

Aubrey's writing has been featured in popular media like the *Montréal Gazette, La Presse,* and *CJN* as well as his most recent books including: *Tangle of Matter & Ghost: Leonard Cohen's Post-Secular Songbook of Mysticism(s) Jewish & Beyond* (2017); *Mystical Vertigo: Kabbalistic Hebrew Poetry Dancing Cross the Divide of Jewish Thinking* (2013); *A New Physiognomy of Jewish Thinking: Critical Theory After Adorno as Applied to Jewish Thought* (2011); *Contemporary Hebrew Mystical Poetry: How It Redeems Jewish Thinking* (2009).

For a fuller list of his publications, see: https://aubreyglazer.academia.edu/